EUTHANASIA, ETHICS AND
PUBLIC POLI

An Argument against Leg

D1535233

Whether the law should permit voluntary euthanasia or physician-assisted suicide is one of the most vital questions facing all modern societies.

Internationally, the main obstacle to legalisation has proved to be the objection that, even if they were morally acceptable in certain hard cases, voluntary euthanasia and physician-assisted suicide could not be effectively controlled; society would slide down a slippery slope to the killing of patients who did not make a free and informed request, or for whom palliative care would have offered an alternative. How cogent is this objection?

This book provides the general reader (who need have no expertise in philosophy, law or medicine) with a lucid introduction to this central question in the debate, not least by reviewing the Dutch euthanasia experience. It will interest readers in any country, whether for or against legalisation, who wish to ensure that their opinions are better informed.

JOHN KEOWN is Senior Lecturer in the Law and Ethics of Medicine, Faculty of Law, University of Cambridge. His previous publications include *Abortion, Doctors and the Law* (1988) and *Euthanasia Examined* (1995).

EUTHANASIA, ETHICS AND PUBLIC POLICY

An Argument against Legalisation

JOHN KEOWN

University of Cambridge

PUBLISHED BY THE PRESS SYNDICATE OF THE UNIVERSITY OF CAMBRIDGE
The Pitt Building, Trumpington Street, Cambridge, United Kingdom

CAMBRIDGE UNIVERSITY PRESS
The Edinburgh Building, Cambridge CB2 2RU, UK
40 West 20th Street, New York, NY 10011-4211, USA
477 Williamstown Road, Port Melbourne, VIC 3207, Australia
Ruiz de Alarcón 13, 28014 Madrid, Spain
Dock House, The Waterfront, Cape Town 8001, South Africa

http://www.cambridge.org

First published 2002

Printed in the United Kingdom at the University Press, Cambridge

Typeface Adobe Minion 10.5/13.5 pt.   *System* LATEX 2_ε [TB]

A catalogue record for this book is available from the British Library

Library of Congress Cataloguing in Publication data
Keown, John.
Euthanasia, ethics and public policy: an argument against legalisation / John Keown.
p.   cm.
Includes bibliographical references and index.
ISBN 0 521 80416 7 – ISBN 0 521 00933 2 (pb.)
1. Euthanasia.   2. Euthanasia – Moral and ethical aspects.   3. Euthanasia – Social aspects.
4. Terminal care – Moral and ethical aspects.   I. Title.
R726 .K465   2002   179.7 – dc21   2001043592

ISBN 0 521 80416 7 (hardback)
ISBN 0 521 00933 2 (paperback)

To VGK and BK

CONTENTS

vii

PREFACE

There are few more momentous and controversial questions facing contemporary society than the legalisation of voluntary, active euthanasia (VAE) and active physician-assisted suicide (PAS). The campaign for their legalisation shows little sign of abating. In January 1997, campaigners for PAS argued their case before the United States Supreme Court. They had persuaded two Federal Appeal Courts that the US Constitution recognised a right of mentally competent, terminally ill patients to PAS. Unanimously, the Supreme Court reversed both decisions.[1]

As the Supreme Court's decisions illustrate, despite the popular support the campaign for legalisation seems to enjoy and the considerable media attention it has generated, the campaign has as yet enjoyed surprisingly little success in changing laws around the world. This is largely because opposition to change remains strong. That opposition is partly based on the view that it is always morally wrong for one person, doctor or not, intentionally to kill another innocent person, even at their request. But it is also rooted in the concern that if VAE/PAS[2] were permitted they would not remain voluntary for long, and that patients who did not really want to die, or who were not suffering severely, or whose suffering could be alleviated by palliative medicine, would nevertheless have their lives terminated. Indeed, fear of this 'slippery slope' is proving to be *the* major obstacle to reform. But is this fear justified or illusory? This is the question which has taken centre-stage in the current political debate, and it is the question which forms the centre-piece of this book.

Many people favour the legalisation of VAE. Their reasons are typically twofold: compassion and autonomy. They think VAE is right because it

---

[1] *Washington v. Glucksberg* 138 L Ed 2d 772 (1997); *Vacco, Attorney-General of New York et al. v. Quill et al.,* 138 L Ed 2d 834 (1997).

[2] Henceforth, to avoid repetition, 'VAE' will be used to include PAS, unless the contrary is apparent from the context.

puts an end to human suffering and because people have a right to decide for themselves when and how to die. Yet how many of those who favour legalisation have seriously explored the counter-arguments? In particular, how many have examined the argument that, whatever the rights and wrongs of VAE, legalising it would be bad public policy, not least because it could not be controlled? How many, for example, have read (or are even aware of) expert reports which have carefully evaluated this major objection?

This book aims to give the general reader, who need have no expertise in philosophy, law or medicine, a lucid introduction to this central issue in the debate. It will be of interest to all those, in any country, who wish to ensure that their opinions, whether currently for or against legalisation, are better informed.

FOREWORD

Forewords do not usually begin with a disclaimer, but there is a reason here, for *Euthanasia, Ethics and Public Policy* uncompromisingly addresses themes which colleagues of the present writer, and occasionally he himself, have tackled in the past, and may have to tackle together in the future. Comity and courtesy make it necessary to avoid the implication that the opinions expressed in this valuable work are necessarily shared in full. This being said, it is a pleasure to welcome a contribution to what is, at present, the most intellectually demanding, the most ethically challenging, and the most important for its contingent effects as well as for its immediate practical impact, of all the points on the line where law, medicine, belief and reason intersect.

The image of the slippery slope is often called up as a warning to those who take an easy step without looking to see where the next may lead, but it also reminds us that in this area the concepts themselves are slippery, escaping sideways from the effort to grasp them. The overlapping problems of accelerated death demand intellectual honesty rather than unfocussed right-thinking, and an emphasis on duties as well as individual rights.

The steepness of the slope, and its treacherous footing, are often concealed by an emollient vocabulary. Thus, the expression 'best interests' conveys an upbeat meaning, at odds with its more chilling implications. So also, the contemporary watchword 'personal autonomy' distracts attention from the duties of those implicated in the rights-based choice of the principal actor. Indeed, so deceptive is the terminology that these two antithetical concepts, authoritarian and libertarian, are quite frequently deployed at the same time: an important example of the need to know what words mean before employing them in debate. The present work uncompromisingly takes this stance, and is right to do so. Equally, it exposes the interchangeable usage of concepts which are not the same: intend/foresee, cause/assist, and so on. This is nothing new in itself, but the emphasis in the present context is a valuable corrective. Again, the sceptical eye cast on expressions which mean different things to different people, such as 'the sanctity of life', will help to discourage their use as common coin.

On the purely jurisprudential side of the debate there is also much to repay study. The unconvincing shifts and expedients in which the courts have taken refuge are clearly exposed. If this makes uncomfortable reading for the professionals, so much the better, so far as the future is concerned.

The book is also an important contribution to the polemic about the feasibility of protection against the abuse of assisted death. Nothing can make up for the paucity of the available data, but the careful analysis of such hard facts as exist will be of value to decision-makers (including the judges) who have to shape policies by reference to pragmatic as well as purely ethical and logical considerations. The debate will continue, but we shall all be better informed.

In sum, we find here a work which displays a consistent and deeply felt ethical purpose, and yet is able to do so in a moderate and scholarly tone. The subject, which requires us to think so deeply about what our lives in society are really about, badly needs contributions of this kind. No doubt it will not persuade everybody, but it is hard to believe that everybody will ever be of the same mind. Rather than try to broker an unattainable unanimity, what we badly need is for our minds to be informed and alert. For this reason I am glad to welcome the book, and to express the hope that many, outside as well as inside the professions whose preoccupations it treats, will take the trouble to read it carefully, and reflect upon what it has to say.

Lord Mustill

ACKNOWLEDGMENTS

I would like gratefully to acknowledge the assistance I have received from several colleagues in writing this book. Professor Luke Gormally, Dr Helen Watt, Wendy Hiscox and Bobbie Sidhu read the whole book in draft; Professor John Finnis, Wesley Smith and Karin Clark read parts. All made helpful suggestions. Wendy Hiscox also checked the references.

Thanks also go to the editors and publishers of several academic books and journals who gave permission to reproduce the following material and thereby bring it to a wider readership. Chapter 4 was published in Donna Dickenson and Mike Parker (eds.), *The Cambridge Medical Ethics Workbook* (2001) 27, and chapters 6 and 19 appeared in the *Law Quarterly Review* ((1997) 113 *LQR* 481). Much of Part III was published as two chapters in Luke Gormally (ed.), *Euthanasia, Clinical Practice and the Law* (1994), a paper in the *Law Quarterly Review* ((1992) 108 *LQR* 51), a paper in (1994) 6(1) *Bioethics Research Notes* 1, and a paper in the *Journal of Medical Ethics* ((1999) 25(1) *J Med Ethics* 16). I should also like to thank the co-author of this paper, Professor Henk Jochemsen, for permission to reproduce it in this book, where it appears as chapter 12. Chapter 20 first appeared in *Legal Studies* ((2000) 20(1) *Legal Stud* 66).

It is also a pleasure to thank the ever-efficient, courteous and unflappable staff at the Squire Law Library, not least David Wills and Peter Zawada.

Finally, I should also like to thank Finola O'Sullivan and Jennie Rubio at Cambridge University Press: Finola for welcoming the book's conception, Jennie for assisting its delivery. Margaret Deith took the pain out of copyediting. Neil de Cort smoothed the production process.

Despite the help I have received from colleagues, I remain solely responsible for the book's argument and accuracy.

TABLE OF CASES

ABBREVIATIONS

A 2d	Atlantic Reporter, 2nd Series
AC	Appeal Cases
All ER	All England Law Reports
Am J Hosp Pall Care	*American Journal of Hospice and Palliative Care*
Am J Law Med	*American Journal of Law and Medicine*
Am J Psychiatry	*American Journal of Psychiatry*
Ann Intern Med	*Annals of Internal Medicine*
BMJ	*British Medical Journal*
BMLR	Butterworths Medico-Legal Reports
Cal Rptr	California Reporter
Camb LJ	*Cambridge Law Journal*
Camb Q Healthc Ethics	*Cambridge Quarterly of Healthcare Ethics*
Cath Med Q	*Catholic Medical Quarterly*
Cm	Command Paper
Cr App R	Criminal Appeal Reports
Crim LR	*Criminal Law Review*
DLR	Dominion Law Reports
Duq L Rev	*Duquesne Law Review*
EHRR	European Human Rights Reports
Fam LR	Family Law Reports
Fam Pract	*Family Practice*
Fitzpatrick	F. J. Fitzpatrick, *Ethics in Nursing Practice*
Gomez	Carlos F. Gomez, *Regulating Death: Euthanasia and the Case of the Netherlands*
Gormally	Luke Gormally, *Euthanasia, Clinical Practice and the Law*
Griffiths	John Griffiths et al., *Euthanasia and Law in the Netherlands*

Guidance	BMA, *Withholding and Withdrawing Life-Prolonging Medical Treatment. Guidance for Decision Making*
Guidelines	KNMG, 'Guidelines for Euthanasia'
Hastings Cent Rep	*Hastings Center Report*
HC	House of Commons
Hendin	Herbert Hendin, *Seduced by Death: Doctors, Patients and Assisted Suicide*
HL	House of Lords
ILRM	Irish Law Reports Monthly
Issues Law Med	*Issues in Law & Medicine*
J Contemp Health Law Policy	*Journal of Contemporary Health Law and Policy*
J Med Ethics	*Journal of Medical Ethics*
J Med Philos	*Journal of Medicine and Philosophy*
J Pall Care	*Journal of Palliative Care*
J R Soc Health	*Journal of the Royal Society of Health*
J R Coll Physicians Lond	*Journal of the Royal College of Physicians of London*
Keown	J. Keown, *Euthanasia Examined: Ethical, Clinical and Legal Perspectives*
L Ed	Lawyers' Edition, United States Supreme Court Reporter
L Med & Health Care	*Law, Medicine and Health Care*
Legal Stud	*Legal Studies*
Lloyd's Rep Med	Lloyd's Law Reports: Medical
Lords' Report	*Report of the Select Committee on Medical Ethics*
LQR	*Law Quarterly Review*
Med J Aust	*Medical Journal of Australia*
Med L Rev	*Medical Law Review*
Med Law	*Medicine and Law*
Minn L Rev	*Minnesota Law Review*
N Engl J Med	*New England Journal of Medicine*
New LJ	*New Law Journal*
NJ	Nederlandse Jurisprudentie
Outline	Ministry of Justice, *Outlines Report Commission Inquiry into Medical Practice with Regard to Euthanasia [sic]*

Parl. Deb.	Parliamentary Debates
QB	Queen's Bench (Law Reports)
QBD	Queen's Bench Division (Law Reports)
Report	*Medische beslissingen rond het levenseinde. Rapport van de Commissie onderzoek medische praktijk inzake euthanasie*
Singapore J Legal Stud	*Singapore Journal of Legal Studies*
Survey	*Medische beslissingen rond het levenseinde. Het onderzoek voor de Commissie Onderzoek Medische Praktijk inzake Euthanasie*
Survey 2	G. van der Wal and P. J. van der Maas, *Euthanasie en andere medische beslissingen rond het levenseinde. De praktijk en de meldingsprocedure*
Task Force	*When Death is Sought: Assisted Suicide and Euthanasia in the Medical Context* (Report of the New York State Task Force on Life and the Law)
U Rich L Rev	*University of Richmond Law Review*
WLR	Weekly Law Reports

Introduction

Despite the major advances in medicine and palliative care witnessed by the last century, many patients, even in affluent Western nations, still die in pain and distress. Some entreat their doctors to put an end to their suffering either by killing them or by helping them to kill themselves. In almost every country in the world, a doctor who complies with such a request commits the offence of murder or assisted suicide and faces a lengthy term of imprisonment and professional disgrace.

Yet many people think it should be lawful for a doctor to end a suffering patient's life on request, either by administering a lethal injection or by assisting the patient to commit suicide.[1] Organisations campaigning for legal reform, such as the Hemlock Society in the USA or the Voluntary Euthanasia Society (VES) in the UK, are not proposing that a doctor should be allowed to kill[2] patients whenever

---

[1] Lord Goff, the former Senior Law Lord, has quoted a poll, conducted on behalf of the Voluntary Euthanasia Society in England, which contained the following proposition: 'Some people say that the law should allow adults to receive medical help to a peaceful death if they suffer from an incurable physical illness that is intolerable to them, provided they have previously requested such help in writing.' His Lordship pointed out that when this was first put to the public in the early 1960s, 50% of those approached agreed with it, but that in 1993 the figure had risen to 79% ('A Matter of Life and Death' (1995) 3 *Med L Rev* 1, 11). His Lordship also pointed out, however, that the proposition raised a number of fundamental questions which cannot be expressed in a simple question suitable for an opinion poll, and that the proposition was ambiguous. What, for example, did those polled understand by 'medical help'?

[2] Some advocates of VAE object to the use of the word 'kill' in this context. They argue that 'killing' is a word which, like 'rape', connotes a lack of consent, and that in discussions of VAE the word 'kill' is misleading and emotive. See Jean Davies, 'Raping and Making Love Are Different Concepts: So Are Killing and Voluntary Euthanasia' (1988) 14 *J Med Ethics* 148. A counter-argument is that the normal definition of 'rape' is sexual intercourse without consent, but that the normal definition of 'kill' is simply 'put to death; cause the death of, deprive of life' (*The New Shorter Oxford English Dictionary* (1993) I, 1487). One can, therefore, kill with or without consent. It makes perfect sense, for example, for a soldier to say, 'My wounded comrade on the battlefield asked me to put him out of his misery, and so I killed him.' And, although it

he[3] feels like it. Mindful of the obvious and gross abuses which might follow were doctors given a completely free hand, such organisations typically propose that doctors should be allowed to end life only if the patient is competent to make a decision, has been informed about alternatives such as palliative care, and has voluntarily asked for life to be ended or to be given the means to commit suicide. Nor do such organisations typically propose that the law should allow doctors to kill patients whenever the *patient* feels like it. The patient should not only have thought seriously about the options but must also be terminally ill or at least experiencing serious suffering. Further, reformers generally put forward some form of procedural safeguards in an attempt to ensure that VAE would only be available to patients whose request was truly voluntary and who were genuinely terminally ill or suffering gravely. Such proposals often include a requirement that the doctor consult an independent doctor beforehand, such as an expert in the illness from which the patient is suffering and/or an expert in palliative care, and they also provide for at least the possibility of official review, as by requiring the doctor, having performed VAE, to report the details of the case to some public authority such as a coroner.

The ethical question whether it can *ever* be right for a doctor to kill a patient, even one who is experiencing severe suffering and who asks for death, continues to generate debate. That important issue of fundamental moral principle has been explored in other books, including *Euthanasia Examined*.[4] Although *Euthanasia, Ethics and Public Policy* outlines these arguments, its focus is different. It asks: even if VAE and PAS were morally acceptable, *could they be effectively controlled?* In other words, if the law were relaxed to permit doctors to administer, or hand, a lethal drug to a patient who was suffering gravely and who freely asked for it, could it effectively limit VAE and PAS to such circumstances? Or would the practice slide down a slippery slope to ending the lives of those who did not really want to die; of those whose severe suffering could be alleviated by palliative care; and of those who were not suffering severely or even at all?

For, although the question of whether VAE and PAS can be justified in principle is important, the question about the likely *effects* of their decriminalisation – not least about whether they would propel society down the

---

is true that the word 'kill' carries potentially emotive overtones, these overtones simply reflect the inherent moral gravity of taking life.

[3] In this book 'he' means 'he or she' unless the contrary is apparent.

[4] *Euthanasia Examined: Ethical, Clinical and Legal Perspectives* (1995) (hereafter 'Keown'). See especially chapters 1–10.

slippery slope – is hardly less important. Indeed, in the worldwide debate as it is unfolding, it is this issue of the slippery slope which has taken centre-stage and which is proving decisive, as it did in the landmark decisions of the US Supreme Court in 1997. Justice Souter, for example, concluded: 'The case for the slippery slope is fairly made out here . . . because there is a plausible case that the right claimed would not be readily containable by reference to facts about the mind that are matters of difficult judgment, or by gatekeepers who are subject to temptation, noble or not.'[5]

However, his rejection of PAS seemed provisional rather than final. Having noted that the advocates of PAS sought to avoid the slope by proposing state regulation with teeth, he concluded that 'at least at this moment' there were reasons for caution in predicting the effectiveness of the teeth proposed. This judge, therefore, seemed open to the possibility of creating a constitutional right to PAS if the dangers of the slippery slope could be avoided.

In the light of the pivotal importance of the slippery slope argument in the current debate, it is essential to consider the experience of three jurisdictions which have taken the radical step of permitting VAE and/or PAS: the Netherlands, the Northern Territory of Australia, and the US state of Oregon. Although this book will consider all three, it will concentrate on the Netherlands because of that country's much longer, and more fully documented, experience of VAE and PAS.

In 1984, the Dutch Supreme Court decided that a doctor who per-formed VAE/PAS in certain circumstances acted lawfully. In tandem with that decision, the Royal Dutch Medical Association, the KNMG, issued guidelines for doctors. Since 1984, thousands of Dutch patients have been euthanised or assisted in suicide. In April 2001 a government bill which essentially gives statutory force to the guidelines, and which had already been passed by the lower house of the Dutch parliament, received the approval of the upper house.[6]

This book considers the lessons the Dutch experience has for other ju-risdictions which may wish to contemplate relaxing their laws to accom-modate VAE and/or PAS. In particular, the book will consider whether, as campaigners for VAE both inside and outside the Netherlands have claimed, the Dutch experience shows that it can be effectively controlled. It

---

[5] *Washington* v. *Glucksberg* 138 L Ed 2d 772 at 828–9 (1997).
[6] *The Daily Telegraph*, 29 November 2000; (2001) 322 *BMJ* 947. The provisions of the bill are discussed in chapter 8.

is appropriate that this book take stock of the Dutch experience. First, given that VAE has been officially tolerated and widely practised in the Netherlands for over fifteen years, a substantial body of empirical evidence and academic commentary[7] has emerged which invites a thorough overview. Secondly, the author is ideally placed to conduct such an overview, having been researching the Dutch experience since 1989. Thirdly, the Dutch experience has provoked wildly divergent interpretations. Such divergence can confuse not only the judicious but even the judicial reader. Justice Souter observed that there was a 'substantial dispute' about what the Dutch experience shows: 'The day may come', he said, 'when we can say with some assurance which side is right, but for now it is the substantiality of the factual disagreement, and the alternatives for resolving it, that matter. They are, for me, dispositive of the . . . claim [for a constitutional right to PAS] at this time.'[8] This book offers a path through the thicket of contradictory interpretations.

Having examined the experience of these three jurisdictions, the book proceeds to review the conclusions of expert bodies – committees, courts and medical associations – in three other jurisdictions – the USA, Canada and the UK – which have thoroughly evaluated the arguments for legalisation. Finally, the book will address an important but often overlooked aspect of the euthanasia debate. This is the issue of *passive* euthanasia (PE): the termination of patients' lives not by an act, but by withholding or withdrawing medical treatment or tube-feeding with intent to kill.

The book is divided into five parts. Part I defines (in chapters 1 and 3) some important terms, such as 'voluntary euthanasia' and 'physician-assisted suicide', and considers (in chapter 2) the moral and legal difference between intended and merely foreseen life-shortening.

Part II outlines (in chapters 4, 5 and 6) three main arguments for permitting VAE, and three counter-arguments. Chapter 7 introduces the slippery slope arguments.

Part III explores the Dutch experience. Chapter 8 outlines the guidelines for VAE. Chapter 9 summarises the empirical evidence generated by a major survey and chapter 10 the extent of non-compliance with the

---

[7] See Carlos F. Gomez, *Regulating Death: Euthanasia and the Case of the Netherlands* (1991) (hereafter 'Gomez'); Herbert Hendin, *Seduced by Death: Doctors, Patients and Assisted Suicide* (1998) (hereafter 'Hendin'); John Griffiths et al., *Euthanasia and Law in the Netherlands* (1998) (hereafter 'Griffiths').

[8] *Washington* v. *Glucksberg* 138 L Ed 2d 772 at 829 (1997).

guidelines disclosed by that survey. Chapter 11 considers evidence of increasing condonation of *non*-voluntary euthanasia (euthanasia of those incapable of asking for it). Chapter 12 summarises the empirical evidence produced by a second major survey. Chapter 13 considers the reliability of Dutch reassurances about the extent to which they control VAE.

Part IV outlines the experience of two other jurisdictions which have relaxed their laws. In 1996, the Northern Territory in Australia decriminalised VAE and PAS, though its legislation was overturned in 1997 by the Australian Federal Parliament. Chapter 14 outlines the Territory's legislation and evidence about its operation during its abbreviated life. In 1994, voters in the US state of Oregon enacted by referendum a law allowing PAS. The law came into force in 1997. Chapter 15 sets out the legislation and reviews its ongoing operation.

In Part V chapters 16, 17 and 18 consider respectively the conclusions of expert committees, supreme courts and medical associations which have scrutinised the case for legalising VAE.

Part VI asks whether jurisdictions such as England, which still prohibit doctors from taking *active* measures to hasten death, nevertheless permit doctors to hasten death *by deliberate omission,* as by the withdrawal of tube-feeding from mentally incapacitated patients with intent to shorten life and, if so, whether the law is morally consistent. Chapter 19 examines the *Bland* case, in which the Law Lords declared lawful the withdrawal of tube-feeding from a patient in a 'persistent vegetative state'. Chapter 20 analyses controversial guidance issued by the British Medical Association in 1999 permitting doctors to withhold/withdraw tube-feeding from patients with other forms of severe mental incapacity, such as advanced Alzheimer's disease. Chapter 21 examines the debate generated by a private member's bill introduced in the House of Commons which sought to prohibit doctors from withholding or withdrawing treatment or tube-feeding if their intention in so doing was to kill the patient.

As the book went to press, a further significant development took place in England. Diane Pretty, a terminally ill woman, sought a judicial ruling than she enjoyed a right to assisted suicide under the European Convention on Human Rights. This important case is considered in the Afterword.

PART I

Definitions

The euthanasia debate is riddled with confusion and misunderstanding. Much of the confusion derives from a failure of participants in the debate to define their terms. Part I seeks to clarify the confusion by noting some of the differing definitions in the current debate, indicating the underlying moral distinctions they reflect, and assessing their relative merits.

1

'Voluntary euthanasia'

'Voluntary'

Campaigners for relaxation of the law typically stress that they are campaigning only for VAE – *voluntary* active euthanasia. VAE is generally understood to mean euthanasia at the request of the patient,[1] and this is how it will be used in this book. VAE can be contrasted with 'non-voluntary' active euthanasia (NVAE), that is, euthanasia performed on those who do not have the mental ability to request euthanasia (such as babies or adults with advanced dementia) or those who, though competent, are not given the opportunity to consent to it. Finally, euthanasia against the wishes of a competent patient is often referred to as 'involuntary' euthanasia (IVAE).

Some commentators lump together the last two categories and classify all euthanasia without request as 'involuntary'. Others (including the author) think that it is preferable to keep the two categories distinct, not least because it helps to avoid unnecessary confusion.

'Euthanasia'

Given the absence of any universally agreed definition of 'euthanasia' it is vital to be clear about how the word is being used in any particular context. The cost of not doing so is confusion. For example, if an opinion pollster asks people whether they support 'euthanasia', and the pollster understands the word to mean one thing (such as giving patients a lethal injection) while the people polled think it means another (such as withdrawing a life-prolonging treatment which the patient has asked to be withdrawn because it is too burdensome), the results of the poll will be worthless. Similarly, if two people are discussing whether 'euthanasia'

---

[1] Or at least with the consent of the patient. Euthanasia would still be voluntary even if the doctor (or someone else) suggested it to the patient and the patient agreed.

should be decriminalised and they understand the word to mean quite different things, their discussion is likely to be fruitless and frustrating.

'Euthanasia', a word derived from the Greek, simply means a 'gentle and easy death'.[2] Used in that wide sense, one hopes *everyone* is in favour of euthanasia: who wants to endure, or wants others to endure, a protracted and painful death? Obviously, however, campaigners for the decriminalisation of euthanasia are not using the word in this uncontroversial sense. They are not simply supporting the expansion of hospices and improvements in palliative care. They are, rather, arguing that doctors should in certain circumstances be allowed to ensure an easy death not just by killing the pain but by killing the patient. Given the variety of ways in which the word 'euthanasia' is used, rather than pretend that there is one universally accepted meaning, it seems sensible to set out the three different ways in which the word is often used, beginning with the narrowest.

All three definitions share certain features. They agree that euthanasia involves *decisions which have the effect of shortening life*. They also agree that it is limited to the *medical* context: 'euthanasia' involves patients' lives being shortened *by doctors*[3] and not, say, by relatives. Moreover, all three concur that characteristic of euthanasia is the belief that *death would benefit the patient, that the patient would be better off dead*, typically because the patient is suffering gravely from a terminal or incapacitating illness or because the patient's condition is thought to be an 'indignity'. Without this third feature, there would be nothing to distinguish euthanasia from cold-blooded murder for selfish motives.

In short, all three definitions concur that 'euthanasia' involves *doctors* making decisions *which have the effect of shortening a patient's life* and that these decisions are *based on the belief that the patient would be better off dead*. Beyond these points of agreement, there are, as we shall see, several major differences.

'Euthanasia' as the active, intentional termination of life

According to probably the most common definition, 'euthanasia' connotes the *active, intentional* termination of a patient's life by a doctor who thinks that death is a benefit to that patient. On this definition, euthanasia is not

---

[2] 'Euthanasia' in *The New Shorter Oxford English Dictionary* (1993) I, 862.
[3] Or, possibly, nurses acting under medical direction.

simply a doctor doing something which he *foresees* will shorten the patient's life, but doing something *intending* to shorten the patient's life. 'Intention' is used here in its ordinary sense of 'aim' or 'purpose'. Such a definition of 'euthanasia' was adopted by the House of Lords Select Committee on Medical Ethics, which was appointed in 1993 to examine euthanasia and related issues. Published in 1994, its report defined 'euthanasia' as: 'a deliberate intervention undertaken with the express intention of ending a life to relieve intractable suffering'.[4] The word 'intervention' connotes some act, rather than an omission, by which life is terminated. Similarly, the New York State Task Force on Life and the Law, which also reported in 1994, defined 'euthanasia' as: 'direct measures, such as a lethal injection, by one person to end another person's life for benevolent motives'.[5] In short, 'euthanasia' is often understood to be limited to the active, intentional termination of life, typically by lethal injection.

The criminal law in most jurisdictions, including the UK and the USA, regards active intentional killing by doctors as the same offence as active intentional killing by anyone else: murder. An example of a doctor falling foul of the law of murder is the prosecution in England in 1992 of Dr Nigel Cox. Dr Cox was a consultant rheumatologist in a National Health Service hospital. One of his elderly female patients, a Mrs Boyes, was dying from rheumatoid arthritis. She was in considerable pain, and pleaded with Dr Cox to end her life. He injected her with potassium chloride and she died minutes later. Surprisingly, he then recorded what he had done in the patient's notes. A nurse who read the notes reported the matter to her superior. The police investigated the matter, and the Crown Prosecution Service decided to take action.

Dr Cox was charged with attempted murder. The charge was attempted murder rather than murder because, according to the Crown Prosecution Service, it was not possible to prove that the potassium chloride had actually caused the victim's death because her corpse had been cremated. The judge directed the jury that it was common ground that potassium chloride has no curative properties and is not used to relieve pain; that injected into a vein it is lethal; that one ampoule would certainly kill,

---

[4] *Report of the Select Committee on Medical Ethics* (HL Paper 21-I of 1993–4) (hereafter 'Lords' Report') para. 20.
[5] *When Death is Sought: Assisted Suicide and Euthanasia in the Medical Context* (Report of the New York State Task Force on Life and the Law (1994)) (hereafter 'Task Force') x.

and that Dr Cox had injected two.[6] In view of the weight of evidence against him, it is not surprising that Dr Cox was convicted. He was, however, given only a suspended prison sentence. The General Medical Council, the medical profession's regulatory body, was also lenient. Although it censured his conduct, it did not erase his name from the medical register and merely required him to undergo a period of re-training.[7] This is just the sort of case that everyone easily recognises as a case of 'euthanasia' (or, at least, *attempted* euthanasia). In short, everyone agrees that 'euthanasia' includes *active, intentional termination of life.* There are some, however (including the author), who use 'euthanasia' in a wider sense.

'Euthanasia' as the intentional termination of life by act or by omission

On this wider definition, 'euthanasia' includes not only the intentional termination of a patient's life by an act such as a lethal injection but also the intentional termination of life by an omission. Consequently, a doctor who switches off a ventilator, or who withdraws a patient's tube-feeding, performs euthanasia *if the doctor's intention is to kill the patient.* Euthanasia by deliberate omission is often called 'passive euthanasia' (PE) to distinguish it from active euthanasia. A good example of PE is the case of Tony Bland.

Tony Bland was a victim of the disaster in 1989 at the Hillsborough football stadium in Sheffield, in which almost 100 spectators were crushed to death. Tony was caught in the crush. Although he survived, he lost consciousness, never to recover it. In hospital, Tony was eventually diagnosed as being in a 'persistent vegetative state' (pvs) in which it was believed he could neither see, hear nor feel. This condition is similar to a coma in that the patient is unconscious but different in that, whereas in coma the patient seems to be asleep, in pvs the patient has 'sleep/wake' cycles. The patient is not, however, thought to be aware, even when apparently awake, which is why pvs has been described as a state of 'chronic wakefulness without awareness'. The consensus among the medical experts who examined him

---

[6] *R. v. Cox* (1992) 12 BMLR 38 at 46.
[7] 'Decision of the Professional Conduct Committee in the Case of Dr Nigel Cox' *General Medical Council News Review (Supplement)*, December 1992.

was that Tony, like most (though not all)[8] patients in pvs, would never regain consciousness. Contrary to some newspaper reports, however, he was neither dead nor dying: his 'brain stem' (that part of the brain necessary for basic bodily functions such as breathing) was still functioning. Nor was he on a 'life-support' machine: he breathed naturally, without any assistance. He also digested normally. However, as he could not feed himself he was fed through a nasogastric tube, a tube threaded into his stomach via his nose. His excretory functions were assisted by a catheter and enemas. Infections were treated with antibiotics.

Tony's parents and his doctor wanted to stop the tube-feeding and antibiotics. His doctor sought the approval of the local coroner but the coroner replied that the doctor might be prosecuted for homicide. In order to obtain an authoritative legal ruling, the Airedale NHS Hospital Trust, which ran the hospital, applied to the High Court for a declaration that it would be lawful to stop the tube-feeding and antibiotics. The application was opposed by the Official Solicitor (an officer of the court who represents those, like Tony, who are incapable of representing themselves). He argued that stopping Tony's feeding would be murder or at least manslaughter: the doctor would be intentionally causing death just as if he severed the air-pipe of a deep-sea diver. Sir Stephen Brown, President of the Family Division of the High Court, disagreed, and granted the declaration. The Official Solicitor appealed to the Court of Appeal, but without success. A further appeal to the House of Lords was also dismissed.

Of the five Law Lords, a majority expressly agreed with the Official Solicitor's submission that the doctor's intention in stopping tube-feeding would be to kill Tony. Lord Browne-Wilkinson said: 'As to the element of intention . . . in my judgment there can be no real doubt that it is present in this case: *the whole purpose of stopping artificial feeding is to bring about the death of Anthony Bland.*'[9]

Why, then, did the Law Lords dismiss the appeal? Why would it not be homicide (murder or manslaughter) to deny Tony food and fluids? The Law Lords held that the doctor would not commit homicide because that offence normally requires an act not an omission. Stopping feeding and antibiotics would be an omission not an act. Lord Goff said that the doctor

---

[8] Another Hillsborough victim, Andrew Devine, emerged from pvs after five years and learned to communicate via a buzzer and to count (*The Times*, 27 March 1997). See p. 250 n. 55.

[9] *Airedale NHS Trust* v. *Bland* [1993] AC 789 at 881 (emphasis added).

would not be killing the patient but would simply be allowing the patient to die as a result of his pre-existing medical condition. Because, in short, there was no *active* termination of life, this was not a case of unlawful killing or 'euthanasia'. Lord Goff said:

> [T]he law draws a crucial distinction between cases in which a doctor decides not to provide, or to continue to provide, for his patient treatment or care which could or might prolong his life, and those in which he decides, for example by administering a lethal drug, actively to bring his patient's life to an end. As I have already indicated, the former may be lawful.

He went on:

> But it is not lawful for a doctor to administer a drug to his patient to bring about his death, even though that course is prompted by a humanitarian desire to end his suffering, however great that suffering may be . . . So to act is to cross the Rubicon which runs between on the one hand the care of the living patient and on the other hand euthanasia – actively causing his death to avoid or end his suffering. Euthanasia is not lawful at common law.[10]

Tony's tube-feeding was stopped and he died some days later.

To those who limit 'euthanasia' to active intentional termination of life (definition (1) above), this was not a case of euthanasia. But on the wider definition of intentional termination of life by act or deliberate omission, it was. Is there any reason to prefer this wider definition? If what characterises euthanasia is an *intention* to kill, it surely makes no *moral* difference if the doctor carries out that intention by an omission rather than by an act. By analogy, if a father were to drown his baby by pushing her head under the bathwater, we would regard this as a clear case of intentional killing and condemn the father's conduct as murder. So too, surely, if the baby, while reaching for a plastic duck, accidentally hit her head on the side of the bath and slipped unconscious beneath the water, and her father deliberately failed to save her with the intention that she should drown. We would hardly excuse the father because he deliberately killed his baby by an omission rather than by an act. On the contrary, we would regard his behaviour in either case as morally equivalent because his *intention* in both cases was the same: that his baby should die. Similarly, in the medical context, there is surely no significant moral difference between a doctor intentionally killing a patient by,

[10] At 865.

say, choking the patient, and by deliberately failing to stop the patient from choking, when the doctor could easily do so, precisely so that the patient should die. Is it not objectionable to define the first as 'euthanasia' but not the second when, in both cases, the doctor's intention (that the patient die) and the result (that the patient dies) are precisely the same?[11]

The *Bland* case raises profound questions of ethics and law, issues which will be discussed in chapter 19. The purpose of mentioning it here is simply to illustrate that, on the second definition under consideration, it was indeed a case of 'euthanasia', albeit PE, euthanasia by deliberate omission. There are those who would adopt an even wider definition.

'Euthanasia' as intentional or foreseen life-shortening

Some, especially many advocates of VAE, tend to adopt an even wider definition which embraces not only the intentional termination of life by act or omission, but also acts and omissions which have the *foreseen* consequence of shortening life. It is common practice, in hospitals and hospices alike, for doctors to administer pain-killing drugs such as morphine to those at the end of life who might otherwise die in pain if not agony. As the patient's body develops an increasing tolerance to the dosage given, the dosage may well have to be increased to achieve the same palliative effect. It is widely believed that a side-effect of administering increasingly large doses is the depression of respiration and the consequent shortening of the patient's life (though experts in palliative care point out that, if properly administered, morphine actually tends to extend life by relaxing the patient).[12] If, however, the popular assumption that morphine shortens life *were* true, would the administration of morphine to ease pain at the end of life, a practice long established in medicine and widely condoned by medical and palliative care associations, constitute 'euthanasia'? On either of the above two definitions, the answer must be 'No' if the doctor's intention is only to alleviate the patient's pain and

---

[11] An added problem with limiting euthanasia to active life-shortening is that it requires a clear distinction to be made between acts and omissions. While the distinction can be black and white, it can also be a murky grey. For example, there is still some disagreement among scholars as to whether switching off a life-support machine should be categorised as an act or an omission.

[12] See e.g. Robert G. Twycross, 'Where There is Hope There is Life: A View from the Hospice' in Keown, 141, 162.

discomfort and not to terminate life. An intention to ease pain is not an intention to shorten life. But, on the third definition, this practice would constitute euthanasia because the acceleration of death is *foreseen* by the doctor.

Similarly, if a doctor withholds/withdraws a life-prolonging treatment, for example by switching off a ventilator, and foresees that the patient will die sooner than would otherwise be the case, is this euthanasia? Again, if the doctor's intention is not to shorten the patient's life but to remove a treatment because it has become too burdensome to the patient, the answer, on either of the first two definitions, is 'No'. An intention to remove a burdensome treatment is not an intention to end life. (It is doubly 'No' on the first definition if the withholding/withdrawal is categorised as an omission.) But on the third definition the answer is 'Yes', because the doctor *foresees* the shortening of the patient's life.

What can be said in favour of this third definition over the first two? Well, at first blush it might well seem that there is very little difference between an intended and a merely foreseen result. If you *know* your conduct is going to have a particular result, isn't this the same as *intending* it? And the *result* is exactly the same, whether it is merely foreseen or intended. However, on closer examination, intention is significantly different from mere foresight. That difference is the subject of the next chapter.

Conclusions

Much of the confusion which besets the contemporary euthanasia debate can be traced to an unfortunate imprecision in definition. Lack of clarity has hitherto helped to ensure that much of the debate has been frustrating and sterile. In an attempt to clarify the confusion, this chapter has distinguished between 'voluntary', 'non-voluntary' and 'involuntary' euthanasia; has set out the three ways in which the word 'euthanasia' is often used; and has foreshadowed the pivotal moral distinction between intended and merely foreseen life-shortening.

It has argued that, although the first definition of 'euthanasia' (the 'active, intentional termination of a patient's life on the ground that death is thought to be a benefit') is the most common, the second (which would also include the intentional termination of life by omission) has more to commend it. As will be argued in the next chapter, it also has more to commend it than the third definition which conflates intended life-shortening with merely foreseen life-shortening. It may be optimistic to expect the emergence of common definitions, at least in the near future, not least as the different definitions reflect different underlying moral presuppositions whose resolution is a prerequisite to definitional consensus. Until such consensus is achieved participants should at least be open and clear about which definition they are employing and why.

2

Intended v. foreseen life-shortening

Distinguishing intention from foresight

In both ordinary language and human experience intention is different from mere foresight. *Aiming* to bring about a consequence is not the same as simple *awareness* that it may or will occur. The difference between the two states of mind is easily illustrated. There can, first, be foresight without intention. To take an example given by the former Law Lord, Lord Goff: when Montgomery ordered his troops to invade France on D-Day, he *foresaw* that many of them would be killed but he obviously did not *intend* that any of them should be killed.[1] Again, the tipsy guest at the wedding reception who drinks too much of the free-flowing fizz foresees the inevitable hangover but hardly intends it. The discomfort of having a tooth extracted by the dentist is always foreseen, never intended.

Conversely, there can be intention without foresight. An assassin may intend to shoot a political leader who is giving a speech hundreds of yards away without foreseeing that the bullet will find its mark. I can intend to make you interested in this sentence without foreseeing that you will be. You can buy a ticket intending to win the lottery without foreseeing that you will.

Moral difference

No less importantly, whether a bad consequence is intended or merely foreseen can make a major difference to the morality of one's conduct. Consider the actions of two dentists, the kindly Mr Fill and the cruel Mr Drill. Mr Fill drills out decay in your tooth and fills the cavity, in accordance with good dental practice, even though both you and Mr Fill foresee that you will suffer some pain. The following week Mr Drill drills

[1] Lord Goff, 'The Mental Element in the Crime of Murder' (1988) 104 *LQR* 30 at 44.

out decay in another of your teeth and fills the cavity. But whereas Mr Fill merely foresaw that you would inevitably suffer pain, Mr Drill *intends* you to suffer pain. Clearly, whereas Mr Fill has done nothing morally questionable, Mr Drill has. And the reason is solely to be found in Mr Drill's *intending* the bad consequence rather than simply foreseeing it as an inevitable side-effect of the good consequence, namely, repairing your tooth. This is irrespective of the fact that the bad consequence, the pain, is precisely the same in both cases.

Similarly, imagine a French tourist who asks two Londoners, Fred and Stan, for directions to Buckingham Palace. Fred says he thinks he knows where it is, but isn't sure, and does his best to give the tourist directions, which turn out to be misleading. The tourist then encounters Stan and asks the way. Stan dislikes French tourists and deliberately sends the tourist the wrong way. There is clearly a significant moral difference between the actions of Fred and Stan. Fred at most foresees he may send the tourist in the wrong direction, but is honestly trying to help. Stan, however, *intentionally* misleads the tourist. Although on the surface it may appear that they have done precisely the same thing (that is, sending the tourist the wrong way), the difference in their respective states of mind (Fred intending to help, Stan to hinder) makes a crucial difference in evaluating the morality of their conduct. So much so that it actually determines the *nature* of their actions. Fred's action may properly be described as 'trying to help the tourist'; Stan's as 'trying to hinder the tourist'. The actions are, again, morally different even though they appear, outwardly, identical.[2]

Or again, imagine two people, Janet and John, living in a tiny apartment with a huge mastiff, Rex. Janet foresees that, because of the relative size of the flat and the dog, she will, sooner or later, trip over Rex. One evening while carrying a tray of cocktail sausages, she accidentally steps heavily on Rex's nose. Rex, not surprisingly, whines in pain. Irritated by Rex's whine, John kicks Rex on the nose. Would you morally equate Janet's accidental trip with John's deliberate kick because the force applied to Rex's nose in each case was the same? Neither would Rex. As the saying goes, even a dog knows the difference between being tripped over and being kicked. The difference is, again, that between intention and foresight.

---

[2] See F. J. Fitzpatrick, *Ethics in Nursing Practice* (1988) 121–2 (hereafter 'Fitzpatrick'); Helen Watt, *Life and Death in Healthcare Ethics* (2000) 7–8; 40.

The principle of 'double effect'

Recognition of the moral difference between intended and foreseen consequences is nothing new. It has, indeed, a very long tradition in Western ethics, not least Western medical ethics. According to this ethical tradition, it is permissible to allow a bad consequence to result from one's actions, even if it is foreseen as certain to follow, provided certain conditions are satisfied. Those conditions are identified by the principle of 'double effect'. According to this ethical principle, it is permissible to produce a bad consequence if:

- the act one is engaged in is not itself bad;
- the bad consequence is not a means to the good consequence;
- the bad consequence is foreseen but not intended; and
- there is a sufficiently serious reason for allowing the bad consequence to occur.[3]

To some, the label 'double effect' sounds fishy, as if it were a form of 'double think'. For this reason, it would perhaps be better if it were called something like the principle of 'unintended bad side-effects'. However, the name is probably too established for it to be easily changed now. In any event, what matters is not how it sounds but what it means. And when properly and fairly understood, it surely makes moral and common sense.

To illustrate its sense, let us apply the principle to the actions of the two dentists we met earlier, Mr Fill and Mr Drill. The principle explains why Mr Fill acted ethically but Mr Drill did not. Mr Fill was engaged in a good or at least morally neutral act (repairing your tooth); the pain was not a means to repairing the tooth but was a side-effect; the pain was foreseen and not intended; and the good of repairing your tooth justified the pain associated with it. Mr Drill, by contrast, acted unethically, since he *intended* you to suffer. Your pain was not merely a foreseen side-effect of his actions: it was his very purpose.

But, it might be argued, is it not artificial to draw a distinction based on intention when it can be so difficult to know what a person's intentions are? How are we to judge whether the dentists intended or merely foresaw your discomfort? The short answer to this objection is that it confuses the

---

[3] See generally Luke Gormally, *Euthanasia, Clinical Practice and the Law* (1994) (hereafter 'Gormally') 48–50; Fitzpatrick, chapter 7.

issue of *what intention is* with the issue of *how to detect it.* It is rather like denying the existence of love because it can be difficult to know whether somebody loves you or not. And, in any event, it is by no means *always* difficult to decide whether someone intends a consequence or not: there is often the evidence of what they say and/or what they do.

Double effect in traditional medical ethics

The principle of double effect was strongly defended in 1994 by the House of Lords Select Committee on Medical Ethics:

> Some witnesses suggested that the double effect of some therapeutic drugs when given in large doses was being used as a cloak for what in effect amounted to widespread euthanasia, and suggested that this implied medical hypocrisy. We reject that charge while acknowledging that the doctor's intention, and evaluation of the pain and distress suffered by the patient, are of crucial significance in judging double effect. If this intention is the relief of severe pain or distress, and the treatment given is appropriate to that end, then the possible double effect should be no obstacle to such treatment being given.[4]

It added:

> Some may suggest that intention is not readily ascertainable. But juries are asked every day to assess intention in all sorts of cases, and could do so in respect of double effect if in a particular instance there was any reason to suspect that the doctor's primary intention was to kill the patient rather than to relieve pain and suffering. They would no doubt consider the actions of the doctor, how they compared with usual medical practice directed towards the relief of pain and distress, and all the circumstances of the case.[5]

Similarly, the New York State Task Force distinguished the intentional termination of life from palliative care, even when the latter foreseeably hastened death. It observed: 'the provision of pain medication is ethically and professionally acceptable even when such treatment may hasten the patient's death, if the medication is intended to alleviate pain and severe discomfort, not to cause death, and is provided in accord with accepted medical practice.'[6] More recently, Raanan Gillon, a philosopher, doctor and

---

[4] Lords' Report, para. 243 (footnote omitted).   [5] Ibid.   [6] Task Force, xvi.

past editor of the *Journal of Medical Ethics*, vigorously defended the distinction between intending to kill and foreseeing that life may be shortened. These states of mind are, he explained, different 'logically, experientially, conceptually, legally and morally'.[7]

Double effect in criminal law

In the *Bland* case, Lord Goff referred to the 'established rule that a doctor may, when caring for a patient who is, for example, dying of cancer, lawfully administer painkilling drugs despite the fact that he knows that an incidental effect of that application will be to abbreviate the patient's life'. He added: 'Such a decision may properly be made as part of the care of the living patient, in his best interests; and, on this basis, the treatment will be lawful.'[8] Although this question was not an issue raised in *Bland*, this statement by an eminent Law Lord clearly carries considerable weight. Moreover, there have been cases in which the issue *has* been raised.

Annie Lindsell

An illustration of how the principle has been recognised by the courts is the case of Annie Lindsell in 1997. She was a former flight attendant, aged 47, with motor neurone disease (the same condition that afflicts Professor Stephen Hawking). This progressive and terminal neurological disease, while leaving the patient mentally alert, gradually and inexorably paralyses the muscles, including the muscles necessary for breathing. With only weeks to live, she sought a court declaration to the effect that when she had lost the ability to swallow and when her anticipation of further deterioration caused her 'severe mental distress accompanied by physical pain', it would be lawful for her general practitioner to administer large doses of diamorphine (heroin) to ease her distress, even if it were also to

---

[7] Raanan Gillon, 'When Doctors Might Kill their Patients: Foreseeing is not Necessarily the Same as Intending' (1999) 318 *BMJ* 1431. See also George J. Annas, 'The Bell Tolls for a Right to Assisted Suicide' in Linda L. Emanuel (ed.), *Regulating How We Die* (1998) 203, 213–14. By contrast, there are philosophers, not least those who advocate a 'consequentialist' ethic, who reject the principle of double effect because they judge the morality of an action solely by its consequences, whether or not those consequences are intended. See, e.g., chapters 1, 3 and 5 in Keown by John Harris.

[8] *Airedale NHS Trust* v. *Bland* [1993] AC 789 at 867.

have the effect of shortening her life. Her doctor was reportedly reluctant to do this without a judicial declaration.

The court invited the Official Solicitor to act as *amicus curiae* ('friend of the court' – an impartial legal advisor to the court). Counsel for the Official Solicitor called an expert in palliative care to assist the court. This expert expressed concern at the proposed course of treatment: Annie Lindsell's doctor had not stated what dosage of diamorphine he proposed to use, and diamorphine was in any event an inappropriate drug for the treatment of mental distress. In his sworn statement, this expert wrote: 'the proposed mode of treatment is not in my view medically sound and, without impugning the motives or intentions of either party in this case, it could as currently described amount to euthanasia'.[9]

Lord Lester QC, counsel for Annie Lindsell, argued that the law was unclear and that if her doctor administered diamorphine, foreseeing that death would probably be hastened, he might be prosecuted for murder. This was because, even though the doctor would not desire her death, he would have performed a positive act which had death as a likely consequence.[10] Lord Lester argued that, 'if the foreshortening of her life is a likely consequence of his actions, he would be at risk of the jury inferring culpable intent'.[11] Counsel for the Official Solicitor disagreed. The law was, he said, clear: 'English law (and, in particular, the English law of murder) undoubtedly recognises and gives effect to the doctrine of double effect.' He added that the doctrine was not confined to the relief of pain but extended in principle to the relief of 'suffering or distress, whether physical or mental'.[12]

Annie Lindsell's doctor revised his proposed treatment, stressing that his aim was to treat both her mental and her physical distress. The expert called by the Official Solicitor informed the court that the revised plan satisfied his concerns.[13] In view of the fact that the evidence before the court indicated that the proposed course of action was in accordance

---

[9] Affidavit of Dr Nigel Sykes of St Christopher's Hospice, London, para. 3.5. I am grateful to Dr Sykes for a copy of his written evidence.

[10] *In the Matter of Ann Lindsell v. Simon Holmes. Plaintiff's Revised Skeleton*, para. 52. I am grateful to Lord Lester QC for sending me a copy of his skeleton argument.

[11] At para. 53(i).

[12] *In the Matter of Ann Lindsell v. Simon Holmes. Skeleton Argument of the Amici Curiae Instructed by the Official Solicitor*, para. 5. I am grateful to Mr James Munby QC (now Mr Justice Munby) for sending me a copy of his skeleton argument.

[13] Report of Dr Nigel Sykes regarding Dr Simon Holmes's fourth Affidavit dated 24 October 1997.

with a responsible body of medical opinion, Lord Lester withdrew the application for a declaration. The judge said that he 'thoroughly approved and endorsed the discontinuance'.[14] Annie Lindsell later died peacefully at home, without needing diamorphine.[15]

The British Medical Association welcomed the outcome of the case because it 'confirmed that doctors, working within the law, can treat the symptoms of terminally ill patients, even if that treatment may have a secondary consequence of shortening the patient's life'.[16] The case illustrates the extent to which the principle of double effect is enshrined not only in medical practice and medical ethics but also in the criminal law. It was, indeed, surprising, in view of earlier case law acknowledging the applicability of the principle, that the application was ever brought. In the *Cox* case, the judge had made it clear to the jury that the law not only permitted doctors so to relieve their patients' suffering, but actually required them to do so. The judge directed that it was 'plainly Dr Cox's *duty* to do all that was medically possible to alleviate her pain and suffering, even if the course adopted carried with it an obvious risk that, as a side effect of that treatment, her death would be rendered likely or even certain'.[17]

Indeed, a case some thirty-five years before *Cox* had also made it clear that the administration of palliative drugs to the terminally ill was lawful, even if it incidentally shortened life. In that case Dr John Bodkin Adams was indicted for the murder of one of his elderly female patients. The prosecution alleged that he had intentionally killed her so that he could inherit property she had left him in her will, and that he had done so by deliberately injecting her with excessively large doses of morphine. Dr Adams pleaded not guilty. The trial judge, Mr Justice Devlin, directed the jury that murder was the 'cutting short of life, whether by years, months or weeks'. He added, however:

> But that does not mean that a doctor who is aiding the sick and the dying has to calculate in minutes or even in hours, and perhaps not in days or weeks, the effect upon a patient's life of the medicines which he administers or else be in peril of a charge of murder. If the first purpose of medicine, the restoration of health, can no longer be achieved, there is still much for a doctor to do, and he is entitled to do all that is proper and necessary to relieve pain and suffering, even if the measures he takes may incidentally shorten life.[18]

---

[14] *The Guardian*, 29 October 1997.   [15] *The Times*, 3 December 1997.
[16] *The Times*, 29 October 1997.   [17] (1992) 12 BMLR 38 at 41 (emphasis added).
[18] Patrick Devlin, *Easing the Passing* (1985) 171.

Dr Adams was acquitted.

After withdrawing Annie Lindsell's application, Lord Lester initiated a debate on the case in the House of Lords. He began by expressing his concern about 'the lack of clarity' in the law.[19] He added that the uncertainty in her case arose because of the early stage at which the treatment was sought to be given, and the probable life-shortening effect it would have.[20] He continued that the court's expert in palliative care had at first objected that the treatment plan amounted to euthanasia, but had later 'changed his mind' (though, as we have seen, the expert changed his mind only because Annie Lindsell's doctor revised his proposed treatment plan).[21] Lord Lester asserted that there was a risk that, where the shortening of life was a probable consequence of the doctor's palliative treatment, the law would usually infer a criminal intent.[22]

The Attorney-General, Lord Williams of Mostyn QC, denied that the law was unclear. He said: 'I do not believe that the doctrine of double effect is at all a sophistry.'[23] He continued: 'The noble Lord, Lord Lester of Herne Hill, indicated that the law was difficult or obscure; it is not . . . The law is perfectly plain.'[24] The Attorney-General could, moreover, have cited the then leading case on intention in the criminal law, the decision of the House of Lords in the case of *Moloney*.[25] In that case, the Law Lords had held that to convict of murder the prosecution had to prove that the accused had intended, and not merely foreseen, death.[26]

Dr David Moor

After the *Lindsell* case any remaining doubt about the law's acceptance of even life-shortening palliative care was still further diminished by the

---

[19] (1997–8) 583 Parl. Deb., HL, col. 720.   [20] At 721.   [21] See p. 23.

[22] (1997–8) 583 Parl. Deb., HL, col. 723.   [23] At 743.   [24] At 743–4.

[25] [1985] AC 905. See also *Re J* [1990] 3 All ER 930 at 938 *per* Lord Donaldson MR.

[26] Or grievous bodily harm. Delivering the leading judgment, Lord Bridge said: 'The first fundamental question to be answered is whether there is any rule of substantive law that foresight by the accused . . . is equivalent or alternative to the necessary intention. I would answer this question in the negative' ([1985] AC 905 at 927–8). He added (at 928): 'I am firmly of opinion that foresight of consequences, as an element bearing on the issue of intention in murder, or indeed any other crime of specific intent, belongs, not to the substantive law, but to the law of evidence.' In other words, the fact that the accused foresaw death did not mean the accused intended death; the accused's foresight was merely evidence for the jury to take into account in deciding whether it was the accused's *purpose* to kill. Cf. Smith and Hogan, *Criminal Law* (9th edn, 1999) 54–5.

unsuccessful prosecution of general practitioner Dr David Moor. Dr Moor
was tried for murdering one of his elderly patients, 85-year-old George
Liddell, who was dying from cancer, by injecting a fatal dose of diamorphine. Dr Moor denied the charge, claiming that he had administered the
drug to ease pain not to shorten life. The trial judge directed the jury that
they had to decide whether Dr Moor was trying to ease pain or whether he
had set out to end his patient's life. The jury acquitted. Outside the court,
Dr Moor made the following statement: 'In caring for a terminally ill
patient, a doctor is entitled to give pain-relieving medication which may
have the incidental effect of hastening death. All I tried to do in treating
Mr Liddell was to relieve his agony, distress and suffering. This has always
been my approach in treating my patients with care and compassion.'[27]

Although the case was, therefore, nothing more than a reaffirmation
of the traditional principle of double effect, the Voluntary Euthanasia
Society (VES) sought to 'spin' the case as a legal endorsement of VAE. A
VES press release described the case as an example of 'slow euthanasia',
and the Society's Vice-Chairman reportedly asked whether the case was
not society's 'wink to euthanasia'. He surely needed his eyes testing. For if
the doctor's intention was, as the doctor himself said it was, to ease pain
and not to shorten life, it was not euthanasia, fast or slow, winked at or
otherwise. Similarly, in a lead letter in *The Times*, Sir Ludovic Kennedy,
President of the VES, claimed that what had brought Dr Moor to court
was his 'brave admission' that he had hastened his patients' deaths. 'This',
added Sir Ludovic, 'has been common practice among doctors in this
country (and other Western countries) for a long time ... Many in the
medical profession will regard Dr Moor's acquittal as a green light for
continuing this practice.' And if the intention and result were the same,
Sir Ludovic asked, where was the moral difference between a slow death
from diamorphine and a quick death from potassium chloride?[28] Again,
this was both confused and confusing. The whole point about the case was
that Dr Moor *denied* an intention to kill, whether quickly or slowly. The
'practice' which was 'common' and to which the case showed a 'green light'
was *not* the intentional termination of life, but the intentional alleviation
of pain.

The upshot of these cases is that the law endorses the established medical
practice of administering palliative drugs to ease pain and distress, even if

---

[27] *The Times*, 12 May 1999.   [28] Ibid., 18 May 1999.

the doctor foresees that life will incidentally be shortened as a result. They underline the important ethical and legal distinction between intending to hasten death, and merely foreseeing death as an unwanted side-effect of palliative care. But why, it may be asked, if the law is so clear, was Dr Moor prosecuted? The answer lies in ambiguous comments Dr Moor had made to a journalist, and in his failure to inform the authorities about the injection of diamorphine until later in their investigation. Taking the unusual step of ordering Dr Moor to pay a third of the defence costs, the trial judge said: 'He has brought this action upon himself. He was very silly, making comments to the press, and he lied to the National Health Service and to the police.'[29]

The law after the Moor case was, then, quite clear, even if campaigners for VAE were somewhat confused. Journalists also often confuse VAE and palliative care, and this confusion may in turn infect their readers' understanding of the distinction. For example, one newspaper reported that a leading facial injuries surgeon who had 'helped some of his terminally ill patients to die' had made a 'deathbed confession' to his family. On closer reading, however, it appeared that all he had said was that when a patient's life was ending anyway, 'enough pain relief should be given to end suffering, even if that would have the effect of shortening life'.[30] This hardly amounted to a confession of VAE. Similarly, newspaper headlines after the *Lindsell* case declaring 'Dying woman wins right to end life in dignity'[31] were also misleading. As we saw, Annie Lindsell won nothing that was not already available in hospitals and hospices up and down the country. Such reports, which could be multiplied, suggest that any confusion lies not so much with judges or doctors as with journalists.

Woollin

Unfortunately, a more recent (non-medical) case may cast doubt on the lawfulness of palliative care which doctors foresee will shorten life. The case of *Moloney*, in which the Law Lords distinguished intention and foresight, now has to be read in the light of their more recent decision in *Woollin*.[32] In that case, the Law Lords appeared to rule that a consequence

[29] Ibid., 12 May 1999.
[30] 'Dying Surgeon in Plea for Compassion', *The Guardian*, 14 June 1997.
[31] *The Guardian*, 29 October 1997.   [32] R. v. *Woollin* [1998] 4 All ER 103.

foreseen as virtually certain is intended. The implications of this for doctors who foresee that their palliative care will shorten life are disturbing: are such doctors now *prima facie* liable for murder?

The question whether a doctor whose actions foreseeably hasten death is guilty of homicide was raised even more recently in the case of the conjoined twins, Jodie and Mary. In that case it was clear that unless the twins were surgically separated both would die, but that if they were separated, the weaker twin, Mary, would die. The Court of Appeal held, following *Woollin*, that because the surgeons who proposed to carry out the operation foresaw Mary's death, they therefore intended to kill her. The court nevertheless held that the separation would not be murder because separation was the lesser of two evils and the surgeons could therefore claim the defence of necessity.[33] It therefore seems that, in the unlikely event that a doctor were to be prosecuted for administering palliative drugs which had the foreseen but unintended effect of hastening death, the courts would, in the light of *Woollin* and the conjoined twins case, hold that the doctor intended to kill. The doctor would have to hope that the courts would hold that the defence of necessity was available on the ground that he had chosen the lesser of two evils.

Woollin is a retrograde step. First, it suggests that doctors engaged in proper palliative care (or surgeons separating conjoined twins) intend to kill – a gross misrepresentation of their state of mind. Had their Lordships in *Woollin* turned their minds to the situation of life-shortening palliative care, and the cases of *Adams*, *Cox* and *Moor*, they would surely have been alerted to the dangers of confusing intention with foresight of virtual certainty. Secondly, *Woollin* raises wholly unnecessary doubts about the lawfulness of proper palliative care. It is hardly an answer to say that the courts would hopefully provide doctors with a defence such as necessity: doctors providing proper palliative care are, as all agree, doing nothing wrong in the first place; are entitled to work free from the fear of prosecution, and should not have to rely for acquittal on the chances of the judicial application of an ancient, vague and uncertain defence.[34] Thirdly,

---

[33] *Re A (Children)* [2000] 4 All ER 961. Unlike the other two judges, Robert Walker LJ did not apply *Woollin*'s artificially stretched meaning of 'intention'. He held (with respect rightly) that as Mary's death was not the surgeons' purpose, they did not intend to kill her. The case is a good illustration of the dangers which *Woollin*'s wide definition of intention poses to doctors.

[34] Or even a new statutory defence protecting 'reasonable' medical conduct. See Andrew Ashworth, 'Criminal Liability in a Medical Context: The Treatment of Good Intentions' in A. P. Simester and A. T. H. Smith (eds.), *Harm and Culpability* (1996) 173.

because of the doubts it creates, *Woollin* may have a chilling effect on the provision of much-needed palliative care and leave patients dying in pain and distress. A ruling which hinders good medicine is clearly bad law.

As we have seen, intention and foresight are distinct states of mind and there are good reasons for ethics and law to embody that distinction. These reasons, and the argument that *Moloney* had distinguished intention from foresight, were not, it appears, even put to the court in *Woollin*. This seriously undermines the authority of the case. The Law Lords appear to have sleepwalked into conflating intention and foresight of virtual certainty, with potentially dire results for palliative care. *Woollin* should be overruled as a matter of urgency.[35]

Intended ends and intended means

Another point. What if a supporter of VAE were to argue: 'I understand and sympathise with the long-standing objection to one person killing another, but VAE doesn't involve intentional killing, since the doctor's intention is simply to ease the patient's pain and suffering?' The reply can be brief. The doctor's intention may well be to ease pain and suffering, but he intends to do this *by terminating the patient's life*. The doctor intends to relieve suffering but also intends to kill. One can intend something as a means to an end as well as intending something as an end. It would hardly do for a burglar caught red-handed in a bank vault, pockets stuffed with wads of banknotes, to say: 'I deny intending to commit burglary. My intention is simply to buy a villa on the Costa Brava and retire from a life of crime.' He may well intend a happy, sun-soaked retirement; but he intends to burgle the bank as a means of paying for it.

'Catch-22'

Finally, the third definition of euthanasia – as embracing both intended and foreseen life-shortening – creates a particularly embarrassing problem

---

[35] For a powerful defence of the distinction drawn in *Moloney* between intended and foreseen effects see J. M. Finnis, 'Intention and Side-Effects' in R. G. Frey and Christopher W. Morris (eds.), *Liability and Responsibility* (1991) 32. See also J. L. A. Garcia, 'Intentions in Medical Ethics' in D. S. Oderberg and J. A. Laing (eds.), *Human Lives: Critical Essays on Consequentialist Bioethics* (1997) 161. Cf. A. P. Simester, 'Why Distinguish Intention from Foresight?' in Simester and Smith, *Harm and Culpability* 71.

for those many supporters of VAE who adopt it and who oppose NVAE. For if:

1 they equate intended death with foreseen death, and
2 they support the administration of palliative drugs to those who are dying in pain but incapable of asking for those drugs, and
3 if those drugs foreseeably shorten life,

why does this not count, on their own definition, as NVAE? In short, supporters of VAE who equate intended and foreseen death surely trap themselves in an intellectual 'catch-22'. Either they must drop their opposition to NVAE or they must object to any palliative care which foreseeably shortens the lives of incompetent patients. There is, of course, a third and more sensible alternative: to drop their equation of intention and foresight.

Conclusion

Chapter 1 argued that much confusion in the euthanasia debate is caused by imprecision in definition. This chapter has suggested that another common source of confusion is the conflation of intention and foresight and has given several reasons for maintaining a clear distinction, in both ethics and law, between intended and merely foreseen life-shortening and for embracing the principle of double effect. It is significant that both the House of Lords Select Committee and the New York State Task Force endorsed the distinction and affirmed the principle.

3

'Physician-assisted suicide'

Whereas in VAE it is the doctor who terminates the patient's life, in PAS he assists the patient to take his or her own life. Assistance may take the form of giving the patient the means to commit suicide, such as supplying a lethal pill to be swallowed or a plastic bag to be put over the head. Or it may take the form of advice about methods, such as which are the most effective. Laws against assisted suicide tend to prohibit not only facilitating suicide ('Here's a plastic bag to put over your head') but also encouraging suicide ('Go on – put the plastic bag over your head and breathe deeply').

A contemporary and striking example of PAS is provided by the bizarre activities of Dr Jack Kevorkian (or 'Dr Death' as the media have dubbed him) in the USA. Dr Kevorkian, a retired pathologist, assisted over forty people to commit suicide in recent years in circumstances which were somewhat removed from regular medical practice. These people travelled to Kevorkian from all over the USA to seek his assistance in suicide. He assisted them, sometimes by attaching them, in the back of his rusting Volkswagen van, to his 'suicide machine', which injected them with lethal drugs when they activated it. Despite being prosecuted for assisted suicide on several occasions, Kevorkian escaped conviction and continued his personal campaign for relaxation of the law in his peculiar way. It was only when he moved from assistance in suicide to euthanasia that he was finally convicted. He filmed himself administering a lethal injection, and the film helped secure his conviction for murder.

The focus of Kevorkian's activities, and the debate he has helped fuel in the USA, is PAS rather than VAE. In recent years campaigners for relaxation of the law in the USA have shifted their focus from VAE to PAS. For example, in the early 1990s, proposals to decriminalise PAS were put to voters in the states of Washington and California, but were narrowly defeated. In 1994, however, such a proposal was passed by voters in the state of Oregon, making that state one of the first jurisdictions in the world to accommodate PAS. We shall return to Oregon in chapter 15.

In 1997, campaigners for PAS argued before the US Supreme Court that laws prohibiting PAS were unconstitutional on the basis that the constitution protected a 'right to die'. The court rejected the claimed right to PAS and upheld the laws against assisted suicide.[1] In rejecting such a right the US Supreme Court followed the Supreme Court of Canada. In 1993, the Canadian Supreme Court was faced with the question of whether legislation prohibiting assisted suicide breached the Canadian Charter of Rights and Fundamental Freedoms.[2] The person who brought the case, Sue Rodriguez, was terminally ill with, and increasingly paralysed by, motor neurone disease. She applied to the courts for permission to be connected by a physician to a line by which she could, at a time of her choosing, self-administer a lethal dose. She argued that the legislation prohibiting PAS breached her rights to autonomy and dignity guaranteed by the Charter. By a narrow majority, the Supreme Court upheld the legislation and rejected her application. These cases serve further to illustrate the recent tendency of campaigners to challenge the law prohibiting assisted suicide rather than the law against murder. Similarly indicative of the trend to distinguish PAS from VAE is the fact that in 1999 the British Medical Association (BMA) initiated a wide-ranging consultation process to reconsider its opposition to PAS. It hosted a conference on PAS in May 2000. One issue raised at the conference was whether there is any significant difference between PAS and VAE. As we shall see in chapter 18, the conference reaffirmed the Association's opposition to PAS.

Why has the focus of debate, particularly in the USA, shifted to PAS? Campaigners for PAS argue that the difference between PAS and euthanasia is morally, and should also be legally, significant. They argue that in PAS it is the patient who makes the final decision and performs the fatal act whereas in VAE it is the doctor who decides whether the patient's life should be ended and who ends it. In other words, it is argued, PAS is an expression of the patient's autonomy, the patient's right to self-determination, and the patient remains in control, whereas VAE is an exercise in medical decision-making, if not medical paternalism, and the doctor is in control.

---

[1] *Washington* v. *Glucksberg* 138 L Ed 2d 772 at 781 (1997).
[2] *Rodriguez* v. *British Columbia (Attorney-General)* (1994) 107 DLR (4th) 342.

Moreover, PAS advocates claim that, unlike VAE, PAS allows time for the patient to change his or her mind.

Many remain unconvinced that there is any significant moral difference between the two and advance a number of counter-arguments. First, they argue that the supposed greater degree of patient control in cases of PAS is overstated. Even in PAS, the patient cannot *require* the doctor's assistance; whether assistance is given will depend on the decision of the doctor, not the patient. And the doctor will not assist unless he first decides that suicide is indeed appropriate in the patient's case. In PAS just as in VAE, they argue, the doctor will not agree to help end the patient's life unless the doctor forms the judgment that the patient's life is no longer worth living; that the patient would indeed be better off dead. So there is a decisive degree of medical control even in PAS.

Secondly, if one of the main moral arguments advanced by campaigners for PAS is respect for the autonomous request of a suffering patient, why should the patient's autonomous request for VAE not carry equal weight? Why should a patient who wants the doctor to administer a lethal injection (and a doctor who wants to comply) not have their autonomy respected? And what if the patient is physically incapable, because of disability, of committing suicide? Do campaigners for PAS value only the autonomy of those who are physically capable of taking their own lives? Do not proposals to decriminalise solely PAS discriminate against those patients with disabilities who are incapable of taking their own lives? And what if the drug taken by the patient does not work, or work quickly enough? Do PAS campaigners believe that doctors should stand idly by while the patient is dying a lingering death and begs the doctor for a swift release?

Thirdly, the physical difference between intentionally ending the patient's life, and intentionally helping the patient to end his or her own life, can be negligible. What, for example, is the supposed difference between a doctor handing a lethal pill to a patient; placing the pill on the patient's tongue; and dropping it down the patient's throat? Where does PAS end and VAE begin? It is easy to see why many conclude that the supposed distinction between PAS and VAE, even when it can be drawn in the physical world, has little significance (if any) in the moral world.[3]

---

[3] See generally Yale Kamisar, 'Physician-Assisted Suicide: The Last Bridge to Active Voluntary Euthanasia' in Keown, 225, 230–3.

Despite the tendency of 'right-to-die' campaigners in North America to urge a moral distinction, campaigners elsewhere, both for and against VAE, do not. In the Netherlands both have been officially condoned and widely practised since 1984. As two Dutch supporters of PAS and VAE have explained: 'In the Netherlands no *distinct moral* difference is maintained between VAE and PAS: No difference is perceived if a physician hands over a cup to drink or gives an injection by needle: In moral terms the act is considered to be identical because intentionally and effectively they both involve actively assisting death.'[4]

One of the authors went on explicitly to criticise the notion that PAS by itself could provide for all cases:

> Thinking that physician-assisted suicide is the entire answer to the question of ending of life of a suffering patient, nevertheless, is a fantasy. There will always be patients who cannot drink, or are semiconscious, or prefer that a physician perform this act. Experience has taught us that there are many cases of assisted suicide in which the suicide fails. Physicians need to be aware of the necessity to intervene before patients awaken.[5]

Commenting specifically on proposals in the USA to allow PAS but not VAE, he added: 'From the above facts, it should be abundantly clear that this limitation is headed for disaster if physicians are forbidden by law to end life actively in cases of failure of the chosen route for assistance.'[6]

Research from the Netherlands has confirmed that not all attempts at PAS are successful and that doctors have not infrequently stepped in to finish the job. A Dutch study reported more problems with the performance of PAS than VAE, and that in no fewer than 18% of cases in which the original intention had been to provide PAS, the doctor administered a lethal injection. The researchers explained:

> In most of these cases, the patient did not die as soon as expected or awoke from coma, and the physician felt compelled to administer a lethal injection because of the anticipated failure of the assisted suicide. In some cases, the

---

[4] Gerrit K. Kimsma and Evert van Leeuwen, 'Euthanasia and Assisted Suicide in the Netherlands and the USA: Comparing Practices, Justifications and Key Concepts in Bioethics and Law' in David C. Thomasma et al., *Asking to Die* (1998) 35, 51 (original emphasis). See also Griffiths, 111–14.

[5] Gerrit K. Kimsma, 'Euthanasia Drugs in the Netherlands' in Thomasma et al., *Asking to Die* 135, 142–3.

[6] Ibid., 143.

physician administered a lethal injection because the patient had difficulty swallowing the oral medication, vomited after swallowing it, or became unconscious before swallowing all of it.[7]

Similarly, in the UK, the alleged distinction has hardly featured in the debate, at least until the BMA consultation and conference. The House of Lords Select Committee on Medical Ethics, having concluded that the law should not be relaxed to permit VAE, simply added, in a brief paragraph, that neither should the law against assisted suicide: 'As far as assisted suicide is concerned, we see no reason to recommend any change in the law. We identify no circumstances in which assisted suicide should be permitted, nor do we see any reason to distinguish between the act of a doctor or of any other person in this connection.'[8]

Why, then, if there is really little to distinguish between PAS and VAE, has a distinction begun to be drawn, particularly among campaigners for reform in North America? The answer appears simply to be a matter of tactics. 'Right-to-die' campaigners may well have calculated that their chances of success are likely to be higher if they press for PAS rather than VAE. Not only might PAS be more easily sold as an exercise of 'patient autonomy' (a slogan with broad appeal, particularly in the USA) but it might more easily enable the campaign to distance itself from the uncomfortable historical baggage associated with euthanasia, not least the monstrous euthanasia programme perpetrated by the Nazi doctors.[9] If this is the thinking of the 'right-to-die' lobby, it is tactically shrewd. For, as the enactment of the law allowing PAS in Oregon illustrates, there appears to have been less reluctance to embrace PAS than VAE.

Conclusions

This chapter has offered a definition of PAS and has suggested that, although there is a current tendency among 'right-to-die' campaigners, especially in North America, to press for the decriminalisation of PAS

---

[7] Johanna H. Groenewoud et al., 'Clinical Problems with the Performance of Euthanasia and Physician-Assisted Suicide in the Netherlands' (2000) 342 *N Engl J Med* 551, 554–5.

[8] Lords' Report, para. 262.

[9] See Robert J. Lifton, *The Nazi Doctors: Medical Killing and the Psychology of Genocide* (1986); Michael Burleigh, *Death and Deliverance: 'Euthanasia' in Germany c. 1900–1945* (1994); Burleigh, *Ethics and Extermination: Reflections on Nazi Genocide* (1997).

rather than VAE, this is essentially a tactical novelty. It has long been accepted among both supporters and opponents of legalisation (even, until recently, in North America) that PAS and VAE raise substantially the same moral issues, that the arguments in favour of the former are essentially the same as for the latter. These arguments are outlined in the next chapter.

PART II

The ethical debate: human life, autonomy, legal hypocrisy, and the slippery slope

Chapter 1 noted that confusion, rather than consensus, surrounds even the definition of 'euthanasia'. The moral debate about whether VAE should be legalised betrays no more consensus and no less confusion. This is partly because of disagreement about terminology. But it is largely due to profound moral disagreement: about the value of human life; about the proper purpose and limits of individual autonomy; and about whether current law and medical practice consistently and effectively prohibit intentional medical killing.

Part II outlines three major arguments for the legalisation of VAE and offers replies to those arguments. The three arguments are:

- that it is right for a doctor intentionally to terminate the life of a patient at the patient's request when death is thought to be a benefit;
- that such a course, as well as recognising that life is sometimes a burden rather than a benefit, also respects the patient's autonomy, the patient's right to make his or her own decisions;
- that the current law is ineffective and inconsistent: not only does it fail to stop the clandestine practice of VAE by some doctors but it hypocritically permits some forms of medical practice, such as administering life-shortening doses of palliative drugs, which are actually a form of euthanasia.

Chapters 4–6 will consider each argument, and corresponding counter-arguments, in turn. Chapter 7 will then consider a major argument *against* decriminalising VAE – the so-called slippery slope argument.

4

The value of human life

The first argument for VAE concerns the value of human life. The argument runs that in certain circumstances, such as where a terminally ill patient requests accelerated death because of serious suffering, it is right for a doctor to comply with the request since death would benefit the patient. Many, however, would reject the claim that life can lose its worth so as to make death a benefit. Indeed, there are two philosophical schools of thought which strongly oppose any such claim. In order to clarify much of the confusion infecting this cardinal dispute, confusion which is rife not only among laypeople but also among doctors and lawyers, it is appropriate here to contrast three schools of thought about the value of human life.

'Vitalism' v. 'sanctity/inviolability of life' v. 'Quality of life'

Three competing views about the value of human life are: 'vitalism'; the 'sanctity/inviolability of life'; and 'Quality of life' (the reason for the capital 'Q' will become apparent below).

Vitalism

Vitalism holds that human life is an absolute moral value. Because of its absolute worth, it is wrong either to shorten the life of a patient or to fail to strive to lengthen it. Whether the life be that of a seriously disabled newborn baby or an elderly woman with advanced senile dementia, vitalism prohibits its shortening and requires its preservation. Regardless of the pain, suffering or expense that life-prolonging treatment entails, it must be administered. In short, the vitalist school of thought *requires human life to be preserved at all costs.*

Sanctity/inviolability of life

The prohibition of intentional killing

The moral and legal principle of the sanctity/inviolability of life is often advocated but much less often understood, even by senior judges who claim to uphold it.[1] In Western thought, the development of the principle has owed much to the Judaeo-Christian tradition.[2] That tradition's doctrine of the sanctity of life holds that human life is created in the image of God and is, therefore, possessed of an intrinsic dignity which entitles it to protection from unjust attack. With or without this theological underpinning, the doctrine that human life possesses an intrinsic dignity grounds the principle that one must never intentionally kill an innocent human being.[3] The 'right to life' is essentially a right not to be intentionally killed.

According to this school of thought, human beings possess dignity or worth because of that radical capacity, inherent in human nature, which normally results in the development of rational abilities such as understanding and choice. In some human beings, most obviously infants, these abilities have not developed. But a radical capacity should not be confused with an exercisable ability: for example, you have the *capacity* but may not have the *ability* to speak Swahili. In other words, you may not be able to speak it now, but you could do so at some point in the future because you have the innate capacity, as a human being, to learn languages. All human beings, moreover, should be presumed to possess the radical capacities characteristic of their nature even though, because of infancy, disability or senility, they may not yet, or ever, or any longer be in possession of the abilities which characteristically flow from those capacities.[4]

As this account of human dignity may suggest, the principle can also be articulated in non-religious terms, in which 'inviolability' would be a more fitting word than 'sanctity' with its religious overtones. Indeed, a prohibition on killing is central to the *pre*-Christian fount of Western

---

[1] See the discussion of the *Tony Bland* case in chapter 19.

[2] Respect for life is, however, also deeply rooted in Eastern thought: see Damien Keown, *Buddhism and Bioethics* (1995).

[3] 'Innocent' excludes anyone contributing to unjust aggression and the principle has, therefore, traditionally allowed the use of lethal force in self-defence, the prosecution of a just war and the execution of capital offenders. This has little relevance, however, to doctors and patients.

[4] See Gormally, 118–19.

medical ethics – the Hippocratic Oath[5] – and the modern reaffirmation of that Oath by the arguably *post*-Christian Declaration of Geneva.[6] Indeed, many non-believers recognise the right of innocent human beings not to be intentionally killed. As Lord Goff noted in the *Bland*[7] case, the sanctity principle has long been recognised in most, if not all, civilised societies throughout the modern world, as is evidenced by its recognition by international conventions on human rights. Article 2 of the European Convention, for example, provides: 'Everyone's right to life shall be protected by law. *No one shall be deprived of his life intentionally* save in the execution of a sentence of a court following his conviction of a crime for which this penalty is provided by law.'[8]

Whether expressed in its religious or secular forms, the principle holds that the right not to be killed intentionally is enjoyed regardless of inability or disability. Rejecting any such distinctions as fundamentally arbitrary and unjust, it asserts that human life is not only an *instrumental* good, a necessary precondition of thinking or doing, but a *basic* good, a fundamental basis of human flourishing. It is, in other words, not merely good as a means to an end but is, like other integral aspects of a flourishing human life, such as friendship and knowledge, something worth while in itself. Of course some people, like those who are pictures of health in the prime of life, participate in the good of life and health to a greater extent than others, such as the terminally ill, but even the sick and the dying participate in this good to the extent they are able. Although human life is a basic good it is not the highest good, a good to which all the other basic goods must be sacrificed in order to ensure its preservation. The sanctity doctrine is not, therefore, vitalistic. The core of the doctrine is the principle which prohibits *intentional killing*; the principle does *not* require the preservation of life at all costs.

Intention and foresight

Sanctity/inviolability prohibits *intentional* life-shortening. Conduct which is intended to shorten a patient's life – 'intention' bearing its ordinary

---

[5] 'To please no-one will I prescribe a deadly drug, nor give advice which may cause his death. Nor will I give a woman a pessary to procure abortion.' Quoted in J. K. Mason and R. A. McCall Smith, *Law and Medical Ethics* (5th edn, 1999) 551.

[6] (As amended in Stockholm in 1994): 'I will maintain the utmost respect for human life from its beginning even under threat, and I will not use my medical knowledge contrary to the laws of humanity' (quoted in ibid., 552).

[7] [1993] AC 789 at 863–4.   [8] Emphasis added.

meaning of purpose – is always wrong. The doctrine embraces the principle of double effect outlined in chapter 2.[9] It therefore accepts that conduct which foreseeably shortens life is not always wrong. Whether it is will turn largely on whether there is a sufficient justification for taking the risk of shortening life. Consequently, according to this approach, a doctor treating a dying cancer patient suffering considerable pain clearly has a sufficient justification for administering reasonable doses of palliative drugs with intent to ease the pain, even though a foreseeable side-effect may or will be the shortening of the patient's life. Similarly, a doctor may properly withhold or withdraw a life-prolonging treatment which is futile (that is, cannot secure a significant therapeutic benefit) or which the patient would find too burdensome, even though the doctor foresees that non-treatment may or will result in the patient's life ending sooner than would otherwise be the case. Doctors may not, on the other hand, take unreasonable risks with patients' lives. It is one thing for a doctor to perform neurosurgery to remove a malignant tumour, even though the operation may prove fatal; quite another to perform it solely to practise surgical skills when there is no possible benefit to the patient.

Acts and omissions

In the medical context, there are no exceptions to inviolability's moral prohibition of intentional killing: the doctor who intentionally shortens the life of a patient, whether a terminally ill adult or a child with Down's syndrome, breaches the principle. It matters not, moreover, whether the shortening is brought about by an act or an omission. Intentionally shortening a patient's life by withholding treatment, or food, water or warmth, is no less wrong than injecting a lethal poison. Nor does a good motive, such as the alleviation of suffering, of the patient or relatives, redeem a bad intent. In short, any conduct which is intended to shorten a patient's life, whether as an end or as a means to an end, and whatever the further motive, offends against the principle.

The worthwhileness of *treatment*: its benefits and burdens

The inviolability doctrine accepts that it is often proper to withhold/ withdraw treatment even though it is foreseen that death will therefore come sooner. That one need not try to preserve life *at all costs* is sometimes

---

[9] See pp. 20–1.

amusingly expressed in the words of A. H. Clough's poem 'The Latest Decalogue'[10] that while one must not kill, one 'needst not strive/ *Officiously* to keep alive'. More precisely, however, the inviolability principle holds that there can be no moral obligation to administer or undergo a treatment which is not worth while.

A treatment may be not worth while either because it offers no reasonable hope of benefit or because, even though it does, the expected benefit would be outweighed by burdens which the treatment would impose, such as excessive pain. Notice, however, that the question is always whether the *treatment* would be worth while, not whether the patient's *life* would be worth while. Were one to engage in judgments of the latter sort, and to conclude that certain lives were 'not worth living', one would forfeit any principled basis for objecting to intentional killing.

Where the benefit of a proposed treatment is not outweighed by the burdens it would impose (or would risk imposing, as with a relatively unproven, experimental therapy), it has traditionally been referred to as 'ordinary' and where the converse is the case as 'extraordinary'. Problems associated with this terminology (not least the fact that 'ordinary' was often mistakenly interpreted to mean 'usual' and 'extraordinary' to mean 'unusual') have resulted in the increasing use of terms such as 'proportionate' and 'disproportionate'. But whichever terms are used, the moral question remains the same: whether a proposed treatment would be worth while, that is, whether its benefits, if any, would outweigh its burdens, if any. What if, by contrast, the decision were based not on whether the *treatment* would be worth while but on whether it was thought that the patient's *life* was worth while? Here we encounter the third school of thought about the value of human life, which may be described as the 'Quality of life' approach.

Quality of life

The doctrine of the Quality of life is not concerned only with assessing the worthwhileness of the treatment but also the worthwhileness *of the patient's life*. It holds that the lives of certain patients fall below a quality threshold, whether because of disease, injury or disability. This valuation

---

[10] In Carl Woodring and James Shapiro (eds.), *The Columbia Anthology of British Poetry* (1995) 615.

of human life grounds the principle that, because certain lives are not worth living, it is right intentionally to end them, whether by act or by deliberate omission. Some who subscribe to this doctrine would require the patient's request as a precondition of termination on the ground that only the patient is in a position to judge whether life is still worth living. Others would not. After all, they argue, if the life of an incompetent patient, such as an elderly woman with advanced dementia, is of such low quality that it is no longer worth living and death would be a benefit, what is wrong with intentionally ending it?

Distinguishing 'Quality of life' from 'quality of life'

'Quality of life' judgments purport to judge the worthwhileness of the patient's life. The inviolability doctrine opposes such attempts and merely takes the patient's condition into account in deciding on the worthwhileness of a proposed treatment. For, in order to decide whether a proposed treatment would be worth while, one must first ascertain the patient's present condition and consider whether and to what extent it would be improved by the proposed treatment. This exercise is often described as involving an assessment of the patient's 'quality of life' now and as it would be after the treatment. At no point in the inviolability assessment is one purporting to pass judgment on the worthwhileness of the patient's life, but the use of the term 'quality of life' clearly risks confusion with its use in that sense. Such confusion is, regrettably, common in ethical and legal discourse. To avoid any misunderstanding here, 'quality of life' will be used to refer to an assessment of the patient's condition as a preliminary to gauging the worthwhileness of a proposed treatment, and 'Quality of life' to refer to an assessment of the worthwhileness of the patient's life. (Hence the use of the capital 'Q' when setting out the three competing approaches.)

Illustrating the distinctions

Given the profound importance of understanding the differences between these three competing approaches to the value of human life, it may be helpful to illustrate the distinctions by way of two hypothetical examples, followed by an elementary diagram.

Mary's case

Mary is a frail old lady, aged 95, who has advanced senile dementia. She has just been admitted to hospital after her third major heart attack and is examined by three consultant physicians, Dr V, Dr Q and Dr I. All three agree about the diagnosis: Mary is suffering from severe coronary disease and advanced Alzheimer's disease. They also agree about the prognosis: Mary's condition is terminal. The coronary disease is progressive and irreversible and she is likely to suffer further heart attacks and to die within weeks if not days. The only way of attempting to extend her life when she suffers her next heart attack would be by cardio-pulmonary resuscitation (CPR). The doctors discuss among themselves (because of her dementia Mary is incompetent to make her own decisions) the right ethical course to take when she suffers her next heart attack. Each doctor explains his ethical approach to the other two. As will appear, the doctors' disagreement about ethics is as pronounced as their agreement about the medical facts.

Dr V(italism)

Dr V explains to Dr Q and Dr I that he thinks that human life is an *absolute* good and that it should be preserved at all costs, regardless of the expense of medical treatment or any pain and discomfort imposed by the treatment. It matters not, he says, whether the patient is young or old, able-bodied or disabled, curable or incurable: the life of every patient has to be preserved as long as possible. In short, Dr V is of the view that it is always unethical to shorten human life or to fail to try to lengthen it. He advocates vitalism. His motto is, he proclaims, 'Long live vitalism! Keep everyone alive!' Applying this vitalistic approach to Mary, he recommends that when she suffers her next heart attack, CPR should be administered. Indeed, he adds, any treatment necessary to preserve her life must be administered to her, regardless of its expense and regardless of any suffering the treatment may cause her.

Dr Q(uality of life)

Dr Q's views are at the opposite ethical pole to those of Dr V. Dr Q states that human life is not an *absolute* good but only an *instrumental* good. It is not absolutely good in itself but is only good in an instrumental way, as a means to an end. That end is leading a 'worthwhile' life, a life of a minimum

'Quality'. 'For of what value is life', asks Dr Q, 'unless as a *vehicle* for a life which is *worth living*?' Serious disability can, he adds, preclude a worthwhile life, particularly if it is mental disability, for an essential requirement of a 'worthwhile' life is the ability to reason, express preferences and make choices. Indeed, if the mental disability deprives the individual of the ability to think rationally, Dr Q adds, what is morally to distinguish the life of that human being from that of a brute animal? A human being who lacks the ability to reason may not even qualify as a 'person'. So, human beings who have not yet developed the ability to reason (such as babies) and those who have never had it (such as those with severe congenital mental handicap) or who have lost it (such as those with advanced senile dementia) may not even qualify as 'persons'. His guiding principle is: 'It is wrong to terminate persons with worthwhile lives, particularly if they want to go on living, but not wrong to kill those whose lives are not worth living, at least if they ask for death or if they lack sufficient mental ability to count as "persons".'

Applying this ethical approach to Mary's case, Dr Q recommends that, given Mary's serious mental disability which renders her unable to think rationally and make decisions, Mary's life is not worth living. Indeed, she does not now, nor will she ever again, qualify as a 'person'. Another reason for allowing Mary to die is, Dr Q continues, that her continuous care is a waste of healthcare resources which could be better spent on someone with intact mental faculties. Consequently, Dr Q advises that Mary should not be resuscitated when she suffers her next heart attack and should instead be 'allowed to die'. Dr Q adds that the ideal option, if only it were permitted by law, would be intentionally to end her life by lethal injection.

Dr I(nviolability of life)

Dr I disagrees with both Dr V and Dr Q, advocating an approach which (as illustrated by the diagram below) offers an ethical 'middle way' between their viewpoints. Dr I explains that human life is neither an *absolute* good nor merely an *instrumental* good but is, rather, a *basic* good. It is a necessary condition of leading a fulfilled life and undoubtedly good in itself. But there is more to a flourishing life than life itself. Life is not the *only* basic good. There are others, such as friendship, knowledge and the enjoyment of art and beauty. That is why Dr I rejects Dr V's elevation of the good of life to the status of the *highest* good which takes priority over the other basic goods. Were life the highest good, it would require us to devote all our time, energies and resources to the preservation of life instead of cultivating friendships, learning, and an appreciation of art and beauty. That would be a stunted rather than a fulfilled life.

It is not the role of the doctor, says Dr I, to prolong life until the last second, but to seek to restore patients to a state of health and, if that is not possible, to alleviate any suffering. There is, moreover, no duty to treat if the treatment is 'disproportionate', either because it is futile (that is, offers no reasonable hope of therapeutic benefit) or because it would involve excessive burdens to the patient (such as excessive pain or expense). In Dr I's view, the doctor's duty to treat is much more limited than Dr V thinks. There is no duty to treat if treatment will not benefit the patient. Treatment will clearly benefit the patient if it will improve the patient's condition or 'quality of life'. In deciding whether a proposed treatment would improve the patient's 'quality of life', Dr I asks: 'Given the patient's present condition, would this treatment improve it?' If it would not, or if it would but it would impose excessive burdens on the patient, then the patient is under no duty to request it or the doctor to provide it. Treatment will also benefit the patient, even if it will not improve the patient's condition, if it will prolong the patient's life when the patient is able to enjoy some of the other basic goods of human life.

Dr I goes on to explain that, just as he avoids Dr V's *absolute* notion of human life at one pole, he also avoids Dr Q's *instrumental* notion of human life at the other pole. He repeats that human life is a basic good, a basic aspect of human flourishing. It is not, like money, of merely in-strumental value. Human life is good in itself, must be respected as such, and must never be intentionally shortened. And although both he and Dr Q use the term 'quality of life', Dr I stresses that he uses it to mean something entirely different from Dr Q. Dr Q uses 'Quality of life' to dis-tinguish between 'worthwhile' and 'worthless' *patients*. That is, Dr Q asks: 'Given this patient's "Quality of life", that is, his or her disabilities, is the patient's *life* worth living or would the patient be better off dead?' But Dr I, who believes that *all* patients are worth while, uses it to distinguish between worthwhile and worthless *treatments*: 'Given the patient's present "quality of life", that is, the patient's condition, would this *treatment* be worth while?' Dr I thinks that the Quality of life philosophy denies the ineradicable value of each patient and engages in discriminatory judg-ments, posited on arbitrary criteria such as physical or mental disability, about whose lives are 'worth while' and whose are not. The arbitrariness is highlighted, he adds, when it is asked *which* disabilities, and to which *degree*, are supposed to make life not worth living.[11] In short, Dr I says that human life is not a mere means to an end and that it must never be intentionally taken. But neither is it an absolute good to be preserved at all costs. Dr I's motto is: 'Life must never be intentionally taken, but it need not be preserved at all costs.'

Applying this approach to Mary, Dr I advises that, contrary to Dr Q's opinion, it would be wrong intentionally to shorten her life, whether by an act or by withholding CPR. There is no moral difference, says Dr I, between withholding a treatment with *intent* to shorten Mary's life and administering a lethal injection to her. Either course of conduct denies her basic human right not to be intentionally killed and treats her life in a merely instrumental way, as a mere means to the end of living a life of a certain 'Quality'. But just because it is wrong to put an end to Mary's life does not mean one must preserve her life at all costs, which is why he disagrees with Dr V's approach. Dr I advises that the doctor's duty is to restore the patient to health if that can be done by treatment which is not disproportionate. Would the treatment be disproportionate? Would it, in other words, offer any reasonable hope of benefit or impose excessive burdens on Mary? Given that Mary is dying, CPR would offer no prospect of improving her quality of life. It would therefore be medically futile. Moreover, the treatment could well impose grave burdens on her. Not only could it prove very distressing to her, but it could easily, in view of her age and frail condition, result in painful fractures. Dr I therefore agrees with Dr Q that CPR should be withheld, though for radically different reasons from those advanced by Dr Q.

Angela

Angela is a baby born with Down's syndrome and an intestinal blockage. Her doctor informs her parents that the blockage can be removed by a straightforward surgical operation and that, if it is not so removed, Angela will die.

Dr V

Dr V, applying the principle that life must be preserved at all costs, argues that the blockage should be removed so that Angela will live.

[11] See Gormally, 123–4.

Dr Q

Dr Q takes the view that life with Down's syndrome is not worth living. Although he recognises that the operation can be performed easily, he advises that the blockage should not be removed in order that Angela will die. His focus is on the worth of Angela's life, not on the efficacy of the treatment. Indeed, the problem arises in Dr Q's view precisely because the treatment would be entirely successful: it would save a life which he thinks is not worth while.[12]

Dr I

Dr I advises that the operation should go ahead: the treatment will clearly benefit Angela by saving her life, and will involve only minimal burdens, such as the usual risks and discomfort associated with a surgical operation. Dr I refuses to allow the fact of Angela's mental retardation to enter into his reasoning about the worthwhileness of the operation: she should be treated just like a little girl of normal mental ability.

This time, therefore, it is Dr V and Dr I who are in agreement, and Dr Q who disagrees.

Conclusion

If one is to make sense of the debate about whether it is right for doctors intentionally to end their patients' lives, it is important to appreciate that there are at least three competing approaches to the valuation of human life. Different people adopt different approaches and this disagreement lies at the heart of the debate about whether it can ever be right in principle for a doctor to perform VAE.

This chapter has sketched three main competing approaches. It has suggested that, while the argument that in certain circumstances patients

---

[12] It is not suggested that all those who subscribe to a Quality of life approach would reach the same conclusion as Dr Q. But in view of the inherent arbitrariness of the Quality of life approach, it is difficult even for its adherents to identify clear criteria by which to judge whose life is 'worth while' and whose is not. And while some Quality of life adherents may regard life with Down's as worth living, others do not. As we shall see in chapter 20, the sedation and starvation of babies with Down's syndrome by doctors in England is far from unknown. Something of the same arbitrariness inherent in the Quality of life approach is evident in the varying indications for eugenic abortion applied by English doctors, which range from spina bifida to harelip and cleft palate.

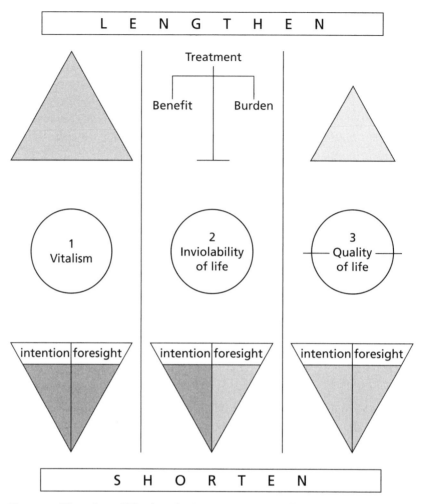

Figure 1   The value of life: three basic positions. *Key:* The triangles (when pointing up) signify conduct which lengthens life and (when pointing down) shortens it. The shading indicates how each approach regards the conduct: dark signifies unethical, light ethical. The light vitalist triangle is larger than the corresponding Quality of life triangle to indicate the former's greater emphasis on preserving life. In place of a triangle, the inviolability approach has a scale to represent the weighing of benefits and burdens in assessing whether a proposed treatment would be worth while. The line bisecting the Quality of life circle represents the level below which that approach judges lives to be no longer worth living.

are better off dead may well exert a certain emotional appeal, particularly in 'hard cases', it is inconsistent with the principle of the inviolability of life (which has historically informed medical ethics and the criminal law), and must also meet the criticism that it is arbitrary and unjust. For it holds that only certain patients, those with certain arbitrarily defined abilities, have a right not to be intentionally killed. The inviolability approach replies that such basic human rights attach because we are human beings, not because we are human beings with a particular degree of a particular mental ability.

Is the criticism of arbitrariness and injustice avoided by allowing *only the individuals affected* to decide that their lives are no longer worth living? Could VAE not be confined to those who came to the judgment that *their own lives* lacked value and that death would be a benefit *for them*? This question will be explored in the next chapter.

5

The value of autonomy

The 'right to choose'

As we saw in chapter 4, the belief that in some circumstances death is better than life, that life is no longer worth living, is an important strand in the argument for VAE. Another strand, hardly less central, is that VAE respects a patient's right to autonomy or self-determination. The bulk of those campaigning for relaxation of the law weave the two strands together. They stress that they support only *voluntary* euthanasia: euthanasia is only ever justifiable *at the request of the patient* as no one but the patient is in a position to judge the worthwhileness of his own life. Only if the *patient* decides that life has lost its value and asks for VAE should it be performed.

Given the rise, particularly in the West, of an almost absolute respect for personal autonomy and the decline of established religious belief on which respect for the inviolability of life has traditionally been based, it is hardly surprising that support for VAE appears to have grown substantially. The traditional consensus has been undermined by liberal pluralism. Many people now reject traditional views about the inviolability of life – views which they often criticise as 'religious', 'authoritarian', 'absolutist' and unfairly 'imposed' by the law on non-believers. They support the relaxation of the law so as to allow individuals to make their own personal decisions about what to value and how to act, particularly when the decision affects so fundamental and personal a matter as when and how to die. If, they argue, a patient thinks that VAE is immoral, he need not ask for it. If, on the other hand, a patient thinks that continued life in a suffering or incapacitated state is an indignity, inconsistent with his own assessment of what makes life worth living, he should be allowed to obtain VAE. As one leading liberal advocate of relaxation has (rather emotively) put it: 'Making someone die in a way that others approve, but he believes a horrifying contradiction of his life, is a devastating, odious form of tyranny.'[1]

Choosing what is right

The purpose and value of autonomy

While placing a high value on autonomy, opponents of VAE argue that its importance is exaggerated by supporters of VAE. The value of individual choice lies, opponents would argue, in the fact that it is through our choices that we are able to promote our own flourishing as human beings (and that of those around us). Such choices, moreover, serve to reinforce dispositions to act in ways conducive to our flourishing. For our choices have internal as well as external effects and serve to shape our character. A's murder of B results not only in B being murdered but in making A a murderer. As the ancient adage attests, an act tends to form a habit, a habit tends to form a character, and a character tends to form a destiny.[2]

The capacity to choose brings with it the responsibility of making not just any old choice, but choices that do in fact promote, rather than undermine, human flourishing. Given the legitimate diversity of lifestyles and life-choices which are consistent with human flourishing, many choices are consistent with human well-being. We should, therefore, think carefully before restricting another's autonomy. But it is difficult to see why patently immoral choices, choices clearly inconsistent with human well-being, merit any respect.

In other words, an exercise of autonomy merits respect only when it is exercised in accordance with a framework of sound moral values. For example, A's decision to murder B is an exercise of autonomy, but it hardly merits respect since it breaches a grave moral norm. This is particularly clear when the decision, such as a decision to murder, seriously harms another person. But it is also true when the decision is morally wrong, whether or not it 'harms' another and whether or not the 'victim' consents. Should we respect decisions to buy and smoke 'crack' cocaine? Or to perform the mutilating procedure of 'female circumcision' on a consenting woman? Or to kill oneself? Opponents of absolute respect for individual autonomy could also cite instances of individual autonomy being

---

[1] Ronald Dworkin, *Life's Dominion* (1993) 217.
[2] See Gormally, 130–1.

restricted by the criminal law even when the act in question is not seriously immoral, such as driving a car without a seatbelt. They would argue that autonomy, far from being a self-justifying end in itself, is more like the pointer in a compass. The pointer itself is of little value, indeed makes little sense, in the absence of the points of the compass. When the pointer indicates a morally valuable course – and there may be a number of morally valuable courses – the choice merits respect. But when the choice is immoral, whether because it would harm another, or oneself, what claim to moral respect can it have? This is *not* to say that *all* immoral choices should be overridden by the law – the law is, for one thing, too blunt an instrument for that – merely that such choices cannot command moral respect. Those making immoral choices certainly have no right to be assisted in carrying them out.

Opponents of VAE would add that much contemporary talk about autonomy consists of little more than the naked assertion that a person's choice merits respect *simply because it is his choice, whatever that choice may be.* They would add that supporters of VAE who reject the inviolability of life as being 'absolutist' are hypocritically trying to supplant it with another moral absolute: an unqualified respect for individual choice, focusing on a self-justifying 'right to choose' rather than on what it is right to choose. The 'right to choose x' often serves as a slogan with powerful emotional appeal. But crude slogans are no substitute for rational reflection, and one can hardly sensibly assert a right to choose 'x' until one has considered whether it is right to choose 'x'; to do otherwise is simply to beg the question. Is there a 'right to choose . . . paedophilia'? Or a 'right to choose . . . cruelty to animals'? Does the mere fact that someone *wants* to blind ponies or to have sex with children carry any moral weight? The 'right to choose' only arguably makes any moral sense in the context of a moral framework which enables us to discern what it is *right* to choose and what choices will in fact promote human flourishing. And not only *our* flourishing, but that of others. For we do not live as atomised individuals, as much loose talk about absolute respect for personal autonomy seems to assume, but in community, where our choices can have profound effects not only on ourselves but on others. As Professor McCall Smith has pertinently observed, we live our lives in the moral company of others, with whom our lives constantly intersect. He cautions that regarding autonomy as the supreme value invites moral pluralism, which easily becomes moral relativism, which is corrosive of moral community. If, by contrast, autonomy is regarded as but one of several important values, then the case for VAE becomes subject to a consideration of those other values.[3]

One of those values is, of course, the value of human life. If the principle of the inviolability of life is accepted, and it has hitherto been a hallmark of civilised societies, its implications for the right to self-determination are patent. If it is seriously immoral intentionally to kill an innocent person, it is difficult to see how a choice to kill, whether another or oneself, can command moral respect. As the Anglican and Catholic bishops stated in their joint submission to the House of Lords Select Committee on Medical Ethics, autonomy is not absolute and is valid 'only when it recognises other moral values, especially the respect due to human life as such, whether someone else's or one's own'.[4] Indeed, the argument continues, given the fundamental value of life, society is fully justified in using the criminal law to deter the implementation of such choices. This is not to say that society must use the law against attempted suicides, who typically need understanding and help rather than condemnation and punishment, but simply that it remains reasonable to use it against those who would assist or encourage suicide.

Opponents of VAE would conclude that, just as the patient's life is not the highest moral value requiring preservation at all costs, neither is the patient's self-determination a moral absolute requiring respect in all circumstances, and certainly not when it involves a choice to kill, whether oneself or another.

The right to refuse futile or excessively burdensome treatments

What role, then, would opponents of VAE accord to individual autonomy at the end of life? While denying that it could ever be right for a patient to judge that his life was no longer worth living, they would defend the patient's right to judge whether a proposed treatment would be beneficial, as for example by improving the quality of his life.

In determining whether a proposed treatment would involve excessive burdens to a particular patient, the views of the patient are clearly crucial. People differ, for example, in their ability to tolerate pain, and what may

---

[3] Alexander McCall Smith, 'Beyond Autonomy' in [1997] 14(1) *J Contemp Health Law Policy* 23, 37–9.

[4] *Euthanasia – No!* (1993) para. 8. On the extent to which the law may properly restrict autonomy to enforce morality see Robert P. George, *Making Men Moral* (1993).

be excessively painful for one patient may not be so for another. Indeed, the distinctions between proportionate and disproportionate treatments were devised by moral thinkers not primarily for the purposes of health-care professionals faced with decisions about which treatments they ought to offer, but for patients facing decisions about which treatments they ought to accept. Moreover, the responsibility for safeguarding and promoting the good of health lies primarily with the *patient*, not with the doctor, at least where the patient is able to make his own decisions. Choices by patients which promote the good of health therefore merit respect and it is reasonable to allow patients considerable leeway, given the considerable variation between patients, in deciding what treatments they would find too onerous.

How autonomous?

There is a further objection that opponents of VAE could raise. *Just how autonomous* are requests for VAE likely to be? Requests are likely to emanate from patients experiencing significant distress at the close of their lives, whose judgment is impaired by the painful effects of terminal illness, clouded by the side-effects of medical treatment, and warped by clinical depression or 'demoralisation'.[5] Even if a patient's capacity for choice were unaffected, how informed is he likely to be about the diagnosis and prognosis and about alternatives such as palliative care? Is there not a genuine danger that many patients would request VAE not because of a clear-headed evaluation that it was the best option for them but because they felt abandoned, or an unwanted burden on relatives, medical and nursing staff, or society? In short, how many requests would reflect the *truly* autonomous wishes of the patient? Significantly, an impressive body of research indicates that a majority of patients who request VAE are indeed suffering from clinical depression or inadequately treated symptoms. Commenting on the psychiatric literature, two experts have observed: 'Studies exploring the motivations that lead to a desire for euthanasia have highlighted the prominent role of depression in its development.'[6]

[5] D. W. Kissane et al, 'Demoralisation Syndrome – a Relevant Psychiatric Diagnosis for Palliative Care' (2001) 17 *J Pall Care* 12.
[6] Annette Street and David Kissane, 'Dispensing Death, Desiring Death: An Exploration of Medical Roles and Patient Motivation during the Period of Legalised Euthanasia in Australia'

Conclusion

The second major argument for VAE, that it respects individual autonomy, is too often advanced as if it were an obvious conclusion rather than a controversial proposition. The counter-argument is that many requests for VAE are not truly autonomous but result from depression or inadequate palliative care and that, in any event, the value of autonomy lies not in making just *any* choice but choices which are consistent with a framework of sound moral values. If this is so, then talk of 'respect for personal autonomy' tends to distract attention from the *fundamental* moral question, raised by the first argument and considered in chapter 4, which is whether doctors are justified in intentionally terminating the lives of patients, even on request.

(1999–2000) 40 *Omega* 231. See also William Breibart and Barry D. Rosenfeld, 'Physician-Assisted Suicide: The Influence of Psychosocial Issues' (1999) 6 *Cancer Control* 146 (also at www.hospicecare.com); H. M. Chochinov et al, 'Will to Live in the Terminally Ill' (1999) 354 *Lancet* 816.

6

Legal hypocrisy?

A third argument prominently deployed in favour of legalising VAE is that the present law is hypocritical. It is argued that, while the law prohibits VAE in theory, it is unenforced in practice, and that this inaction against what is a common practice betrays tacit approval. In other words, while the law ostensibly sets its face against VAE, it nevertheless winks at it. The law's alleged hypocrisy is compounded, the argument continues, by the fact that while it prohibits doctors from administering or handing lethal drugs to patients it nevertheless allows doctors intentionally to end patients' lives, and help patients end their own lives, in other ways.

The current law

VAE as murder

Before evaluating these criticisms, we need first to consider what the state of the law is. We shall outline the law in England, though the law in other jurisdictions whose law is derived from English law, such as the USA, Canada, Australia and New Zealand, is similar.[1] To begin with, we shall consider which of the three competing moral approaches outlined in chapter 4 the law adopts.

The law has never adopted vitalism: doctors have never been under a duty to preserve life at all costs.[2] Nor has the law historically accepted the 'Quality of life' approach – that only those with 'worthwhile' lives have a right not to be killed. Rather, the law has traditionally adopted the inviolability principle. In particular, it has always been murder for a doctor actively and intentionally to hasten a patient's death. It is murder,

---

[1] See generally Margaret Otlowski, *Voluntary Euthanasia and the Common Law* (1997).
[2] See p. 231.

however compassionate the motive of the doctor,[3] and whatever the age, medical condition or wishes of the patient. It is as much murder so to kill an aged terminally ill cancer patient who pleads for death as it is to kill a young person in the prime of life who strenuously clings to life. Nor is it a defence for a doctor to plead that terminating the patient's life was a reasonable and proportionate way of securing a higher good recognised by the law (the defence of necessity)[4] or that he or she felt compelled to terminate the patient's life by threats of death or serious injury made by the patient or relatives (the defence of duress).[5]

Nor is the criminal law concerned only to punish *active* killing. Although there is, generally, no liability for an omission to preserve life, it is well established that it is murder to omit to discharge a duty to preserve life with intent to kill. Examples are a parent's omission to feed a child,[6] or a doctor's to feed a patient, with such intent.

The law also punishes assisting or encouraging another to commit suicide. The Suicide Act 1961 provides a maximum penalty of fourteen years imprisonment for aiding, abetting, counselling or procuring suicide. This is less than the penalty prescribed for murder: a mandatory sentence of life imprisonment.[7]

---

[3] As Lord Goff has pointed out: 'if I kill you from the motive of compassion (so-called mercy killing) I nevertheless intend to kill you and the crime is one of murder' (Lord Goff, 'The Mental Element in the Crime of Murder' (1988) 104 *LQR* 30 at 42 (footnote omitted)).

[4] In *Dudley and Stephens* (1884–5) 14 QBD 273, Lord Chief Justice Coleridge, rejecting necessity as a defence to murder, observed (at 287): 'It is not needful to point out the awful danger of admitting the principle which has been contended for. Who is to be the judge of this sort of necessity? By what measure is the comparative value of lives to be measured? Is it to be strength, or intellect, or what?' Cf. *Re A (Children)* [2000] 4 All ER 961.

[5] In *Howe* [1987] AC 417 Lord Mackay said (at 456):

> It seems to me plain that the reason that it was for so long stated by writers of authority that the defence of duress was not available in a charge of murder was because of the supreme importance that the law afforded to the protection of human life and that it seemed repugnant that the law should recognise in any individual in any circumstances, however extreme, the right to choose that one innocent person should be killed rather than another.

He concluded that the law should continue to deny that right. See also *McKay* v. *Essex AHA* [1982] QB 1166. The courts' misunderstanding of the inviolability of life in several leading medico-legal cases over the last twenty years is considered in chapter 19.

[6] *R.* v. *Gibbins and Proctor* (1918) 13 Cr App R 134.

[7] There is considerable support for the abolition of the mandatory life sentence to enable judges to pass sentences calibrated to the moral blameworthiness of the particular defendant. See, e.g.,

The inviolability principle, it will be recalled, prohibits conduct *intended* to shorten life; conduct which is *foreseen* as certain to shorten life may or may not be culpable, depending on the circumstances. Inviolability incorporates the principle of double effect. Similarly, the criminal law also generally distinguishes intention from foresight. Intentional killing is punished as murder, but conduct which foreseeably shortens life is at most manslaughter and may be perfectly lawful, depending on the reasonableness of the doctor's conduct. As our discussion in chapter 2 of cases such as *Cox* and *Moor* showed, a doctor who follows reasonable medical practice in administering palliative drugs to a dying patient, intending thereby to alleviate suffering, acts lawfully, even if the drugs hasten death as an unintended side-effect. As we also noted in that chapter, however, the apparently unargued and, with respect, erroneous equation by the Law Lords in *Woollin* of intention with foresight of virtual certainty casts unnecessary and regrettable doubt on these cases. To equate trying to kill pain with trying to kill patients[8] is bad ethics which produces bad law which can only impede good medical practice.

Autonomy and the law

The law has historically embodied the 'middle way' not only on the value of life but also on individual autonomy. While placing a high value on autonomy, it has declined to afford it absolute respect. Consequently, it has proscribed, and continues to proscribe, many exercises of autonomy on the ground that they are wrongful. Their wrongfulness often inheres

Report of the Select Committee (Paper 78-I of 1988–9), *Murder and Life Imprisonment*; Lords' Report, para. 261. There is clearly something to be said for punishing those who kill out of compassion less severely than those who kill for selfish motives. Another means of enabling judges to do so would be to create a separate offence of 'mercy killing'. This was considered, and rejected, by the Criminal Law Revision Committee in 1980: see Roger Leng, 'Mercy Killing and the CLRC' (1982) 132 *New LJ* 76. It was also opposed by the House of Lords Select Committee on Medical Ethics:

> To distinguish between murder and 'mercy killing' would be to cross the line which prohibits any intentional killing, a line which we think it essential to preserve. Nor do we believe that 'mercy killing' could be adequately defined, since it would involve determining precisely what constituted a compassionate motive. For these reasons we do not recommend the creation of a new offence.

Lords' Report, para. 260

[8] For another example of this confusion see Ian Kennedy, 'The Quality of Mercy: Patients, Doctors and Dying' (The Upjohn Lecture, 1994).

in their infliction of harm upon others or in the exposure of others to the risk of harm, whether or not, as in, say, duelling, the other consents to the risk of harm.[9] But an exercise of autonomy may also be prohibited because it exposes oneself to harm, or to the risk of harm, such as snorting cocaine or, less seriously, driving a vehicle without wearing a seatbelt. In short, the law has, historically, provided scant support for an absolutist understanding of individual autonomy.

Five criticisms of the current law

The charge of hypocrisy subsumes five criticisms.

Ineffective?

The first criticism is that VAE and PAS are common, that the legal prohibition is largely unenforced, and that the lack of enforcement betrays an attitude of hypocritical sympathy. There are a number of problems with this criticism. First, it needs to show that VAE and PAS are common. While there is some evidence that they occur, there appears to be little hard evidence that they are at all frequent. In a survey commissioned by BBC Scotland and carried out in 1996, 1,000 health professionals (including pharmacists) were asked about their experience of PAS: 60% said they had treated a patient who had considered suicide[10] and 28% had been asked to provide the means.[11] Twelve per cent of respondents said that they personally knew another health professional who had assisted suicide,[12] and 4% that they had themselves assisted suicide, providing either drugs or advice.[13] While 4% is not an insignificant percentage, it hardly shows that PAS is commonplace.

Another, less detailed, survey took the form of a postal questionnaire sent to 424 English doctors. It asked: 'Have you ever taken active steps to bring about the death of a patient who asked you to do so?' Thirty-eight (9%) replied affirmatively.[14] Again, while 9% is not an insignificant proportion, it is a long way from a majority. There is, moreover, some doubt

---

[9] See also *R. v. Brown* [1991] 2 All ER 75.

[10] Sheila A. M. McLean and Alison Britton, *Sometimes a Small Victory* (1996) Appendix III, table 17, 31–2.

[11] Ibid., table 19, 35–6.   [12] Ibid., table 20, 37–8.   [13] Ibid., table 18, 33–4.

[14] B. J. Ward and P. A. Tate, 'Attitudes among NHS Doctors to Requests for Euthanasia' (1994) 308 *BMJ* 1332.

about the reliability of this response. Asked if they would be 'prepared to withdraw or withhold a course of treatment from a terminally ill patient, knowing the treatment might prolong the patient's life', 276 (65%) replied affirmatively. The authors of the survey described these percentages as disclosing the incidence of 'active euthanasia' and 'passive euthanasia'. These inferences must, however, be treated with caution. First, it is doubtful whether the respondents all shared the same understanding of 'euthanasia'. The survey's definition of 'passive euthanasia' was clearly over-broad: it included withholding/withdrawing treatment which results in a foreseen but not intended hastening of death. Some respondents may well, particularly in the light of this extensive definition of passive euthanasia, have understood active euthanasia to include the provision of palliative care which foreseeably, rather than intentionally, hastened death. Given that the survey took the form of an anonymous postal questionnaire rather than an interview, there was no opportunity to ensure that the respondents all shared the same understanding of 'euthanasia' as the intentional termination of life.[15]

A survey from the USA has also suggested that VAE and PAS are not common. A questionnaire was sent to 3,102 physicians under the age of 65. Of the 1,902 who replied, 11% said they had received a request for VAE and 18% a request for PAS; 5% said they had administered a lethal injection and 3% that they had written a prescription for lethal drugs. Since some doctors had done both, the cumulative total of doctors who had performed VAE or PAS was 6%.[16] The co-author of the survey observed: 'This is really not happening very often. That's the most important finding. It's a rare event.'[17]

In short, then, there appears to be little hard evidence that health professionals commonly take steps intentionally to end, or help end, patients' lives. Nor is this surprising: a doctor who did so would be liable to a lengthy term of imprisonment and erasure from the medical register.

---

[15] Moreover, 146 respondents (34%) thought that the law in England should permit VAE as it does in the Netherlands: the possibility that at least some of these doctors exaggerated their practice of euthanasia so as to try to make the law appear ineffective cannot be ruled out.

[16] Diane E. Meier et al., 'A National Survey of Physician-Assisted Suicide and Euthanasia in the United States' (1998) 338 *N Engl J Med* 1193.

[17] Associated Press, 23 April 1998. See (1998) 8(3) *Life at Risk* 1; Paul van der Maas and Linda L. Emanuel, 'Factual Findings' in Linda L. Emanuel (ed.), *Regulating How We Die* (1998) 151, 159 ('the proportion of deaths in the United States that involve physician-assisted suicide and euthanasia is likely to be small').

Secondly, this first argument needs to show that the law is largely un-enforced. There are two criteria applied by the Crown Prosecution Service (CPS) in deciding whether to launch a criminal prosecution: first, whether there is sufficient evidence to provide a realistic prospect of conviction; secondly, whether prosecution would be in the public interest.[18] As the prosecutions of Dr Cox and Dr Moor indicate, the CPS is willing to prosecute if these criteria are satisfied in cases of VAE.

Thirdly, even if it could be shown that VAE and PAS were relatively common, many criminal laws are regularly broken. Not only are relatively minor offences such as speeding common, but also more serious offences such as rape. Is the fact of their frequent commission a reason for repealing the laws which prohibit them? Further, while some doctors have undoubt-edly committed VAE, it is no doubt equally true that other doctors have performed NVAE. Is this an argument for repealing the law against not only VAE but also NVAE? Surely, the mere fact that a law is broken is not in itself an argument for repealing it. It may, on the contrary, be more of an argument for making the law itself stricter or making its enforcement more rigorous. It is sometimes claimed that if guidelines permitted VAE, it would be 'brought out into the open' and doctors would comply with guidelines permitting it. But if some doctors are currently prepared to disregard the law of murder, why should we expect them to comply with guidelines?

Supporters of VAE may reply that what singles out VAE as a particularly good candidate for decriminalisation is that, unlike rape, it is a 'victim-less' crime. In other words, the supposed victim at least consents if not requests its commission and so no one is 'harmed'. However, it does not follow that because something is consensual it should not be illegal. The law prohibits duelling, possessing cocaine or child pornography, bestial-ity, and female circumcision. And the voluntariness of many requests for euthanasia is, as the last chapter indicated, far from unproblematic. Even if all such requests were truly free there remains the argument that the principle of the inviolability of life is of such foundational importance to any civilised society that it should never be compromised, even at an individual's free request, any more than society's prohibition on slavery should be compromised, even at an individual's free request. Should the

---

[18] *Select Committee on Medical Ethics* (21-III of 1993–4) 79 (Memorandum by the Crown Pros-ecution Service).

law allow employers to treat their black employees less favourably than their white workers, even if the black employees were freely to choose, for whatever reason, to work for such employers?

Nor would the argument for repeal necessarily be the stronger if any lack of enforcement were attributable to tacit official condonation rather than the very real difficulties of gathering evidence and proving guilt. It may well be the case that domestic violence is common, that enforcement is lacking, and that prosecutorial policy is lax. There is evidence that so-called 'domestics' were long treated far less seriously by the police and prosecuting authorities than violence against strangers. This was hardly, however, an argument for relaxing the law to permit partner abuse.

Palliative care and euthanasia

As we saw in chapter 2, advocates of VAE often accuse the law of hypocrisy by prohibiting doctors from intentionally hastening patients' deaths while allowing them foreseeably to do so, either by administering palliative drugs which may or will, as a side-effect, shorten life. But, as we also saw, this criticism only holds water if one equates intention and foresight, an equation which was rejected as forced and false. As we also saw, it lands supporters of VAE in a 'catch-22' situation, requiring them either to criticise palliative care of incompetent patients which will, as a side-effect, shorten life, or to condone NVAE.

A right to commit suicide?

A third allegation of hypocrisy relates to the law's prohibition of PAS. The argument is that the Suicide Act 1961 created an inconsistency by decriminalising suicide but prohibiting assisted suicide. How, the argument runs, can the law create a right to commit suicide and at the same time make it an offence to assist or encourage someone to exercise that right? In support of this argument, VAE advocates could cite Lord Justice Hoffmann, who expressed the opinion in the *Bland* case that the Suicide Act represented the triumph of the right to self-determination over the sanctity of life.[19] If he is accurate, surely the Act is inconsistent in limiting

---

[19] *Airedale NHS Trust v. Bland* [1993] AC 789 at 827.

the right of self-determination to cases of self-termination? By analogy, if an Act conferred a right to walk dogs, how could it consistently prohibit petshop owners from selling leads?

Were the premises of this argument sound, so too would be its conclusion; but they are not, and it is not. First, although the Suicide Act 1961 did indeed decriminalise suicide, it did not create a 'right' to suicide. Suicide, though no longer a criminal offence, remains 'unlawful'.[20] It does not follow that, because conduct is not, or is no longer, a criminal offence, it is 'lawful', let alone that one has a 'right' to engage in that conduct. Consider, for example, breach of contract. It is not a criminal offence to breach a contract but to claim that such conduct is lawful, or that there is a 'right' to breach a contract, is clearly misleading. Moreover, the law regards certain contracts, such as agreements to engage in sexual immorality, as 'illegal' contracts, even though their performance would not involve the commission of a criminal offence.[21] Similarly, it is not a criminal offence negligently to injure another. But to claim that such conduct is 'lawful', or that there is a 'right' negligently to injure another, is misguided. The law regards a whole panoply of conduct which is not criminal as unlawful or contrary to public policy and seeks to discourage such conduct by means other than the criminal sanction.

Secondly, the legislative history of the Suicide Act demonstrates that it was not Parliament's intention to condone suicide; quite the contrary. The Parliamentary debates show conclusively that the purpose of the legislation was not to help the suicidal *to* commit suicide, but to help them *not* to. The legislation was enacted because it was felt, quite reasonably, that the suicidal need help, not punishment. Responding to concerns that the Act might be perceived as condoning suicide, the government minister who steered the legislation through the House of Commons solemnly stated

---

[20] See *Hyde* v. *Tameside AHA* (1981, LEXIS) *per* Lord Denning MR. Cf. Lord Goff, 'A Matter of Life and Death' (1995) 3(1) *Med L Rev* 1, 10. Lord Goff did not, however, consider the argument advanced in the text.

[21]
Illegality in the law of contract is not coterminous with illegality in the criminal law, for a contract may be illegal without involving any breach of the criminal law at all. The most obvious illustration of this possibility is a contract involving sexual immorality. For instance, although prostitution is not, as such, criminal, a prostitute cannot sue her clients in a court for remuneration for her professional services.

P. S. Atiyah, *An Introduction to the Law of Contract* (1995) 344

that suicide remained a grave wrong. Moving the bill's third reading, the Joint Under-Secretary of State for the Home Department said:

> Because we have taken the view, as Parliament and the Government have taken, that the treatment of people who attempt to commit suicide should no longer be through the criminal courts, it in no way lessens, nor should it lessen, the respect for the sanctity of human life which we all share. It must not be thought that because we are changing the method of treatment for those unfortunate people we seek to depreciate the gravity of the action of anyone who tries to commit suicide.[22]

Addressing fears that decriminalisation might give the impression that suicide was no longer regarded as wrong, he stated:

> I should like to state as solemnly as I can that that is certainly not the view of the Government, that we wish to give no encouragement whatever to suicide . . . I hope that nothing that I have said will give the impression that the act of self-murder, of self-destruction, is regarded at all lightly by the Home Office or the Government.[23]

Reinforcing that message, the Act provides that anyone who intentionally assists or encourages suicide commits an offence punishable by up to fourteen years' imprisonment. In short, the Suicide Act created neither a right to commit suicide, nor a right to be assisted in suicide. On the contrary, it reaffirmed the unlawful nature of the act and underlined the prohibition on assisting or encouraging another to commit it.

A right to commit suicide by refusing treatment?

A fourth charge of hypocrisy levelled at the present law is related to the third and concerns the patient's right to refuse medical treatment. The courts appear to have granted competent adult patients an absolute right to refuse medical treatment, including life-saving medical treatment, even if the refusal will result in the patient's earlier death.[24] The law evidently requires doctors to respect such refusals, and to withhold/withdraw even life-saving treatment which has been competently refused. Is the law not thereby allowing patients to commit suicide by such refusals and allowing – indeed requiring – doctors to assist such suicidal refusals? If so, how can the law consistently allow doctors to assist suicide by omission while

---

[22] (1960–1) 645 Parl. Deb., HC, cols. 822–3 (Mr Charles Fletcher-Cooke MP).
[23] (1960–1) 644 Parl. Deb., HC, cols. 1425–6.
[24] See e.g. *Re T (Adult: Refusal of Medical Treatment)* [1992] 3 WLR 782.

prohibiting them from assisting suicide by a positive act, such as handing the patient a syringe filled with potassium chloride?

There are a number of counter-arguments, the first being that the patient's intention in refusing treatment and the doctor's intention in withholding/withdrawing that treatment need not be *to end life*. The patient may refuse treatment not in order to hasten death but to avoid a treatment which would not be worth while, as being either futile or too burdensome. In withholding/withdrawing the treatment, the doctor's intention may be simply to respect the patient's refusal of a disproportionate treatment. If the law respects, and requires doctors to respect, only refusals of treatment which are not suicidal, then there is no inconsistency in the law: it consistently sets its face against assistance in suicide, whether by act or omission.[25] Indeed, it is arguable that, in order to avoid the injustice of doctors forcing treatment on patients who are wrongly suspected of refusing treatment with intent to kill themselves, the law could properly require doctors to respect *all* competent refusals of treatment, without in any way endorsing those which are suicidal.

If, by contrast, the law were to require or even allow doctors *intentionally to assist* refusals of treatment which are clearly suicidal, then the law would indeed have fallen into serious inconsistency. How could the law consistently tell doctors that they must on no account intentionally assist a patient to commit suicide by an act, but that they may lawfully intentionally assist a patient to commit suicide by withholding/withdrawing life-saving treatment? If a patient says to a doctor: 'Doctor, I want to hasten my death. Please help me', what is the moral difference between the doctor intentionally doing so by, on the one hand, giving the patient a lethal pill and, on the other, switching off the patient's life-support machine? As we asked in chapter 1, if the doctor's *intention* is the same in both cases, where is the moral difference? The distinction between acts and omissions is, where the doctor's intention is identical, a distinction without a difference.

As we shall see in Part VI of the book, it may be that the law is seriously inconsistent in this respect. Although the law is far from clear on this point, it is open to the interpretation of requiring doctors to assist all refusals of

---

[25] Cf. David P. T. Price, 'Assisted Suicide and Refusing Medical Treatment: Linguistics, Morals and Legal Contortions' (1996) 4(3) *Med L Rev* 270. Price rightly accepts that a patient who refuses life-sustaining treatment with the intention of hastening death commits suicide, and that a doctor who intentionally assists this purpose, by withholding or withdrawing the treatment, assists suicide. However, Price goes awry when, conflating intention and foresight, he argues that this is also true of refusals when death is merely foreseen and not intended.

life-saving treatment by competent adults even if they are clearly suicidal. It does not follow, however, that any such inconsistency in the law should be resolved by relaxing the law to permit doctors *actively* to assist patients to commit suicide rather than by restricting the law to prevent them from *passively* doing so.

Active and passive euthanasia

A final allegation of inconsistency is that the law prohibits active, intentional termination of life, but permits intentional termination of life by deliberate omission, at least in the case of incompetent patients such as Tony Bland. This argument tends not to form part of the case for reform advanced by advocates of VAE. This may well be because such cases of passive euthanasia are instances not of VAE but of NVAE. Were supporters of VAE to invoke such cases of NVAE as part of their campaign, it would undercut their claim that they support only VAE. As we shall argue in Part VI, however, the argument does have considerable force: the law is indeed inconsistent in the way alleged. As we shall also argue, it by no means follows that the inconsistency should be resolved by relaxation, rather than restriction, of the law.

Conclusion

Part II has sketched some of the major arguments advanced in favour of the decriminalisation of VAE, and some of the counter-arguments which can be raised against them. There are three main arguments in favour:

- that life is not always a benefit and that it is justifiable to terminate the life of a patient on request when the patient would be better off dead;
- that VAE and PAS are required by respect for patient autonomy;
- that the present law exhibits several inconsistencies in its prohibition of VAE and PAS, and that those inconsistencies are a good argument for relaxing the present prohibition. In particular, if the present law allows passive VAE and PAS, it should also allow active VAE and PAS.

Part II has suggested, however, that when viewed against the counter-arguments, these arguments are much less persuasive than they might appear at first blush. Part II has not attempted a treatise on the philosophical ethics of VAE and PAS; it has, much more modestly, sought simply to canvass and briefly evaluate the main ethical arguments and counter-arguments so that the reader is better informed about what the issues of principle are.

It is now time to turn our attention to the argument, or rather the two arguments, against decriminalisation which are proving of pivotal importance in the current debate, arguments which must be countered by any supporter of VAE and which form the centrepiece of this book, namely, the slippery slope arguments. Even if VAE and PAS were right in principle in certain hard cases, could they be effectively controlled and limited to those cases?

7

The slippery slope arguments

VAE in principle and in practice

The prohibition of VAE by the criminal laws of almost all countries and by the ethical codes of virtually all medical associations testifies to the historic and enduring appeal of the principle of the inviolability of human life. Many people continue to judge that it is wrong intentionally to take the life of another person, even if that person earnestly requests death to avoid pain and suffering. Many, therefore, continue to oppose VAE in principle.

But many do not. They believe that in principle, VAE (or at least PAS) is morally justifiable provided that the patient's request is free and informed, and that the patient is suffering from an illness resulting in unbearable suffering which can only be ended by terminating the patient's life. However, it does not follow that they also believe that the law should therefore be relaxed to permit VAE or PAS. Many such people oppose relaxation of the law because they believe it would result in (or would involve an unacceptable risk of resulting in) two undesirable consequences. The first is a slide from PAS to VAE and from VAE to NVAE and possibly even IVAE. The second is a slide from VAE as a last resort to its use as a standard and premature alternative to palliative care. In short, many of those who see nothing wrong with VAE *in principle* do not want the law to permit it *in practice* because they think it would be likely to result in a slide down a slippery slope from something they condone – ending patients' lives at their request as a last resort – to something they oppose – ending their lives without request or where less extreme alternatives exist. The slippery slope argument about what is likely to happen in practice has taken centre-stage in the contemporary debate. It therefore merits close consideration.

The nature of the slippery slope argument

The slippery slope argument holds that if a proposal is made to accept A, which is not agreed to be morally objectionable, it should nevertheless be rejected because it would lead to B, which is agreed to be morally objectionable.[1] An illustration would be the argument that it is wrong to permit abortion, even on health grounds, because even if abortion on health grounds were morally acceptable, allowing it will tend to lead to abortion for social convenience, which is not. This very example was cited some years ago by the then Bishop of Durham, Dr John Habgood, who was later to become Archbishop of York and a member of the House of Lords Select Committee on Medical Ethics. In 1974 he wrote:

> Legislation to permit euthanasia would in the long run bring about profound changes in social attitudes towards death, illness, old age and the role of the medical profession. The Abortion Act has shown what happens. Whatever the rights and wrongs concerning the present practice of abortion, there is no doubt about two consequences of the 1967 [Abortion] Act:
>
> (a) The safeguards and assurances given when the Bill was passed have to a considerable extent been ignored.
> (b) Abortion has now become a live option for *anybody* who is pregnant. This does not imply that everyone who is facing an unwanted pregnancy automatically attempts to procure an abortion. But because abortion is now on the agenda, the climate of opinion in which such a pregnancy must be faced has radically altered.

One could, he added, expect 'similarly far-reaching and potentially more dangerous consequences from legalized euthanasia'.[2] Even ardent pro-choicers would have to concede that, although the Abortion Act 1967 permits abortion for medical but not social reasons, abortion for social reasons has become the norm, or at least commonplace.[3]

---

[1] See generally David Lamb, *Down the Slippery Slope: Arguing in Applied Ethics* (1988); Douglas N. Walton, *Slippery Slope Arguments* (1992).

[2] Rt. Revd J. S. Habgood, 'Euthanasia – A Christian View' (1974) 3 *J R Soc Health* 124, 126 (original emphasis). See also Lord Goff, 'A Matter of Life and Death' 14. Commenting on the difficulty of drawing a defensible line permitting VAE in certain restricted conditions, his Lordship observed: 'An indication that there may well be no such defensible line may be drawn from experience of the legalisation of abortion in England which, though introduced for the main purpose of attacking the perceived evil of back street abortions, now extends to permit abortion in practically all circumstances.'

[3] For evidence of the prevalence of abortion for social reasons see John Keown, *Abortion, Doctors and the Law* (1988) chapter 5.

Sometimes the empirical argument can be misapplied. It would clearly be pressing the argument too far to argue that no one should touch a drop of alcohol because of the risk of alcoholism. The vast majority of people are able to make common-sense judgments about how much they can safely drink without becoming addicted. Nor is the taking of alcohol as such a morally contested issue (at least in secular society). Abortion is, however, a hotly disputed moral issue, and the difficulty of justifying, drawing and policing a distinction between 'medical' and 'social' grounds for abortion gives the slippery slope argument against allowing abortion for 'medical' reasons much greater purchase. In short, the slippery slope argument sometimes has force, and sometimes lacks force. The question here is whether it has force in relation to the legalisation of VAE.

Empirical and logical slopes

The slippery slope argument is often thought of as one argument but it is more accurately understood as comprising two independent arguments: the 'logical' and the 'empirical'.

The empirical argument

The empirical slippery slope argument runs that even if a line can in principle be drawn between VAE and NVAE, and between VAE as a last resort and as an earlier resort, a slide will occur in practice because the safeguards to prevent it cannot be made effective.[4] In other words, purely as a *practical* matter, VAE resists effective regulation.[5] Try as one may to devise procedures to ensure that it is only performed after a clear and considered request by the patient, and only where it is a last resort, there will in practice be an inevitable tendency for it to be performed in cases where the request is neither clear nor considered, and where alternatives are available but are overlooked or even deliberately ignored. And the reason that the empirical argument has force in relation to VAE, it may be claimed, is that it is no more possible to frame precise guidelines for VAE,

---

[4] See generally Luke Gormally, 'Walton, Davies, Boyd and the Legalization of Euthanasia' in Keown, chapter 10; Yale Kamisar, 'Some Non-Religious Views against Proposed "Mercy-Killing" Legislation' in Dennis J. Horan and David Mall (eds.), *Death, Dying and Euthanasia* (1980) 406 (originally published in (1958) 42 *Minn L Rev* 969).
[5] Kamisar, 'Some Non-Religious Views' *passim.*

and to police doctors' interpretation and application of those guidelines, than it is possible to frame and police guidelines for 'therapeutic' abortion.

Any attempt at effective legal regulation of VAE will break down, the argument runs, because some – perhaps many – doctors will fail to ensure that requests are genuine, free and considered, and that there are no alternatives. Some doctors will fail because, although they are conscientious practitioners with the best interests of their patients at heart, they simply lack the psychiatric expertise to discern when a request is the result not of the patient's free and considered judgment but of clinical depression. Others will fail because, although they may have, or have theoretical access to, the required expertise, they lack the time or resources to apply or access it in practice. Still others will fail because they are not sufficiently conscientious to consider the quality of the patient's request.

Equally, some doctors will fail to ensure that VAE is used only as a last resort. In some cases, patients will be misdiagnosed and inaccurately told their condition is terminal. Other patients will be correctly diagnosed but will be given a false prognosis: the doctor will mistakenly tell the patient there is no hope of a cure. And in some cases, even when the doctor arrives at a correct diagnosis and prognosis, he will simply lack sufficient expertise in palliative care to know what relief it can offer the particular patient.

Again, the parallel with abortion may assist. How many doctors have the expertise, commitment, time and resources to consider the quality of each request for abortion in appropriate depth? Surely some, perhaps many if not most, approve requests for abortion after a relatively brief consultation and without any expert psychiatric evaluation of the woman. How many requests for abortion have been granted which were really the result of clinical depression or pressure from spouses, partners or relatives? And how many women experience lasting psychological harm and psychiatric illness as a result of abortions which were really someone *else's* choice? In VAE, of course, the quality of the decision is no less crucial and merits no less attention given the particular vulnerability to pressure of the elderly dying and the significant proportion of patients requesting VAE who are in fact clinically depressed.[6]

Again, in how many cases is abortion used truly as a last resort? In how many cases are women presented with realistic alternatives, whether it be in the form of help from social services, or specialist advice about bringing

[6] See p. 56 n. 6.

up a disabled child? If VAE were to follow in the footsteps of abortion, would it not frequently be performed with inadequate examination of the quality of the request and little if any exploration of alternatives? And given that in the VAE debate, unlike the abortion debate, there is no dispute that the life at stake is that of a full human being, the argument for caution is recognisably clearer. The analogy between abortion and VAE is not exact, but if anything the differences (the particular vulnerability of the debilitated and dying elderly, who would, at least initially, tend to be the prime candidates) serve only to sharpen the slippery slope argument against VAE. In short, Lord Habgood's caution seems prudent.

Could it not be argued, however, that appropriately strict guidelines would forestall any slide down the empirical slope? Guidelines which would ensure that each request was properly checked, that the diagnosis and prognosis were confirmed, that alternatives were fully investigated, and that the patient's suffering was truly unbearable? The empirical argument questions the possibility of drafting and enforcing such safeguards. How, for example, does a guideline purport to ensure that a request is truly 'voluntary'?[7] How can a doctor know whether the request reflects the true, considered and informed wishes of the patient, or is a result of pressure from relatives? And how can a guideline ensure that the patient's suffering is truly 'unbearable'?

Surely, guidelines would end up granting considerable leeway to the opinion of the doctor as to whether the request was voluntary, and to the feelings of the patient as to whether the suffering was unbearable. Both of these are recalcitrant to external regulation. Moreover, even if precise guidelines could be formulated, specifying what qualifies as a 'voluntary' request and 'unbearable' suffering, how could the guidelines be effectively enforced?

Here advocates of VAE appear to encounter yet another 'catch-22'. One approach to regulation is to avoid independent scrutiny of the doctor's

---

[7] It has been argued that a number of demanding conditions must be satisfied before a decision to refuse life-sustaining treatment in advance of incompetence can be said to be truly 'autonomous': see Julian Savulescu, 'Rational Desires and the Limitation of Life-Sustaining Treatment' (1994) 8 *Bioethics* 191. Savulescu argues that for a desire to be an expression of a person's autonomy, it must be or satisfy that person's 'rational desires'. A person rationally desires a course of action if that person 'desires it while being in possession of all available relevant facts, without committing relevant error of logic, and "vividly imagining" what its consequences would be like for her'. It could be argued that, if such conditions should apply in relation to anticipatory treatment refusals, they should apply with no less force to requests for VAE.

actions and to trust to the doctor's competence and good faith. But then how is either incompetence or dishonesty to be prevented? A stricter approach is to build in stringent independent checks, such as the prior, or at least retrospective, approval of an independent person or body, such as a lawyer or a court. But how many doctors are likely to submit themselves and their patients to an independent review, particularly by a lawyer? Any middle approach, such as requiring consultation with an independent doctor, might well prove to be more form than substance. Though a doctor would be less reluctant to consult another doctor than a judge, how likely is the second doctor to conduct an independent examination of the patient, familiarise himself with all the facts of the case, and rigorously scrutinise the competence and good faith of the first doctor? The tendency of some second-opinion doctors to 'rubber-stamp' the opinion of the first is certainly far from unknown in other contexts. Although the Abortion Act 1967 requires a second doctor to certify that the grounds for abortion stated in the Act have been met, it does not even require the second doctor to see the woman. Moreover, the tendency of doctors to overlook their colleagues' unprofessional behaviour is well documented.[8]

After a comprehensive review of proposals to decriminalise PAS in the USA, philosopher Daniel Callahan and lawyer Margot White concluded that *none* of the proposals would have ensured effective regulation. They observed: 'The fundamental problem with legalization of PAS and euthanasia lies in the nature of the physician–patient relationship – that it is conducted in private and protected by ethical and legal requirements of confidentiality. Therefore, it is inherently inconsistent with on-site procedural requirements.'[9]

They added that legalisation could serve only to protect the physician, not the patient: 'It will not, and cannot, achieve the goal of protecting patients or of preventing or limiting abuse. If protection of patients and meaningful regulation of PAS/euthanasia is the goal, no legislation can achieve it.'[10]

---

[8] See e.g. Eliot Freidson, *The Profession of Medicine* (1970) chapters 7 and 8. A raft of recent scandals in England exposing long-standing medical misconduct, from Dr Harold Shipman's serial killing in Stockport, to inadequate paediatric surgery in Bristol, and the retention of children's organs without parental consent in Liverpool, have gravely undermined public confidence in the ability and willingness of the medical profession effectively to regulate itself.

[9] Daniel Callahan and Margot White, 'The Legalization of Physician-Assisted Suicide: Creating a Regulatory Potemkin Village' (1996) 30 *U Rich L Rev* 1 at 66.

[10] Ibid., 69.

Years ago, in his classic article refuting the case for the legalisation of VAE, Professor Yale Kamisar, the distinguished liberal scholar of US constitutional law, noted that campaigners for VAE were seeking a goal which is inherently inconsistent: a procedure for death which provides ample safeguards against abuse and mistake, and one which is 'quick' and 'easy' in operation.[11]

In short, the empirical argument maintains that guidelines, whether lax or strict, cannot guarantee effective regulation of the doctor's decision-making. Indeed, stricter guidelines may serve to make doctors even *less* compliant. Hence, the regulatory 'catch-22' which appears to beset any attempt to permit VAE subject to 'guidelines' or 'safeguards': any attempt to close the hand of regulation more tightly may well result in more cases slipping, unregulated, through its fingers. Even leaving aside the grave difficulty if not practical impossibility of policing VAE, there remains another reason why, it is argued, a slide will occur. This brings us to the *logical* slippery slope argument.

The logical argument

In the current debate, the limelight is taken by the empirical argument at the expense of its sister argument. This is unfortunate, since the logical argument is even more formidable. It holds that, even if precise guidelines could be framed which sought to permit only VAE in cases of unbearable suffering, those guidelines would soon give way, not (or not only) because of practical difficulties of enforcement *but because the case for euthanasia with those limitations is also, logically, a case for euthanasia without them.*[12]

Voluntariness

The logical argument runs that acceptance of VAE leads to acceptance of NVAE because the former rests on the judgment that some patients would be better off dead, which judgment can logically be made even if the patient is incapable of making a request. The proposals currently advanced by advocates of VAE and PAS envisage a central role for doctors, not only in the termination of life itself, but also in the decision to terminate life.

[11] Kamisar, 'Some Non-Religious Views' 418–19.
[12] See Gormally, 131–3; Gormally in Keown, chapter 10, 115; Daniel Callahan, 'When Self-Determination Runs Amok' (1992) 22(2) *Hastings Cent Rep* 52, 53.

They are not proposals for 'euthanasia on demand', that is, simply at the patient's request and without the considered assessment, judgment and approval of a responsible doctor.

Doctors are not robots who mindlessly comply with their patients' wishes. They are professionals who form their own judgment about the merits of any request for medical intervention. A responsible doctor would not agree to kill a patient just because the patient autonomously asked, any more than the doctor would prescribe anti-depressant drugs for a patient just because the patient autonomously requested them. The doctor, if acting professionally, would decide in each case whether the intervention was truly in the patient's best interests. Therefore, a responsible doctor would no more kill a patient who had, in the doctor's opinion, 'a life worth living' than prescribe anti-depressants for a patient who, in the doctor's opinion, was not depressed. Advocates of VAE would surely agree. They typically propose VAE only for those who meet certain conditions, whether 'terminal illness', or 'unbearable suffering', which it is thought makes their lives no longer worth living.

Consequently, the real, rather than the rhetorical, justification for VAE is not the patient's autonomous request *but the doctor's judgment that the request is justified because death would benefit the patient.* True, in the proposals currently advanced by campaigners for VAE, this judgment would not be made without a prior, autonomous request by the patient. But even under such proposals the autonomous request is not decisive. It serves merely to trigger the *doctor's* judgment about the merits of the request. To put the point more crudely, the patient proposes but the *doctor* disposes. The *doctor* decides whether the request is justified, that is, whether the patient would indeed be better off dead. And if a doctor can make this judgment in relation to an autonomous patient, a doctor can, logically, make it in relation to an incompetent patient. Moreover, if death is a 'benefit' for competent patients suffering from a certain condition, why should it be denied incompetent patients suffering from the same condition?

If VAE were to be made available to competent people who requested it, it would soon be argued that it should be extended to the incompetent, either on the ground that it would be discriminatory to deny them this benefit because of their incompetence or because VAE is what they would have wanted had they been competent to ask for it. The latter approach, which constructs what is called a 'substituted judgment' on behalf of the incompetent, is already well established in the law relating to the treatment of incompetent patients in parts of the USA. And, in England, government proposals for legislation concerning treatment of the incompetent would accord weight to the incompetent person's 'past and present wishes' and 'the factors the person would consider if able to do so'.[13]

VAE supporters may well disagree, and press the argument that it is ultimately the *patient* who decides whether his life is worth while, but this argument sits uneasily with their own typical legislative proposals which require a *doctor*, exercising independent judgment, to approve the patient's request. The doctor's role is not envisaged simply as one of ensuring that the patient's request is autonomous (indeed, a psychologist or counsellor would surely discharge that function at least as well), but as one of considering the *merits* of the request. What could those merits be other than a judgment that the patient would indeed be better off dead? And once doctors began to make comprehensive judgments of that sort in relation to competent people, why would they not think themselves equally qualified to make such judgments in relation to incompetent patients? Why should they deny their incompetent patients the benefit of euthanasia when they are in exactly the same situation as their competent patients, except for their ability to request that benefit? Is there any other situation in medical practice where doctors deny treatment which they think beneficial simply because the patient cannot request it?

Imagine two patients of Dr A: X and his brother Y. They are identical twins, with an identically painful terminal illness and suffering to an identical degree. They lie, side by side, in hospital. X, who is competent, pleads with Dr A for a lethal injection of potassium chloride because the 'suffering is unbearable'. Dr A agrees that death would indeed be a benefit for X and agrees to administer the injection to give him a 'merciful release'. X requests the same for his brother Y, who is incompetent, on the ground that he, too, must be experiencing 'unbearable and useless' suffering. Is Dr A to deny Y the same benefit he has agreed to confer on X? If so, what has become of the doctor's duty to act in the best interests of his patient?

---

[13] *Making Decisions. The Government's Proposals for Making Decisions on Behalf of Mentally Incapacitated Adults* (Cm 4465, 1999) para. 1.11.

Confirming the logical link between VAE and NVAE, many leading philosophical advocates of VAE, such as Peter Singer and Helga Kuhse,[14] Jonathan Glover[15] and John Harris,[16] also condone NVAE.

'Unbearable suffering'

Those advocates of VAE who insist that what is decisive in justifying VAE is respect for individual autonomy encounter a logical problem if they also insist that VAE be limited to patients who are suffering unbearably. For if VAE is justified by respect for patient self-determination, how can it be right to deny it to any patient who autonomously asks for it, whether or not they are experiencing 'unbearable suffering'?[17] Why need their suffering be 'unbearable'? Why should suffering which is bearable but which the patient does not want to bear not qualify? What if a patient earnestly asks for VAE because, say, he is suffering from some incurable condition such as severe arthritis, which is painful and debilitating and which, even though it may be bearable, he does not want to bear? The case would be even stronger if he had previously led a life in which physical activity, such as outdoor pursuits, had played a central part. Indeed, the patient may have a condition which involves relatively little physical suffering. Imagine a rock-climbing fanatic who has been paralysed from the neck down in a climbing accident and who requests VAE because he says that he 'does not want to live trapped in a useless body'. Why should he be denied release if he believes that life has lost its value? Some prominent writers on medical ethics have argued that what gives a person's life value is its being valued by that person.[18] If a patient no longer thinks that life has value, they argue, then it no longer has value.

If the core justification for VAE is thought to be respect for patient autonomy, this is surely logically inconsistent with a requirement that the patient be suffering unbearably, bearably, or at all.

---

[14] Peter Singer and Helga Kuhse, *Should the Baby Live?: The Problem of Handicapped Infants* (1985).

[15] Jonathan Glover, *Causing Death and Saving Lives* (1977).

[16] John Harris, *The Value of Life* (1992). Historically, moreover, more than a few of those involved in the campaign for VAE have seen it as a tactical first step towards their goal of NVAE. See Gormally, 31–2; Alexander M. Capron, 'Euthanasia and Assisted Suicide' (1992) 22(2) *Hastings Cent Rep* 30. See also Kamisar, 'Some Non-Religious Views' 464–7.

[17] See Callahan and White, 'The Legalization of Physician-Assisted Suicide' 54.

[18] See e.g. John Harris, *The Value of Life* (1992).

Conclusion

This chapter has outlined the two slippery slope arguments against VAE: the empirical argument and the logical argument. The arguments hold that, even if VAE were morally acceptable to relieve a patient from 'unbearable suffering' at the patient's 'free and informed request', relaxation of the law to cater for such admittedly difficult cases would, sooner or later, result in its extension by law to patients who are incompetent and who are not suffering unbearably. The empirical argument holds that this slide will result because of the practical grave difficulty if not impossibility of framing and enforcing safeguards to prevent the slide. The logical argument holds that the slide will occur because the argument for accepting the one is also, when taken to its logical conclusion, an argument for accepting the other.

'Hard cases', say lawyers, 'make bad law.' However tempting it may be to make exceptions in difficult cases, the effect of so doing may be that the exception swallows the rule. The temptation to pull shipwreck survivors into a full lifeboat may be strong, but it should be resisted lest the lifeboat capsize. Both of the slippery slope arguments urge that, however tempting it may be for the law to accommodate 'mercy killing' in extreme circumstances, yielding to the temptation would subvert the law's protection of all. As we shall see, the argument has persuaded many that legalisation would be a mistake – even many of those who support VAE in principle.

PART III

The Dutch experience: controlling VAE? condoning NVAE?

To many, the slippery slope arguments are obviously persuasive. To others, however, they remain unconvincing, and no basis for resisting the decriminalisation of VAE in certain 'hard cases'. Why, it is asked, should the possibility of future abuse trump the certainty of present suffering?

As VAE has historically been illegal around the world, the empirical argument has, inevitably, lacked evidential support. (The logical argument, being philosophical rather than practical, does not rely on empirical evidence, though evidence of a shift in practice from condonation of VAE to condonation of NVAE would certainly illustrate its cogency.) More recently, that situation has changed. In 1984, the Supreme Court in one jurisdiction – the Netherlands – declared that doctors could lawfully carry out VAE in certain circumstances. Since that time a substantial body of evidence has accumulated which allows the empirical version of the slippery slope argument to be tested. Given the cardinal importance of the Dutch experience to the debate, the following chapters consider whether the evidence from the Netherlands indicates that VAE is, as the Dutch claim, effectively controlled, and whether there has been a shift towards condonation of NVAE.

By way of preamble, it is worth noting that the Dutch experience is a matter of some dispute. Its defenders (who are usually but not exclusively Dutch) claim that VAE has been successfully 'brought out into the open' and effectively controlled. Its critics (usually but not exclusively outside the Netherlands) dispute this and maintain that VAE remains beyond effective control. It is no easy matter for someone unfamiliar with the mass of evidence to discern where the truth of the matter lies. The difficulty is compounded by superficial and misleading reports in the mass media. This section of the book draws on the author's own research over ten years into the Dutch experience.

Chapter 8 will outline the Dutch guidelines and consider whether they are, as claimed by the Dutch, precise and strict. It will also outline the provisions of a government bill which was enacted in 2001 and which gives the guidelines statutory force. Chapter 9 will consider the evidence contained in a large-scale survey about end-of-life decision-making by Dutch doctors in 1990 and chapter 10 will consider the extent to which their decision-making complied with the legal and professional guidelines. Chapter 11 will identify a shift towards official condonation of NVAE. Chapter 12 will consider the evidence of a repeat survey about decision-making in 1995. Chapter 13 will suggest that confusion about the Dutch experience is at least partly due to misleading interpretations of the evidence by the Dutch themselves.

The key conclusion of Part III is that the evidence from the Netherlands reveals not only a serious lack of control – which lends support to the empirical argument – but also a growing condonation of NVAE – which illustrates the force of the logical argument.

8

The guidelines

The Dutch law

The Netherlands is the only country in which VAE is legally permitted and widely practised. Although it is a specific offence under the Dutch Penal Code to kill another person at his request, the Dutch Supreme Court held in 1984 that a doctor who ends the life of a patient may in certain circumstances successfully invoke the defence of 'necessity', also contained in the Code. This defence operates to justify (though in some other jurisdictions it serves only to excuse)[1] the actions of a person who has broken the law, but who has acted reasonably and proportionately in doing so to secure a higher value recognised by the law. A simple example would be the action of pulling a jaywalker from the path of an oncoming car. The law, upholding the values of human autonomy and bodily integrity, generally prohibits touching others without their consent. But it condones the action of one who pulls a jaywalker to safety even though there is no time to seek his consent.

A few months before the landmark case in 1984, the Royal Dutch Medical Association (KNMG) published guidelines for VAE, guidelines which were considered by the Supreme Court in arriving at its decision.[2] Since that time the lives of tens of thousands of Dutch patients have been actively and intentionally shortened by their doctors. A requirement central to both the legal and medical guidelines has been the free and explicit request of the patient. Defenders of the guidelines have claimed that they permit VAE but not NVAE, that they are sufficiently strict and precise to prevent any slide down a slippery slope to euthanasia without request, and that there has been no evidence of any such slide in the Netherlands.

---

[1] A justificatory defence (such as self-defence) justifies the act; an excusatory defence (such as provocation) merely excuses the actor from punishment for a wrongful act.

[2] The guidelines were published in English by the KNMG in 1986 as *Vision on Euthanasia*.

Before considering the guidelines and their effectiveness, it is important to note the peculiarly narrow Dutch definition of 'euthanasia'. As we saw in chapter 1, a typical definition of 'euthanasia' would be 'the intentional putting to death of a person with an incurable or painful disease'.[3] However, the Dutch definition corresponds to what is normally called 'voluntary, active, euthanasia' (VAE). This definition therefore excludes cases of the intentional, active termination of life *without request* as well as intentional killing *by deliberate omission*. This will prove significant when Dutch claims about the incidence of 'euthanasia' in their country are being interpreted.

'Strict safeguards'?

The guidelines

Taking the life of another person at his request is an offence contrary to Article 293 of the Penal Code; assisting suicide is prohibited by Article 294. In 1984, however, in a case often referred to as the *Alkmaar* case (after the town where the case was first heard) or the *Schoonheim* case (after the name of the defendant doctor), the Dutch Supreme Court allowed a doctor's appeal against conviction for actively and intentionally ending the life of one of his elderly patients at her request. The court held that the lower courts, which had convicted the doctor, had wrongly failed to consider the defence of necessity. They should have considered whether he had been faced with a 'conflict of duties'[4] (his duty to obey Article 293 on the one hand against his duty to relieve his patient's suffering on the other); whether according to 'responsible medical opinion'[5] and the 'prevailing standards of medical ethics'[6] a situation of 'necessity'[7] existed; and whether he had, therefore, been entitled to the defence of necessity contained in Article 40 of the Penal Code.[8]

This decision was remarkable. First, the necessity defence has traditionally been understood as justifying an ostensible breach of the law in order to *save* life (as, to return to the example we used earlier, by pulling someone out of the path of an oncoming car), not to *take* life. Secondly, the judgment failed to explain *why* the doctor's duty to alleviate suffering overrode his duty not to kill. Doctors in other countries see no conflict

---

[3] *Stedman's Medical Dictionary* (25th edn, 1990) 544.
[4] Nederlandse Jurisprudentie (hereafter 'NJ') (1985) No. 106, 451 at 452. See also I. J. Keown, 'The Law and Practice of Euthanasia in the Netherlands' (1992) 108 *LQR* 51, 51–7.
[5] NJ (1985) No. 106, 453.   [6] Ibid.   [7] Ibid.   [8] Ibid.

at all between their duty not to kill and their duty to alleviate suffering. Finally, the court appeared to abdicate to doctors the power to determine the circumstances in which VAE attracted the necessity defence. What qualifies *doctors* to decide when it is right to kill patients?

In a series of decisions straddling this landmark case, lower courts laid down a number of conditions which have since been thought to be essential if a doctor is to enjoy the defence of necessity, though, as we shall see later, it was far from clear which of these conditions, if any, was essential. Subject to this important caveat, these conditions were listed in 1989 by Dr Els Borst, then Chairwoman of the Dutch Health Council and later Minister of Health, as follows:

(i) The request for euthanasia [i.e., VAE] must come only from the patient and must be entirely free and voluntary.

(ii) The patient's request must be well considered, durable and persistent.

(iii) The patient must be experiencing intolerable (not necessarily physical) suffering, with no prospect of improvement.

(iv) Euthanasia must be a last resort. Other alternatives to alleviate the patient's situation must have been considered and found wanting.

(v) Euthanasia must be performed by a physician.

(vi) The physician must consult with an independent physician colleague who has experience in this field.[9]

Moreover, having performed VAE, the doctor must *not* certify death by 'natural causes'. To do so would involve the criminal offence of falsifying the death certificate since death has been caused not by nature but by the doctor. Rather, the doctor must leave the death certificate incomplete and call in the local medical examiner to investigate. The medical examiner should carry out an external examination of the corpse, interview the doctor, and file a report with the local prosecutor. Only if it appeared that the guidelines had not been followed was the prosecutor likely to initiate an investigation. The reporting procedure was formally agreed between the Ministry of Justice and the KNMG in 1990 and given statutory force in 1994.

Since 1998, when the reporting procedure was revised, the medical examiner has sent both the physician's report and his own report to one of five regional, interdisciplinary VAE review committees. The medical examiner informs the prosecutor that a case of VAE has taken place and

---

[9] Keown, 'The Law and Practice of Euthanasia in the Netherlands' 56.

indicates (but without sending the full reports) whether the guidelines appear to have been followed. If the indication is positive, the prosecutor will give permission for the corpse to be buried or cremated. The interdisciplinary committee examines the case within six weeks; only when in the committee's opinion the guidelines have not been satisfied does it notify the Board of the Chief Prosecutors and the regional health care inspector, who may further investigate the case.

The criteria published by the KNMG before the Supreme Court decision[10] are substantially similar to the conditions just listed. They require a voluntary request by the patient which is well considered and persistent; unacceptable suffering by the patient; and consultation by the doctor with a colleague working in the same institution and then with an independent doctor.[11] The KNMG subsequently published similar guidelines in collaboration with the National Association of Nurses.[12]

'Precisely defined' and 'strict'?

Before we consider the evidence which indicates the extent to which medical practice conforms to the above requirements, some comment is called for on the nature of those requirements and particularly the extent to which they are *capable* of closely regulating VAE. A leading Dutch defender of VAE has claimed that the guidelines are 'strict' and 'precise'.[13] The claim is not, however, easy to sustain. For one thing, it is unclear which *are* legal requirements: the courts have never laid down a definitive list. As we shall see, for example, it has long been doubtful whether consultation is a legal requirement, and relatively recent court decisions have held that a request is not always essential. Secondly, even if all six guidelines set out by Dr Borst were requirements rather than recommendations, they are far from unambiguous. A recent survey of public prosecutors highlighted their vagueness, revealing substantial differences of opinion among prosecutors as to whether certain hypothetical cases breached the guidelines and should result in prosecution.[14] Thirdly, as Professor Leenen, a leading Dutch health

---

[10] *Vision on Euthanasia.*   [11] Ibid., 8–11.

[12] 'Guidelines for Euthanasia' (translated by W. Lagerwey) (1988) 2 *Issues Law Med* 429. Hereafter 'Guidelines'.

[13] Henk Rigter, 'Euthanasia in the Netherlands: Distinguishing Facts from Fiction' (1989) 19(1) *Hastings Cent Rep* 31.

[14] J. M. Cuperus-Bosma, G. van der Wal et al., 'Assessment of Physician-Assisted Death by Members of the Public Prosecution in the Netherlands' (1999) 25 *J Med Ethics* 8.

lawyer (and supporter of VAE), has observed, concepts such as 'unbearable pain' (and no less so, one might add, 'unbearable suffering') are open to subjective interpretation and are incapable of precise definition.[15]

An illustration of the elasticity of the guidelines is provided by the interpretation placed on them by a leading Dutch practitioner of VAE. Presented with an imaginary case of an old man who requested VAE because he felt a nuisance to his relatives who wanted him dead so that they could enjoy his estate, this doctor was asked whether he would rule out VAE in such a case. The doctor replied: 'I . . . think in the end I wouldn't, because that kind of influence – these children wanting the money now – is the same kind of power from the past that . . . shaped us all. The same thing goes for religion . . . education . . . the kind of family he was raised in, all kinds of influences from the past that we can't put aside.'[16]

If an experienced practitioner of VAE (and one who has given lectures to Dutch police on how to deal with cases of VAE) can interpret the guidelines requiring an 'entirely free and voluntary request' and 'unbearable suffering' as possibly extending to such a case, little more need be said about their supposed precision.

Moreover, in a real case decided in 1994 in which a psychiatrist, Dr Chabot, was prosecuted for assisting in suicide a 50-year-old woman because of her persistent grief at the death of her two sons, the Supreme Court held that such mental distress could amount to 'unbearable suffering'.[17] No less remarkably, in a case decided in 2000, a court in Haarlem acquitted a doctor, Dr Sutorius, who had assisted in suicide an 86-year-old patient, a Mr Brongersma, who reportedly wanted to die not because he had any serious physical or mental illness, but because he felt his life to be 'pointless and empty'.[18]

Nor are the guidelines 'strict', in the sense of imposing exacting checks on the physician. The only external checks on a doctor's decision-making are consultation with a colleague and an interview with the local medical examiner. Even if consultation has always been legally required, it was, at least until relatively recently, apparently satisfied by a telephone conversation with a compliant (or even a non-compliant) colleague. Although

---

[15] H. J. J. Leenen, 'The Definition of Euthanasia' (1984) 3 *Med Law* 333, 334.

[16] Interview by author with Dr Herbert Cohen, 26 July 1989.

[17] Hoge Raad, 21 June 1994, Strafkamer, no. 96,972. For a discussion of the case see Hendin, chapter 3.

[18] Tony Sheldon, 'Dutch GP Cleared after Helping to End Man's "Hopeless Existence"' (2000) 321 *BMJ* 1174; (2000) 7(6) *Pro Vita Humana* 196.

revised guidelines issued by the KNMG in 1995[19] explained that consultation means a formal discussion with an independent colleague who has examined the patient, the very fact that this had to be spelled out is revealing.

Nor can the interview with the local medical examiner act as an effective check. For one thing, it is left to the doctor to call in the medical examiner and to provide the relevant information. One senior Dutch prosecutor (who supports VAE) has complained that the medical examiner (who is a physician) does not have the necessary investigative expertise, conducts an inquiry which is 'just a chat between doctors and no inquiry at all' and that the reporting procedure requires prosecutors to lower their professional standards below the 'absolute minimum'.[20] John Griffiths, a professor of the sociology of law at a Dutch university, and another supporter of VAE, has acknowledged the 'intrinsic ineffectiveness of control based on self-reporting'.[21]

The government bill

A Dutch government bill which has given statutory force to the guidelines permitting VAE (and PAS) was passed by the lower house of the Dutch Parliament in November 2000 and by the upper house in April 2001.[22]

The Act provides:

1 VAE must be performed in accordance with 'careful medical practice'. Requests must be voluntary, well considered, persistent, and emanate from patients who are experiencing unbearable suffering without hope of improvement, and the doctor and the patient must agree that VAE is the only reasonable option. At least one independent physician must be consulted, who must see the patient and give a written opinion on the case.

---

[19] W. R. Kastelijn, *Standpunt hoofdbestuur KNMG inzake euthanasie* [Position of the Central Committee of the KNMG with respect to euthanasia] (1995).

[20] Interview by author with (anonymous) public prosecutor, 7 December 1989.

[21] Griffiths, 257.

[22] Wet Toetsing levensbeëindiging op verzoek en hulp bij zelfdoding [Legal assessment of life termination on request and assisted suicide] (Tweede Kamer 1998–9, 26691, no. 3, 10). See Henk Jochemsen, 'Legalizing Euthanasia in the Netherlands' (1999) 5 *Dignity: The Newsletter of the Center for Bioethics and Human Dignity* 1; Jochemsen, 'Update: The Legalization of Euthanasia in the Netherlands' (2000) 17(1) *Ethics & Medicine* 7. A copy of the Act is available on the Justice Ministry's website: www.minijust.nl:8080/a_beleid/fact/suicide.htm

2 All cases must be reported to and evaluated by regional committees consisting of a lawyer, a doctor, an ethicist or another professional who is accustomed to dealing with ethical issues. (For each member there is a substitute member.)

3 VAE will not be punishable if performed by a doctor who has complied with the requirements listed in (1) and who has reported the case to the local medical examiner.

4 The local medical examiner must send his or her report as well as the physician's report to the regional review committee. The medical examiner sends a form to the prosecutor informing the prosecutor about the case and seeking permission for burial or cremation. In the event of any serious infringement reported by the medical examiner or anyone else, the prosecutor will withhold permission for burial or cremation until a further investigation has been conducted. The reports to the regional committee must demonstrate that all the requirements have been met.

In addition to these established criteria, the Act contains provisions concerning children and advance directives:

5 A doctor may agree to a request for VAE by a child between 12 and 16 but only with the parents' consent. Requests by children aged 16–17 do not require parental consent, though parents should be involved in the decision-making process.

6 Doctors may terminate the life of an incompetent patient who has made his or her request for VAE by way of a signed advance directive.

The guidelines contained in the new legislation seem no more precise and strict than those laid down by the courts. Commenting on earlier legislative proposals, Professor Gevers, a professor of health law in the Netherlands and supporter of VAE, observed: 'It is impossible to delineate precisely the situations in which euthanasia should be allowed; therefore, a new law cannot add very much to what has already been developed by courts, and will only partially reduce legal uncertainty.'[23]

Similarly, Professor Griffiths has written:

the most important argument for legalization lies in the idea that it would increase the legal security of doctors, thereby (among other things) increasing their willingness to report. But putting the rules which have emerged in

---

[23] J. K. M. Gevers, 'Legal Developments concerning Active Euthanasia on Request in the Netherlands' (1987) 1 *Bioethics* 156 at 162.

the case law into the Criminal Code does not change the conditions under which euthanasia can be legally performed. It is therefore not clear why such legalization would have the desired effect on the rate of reporting.[24]

Moreover, even under the law as amended, the relevant information is still to be provided by the doctor, and only an unusually honest or an unusually stupid doctor would report that he had broken the guidelines. The legislation seems more a change in form than substance.

Conclusion

The Dutch claim that their guidelines for VAE are precise and strict and therefore capable of ensuring effective control fails to pass muster. The elasticity of the guidelines and the absence of a rigorous independent oversight of the doctor's decision-making suggest the contrary. We now turn to consider whether this suggestion is confirmed by the empirical evidence.

[24] Griffiths, 282.

9

The first Survey: the incidence of 'euthanasia'

Since the Dutch Supreme Court declared VAE lawful in 1984, a substantial body of empirical data has emerged concerning its practice. Much of this data has helpfully been generated by the Dutch themselves in the form of two major surveys. The first survey examined practice in 1990; the second practice in 1995. This chapter will consider the incidence of VAE and of other forms of intentional life-shortening (in particular NVAE and PE or passive euthanasia) in 1990.

The Remmelink Report and the Van der Maas Survey

The Dutch coalition government which assumed office in 1989 decided to appoint a commission to report on the 'extent and nature of medical euthanasia practice'.[1] A commission under the chairmanship of the Attorney-General, Professor Remmelink, was appointed on 17 January 1990 by the Minister of Justice and the State Secretary for Welfare, Health and Culture and charged to report on the practice by physicians of 'performing an act or omission... to terminate [the] life of a patient, with or without an explicit and serious request of the patient to this end'.[2] The Commission asked P. J. van der Maas, Professor of Public Health and Social Medicine at the Erasmus University, to carry out a survey which would produce qualitative and quantitative information. The Commission and Van der Maas agreed that the survey should embrace *all* medical decisions affecting the end of life so that VAE could be seen within that broader context. Their umbrella term 'Medical Decisions concerning the End of Life' ('MDELs') included 'all decisions by physicians concerning courses of action aimed at hastening the end of life of the patient or courses

---

[1] *Medische beslissingen rond het levenseinde. Het onderzoek voor de Commissie onderzoek medische praktijk inzake euthanasie* (1991) (hereafter 'Survey') 3.
[2] Ibid., 4.

of action for which the physician takes into account the probability that the end of life of the patient is hastened'.[3] MDELs comprised the administration, supply or prescription of a drug, the withdrawal/withholding of a treatment (including resuscitation and tube-feeding), and the refusal of a request for VAE.[4] The Commission's Report[5] and the Survey[6] were published in Dutch in September 1991. One year later, the Survey was published in English.[7]

The findings of the Survey

In addressing the incidence of 'euthanasia', our attention will focus on the Survey rather than the Report: the Report contains the Commission's conclusions in the light of the Survey but the Survey is a comprehensive empirical study which stands independently of the Report, and the conclusions drawn in the Report are not infrequently difficult to square with the findings of the Survey.

Methodology

Before we turn to the Survey's findings, a summary of its methodology is appropriate. The Survey comprised three studies.

The retrospective study[8]

A sample of 406 doctors was drawn from GPs, specialists (concerned with MDELs) and nursing home doctors, of whom 91% agreed to participate. The doctors were interviewed on average for two and a half hours and almost always by another doctor.[9] Respondents were asked about relevant types of decision. If they had made a decision of a given type, the last

---

[3] Ibid., 19–20.   [4] Ibid., 20.

[5] *Medische beslissingen rond het levenseinde. Rapport van de Commissie onderzoek medische praktijk inzake euthanasie* (1991) (hereafter 'Report').

[6] Survey.

[7] P. J. van der Maas, J. J. M. van Delden and L. Pijnenborg, *Euthanasia and Other Medical Decisions concerning the End of Life* (1992). Oddly, the Report has not been translated, though a brief English summary was produced by the Ministry of Justice: *Outlines Report Commission Inquiry into Medical Practice with Regard to Euthanasia [sic]* (n.d.) (hereafter 'Outline'). Dr Richard Fenigsen's unpublished 'First Reactions to the Report of the Committee on Euthanasia' (1991) contains a translation of key passages of the Report. For a more concise summary see his 'The Report of the Dutch Governmental Committee on Euthanasia' (1991) 7 *Issues Law Med* 339.

[8] See generally Survey, Part II (chapters 4–10).   [9] Ibid., 14–17; 191.

occasion on which they had done so was discussed in greater detail. At most, ten cases were discussed with each.[10]

The death certificate study[11]

This study examined a stratified sample of 8,500 deaths occurring in the Netherlands from July to November 1990 inclusive. The treating doctor was identified from each death certificate and was sent a short question-naire which could be returned anonymously. The response rate was 73%.[12]

The prospective study[13]

Each of the doctors interviewed in the retrospective study was asked to complete a questionnaire about each of their patients who died in the fol-lowing six months. This study had several advantages: there would be little memory distortion because the questionnaire would be completed soon after the death; it would provide additional information to strengthen the quantitative basis of the interview study; and the carefully planned selection of respondents meant that the responses were representative of 95% of all deaths. The study ran from mid-November 1990 to the end of May 1991. Eighty per cent of those involved in the first study participated, completing over 2,250 questionnaires.[14] In all, some 322 doctors supplied information about, on average, seven deaths.[15] The method of data col-lection in all three studies was such that anonymity of participants could be guaranteed.[16]

How much 'euthanasia'?

VAE

In 1990, the year covered by the Survey, there were almost 130,000 deaths in Holland from all causes, of which 49,000 involved a MDEL.[17] Both the Report and the Survey adopted the Dutch definition of 'euthanasia' as VAE, that is: 'the intentional action to terminate a person's life, performed by somebody else than the involved person upon the latter's request'.[18] How many cases were there in 1990?

---

[10] Ibid., 33.   [11] See generally ibid., Part III (chapters 11–13).   [12] Ibid., 15; 121–5; 191.
[13] See generally ibid., Part IV (chapters 14–15).   [14] Ibid., 15; 149–51; 192.
[15] Ibid., 160.   [16] Ibid., 16.   [17] Report, 14.
[18] Ibid., 11 (see also Outline, 2); 'the purposeful acting to terminate life by someone other than the person concerned upon request of the latter' (Survey, 5; see also 23; 193).

The three studies differed as to the incidence of VAE, yielding respective figures of 1.9%, 1.7% and 2.6% of all deaths. The researchers felt that the difference between the second and third estimates was 'probably due to the existence of a boundary area between "euthanasia" and intensifying of the alleviation of pain and/or symptoms'[19] and to the probability of the third study counting cases of pain alleviation as cases of VAE, thereby exaggerating its incidence.[20] The researchers concluded that, in the light of all three studies, VAE occurred in about 1.8% of all deaths, or about 2,300 cases,[21] and that there were almost 400 cases of PAS, some 0.3% of all deaths.[22] More than half the physicians regularly involved with terminal patients indicated that they had performed VAE or PAS and only 12% of doctors said they would never do so.[23]

Other cases of 'euthanasia'

So much for 'euthanasia' in its narrowest, Dutch sense: the intentional, *active* termination of life *at the patient's request*. But the authors of the Survey themselves went on, rightly, to consider cases of the intentional hastening of death, whether by act *or by omission*, and whether with *or without* a request by the patient.

They estimated that in a further 1,000 cases (or 0.8% of all deaths) physicians administered a drug 'with the explicit purpose of hastening the end of life without an explicit request of the patient'.[24] And beyond this, there lies a range of evidence yielded by the Survey, but not adequately

---

[19] Survey, 178.   [20] Ibid.   [21] Ibid.

[22] Ibid., 179. Of the three studies it is, however, arguably the third which produced the most accurate estimate of VAE. As the authors of the Survey pointed out, the respondents in the second study had no information other than the questionnaire and an accompanying letter, whereas those in the third had participated in the physician interviews, discussing one or more cases from their practice and the crucial concepts in the questionnaire for over two hours with a trained interviewer. The authors, noting that a 'great number' (Survey, 162) of interviewees commented that the interview had clarified their thinking about MDELs, suggested the possibility of a learning effect: familiarity with the questionnaire, in which the question about VAE followed those relating to other MDELs, may have led the respondents to reply negatively to the earlier questions knowing that the question about VAE was to come. The authors concluded that the most important fact was that the respondents in the third study 'changed their approach with respect to their intention when administering morphine due to their recent intensive confrontation with thinking about this complex of problems' (ibid.). If, however, the thinking of participants in the third study had been clarified by their participation in the first study, their responses were surely more likely to have been reliable than those in the second study, particularly as, the second study being retrospective, there was less risk of memory distortion.

[23] Ibid., 40, table 5.3.   [24] Ibid., 182. The third study returned a figure of 1.6% (ibid., 181).

considered by the authors in their commentary. For many other MDELs also involved an intent to hasten death. Palliative drugs were administered in 'such high doses . . . that . . . almost certainly would shorten the life of the patient'[25] in 22,500 cases (17.5% of all deaths).[26] In 65% (or 14,625) of these cases the doctor administered the medication merely 'Taking into account the probability that life would be shortened',[27] but in 30% (or 6,750 cases) it was administered 'Partly with the purpose of shortening life'[28] and in a further 6% (or 1,350 cases) 'With the explicit purpose of shortening life'.[29]

Moreover, doctors withheld/withdrew treatment without request in another 25,000 cases and, by the time of the Survey, some 90%, or 22,500, had died.[30] In 65% (or 16,250 cases) the treatment was withdrawn or withheld 'Taking into account the probability that life would be shortened',[31] but in 19% (or 4,750 cases) it was withdrawn/withheld 'Partly with the purpose to shorten life'[32] and in a further 16% (or 4,000 cases) 'With the explicit purpose to shorten life'.[33] The above figures are reproduced in Table 1.

2,700 or 9,050?

The Commission stated that the figure of 2,700 cases of VAE and PAS did not 'warrant the assumption that euthanasia in the Netherlands occurs on an excessive scale'.[34] However, it is clear that the total number of cases of intentional life-shortening in 1990 was in reality significantly higher than 2,700. To clarify and confirm this conclusion it is necessary to look more

---

[25] Ibid., 71. The authors were not concerned with cases where palliative drugs were used which had no chance of shortening life (ibid., 72). Life was shortened by up to one week in 70% of cases and by one to four weeks in 23% (ibid., 73, table 7.3).

[26] Ibid., 183.   [27] Ibid., 72, table 7.2.   [28] Ibid.   [29] Ibid.

[30] Ibid., 85; 90, table 8.14.   [31] Ibid., 90, table 8.15.   [32] Ibid.

[33] Ibid. Physicians received some 5,800 requests to withdraw/withhold treatment when it was the intention of the *patient* at least in part to hasten death (ibid., 81). In 74% of these cases the doctor withdrew or withheld treatment when it was partly the intention of the patient to shorten life, and in 26% of cases when it was the patient's primary intention to shorten life (ibid., 84, table 8.7). By the time of the interview, some 82% (or 4,756) had died (ibid., 82, table 8.6). The Survey notes that 'The patient's intention does not have to agree with that of the physician' (ibid., 83). Because the doctor's intention may have been to respect the patient's legal right to refuse treatment rather than to shorten the patient's life, it is unclear how many of these cases could properly be categorised as cases of intentional life-ending. Interestingly, by no means all of the patients from whom treatment was withdrawn on request were terminal. Life was shortened by one to four weeks in 16%, by one to six months in 34% and even longer in 13% (ibid., 82, table 8.6).

[34] Report, 31; Outline, 2.

Table 1. *Medical decisions concerning the end of life in 1990*

	Acts or omissions with intent to shorten life (cases of 'explicit' intent to shorten life in bold; cases without explicit request in parenthesis)
Total deaths (all causes)	129,000
'Euthanasia'^ (i.e. VAE)	**2,300**
Physician-assisted suicide	**400**
Intentional life-terminating acts without explicit request+	**1,000 (1,000)**
Alleviation of pain/symptoms~	22,500
with the 'explicit purpose' of shortening life	**1,350 (450)**
'partly with the purpose' of shortening life	6,750 (5,058)
Withdrawal/withholding of treatment without explicit request*	25,000
with the 'explicit purpose' of shortening life	**4,000 (4,000)**
'partly with the purpose' of shortening life	4,750 (4,750)
Withdrawal/withholding of treatment on explicit request** had where the *patient*	5,800
the 'explicit purpose' of shortening life	1,508
'partly ... the purpose' of shortening life	4,292
Sub-total#	**9,050 (5,450)**
Total##	20,550 (15,258)

^No shortening of life occurred in 1% of these cases (Survey, 49, table 5.13).

+No shortening of life occurred in 4% of these cases (ibid., 66, table 6.10).

~No shortening of life occurred in 8% of these cases (ibid., 73, table 7.3).

*90% of these patients (22,500) had died by the time of the interview and there had been no shortening of life in 20% of these cases (ibid., 90, table 8.14).

**82% of these patients (4,756) had died by the time of the interview and there had been no shortening of life in 19% of these cases (ibid., 82, table 8.6).

#This sub-total refers to cases where doctors 'explicitly' intended to shorten life by act or omission.

##This total refers to cases where doctors intended ('explicitly' or 'partly') to hasten death by act or omission. Both it and the preceding sub-total therefore include (as does the Survey) cases where life may not in fact have been shortened and cases in the asterisked categories where patients had not died by the time of the Survey.

closely at the definitions used by the authors of the Survey in arriving at their figure of 2,700.

It will be recalled that the definition of 'euthanasia' adopted by the Commission was an 'intentional action to terminate a person's life, performed by somebody else than the involved person upon the latter's request'.[35] Similarly, the definition adopted in the Survey was 'the purposeful acting to terminate life by someone other than the person concerned upon request of the latter'.[36] The authors of the Survey distinguished the following states of mind:

(acting with) the explicit purpose of hastening the end of life;
(acting) partly with the purpose of hastening the end of life;
(acting while) taking into account the probability that the end of life will be hastened.[37]

They explained that the first category, unlike the third, applied where the patient's death was the intended outcome of the action. The second category was used because sometimes an act was performed with a particular aim (such as pain relief) but the side effect (such as death) was 'not unwelcome'.[38] The Dutch definition of 'euthanasia' as active, voluntary, *intentional* killing indicates that the Dutch agree that intention, and not foresight, is the badge of 'euthanasia'. The distinction the researchers drew between intentional and foreseen life-shortening is therefore understandable.[39] For the reasons given in chapter 1, it is also welcome.

As Table 1 reveals, the Survey disclosed that doctors intended to accelerate death in far more than the 2,700 cases classified by the Commission as 'euthanasia' and assisted suicide. This total ignores the 1,000 cases of

[35] Report, 11.   [36] Ibid.

[37] Survey, 21. 'Explicit' is the translation in the English version of the Survey of the Dutch *uitdrukkelijk*. 'Primary' would have been a better word to have used than 'explicit': an intention may be explicit yet secondary, or primary yet implicit.

[38] Ibid. They felt that such an effect should be categorised as intentional because to count as *un*intentional a death 'should not in fact have been desired'. The category related to a situation in which the 'death of the patient was not foremost in the physician's mind but neither was death unwelcome' and was regarded by the researchers as a 'type of intention' (ibid.).

[39] Their explanation of the distinction between the two states of mind is not as clear as it could have been. This is illustrated not only by their questionable interpretation, in the preceding note, of a consequence as 'partly' intended, but also by their comment that, in the third category, death 'may not' have been intended. It would have been clearer had they distinguished between the hastening of death as the doctor's 'sole or primary purpose'; the doctor's 'secondary purpose'; and as merely 'foreseen'.

intentional life termination without request. It also excludes two other categories in which doctors said their primary purpose had been to shorten life: the 1,350 cases involving the administration of palliative drugs, and the 4,000 cases of withholding or withdrawing treatment without request.[40] Adding these 1,000, 1,350 and 4,000 cases to the Commission's total of 2,700 yields a total of 9,050 cases in which doctors said it was their primary purpose to shorten life by act or omission, with or without request.

It could be replied that the cases in excess of 2,700 should not be counted as they were not cases of VAE. There are, however, two counter-arguments. First, some of them clearly *were*. In relation to the 1,350 cases in which it was the explicit purpose of the doctor to shorten life by increasing the dosage of palliative drugs, the Survey discloses: 'In all these cases the patient had at some time indicated something about terminating life and an explicit request had been made in two thirds of the cases.'[41] Indeed, the authors comment: 'This situation is therefore rather similar to euthanasia.'[42] It is unclear, therefore, why the Commission did not regard these as cases of VAE: they seem to fall squarely within its definition.[43] The second counter-argument is that the true scale of intentional life-shortening can only properly be gauged when the Commission's unusually narrow definition of 'euthanasia' as VAE is replaced by a wider definition, such as the intentional termination of a patient's life by act or omission.[44] A broader definition yields a higher total. And a broader definition including cases where doctors said their primary purpose was to shorten life, by act or omission, with or without request, produces a total of 9,050.

Would it be reasonable to add to this total of 9,050 the further 11,500 cases (the 6,750 cases of administering palliative drugs and the 4,750 of withdrawing treatment without request) in which hastening death was 'partly' the doctor's intention?[45] Although it may well be that the doctor's

---

[40] The cases of withholding/withdrawing treatment at the explicit request of the patient where it was the intention of the patient, either primary or secondary, to shorten life, are excluded from consideration here for the reason given in note 33.

[41] Survey, 72.   [42] Ibid.

[43] A member of the Commission (who in fact wrote the Remmelink Report) later agreed with the proposition that those cases where doctors had administered palliative drugs, with the explicit purpose of shortening the patient's life and at the patient's explicit request, could properly be categorised as 'euthanasia' (interview by author with Mr A. Kors, Ministry of Justice, The Hague, 29 November 1991).

[44] See pp. 12–15.

[45] If they are added, the total rises to 20,550 cases in which it was the doctors' primary or secondary intention to shorten life by act or omission, with or without request. On this total, the incidence of intentional termination of life rises to over 15% of all deaths.

intention in most if not all of these cases was to shorten life, the possibility that it was not, given the researchers' unclear explanation of this category, cannot be ruled out.[46]

Even if these cases are not included, however, the total number of life-shortening acts and omissions where the doctor's 'explicit' or primary intention was to shorten life, and which are therefore indubitably euthanasiast, was 9,050. This figure comprises the 2,700 cases categorised as 'euthanasia' and assisted suicide by the Survey; plus the 1,000 cases of life-termination without explicit request; plus the 1,350 cases involving the administration of palliative drugs with intent to shorten life; plus the 4,000 of withholding or withdrawing treatment without request with intent to end life. In *all* those cases, doctors said their explicit purpose was to shorten life. The figure of 9,050 is over three times the Survey's total of 2,700 and amounts to over 7% of all deaths that year. In other words, in around 1 in 15 of all deaths in the Netherlands in 1990, doctors said their explicit purpose had been to end the patient's life.

'Dances with data'?

The authors of the Van der Maas Survey have argued that some observers (including the author) have misinterpreted their findings.[47] One of their main criticisms is that we have inaccurately inflated the total number of cases of 'euthanasia' and PAS disclosed by their Survey. Their main

---

[46] On the one hand, these cases were distinguished in the Survey from those where the doctor merely foresaw the acceleration of death (where the doctor proceeded 'Taking into account the probability that life would be shortened' (Survey, 73, table 7.2; 90, table 8.15)). If the doctor's purpose in these cases was, albeit partly, to hasten death, then it does not seem inappropriate to regard them as instances of 'euthanasia' on the second definition of 'euthanasia' considered, and favoured, in chapter 1. By analogy, if racial discrimination is the intentional (purposeful) treating of one person less favourably than another on racial grounds and, say, an employer takes advantage of a need to make redundancies in order to get rid of his black workers, he may be said to have acted partly with a view to doing just that, even though his primary purpose is to save his company by reducing expenditure on wages.

On the other hand, it is arguable that these disputed cases were not necessarily cases in which it was even the doctor's secondary purpose to hasten death. Notwithstanding the researchers' classification of these as cases of intentional killing, their vague explanation of this category and in particular their imprecise understanding of the concept of 'purpose' (see note 39) in fact leave the matter unclear. The implication in their explanation that death in these cases was 'desired' does indeed suggest that the doctor intended to shorten life, but the reference to death as a 'not unwelcome' consequence suggests that death, while not regretted, may not, in some of these cases, have been any part of the doctor's purpose or goal.

[47] J. J. M. van Delden et al., 'Dances with Data' (1993) 7 *Bioethics* 323.

argument is that 'intentions cannot carry the full weight of a moral evaluation on their own'[48] because 'intentions are essentially private matters.
Ultimately only the agent "decides" what his intentions are, and different
agents may describe the same actions in the same situations as performed
with different intentions'.[49] And, they add, the agent's purpose may change
over time, so what is to count as the 'definitive description'?[50]

This argument is odd. The authors agree that VAE is to be distinguished
from other MDELs in that it involves the intentional ('purposeful') shortening of life; indeed, one of the welcome features of their meticulous
Survey is the care they took to ascertain the doctors' state of mind when
hastening death. They specifically *asked* whether the doctors shortened life
with the 'explicit purpose' of so doing; or 'partly with the purpose' of so
doing; or merely 'taking into account the probability' of so doing and the
doctors *replied* that in some 9,050 cases it had been their 'explicit' intention
to shorten life. Why, then, are the doctors' own answers not taken as the
'definitive description' of their intention? If the authors thought it impossible to discern the doctors' intention, why did they bother asking them?

The authors add that no doctor who performs VAE does so with the
sole intent to kill: 'His or her intention can always be described as trying
to relieve the suffering of his or her patient. This is exactly what infuriates
Dutch physicians when, after reporting the case they are treated as crimi-
nals and murderers.'[51] However, while the doctors' ultimate intention may
be to relieve suffering, they intend to do so *by shortening the patient's life*,
which is precisely why, in most jurisdictions, the doctor who intentionally
kills a patient, even to end suffering, is liable for murder. If an heir kills
his rich father by slipping a poison into his tea, would the authors deny
that this was murder on the ground that the heir's intention was not to
kill and 'can always be described as' trying to accelerate his inheritance?

They continue that it is wrong to rest a moral evaluation entirely on
intention: 'For a moral evaluation, more is to be taken into account, such
as the presence of a request of the patient, the futility of further medical
treatment, the sequelae of the decision to stop treatment (e.g. will this
cause heavy distress?), the interests of others involved such as family and
so on.'[52] Their reasoning is, again, muddled. The question at issue here is
not the *moral evaluation* of cases of euthanasia but their *incidence*, and this
is a matter of definition, not evaluation.

[48] Ibid., 325.   [49] Ibid.   [50] Ibid.   [51] Ibid.   [52] Ibid., 325–6.

A further argument they advance is that if the 'context' is taken into account, it can be questioned whether the intention was to end life. As an example they cite the 6% of cases of alleviation of pain and symptoms in which doctors stated that their explicit intention was to shorten life. The authors seek to distinguish these cases from VAE on the ground that they involve a failure of palliative care followed by the use of higher doses which may lead to a point at which 'the physician realizes that he or she actually hopes that the patient dies'.[53] His or her intention is 'not necessarily'[54] the same as with VAE, where the physician would surely try another lethal drug if the first failed, which would 'never'[55] happen with the administration of opioids. This argument, too, fails. First, in these 6% of cases doctors stated it was their *explicit*, not partial, intention to shorten life; the authors give no reason to doubt the accuracy of this response. Secondly, their argument appears to rest on the speculation that, had the higher dose failed to shorten life, the doctor would not have resorted to another method. Even if this were so, the argument is specious, resting on a patent *non sequitur*. If A attempts to kill B by method M1, which fails, A's decision not to resort to method M2 in no way establishes A did not intend to kill by method M1.

In sum, the criticisms advanced by the Survey authors against those who arrive at a higher total are quite unpersuasive.

Conclusion

In view of the moral significance of intention (noted in chapter 2) in distinguishing 'euthanasia' from other MDELs, a significance accepted by the Dutch in their definition of 'euthanasia', there is good reason to count as 'euthanasia' *all* cases in which doctors stated that their primary purpose (and even secondary purpose) was to kill. To exclude, as do the Dutch, cases in which doctors carried out that purpose by deliberate omission and cases in which patients had made no explicit request for death, seems arbitrary and liable significantly to underestimate the incidence of euthanasia, at least as understood by many people outside the Netherlands.

All this illustrates the importance, stressed in chapter 1, of clarity in definition. The Dutch adopt a peculiarly narrow definition of 'euthanasia'

---

[53] Ibid., 326.   [54] Ibid.   [55] Ibid., 327.

as VAE which results in an unduly restricted perception of the extent to which Dutch doctors intentionally kill their patients. Applying their narrow definition, the Dutch arrived at a figure of 2,700. A wider definition, which more accurately reflects the moral importance of the *intentional* termination of life, and which includes NVAE and PE (passive euthanasia), yields a total of 9,050.

This chapter has suggested that the Dutch total is on the low side, even if the narrow Dutch definition is applied. It has also replied to Dutch criticism of a higher total. Had Professor Van der Maas simply accepted that the higher total reflects a wider definition of 'euthanasia', there would have been much less room for disagreement about its incidence. By criticising the wider definition's emphasis on intention, however, he contradicts the importance attached to it by his very own Survey.

10

Breach of the guidelines

In how many cases of VAE was there a 'free and voluntary' request which was 'well-considered, durable and persistent'? In how many was there 'intolerable' suffering for which VAE was a 'last resort'? In how many did the doctor consult with another doctor and subsequently report to the authorities?[1] The Survey contained telling evidence also about the extent to which Dutch doctors did, and did not, comply with the guidelines. This chapter will summarise that evidence, which betrays widespread non-compliance with the guidelines, not least the practice of NVAE.

An explicit request

An 'entirely free and voluntary' request which was 'well considered, durable and persistent'?

Doctors stated that in the 2,700 cases of VAE and PAS there was an 'explicit request'[2] in 96%; which was 'wholly made by the patient'[3] in 99% of cases and 'repeated'[4] in 94%; and that in 100% of cases the patient had a 'good insight'[5] into his disease and its prognosis. Oddly, no specific question was put about the voluntariness of the request and there is no evidence of any mechanism which could have guaranteed that the request was voluntary. Moreover, the request was purely oral in 60% of cases[6] and, when made to a GP in cases where a nurse was caring for the patient, the GP more often

---

[1] Ninety-eight per cent of doctors stated that they were aware of the 'rules of due care' formulated by the KNMG, the Health Council and the government. When asked what they were, 89% mentioned consultation; 66% the need for a seriously considered request; 42% a voluntary request; 37% 'unacceptable' suffering, and 18% a long-standing desire to die (Survey, 95–6, table 9.1). By contrast, when shown fourteen guidelines and asked to rank them in importance, 98% mentioned voluntariness and only 67% consultation (ibid., table 9.2).

[2] Ibid., 50, table 5.15.   [3] Ibid.   [4] Ibid.   [5] Ibid.   [6] Ibid., 43.

than not failed to consult her.[7] There is no way of gauging the accuracy of the doctors' statements, which were uncorroborated, about the patients' requests. Even if they were true, however, the Survey data showed that in the majority (60%) of the 9,050 cases in which it was the doctor's primary purpose to hasten death by act or omission, there was no explicit request from the patient.

'Life-terminating acts without the patient's explicit request'

It will be recalled from the previous chapter that the Survey disclosed a remarkable incidence of NVAE: 'On an annual basis there are, in the Netherlands, some 1,000 cases (0.8% of all deaths) in which physicians prescribe, supply or administer a drug with the explicit purpose of hastening the end of life without an explicit request of the patient.'[8] In over half these cases, the decision was discussed with the patient or the patient had previously indicated a wish for the hastening of death, but in 'several hundred cases there was no discussion with the patient and there also was no known wish from the patient for hastening the end of life'.[9] Virtually all cases, wrote the researchers, involved seriously ill and terminal patients who obviously were suffering a great deal and were no longer able to express their wishes, though there was a 'small number'[10] of cases in which the decision could have been discussed with the patient.

The fact that doctors intentionally administered a lethal drug without an express request in 1,000 cases is striking. So too was the Commission's reaction to this disturbing statistic. The Commission observed that the ('few dozen')[11] cases in which the doctor killed a *competent* patient without request 'must be prevented in future',[12] and that one means would be 'strict compliance with the scrupulous care'[13] required 'including the requirement that all facts of the case are put down in writ[i]ng'.[14] However, the Commission *defended* the other cases of unrequested killing, stating that 'active intervention'[15] by the doctor was usually 'inevitable'[16] because of the patient's 'death agony'.[17] That is why, it explained, it regarded

---

[7] Ibid., 108, table 10.3. By contrast, 96% of specialists and nursing home doctors consulted nursing staff (ibid.). Further, two-thirds of GPs said they felt it was up to the doctor in certain circumstances to raise the topic of VAE (ibid., 101).
[8] Ibid., 182.   [9] Ibid.   [10] Ibid.   [11] Outline, 3.   [12] Ibid.
[13] Ibid.   [14] Ibid.   [15] Ibid.   [16] Ibid.   [17] Ibid.

these cases as 'care for the dying'.[18] It added that the ultimate justification for killing in these cases was the patient's 'unbearable suffering'.[19]

The Commission's assertion that most of the 1,000 patients were incompetent patients in their 'death agony' should not pass unchallenged. The physician interviews indicated that 14% of the patients were totally competent and a further 11% partly competent.[20] They also disclosed that 21% had a life expectancy of one to four weeks and 7% of one to six months (the Survey classed patients as 'dying' if their life had been shortened only by 'hours or days', not by 'weeks or months').[21] Moreover, doctors did not list 'agony' as a reason for killing these patients. The reasons given by doctors were the absence of any prospect of improvement (60%); the futility of all medical therapy (39%); avoidance of 'needless prolongation' (33%);[22] the relatives' inability to cope (32%), and 'low quality of life' (31%).[23] Pain or suffering was mentioned by only 30%.[24] Even in relation to these 30%, if they were essentially cases of increasing pain or symptom treatment with the explicit intent to shorten life, why did the doctors not classify them under that heading?[25]

In short, the Commission's defence of these 1,000 cases would appear to be based on a shaky factual foundation and to amount to little more than a bare assertion that ending patients' lives without request, a practice in breach of a cardinal guideline, is morally acceptable. On the basis of this assertion, the Commission proceeded to recommend that doctors should report such cases in the same way as they report cases of VAE.[26] This

[18] Ibid. [19] Ibid.
[20] Seventy-five per cent of the patients were 'totally unable to assess the situation and take a decision adequately'. However, 14% were totally, and 11% partly ('not totally') able to do so (Survey, 61, table 6.4). The authors described a person 'not totally able' as 'partially able to assess the situation and on this basis adequately take a decision' (ibid., 23). According to the death certificate study, 36% were competent (Loes Pijnenborg et al., 'Life-Terminating Acts without Explicit Request of Patient' (1993) 341 *Lancet* 1196, 1198, table II).
[21] Survey, 66, table 6.10. According to the Survey's (tentative) definition of 'dying' (ibid., 24), therefore, in only 29% of the 2,700 cases of VAE and PAS was the patient dying (ibid., 49, table 5.13).
[22] Ibid., 64, table 6.7. [23] Ibid.
[24] Ibid. Surprisingly, no question was asked about the doctor's intention which, as the authors noted, 'complicates the interpretation of the results' (ibid., 57).
[25] Henk Jochemsen, 'Euthanasia in Holland: An Ethical Critique of the New Law' (1994) 20 *J Med Ethics* 212, 213.
[26] Outline, 6. The Commission excepted from this recommendation cases where 'the vital functions have already and irreversibly begun to fail' on the ground that in such cases a natural death would have ensued anyway (ibid.). The government rejected this exception: see J. K. M.

recommendation was implemented when in 1993 the government incorporated the reporting procedure into the statute regulating the disposal of the dead. The amended legislation, which came into force the following year, made it clear that the reporting procedure was to be followed whether or not the patient had explicitly requested death.[27]

Other cases lacking an explicit request

In addition to the 1,000 cases, many other cases of intentional life-shortening involved no explicit request by the patient. In 59% (or 4,779) of the 8,100 cases in which doctors were said to have intended to hasten death by pain-killing drugs, the patient had 'never indicated anything about terminating life',[28] and there had been no explicit request in a further 9% (or 729),[29] making 5,508 cases in which there had been no explicit request.[30] Of the 1,350 cases in which it had been the doctor's explicit purpose to hasten death, there had been no explicit request from the patient in 450 cases.

Additionally, there were 8,750 cases in which treatment was said to have been withheld/withdrawn without explicit request and intentionally to shorten life, in 4,000 of which it was the doctor's explicit purpose to end life.[31] The Commission represented these as cases of omitting to provide futile treatment. It stated:

> After all, a doctor has the right to refrain from (further) treatment, if that treatment would be pointless according to objective medical standards. The commission would define a treatment without any medical use as therapeutical interference that gives no hope whatsoever for any positive effect upon the patient. To the application of this kind of futile medicine, no one is entitled. It is undisputed that the medical decision whether a particular action is useful or not, belongs to normal medical practice.[32]

Gevers, 'Legislation on Euthanasia: Recent Developments in the Netherlands' (1992) 18 *J Med Ethics* 140.

[27] Gevers, 'Legislation on Euthanasia' 139–40.

[28] Survey, 76, table 7.9.   [29] Ibid.

[30] In 17% of cases, the patient had indicated something about life termination but the 'request was not strongly explicit' (ibid.). If these cases are included, the number of cases of life-shortening without explicit request becomes 6,885. In only 15% of cases, therefore, was there a 'strongly explicit' request (ibid.).

[31] Survey, 90, table 8.15. In 18% of cases the patient had 'indicated something at some time about terminating life' and in a further 13% there had been some discussion with the patient (Survey, 88, table 8.11).

[32] Outline, 3–4.

The Commission was surely confused. First, the Survey did not use the concept of futile treatment in relation to the withholding/withdrawal of treatment as the authors felt its meaning was open to 'variable' interpretation.[33] Secondly, the preamble to the relevant questions suggested that they were not asking about the withholding/withdrawal of futile *treatment*, that is, treatment which was incapable of achieving its normal therapeutic purpose, but rather about the withholding/withdrawal of treatment which was preserving what were deemed to be futile *lives*, that is, lives which were thought not to be worth preserving. The preamble read:

> In most instances this [decision to withhold/withdraw treatment] concerns situations in which the treating physician does not expect or does not observe sufficient success. However, there are situations in which a considerable life-prolonging effect can be expected from a certain treatment while the decision can nevertheless be made to withhold such treatment or to withdraw it. This implies that under such circumstances considerable prolongation of life is considered undesirable or even futile. 'Considerable' is taken to mean more than one month.[34]

That the questions were concerned with 'futile' lives rather than ineffectual treatment is further suggested by the authors' explanation of this series of questions:

> Briefly, two types of situations are discussed here. On the one hand therapies are involved which will probably meet with little or no success. Such treatment can be withdrawn or withheld for this reason. On the other hand there are cases in which therapies which can have a considerable (more than one month) life-prolonging effect but in which prolongation of life is undesirable or pointless and treatment is withdrawn or withheld for this reason.[35]

They add that doctors were asked to discuss 'only the second type'[36] of situation. Thirdly, it seems clear that the question was so understood by those respondents who said that their intention had been to hasten death, not to withdraw a futile treatment.[37]

That the lives of so many patients were shortened without explicit request is striking. Hardly less striking is the fact that by no means all of the patients killed without request were incompetent. It will be recalled that of the 1,000 actively and intentionally killed without request by the

---

[33] Survey, 24.   [34] Ibid., 84–5.   [35] Ibid., 85.   [36] Ibid.   [37] See p. 106.

administration of a lethal drug, 14% were (according to the physician in-terviews) totally competent and a further 11% partly competent. Van der Wal, a Dutch health inspector and leading medical supporter of VAE, has rightly observed that in these cases the right to self-determination was 'seriously undermined'.[38] Moreover, of the 8,100 patients whose deaths were said to have been intentionally accelerated by palliative drugs, 60% (or 2,867) of those who had never indicated anything about life termina-tion were competent.[39] Finally, the patient was totally competent in 22%, and partly competent in a further 21%, of all the cases where treatment was withheld or withdrawn without request.[40]

The Commission concluded that the Survey 'disproves the assertion often expressed, that non-voluntary active termination of life occurs more frequently in the Netherlands than voluntary termination'.[41] This may well be so if 'euthanasia' is defined as the *active* termination of life. However, if intentional termination *by omission* is included, the Survey disclosed that in 1990 doctors intentionally sought to shorten more lives without than with an explicit request. It was their 'explicit' (primary) aim to end the lives of 9,050 patients. Of that total, 5,450 (or 60%) had made no explicit request to have their lives ended: the 1,000 given lethal injections; the 450 given overdoses of pain-killers; and the 4,000 from whom treatment was withheld or withdrawn. Even applying the Commission's narrower definition of 'euthanasia' as VAE, 27% of patients whose lives were actively and intentionally ended (1,000 of 3,700) were killed without an explicit request: no small proportion.

Unbearable suffering and last resort

Unbearable suffering?

The Survey threw doubt on whether VAE was confined to patients who were 'suffering unbearably' and for whom it was a 'last resort'.[42] For exam-ple, doctors were asked in interview which reason(s) patients most often

[38] Gerrit van der Wal, 'Unrequested Termination of Life: Is it Permissible?' (1993) 7 *Bioethics* 330, 337.

[39] Survey, 77.

[40] Ibid., 88. The Survey did not appear to provide separate figures for those whose lives were intentionally shortened by the withholding/withdrawal of treatment.

[41] Outline, 3; Report, 33.

[42] The Commission stated that Dutch doctors regarded the 'intolerable suffering of the patient and/or his natural desire for a quiet death' as the only grounds for VAE (ibid., 32). The reference

gave for requesting VAE. Their replies to this question (and to that about the most important reasons for ending life without request)[43] showed that in most cases, 57%, it was 'loss of dignity'; in 46% 'not dying in a dignified way'; in 33% 'dependence' and in 23% 'tiredness of life'. Only 46% mentioned 'pain'.[44]

As we noted in chapter 8 when outlining the guidelines, two court cases have illustrated the elastic meaning of 'unbearable suffering'. In the *Chabot* case, decided in 1994, in which the defendant doctor was charged with assisting in suicide a woman suffering from severe grief after the death of her two sons, the Supreme Court held that the patient need have no physical, let alone terminal, illness. The suffering which was considered sufficient in that case was purely mental, resulting from a 'depression in a particular sense without psychotic characteristics in the context of a complicated grieving process'.[45]

More recently, the *Sutorius* case appears to have stretched the guideline even further.[46] In 2000, a court in Haarlem acquitted Dr Philip Sutorius for assisting Edward Brongersma, his 86-year-old patient, to commit suicide. The patient had asked Dr Sutorius for death on at least eight occasions since 1986. A month before committing suicide in April 1998 the patient, who was obsessed with his 'physical decline', had said that death had 'forgotten' him, that his friends and relatives were dead, and that he experienced 'a pointless and empty existence'.[47] A second opinion confirmed that he was suffering hopelessly and a psychiatrist judged that the patient had no treatable psychiatric illness. The prosecutor argued that the requirement of 'hopeless and unbearable suffering' was not satisfied

---

to these grounds in the alternative, without disapproval, is revealing: it implies that doctors and the Commission regarded NVAE as permissible.

[43] Survey, 64, table 6.7.   [44] Survey, 45, table 5.8.

[45] '. . . een depressie in engere zin, zonder psychotische kenmerken, in het kader van een gecompliceerd rouwproces' (Hoge Raad, 21 June 1994, Strafkamer, no. 96.972 para. 4.5 (see p. 87 n. 17)). The Supreme Court rejected the prosecution's submissions that necessity required somatic pain and that a psychotic patient could not make a genuine request for death. It held, however, that in cases where the suffering was not somatic, a proper factual basis for the necessity defence could be laid only where the patient had been examined by an independent doctor who had assessed the gravity of the suffering and other possibilities for its alleviation. As the Appeal Court had not made such a finding in this case it had not been in a position to conclude that a situation of necessity existed. Although Dr Chabot was convicted, he was not punished. He was later admonished by a Medical Disciplinary Court.

[46] Tony Sheldon, 'Dutch GP Cleared after Helping to End Man's "Hopeless Existence"' (2000) 321 *BMJ* 1174. See p. 87 n. 18.

[47] Ibid.

and called for Dr Sutorius to be given a three-month suspended prison sentence. However, three medical experts asked to review the case testified that the patient was suffering unbearably and that there was no possible medical treatment. The court accepted that the defendant had made a justifiable choice between his duty to preserve life and his duty to relieve suffering.

Even the KNMG has criticised this decision, a spokesman saying that the notion of unbearable suffering had been 'stretched too far'. He added: 'What is new is that it goes beyond physical or psychiatric illness to include social decline.'[48] Similarly, the Minister of Justice commented that being 'tired of life' is not a sufficient ground and the prosecution evidently intends to appeal. On the other hand, in April 2001, Els Borst, the Health Minister, expressed her opinion that very old people who are simply 'tired of life' should be allowed to obtain a suicide pill.[49] Citing the example of two 95-year-olds she had known, she said: 'They were bored stiff, but, alas, not bored to death – because that was indeed what they wanted most of all.'[50]

Last resort?

Nor does it appear that VAE was invariably a 'last resort'. Doctors said that treatment alternatives remained in one in five cases (21%) but that, in almost all of these cases, they were refused.[51] Moreover, one in three GPs who decided that there were no alternatives had not sought advice from a colleague.[52] And when asked to rank the guidelines in order of importance, only 64% of respondents said absence of treatment alternatives was '(very) important'.[53]

Even in the four out of five cases in which the doctors said there were no treatment alternatives, this appeared to mean 'alternatives to the current treatment' rather than 'alternatives to VAE', an interpretation supported both by the question asked ('Were alternatives available *to the treatment given*? Here I consider other therapeutic possibilities or possibilities to alleviate pain and/or symptoms')[54] and by the doctors' response to another

---

[48] Ibid.   [49] CNN.COM./WORLD 14 April 2001.   [50] Ibid.   [51] Survey, 45, table 5.7.
[52] Ibid., 43. Even in those cases where the doctors (two-thirds of GPs and 80% of specialists) did consult, there is nothing to suggest that the colleague consulted was a specialist in palliative medicine.
[53] Ibid., 96, table 9.2.   [54] Ibid., 43 (emphasis added).

question about the aim of the treatment at the time when the decision to carry out VAE was made: 77% replied that it was palliative, 10% life-prolonging, and 2% curative; only 14% said there was no treatment.[55] In other words, just because there may have been no treatment alternatives to the existing treatment does not mean that the existing treatment was not an alternative to VAE.

But even *if* the palliative treatment given in 77% of cases was not pre-venting unbearable suffering and was so ineffectual that VAE was thought to be the only alternative, does this (and the fact that in 46% of cases pain was one of the reasons given by patients for wanting VAE) not raise questions about the quality of the palliative care that the patients were receiving? Revealingly, a report on palliative care published in 1987 by the Dutch Health Council concluded that a majority of cancer patients in pain suffered unnecessarily because of health professionals' lack of expertise.[56] Similarly, research published two years later into pain management at the Netherlands Cancer Institute, Amsterdam, contained the 'critical and worrisome overall finding . . . that pain management was judged to be in-adequate in slightly more than 50% of evaluated cases'.[57]

Forty per cent of the doctors interviewed in the Van der Maas Survey ex-pressed agreement with the proposition that 'Adequate alleviation of pain and/or symptoms and personal care of the dying patient make euthana-sia unnecessary'.[58] Yet the Commission concluded that its total of 2,700 cases showed that VAE and PAS were not being used as an alternative to

---

[55] Ibid., 45, table 5.6. Why 14% were receiving no treatment is unexplained.

[56] I. J. Keown, 'The Law and Practice of Euthanasia in the Netherlands' (1992) 108 *LQR* 51, 65. The British Medical Association Working Party on Euthanasia commented that palliative care in the Netherlands was not as advanced as in Britain: *Euthanasia: Report of the Working Party to Review the British Medical Association's Guidance on Euthanasia* (hereafter '*Euthanasia*') (1988) 49.

[57] Karin L. Dorrepaal et al., 'Pain Experience and Pain Management among Hospitalized Cancer Patients' (1989) 63 *Cancer* 593, 598. Referring to this study, Zbigniew Zylic, a leading hospice doctor in the Netherlands, commented that it did not warrant a general judgment about terminal care in the Netherlands but should be taken as a warning and a stimulus for further studies. He noted that 'cancer pain treatment and symptom control does not receive enough attention and, in many places, it is practised at a very poor level. As yet, there is no specific training available in palliative care' ('The Story behind the Blank Spot' (July/August 1993) *Am J Hosp Pall Care* 30, 32). He added that there were no comprehensive hospices in Holland because the high standard of care in hospitals and nursing-homes and the government's policy to reduce institutional beds have combined to discourage the hospice system. While hospitals were officially encouraged to provide hospice care, the necessary resources were not provided. Zylic urged the establishment of more hospices (ibid., 33–4). See also pp. 140–1 nn. 16–23.

[58] Survey, 102, table 9.7.

palliative medicine or terminal care.[59] Moreover, the Commission's conclusion sits uneasily with its later observation about the inadequacy of
such care in the Netherlands:

> The research report shows that the medical decision process with regard to
> the end of life demands more and more expertise in a number of different
> areas. First of all medical and technical know-how, especially in the field
> of the treatment of pain, of prognosis and of alternative options for the
> treatment of disorders that cause insufferable pain.[60]

The Commission added:

> Especially doctors, but nurses as well, will have to be trained in terminal
> care ... Optimal care for someone who is dying implies that the doctor has
> knowledge of adequate treatments for pain, of alternatives for the treatment
> of complaints about unbearable pain and that he is aware of the moment
> when he must allow the process of dying to run its natural course. Doctors
> still lack sufficient knowledge of this care ... In a country that is rated among
> the best in the world when it comes to birth care, knowledge with regard to
> care for the dying should not be lacking.[61]

If there was such a lack of knowledge, does this not fortify the impression
that VAE was being used, at least sometimes, as an alternative to palliative
care?[62]

Consultation and reporting

Consultation

Doctors stated that they had consulted a colleague in 84% of cases of VAE
and PAS.[63] The Survey did not explain the form, substance or outcome of
the consultations. Again, in respect of the 1,000 acts of NVAE – cases where

---

[59] Outline, 2; Report, 31.   [60] Outline, 7.   [61] Ibid.

[62] An expert committee of the World Health Organisation concluded: 'now that a practicable
alternative to death in pain exists, there should be concentrated efforts to implement programmes of palliative care, rather than a yielding to pressure for legal euthanasia' (*Cancer Pain
Relief and Palliative Care* (1990)). Dr Pieter Admiraal, one of Holland's leading practitioners
of VAE, has written that 'in most cases, pain can be adequately controlled without the normal
psychological functions of the patient being adversely affected' ('Justifiable Euthanasia' (1988)
3 *Issues Law Med* 361, 362).

[63] Survey, 47, table 5.9.

it might be thought that consultation assumed especial importance – only a minority (48%) of doctors had consulted a colleague.[64] Moreover, 40% of GPs stated that they did not think that consultation was very important.[65]

Reporting

Of the 2,700 cases of VAE and PAS in 1990, only 486 were reported to the legal authorities; 82% of cases were, therefore, illegally certified by doctors as death by 'natural causes'.[66] Doctors gave as their three most important reasons for falsifying the certificate the 'fuss' of a legal investigation (55%); a desire to protect relatives from a judicial inquiry (52%); and a fear of prosecution (25%).[67] Similarly, virtually all of the 1,000 acts of life termination without request were certified as natural deaths. The most important reasons given by the doctors were the 'fuss' of a legal investigation (47%); the (remarkable) opinion that the death was in fact natural (43%), and the desire to safeguard the relatives from a judicial inquiry (28%).[68]

Interestingly, only 64% of doctors thought that each case of VAE should somehow be examined, and the most favoured form of review was by other doctors.[69]

---

[64] Ibid., 64, table 6.8. The reason given for not doing so in 68% of cases was that the doctor felt no need for consultation because the situation was clear (ibid., 65). Before withholding/withdrawing a treatment without request, doctors consulted a colleague in 54% of cases (ibid., 89, table 8.13). (When there was a request the figure was 43% (ibid., 82, table 8.5).) Before administering palliative drugs in such doses as might shorten life, doctors consulted in 47% of cases (ibid., 73, table 7.4).

[65] Ibid., 96, table 9.2.

[66] G. van der Wal and P. J. van der Maas, *Euthanasie en andere medische beslissingen rond het levenseinde. De praktijk en de meldingsprocedure* [Euthanasia and other medical decisions concerning the end of life. Practice and reporting procedure] (1996) (see p. 125 n. 1), tables 11.1 and 11.2.

[67] Survey 2, 48. The authors added that 23 doctors actually stated that they had regarded the death as natural.

[68] Ibid., 65. Deaths hastened by withholding/withdrawing a treatment without request were almost all certified as natural deaths (ibid., 89). So too were all deaths hastened by the administration of palliative drugs, in over 90% of cases because the doctor felt the death was natural, but in 9% because the doctor felt that reporting an unnatural death would be 'troublesome' (ibid., 74).

[69] Ibid., 97, table 9.3; 98. It merits mention that in a small number of cases, the lethal drug was administered by someone other than the doctor, nurse or patient (see ibid., 140, table 13.10; 143; 193).

Conclusion

The Survey disclosed that the guidelines had been widely breached. In many cases, doctors had intentionally shortened lives without an explicit request from patients: the 1,000 cases vividly illustrated the reality of NVAE in Dutch medical practice.

Moreover, in a significant proportion of cases, the reasons doctors gave for performing VAE suggested an elastic interpretation of 'unbearable suffering'. The *Chabot* case illustrated how 'unbearable suffering' could include even non-terminal, non-somatic illness, and the *Sutorius* case has evidently stretched it still further to include 'social decline'. Further, the Survey showed that VAE was by no means always a 'last resort' and was applied even though palliative care could have offered an alternative.

Finally, the failure by the vast majority of doctors to report deprived the authorities of even the *opportunity* of review and control. Even in relation to those cases which *were* reported, it must be doubted, in view of the lax system of investigation – not least the extent to which it relies on doctors to expose their own wrongdoing – whether the authorities had any realistic hope of detecting abuse of the guidelines.

11

The slide towards NVAE

The Remmelink Report

The Survey revealed that the Dutch system of regulation had failed to prevent major non-compliance with the guidelines. Nor is this surprising: the system could never realistically hope to detect doctors who ignored the guidelines since it essentially relied on them to expose their own non-compliance. It is therefore puzzling that the Remmelink Commission should have concluded that the 'medical actions and decision process concerning the end of life are of high quality'.[1] No less puzzling, given the failure of a large majority of doctors to report cases, was Professor Van der Maas's observation that the Survey showed that doctors were 'prepared to account for their decisions'.[2]

Moreover, the Remmelink Report's narrow categories of 'euthanasia' and 'intentional killing without request' may have suggested to those who had not considered it before a neat way of side-stepping the reporting procedure. A doctor might end life not by intentionally administering a lethal drug, which the guidelines would require to be reported, but by an overdose of morphine or by withdrawing treatment, and then claim (in the most unlikely event of being challenged) that this was not 'euthanasia' but 'normal medical practice'.

Even though later statistics have indicated, as we shall see in the next chapter, a significant increase in the number of cases reported (for example, 1,303 were reported in 1993),[3] it was always likely, because of the

---

[1] Outline, 6. Remarkably, Van der Maas also regarded them as of 'good quality' (Survey, 199).
[2] Survey, 205.
[3] *Jaaverslag Openbaar Ministerie 1993* (1994) Appendix 1, table 'Number of reported cases of euthanasia and assisted suicide'. Although this number was almost three times the number for 1990, it is 15 fewer than for 1992. The table also indicated that only 14 cases were prosecuted in 1993. In a dozen of these cases the prosecution was brought because the patient had not been

absence of any effective independent check, that the reporting procedure would remain a wholly inadequate regulatory mechanism and that the reports filed would continue to provide a misleadingly reassuring picture. Any reports of ending life without explicit request would continue to be particularly unrepresentative: how many doctors would be likely to report a practice which was outside the guidelines and which had not been declared lawful by the courts? Further, even if *all* cases, with or without request, were reported, this would still provide no guarantee of propriety. Indeed, were all to be reported, it is doubtful whether prosecutors would have the resources to subject them even to the largely formal consideration which reports have hitherto received.

The Report used the finding that doctors refused some 4,000 serious requests[4] to argue that VAE was not used excessively and as an alternative to good palliative care.[5] Leaving aside the evident shortcomings in Dutch terminal care, this is simply illogical, particularly when viewed against the 9,050 occasions on which it was the doctor's primary purpose to end life. Moreover, the incidence of NVAE disclosed by the 1,000 cases was striking. Nor were these patients killed by a minority of maverick doctors: *a majority* of doctors admitted that they either had killed without request or would be prepared to do so.[6]

It has become increasingly clear that not only the majority of individual doctors, but also the legal and medical authorities in the Netherlands, condone NVAE in certain circumstances. The Remmelink Report defended, it will be recalled,[7] the vast majority of the 1,000 cases of termination without request as 'care for the dying'.[8] Stating that the absence of a request served only to make the decision more difficult than when there was a request, it added:

> The ultimate justification for the intervention is in both cases the patient's unbearable suffering. So, medically speaking, there is little difference between these situations and euthanasia, because in both cases patients are involved who suffer terribly. The absence of a special request for the termination of life stems partly from the circumstance that the party in question

---

terminally ill. After the decision of the Supreme Court in the case of Dr Chabot that a terminal illness was not required to justify VAE, the prosecution in these cases was discontinued.
[4] Survey, 52.   [5] Outline, 2.   [6] Survey, 58, table 6.1.   [7] See pp. 104–5 nn. 15–19.
[8] A member of the Commission informed me that these killings came as a 'terrible shock' to its members, who had hoped that they did not exist. Interview by author with Mr A. Kors, 29 November 1991. This makes the Commission's defence of the bulk of these killings all the more puzzling.

is not (any longer) able to express his will because he is already in the terminal stage, and partly because the demand for an explicit request is not
in order when the treatment of pain and symptoms is intensified. The degrading condition the patient is in confronts the doctor with a case of force
majeure [necessity]. According to the commission, the intervention by the
doctor can easily be regarded as an action that is justified by necessity, just
like euthanasia.[9]

The classification of killing without request as 'care for the dying' could be
criticised as tendentious euphemism and is inconsistent even with established Dutch terminology.[10] Moreover, in view of the importance which
has long been attached by many Dutch proponents of VAE to the need
for a request by the patient, it is remarkable that the Commission, rather
than setting out a reasoned ethical case seeking to justify NVAE, should
do scarcely more than assert that a request was no longer a requirement
in all cases.

Nevertheless, as we noted in chapter 10, the Dutch Parliament implemented the Commission's recommendation that the reporting procedure
for VAE should clearly extend to NVAE. It amended the Burial Act 1955 to
set out the reporting procedure in statutory form, a form which made it
clear that the procedure was to be followed even in cases of NVAE.[11] The
amendment, which came into force in June 1994, did not purport to make
either VAE or NVAE lawful but simply enshrined the reporting procedure
in statutory form. Different forms were provided for VAE and NVAE and
both the government and Parliament left it to the courts to determine the
legal status of NVAE in each case reported.

The KNMG

Further evidence of a willingness to accommodate NVAE is provided by developments within the KNMG. A committee established by the KNMG to
consider NVAE has condoned the termination, in certain circumstances, of
incompetent patients including babies and patients in persistent coma, and
has canvassed opinion on the killing of patients with severe dementia.[12]

---

[9] Outline, 3.   [10] See pp. 84 and 93.
[11] See pp. 105–6; Lords' Report, Appendix 3, 65.
[12] Henk Jochemsen, 'Life-Prolonging and Life-Terminating Treatment of Severely Handicapped
Newborn Babies...' (1992) 8 *Issues Law Med* 167; Nederlandse Vereniging voor Kindergeneeskunde, *Doen of laten?* (1992) 13; 'Dutch Doctors Support Life Termination in Dementia'
(1993) 306 *BMJ* 1364. See also Griffiths, chapter 3.

It was only a matter of time before such 'responsible' medical opinion received judicial approval which, as we shall see below, it now has. Indeed, if the criterion for the availability of the defence of necessity is what accords with 'responsible' medical opinion, it is difficult to see how the courts could logically withhold their endorsement.

Prosecutors

The authors of the Van der Maas Survey, referring to the 1,000 cases of termination of life without explicit request, wrote that legally speaking there was no question that these cases should be seen as anything but murder. They added, however, that 'the possibility that a court will accept an appeal to force majeure in circumstances of exceptional suffering cannot be ruled out'.[13] Similarly, Professor Leenen has expressed the opinion (which seems to contradict his earlier opinion,[14] to which he does not refer) that in 'exceptional' cases NVAE attracts the defence of necessity.[15] Moreover, the Chief Prosecutors have already declined to prosecute in a number of cases of termination without request.

One such case involved a patient in a permanent coma after a heart attack. The local Chief Prosecutor, mindful of the Remmelink Commission's recommendation that such cases should be dealt with in the same way as killing on request, decided against prosecution. After questions had been raised in Parliament, his decision was affirmed at a meeting of all the Chief Prosecutors in February 1992.[16] Another case concerned a dying, comatose 71-year-old man who had not asked for his life to be shortened. At a meeting in November 1992 the Chief Prosecutors decided against prosecution since 'the action taken . . . amounted to virtually the same as suspending ineffectual medical treatment',[17] even though

---

[13] Johannes J. M. van Delden et al., 'The Remmelink Study: Two Years Later' (1993) 23(6) *Hastings Cent Rep* 24, 25; cf. Loes Pijnenborg et al., 'Life-Terminating Acts without Explicit Request of Patient' (1993) 341 *Lancet* 1196, 1199, where they write that, when all the 'safeguards' are respected and 'only the best interests of the patient are taken into account' such killings are 'certainly not murder'.

[14] See p. 121.

[15] H. J. J. Leenen and Chris Ciesielski-Carlucci, '*Force Majeure* (Legal Necessity): Justification for Active Termination of Life in the Case of Severely Handicapped Newborns after Forgoing Treatment' (1993) 2(3) *Camb Q Healthc Ethics* 271, 274.

[16] Personal communication, Staff Office of the Public Prosecutor, The Hague, 12 February 1993.

[17] Ibid.

they regarded the case as 'potentially extending the boundaries of current practice'.[18]

Courts

More recently, and more significantly still, NVAE has been approved by the courts. In 1996, such a case came before the Court of Appeal in Amsterdam.[19] It concerned a disabled newborn baby with spina bifida, hydrocephalus, a spinal cord lesion and brain damage. The specialists decided not to operate on the spina bifida because of a bad prognosis. It was thought that the baby was suffering severe pain. Her parents asked for her life to be ended and, three days after her birth, she was killed by the defendant gynaecologist, after consultation with other specialists who had examined the baby.[20]

The District Court at Alkmaar held that the doctor was not guilty of murder as he enjoyed the defence of necessity. The court laid down the conditions which attracted the defence in such a case. First, the infant is suffering intolerably with no prospect of improvement; the suffering is incurable and cannot be alleviated, at least not in a 'medically meaningful way' (by which the court appeared to mean that the suffering could only be alleviated by total sedation). Secondly, the procedure leading to the decision to terminate the baby's life and the termination itself should meet the requirements of care and precision. Thirdly, the doctor should comply with responsible medical opinion and prevailing medical ethics. Fourthly, termination should only be carried out at the explicit, repeated and consistent wish of the parent(s).[21]

The Amsterdam Court of Appeal affirmed the District Court's decision, for broadly the same reasons. With respect to the first condition, the Appeal Court observed that an operation was not proportional and palliative care was 'medically meaningless' because, first, it would require such doses that the baby would be 'floating between heaven and earth';

---

[18] Ibid. A third case involved the killing of a 4-year-old handicapped child who was dying. Charges were dropped 'in view of the specific and unusual circumstances of the case, despite the fact that the patient had not expressly requested intervention' (ibid.).

[19] This case and the following case are discussed by Henk Jochemsen, 'Dutch Court Decisions on Nonvoluntary Euthanasia Critically Reviewed' (1998) 13(4) *Issues Law Med* 447. See also Griffiths, 83–4.

[20] Ibid., 451.   [21] Ibid., 452.

secondly, because such palliative care would in fact be aimed at hastening death as the decision not to treat could be interpreted as a 'choice against the life of the baby'; thirdly, because allowing the baby to live would have led to complications (especially expansion of the hydrocephalus) which would have produced doubts about the appropriateness of that course, which would in turn have caused burdensome uncertainty for the parents, doctors and nurses; and fourthly, because if a course of non-treatment had later been reversed in favour of curative treatment, the baby would have been worse off than if she had been given curative treatment immediately.[22]

In the same year, a similar case fell for decision before the Court of Appeal in Leeuwarden. This case concerned a newborn baby with trisomy 13, a syndrome which manifested itself in a number of disorders including deformities of the skull, face and hands, malformation of the heart and kidney, and brain damage. The baby was given six months to a year to live. She was taken home and looked after by her parents. After a short time, some tissue protruded from an opening in the skull and appeared to be very sensitive. The defendant family doctor treated the pain, but the treatment did not appear fully effective. After a few days, with the consent of the parents (though whether at their request is unclear), the doctor, having consulted with a paediatrician who had seen the baby, gave the baby a lethal injection.[23]

Affirming the doctor's acquittal by the Groningen District Court, the Leeuwarden Court of Appeal applied the same reasoning as the Amsterdam Appeal Court. The Leeuwarden court mentioned that the consent of the parents was essential to the defence of necessity. Also important were, first, the fact that there must be no doubt about diagnosis and prognosis; secondly, the doctor must consult colleagues; thirdly, death must be brought about carefully; and fourthly, the doctor must report the case.[24]

The speed of the slide

The growing condonation of NVAE, reflected by the above decisions of prosecutors and courts, contrasts markedly with pronouncements made

---

[22] Ibid., 452–3.   [23] Ibid., 451.   [24] Ibid., 453–4.

not so long ago by Dutch supporters of VAE. There was relatively little support for NVAE in 1984. As we saw in chapter 8, the very definition of 'euthanasia' adopted by the Dutch incorporated the need for a request. Moreover, the KNMG Report of that year was careful to confine itself to VAE and three of its five guidelines sought to ensure not only that there was an explicit request by the patient, but that it was free, well considered and persistent. Similarly, in 1985 a State Commission on Euthanasia concluded that third parties should not be permitted to request the termination of life on behalf of (incompetent) minors and 'other persons incapable of expressing their opinion, such as the mentally handicapped or senile elderly people'.[25] Its vice-chairman, Professor Leenen, later commented that the Commission proposed an amendment to the Penal Code to prohibit the intentional termination of an incompetent patient's life on account of serious physical or mental illness and that it did so in order to 'underline the importance of the request of the patient'.[26] In 1989, Leenen reaffirmed that a request was 'central' to the Dutch definition, adding:

> *Without it the termination of a life is murder.* This means that the family or other relatives, parents for their children, or the doctor cannot decide on behalf of the patient. *People who have become incompetent are no longer eligible for euthanasia,* unless they have made a living will prior to their becoming incompetent, in which they ask for the termination of life.[27]

He added that Article 2 of the European Convention for the Protection of Human Rights and Fundamental Freedoms, which provides that everyone's right to life shall be protected by law, did not (in his view) prohibit the killing of a patient who freely wishes to die but that it '*prohibits the State and others from taking another's life without his request*'.[28] Rejecting the argument that VAE would undermine the public's trust in doctors, he stated: 'People's trust in health care will not decrease if they are sure that euthanasia will not be administered *without their explicit request.*'[29]

---

[25] H. J. J. Leenen, 'Euthanasia, Assistance to Suicide and the Law: Developments in the Netherlands' (1987) 8 *Health Policy* 197, 204.

[26] Ibid.

[27] H. J. J. Leenen, 'Dying with Dignity: Developments in the Field of Euthanasia in the Netherlands' (1989) 8 *Med Law* 517, 520 (emphasis added; footnote omitted).

[28] Ibid., 519 (emphasis added). The English courts' view as to whether the Convention contains a right to assisted suicide is considered in the Afterword.

[29] Ibid., 520 (emphasis added).

Leenen was echoed in the same year by Henk Rigter, of the Dutch Health Council, who wrote in the bioethics journal *The Hastings Center Report*: 'In the absence of a patient request the perpetrator renders him or herself guilty of manslaughter or murder.'[30] In the letters page of the same journal, Rigter's paper received ringing endorsement from a galaxy of leading Dutch VAE advocates. The Secretary of the Dutch Society of Health Law, C. J. van der Berge, reported that the Society's General Assembly had unanimously rejected the criticism that Dutch doctors 'who terminate the lives of patients without their request remain unpunished'.[31] The Board of the Dutch Society for Voluntary Euthanasia asserted that NVAE[32] was 'murder, and will be prosecuted and sentenced as such'.[33] The Board added that whoever wanted a lethal injection would 'have to "fight" urgently and persistently for it' and that in the Netherlands 'proper terminal care precedes proper euthanasia'.[34] A letter signed by many of the most prominent defenders of VAE in the Netherlands stated that 'problems concerning the termination of life of incompetent patients, either comatose or newborn, are *not* a part of the euthanasia problem'.[35] One, the Director of the National Hospital Association, wrote that 'euthanasia' meant killing on request, adding:

> Consequently, it is impossible for people who do not want euthanasia to be maneuvered or forced into it. The requirement of voluntariness means no one need fear that his or her life is in danger because of age or ill health, and that those who cannot express their will, such as psycho-geriatric patients or the mentally-handicapped, shall never be in danger as long as they live.[36]

---

[30] Henk Rigter, 'Euthanasia in the Netherlands: Distinguishing Facts from Fiction' (1989) 19(1) *Hastings Cent Rep* 31.

[31] C. J. van der Berge, letter in 'Mercy, Murder, and Morality' (1989) 19(6) *Hastings Cent Rep* 47.

[32] The letter uses the words 'involuntary euthanasia', but it is clear from the context that the Board meant mainly if not exclusively ending the lives of incompetent, rather than competent, patients without request. The Board's letter was criticising a paper which had been published in the same journal by Dr Richard Fenigsen in which he claimed that 'involuntary' euthanasia was practised in the Netherlands: 'A Case against Dutch Euthanasia' (1989) 19(1) *Hastings Cent Rep* 22. By 'involuntary' euthanasia, Fenigsen meant the intentional termination without request of incompetent, and not just competent, patients. For example, he referred (at 28) to the 'involuntary' euthanasia of 'the newborn, the demented, the comatose'.

[33] Board of the Dutch Society for Voluntary Euthanasia, letter in 'Mercy, Murder, and Morality' 49.

[34] Ibid.   [35] J. G. M. Aartsen et al., ibid., 48 (original emphasis).

[36] Herman H. van der Kloot Meijburg, ibid., 48.

The argument that 'euthanasia' cannot, by definition, be forced on patients, and that NVAE is not, therefore, part of the 'euthanasia' problem,
is unimpressive. If an advocate of abortion on health grounds were to
define 'abortion' as 'therapeutic abortion' and dismiss arguments that its
legalisation might lead to abortion for social reasons, or to women being
pressured into abortion, on the ground that these would not be 'abortion'
and are not, therefore, 'part of the abortion problem', he or she would
rightly be given short shrift. The suggestion, made not infrequently in the
Netherlands, that the slippery slope argument can be rebutted by definitional *fiat* serves only to illustrate the intellectual poverty of the case for
VAE which has come to prevail there.

The widespread willingness among Dutch doctors to end life without
explicit request contrasts starkly with their refusal of many serious requests
for VAE, and serves further to underline the secondary role of patient
autonomy in the reality, if not the rhetoric, of the Dutch experience. As
two of the (very few) Dutch academic critics of the Dutch experience
have shrewdly pointed out, acceptance of VAE has resulted not in greater
patient autonomy but in doctors 'acquiring even more power over the life
and death of their patients'.[37]

The hard evidence of the Survey indicated that within six years of the
promulgation of the guidelines for VAE, NVAE was not uncommon. This is
partly because of the inability of the vague and loose guidelines for VAE to
ensure compliance. It is also partly because the underlying justification
for VAE in the Netherlands appears not to be patient self-determination
but the principle that it is right to end the lives of certain patients because
they are not worth living. Acceptance of that principle seems implicit
in the views – on what are obvious cases of NVAE – of the Remmelink
Commission, the KNMG, prosecutors and courts. Indeed, the authors
of the Van der Maas Survey lent support to this thesis when they wrote:
'[Is] it not true that once one accepts euthanasia and assisted suicide,
the principle of universalizability forces one to accept termination of life
without explicit request, at least in some circumstances, as well? In our
view the answer to this question must be affirmative.'[38]

---

[37] Henk A. M. J. ten Have and Jos V. M. Welie, 'Euthanasia: Normal Medical Practice?' (1992)
22(2) *Hastings Cent Rep* 34, 38. See also Jos V. M. Welie, 'The Medical Exception: Physicians,
Euthanasia and the Dutch Criminal Law' (1992) 17 *J Med Philos* 419, 435.

[38] Van Delden et al., 'The Remmelink Study' 26.

Conclusion

The fact that NVAE is far from uncommon in the Netherlands has emerged from the mouths of Dutch doctors themselves. In recent years it has become increasingly clear that it is not only widely practised but now appears to enjoy, at least in certain circumstances, the support of the Dutch political, legal and medical establishment. This fact illustrates the force not only of the empirical, but also of the logical, slippery slope argument.

12

The second Survey

This chapter outlines and analyses the data from a second major Survey, carried out by Professor Van der Maas and Professor Van der Wal (an inspector of health), covering medical practice in the year 1995. A summary of the Survey was published in English the following year.[1] The Survey sought particularly to ascertain the incidence of intentional life-shortening by doctors; the extent to which they complied with their duty to report such cases (in accordance with the procedure which was agreed between the KNMG and the Ministry of Justice in 1990 and given statutory force in 1994); and the quality of their reporting. The main purpose of the reporting procedure is, as the authors of the Survey acknowledged, to provide for possible scrutiny of the intentional termination of life by doctors and to promote careful decision-making in such cases.[2] The most important quantitative data generated by the Survey are reproduced in Table 2.

It is important to note that, as with the first Survey, the only objectively verifiable figures are those concerning the total number of deaths and the total number of cases reported. All the other figures are based on the responses of the physicians concerning cases in which they said they had recently been involved. It is no less important to stress that this chapter does not question the methodology used by the researchers to obtain their data, namely, interviews with 405 physicians and postal questionnaires mailed to physicians who had attended 6,060 deaths identified from death certificates. The chapter uses the researchers' own data and standardly

---

[1] G. van der Wal and P. J. van der Maas, *Euthanasie en andere medische beslissingen rond het levenseinde. De praktijk en de meldingsprocedure* [Euthanasia and other medical decisions concerning the end of life. Practice and reporting procedure] (1996) (hereafter 'Survey 2'). For summaries of the research in English see P. J. van der Maas, 'Euthanasia, Physician-Assisted Suicide, and Other Medical Practices Involving the End of Life in the Netherlands, 1990–1995' (1996) 335 *N Engl J Med* 1699; G. van der Wal, 'Evaluation of the Notification Procedure for Physician-Assisted Death in the Netherlands' (1996) 335 *N Engl J Med* 1706.

[2] Survey 2, 25.

Table 2. *End-of-life decisions by doctors in the Netherlands 1990–1995*

	1990	1995
Deaths in the Netherlands	129,000 (100%)	135,500 (100%)
Requests for euthanasia	8,900 (7%)	9,700 (7.1%)
Euthanasia (i.e. VAE)	2,300 (1.8%)	3,200 (2.4%)
Physician-assisted suicide	400 (0.3%)	400 (0.3%)
Life-terminating acts without explicit request	1,000 (0.8%)	900 (0.7%)
Intensification of pain and symptom treatment	22,500 (17.5%)	20,000 (14.8%)
a. explicitly intended to shorten life	1,350 (1%)	2,000 (1.5%)
b. partly intended to shorten life	6,750 (5.2%)	2,850 (2.1%)
c. taking into account the probability that life will be shortened	14,400 (11.3%)	15,150 (11.1%)
Withdrawing/withholding treatment (incl. tube-feeding)	22,500 (17.5%)	27,300 (20.1%)
a. at the explicit request of the patient	5,800 (4.5%)	5,200 (3.8%)
b. without the explicit request of the patient		
b1. explicitly intended to shorten life	2,670 (2.1%)	14,200 (10.5%)
b2. partly to shorten life	3,170 (2.5%)	—
b3. taking into account the probability that life will be shortened	10,850 (8.4%)	7,900 (5.8%)
Intentional termination of neonates		
a. without withholding/withdrawing treatment	—	10
b. withholding/withdrawing treatment plus administration of medication explicitly to shorten life	—	80
Assisted suicide of psychiatric patients	—	2–5

Note: A dash indicates that no figures are available.

cites their 'best estimate' (though in some cases numbers have been arrived at on the basis of percentages and numbers used in the survey and, in such cases, the numbers have then been rounded off). Like chapter 9, which examined the first Survey, this chapter, while not questioning the researchers' methodology, does question their interpretation of some of the evidence they unearthed.

The data

VAE and PAS

Between 1990 and 1995 the number of explicit requests for VAE and PAS rose by 9%, and the number of requests granted rose from 30% to 37%.[3] Cases of VAE and PAS rose from 2,700 cases in 1990 to 3,600 in 1995, comprising 3,200 cases of VAE and 400 cases of PAS. This was a rise of one-third.

According to the attending physicians, there were treatment alternatives in 17% of these cases but in almost all the patients did not want them.[4] However, in 1994 the Dutch Supreme Court held that doctors should not hasten death whenever the alternative of palliative treatment was available, at least in cases of mental suffering[5] and the Ministers of Justice and Health,[6] and the KNMG,[7] decided that the same restriction should apply in cases of somatic suffering. The above cases appear, therefore, to have breached this guideline.

Life was shortened by one to four weeks in 31% of cases of VAE and 45% of PAS and by more than a month in 7% of cases of VAE and in 30% of cases of PAS.[8] Physicians stated that the main reason why patients asked for VAE was 'intolerable suffering without prospect of improvement' (74%),[9] which has become the standard terminology to describe the seriousness of the condition required by the law. But the next most common reasons were 'to prevent loss of dignity' (56%) and 'to prevent further suffering' (47%).

---

[3] Survey 2, tables 5.3; 6.2; 9.1; Paul van der Maas and Linda L. Emanuel, 'Factual Findings' in Linda L. Emanuel (ed.), *Regulating How We Die* (1998) 151, 159.

[4] Survey 2, table 5.5.

[5] Nederlands Juristenblad 1994, 69 no. 26: 895ff. See also H. Jochemsen, 'The Netherlands Experiment' in J. F. Kilner et al. (eds.), *Dignity and Dying* (1996) chapter 12.

[6] W. Sorgdrager and E. Borst-Eilers, 'Euthanasie – de stand van zaken' (1995) 12 *Medisch Contact* 381–4.

[7] W. R. Kastelijn, *Standpunt hoofdbestuur KNMG inzake euthanasie* (1995).

[8] Survey 2, table 5.4.   [9] Ibid., table 5.6.

It must be doubted whether either of these reasons, by itself, satisfies the requirement of 'unbearable suffering'.

Interestingly, one of the most important reasons for rejecting a request for VAE (cited by 35% of physicians) was the physician's opinion that the patient's suffering was not intolerable.[10] This again suggests that, despite the emphasis placed on patient autonomy by advocates of VAE, the application of VAE continued to be more a function of the *physician's* judgment about the quality of the patient's life than of respect for the patient's autonomy. This suggestion is fortified by the evidence about the extent to which Dutch doctors continued to terminate the lives of patients without an explicit request.

Active termination of life without explicit request

The Survey confirmed that NVAE remained far from uncommon. Nine hundred patients were so killed in 1995, representing 0.7% of all deaths, only a slight decrease on the 0.8% whose lives were so terminated in 1990.[11] In other words, of the 4,500 (3,200 + 400 + 900) cases in which doctors admitted they actively and intentionally terminated life, one in five involved no explicit request.

The main reason for not discussing the issue with the patient was stated to be the patient's incompetence (due, for example, to dementia). But by no means all patients whose lives were terminated without an explicit request were incompetent. In 15% of cases where no discussion took place but could have done, the doctor did not discuss the termination of life because the doctor thought that termination was clearly in the patient's best interests.[12] Furthermore, in over a third (37%) of the 900 cases, there had been a discussion with the patient about the possible termination of life, and some 50% of this subgroup of patients were fully competent, yet their lives were terminated without an explicit, contemporaneous request. Moreover, in 17% of the 900 cases, treatment alternatives were thought to be available by the attending physician.[13] The physicians thought that life was shortened by one to four weeks in 3% of cases but by more than a month in 6%.[14] Finally, physicians had not discussed their action with a

---

[10] Ibid., table 5.12.   [11] Ibid., table 6.2; 92.

[12] Ibid., table 6.5. The distinction between 'discussion' and 'request' is made in chapter 10 of the Survey, and implies that, when an earlier discussion about a life-ending act had taken place with the patient, the patient had expressed a wish for it.

[13] Ibid., table 6.4.   [14] Ibid., table 6.3.

colleague in 40% of cases, with a close relative in 30% of cases, and anyone at all in 5%.[15]

Intensification of pain and symptom treatment

In 20,000 cases (according to the physician interviews) or 25,800 cases (according to the death certificate survey), palliative drugs were administered in doses which almost certainly shortened life. In some 2,000 of these cases the doctor 'explicitly' (primarily) intended, and in a further 2,850 cases, partly intended, to shorten life.[16] The researchers estimated that the grey area between intending to alleviate pain and symptoms and intending to shorten life was about 2% of all deaths, the same as in 1990.[17]

Where doctors administered palliative drugs partly in order to shorten life, they had discussed it with the patient in just over half of the cases (52%) and in only 36% of cases was there an explicit request for life-shortening doses by the patient. The physicians stated that eighty-six patients (3%) with whom they had not discussed this treatment were fully competent.[18] Moreover, in only 36% of these cases had the doctors consulted a colleague. Life was shortened by an estimated one to four weeks in 7% of cases and by more than a month in 1%.[19]

Withholding/withdrawing treatment

In some 27,300 cases a treatment was withheld or withdrawn (in 5,200 cases at the patient's explicit request) taking into account a probable shortening of life. In 18,000 of these cases (14,200 of which involved no explicit request by the patient) it was the physician's explicit intention to shorten life.[20] However, a note to the relevant question states that an intention to 'hasten the end of life' could also be understood as an intention 'not to prolong life'.[21] This creates an unfortunate ambiguity and an obstacle to ascertaining how many of these cases could reasonably be classified as intentional life-shortening by deliberate omission, or PE. An intention not to prolong life is not the same as an intention to end it. In many of these cases

---

[15] Ibid., table 6.6.
[16] Ibid., table 7.2. This figure is calculated from the researchers' percentages and estimates at pp. 92–3. In fact, the figure of 2,000 is conservative as it is derived from the total number of 20,000 cases yielded by the physician interviews rather than from the larger total of 25,800 in the death certificate study.
[17] Ibid., 93.   [18] Ibid., table 7.4.   [19] Ibid., table 7.3.   [20] Ibid., tables 8.1; 8.3; 8.4.
[21] Ibid., 297.

doctors may have intended to withhold/withdraw treatment not to end the patient's life, but because the treatment was futile or too burdensome.

In the majority of cases in which no discussion with the patient had taken place, the physicians stated that the patient was either incompetent or only partly competent. However, in 1% of these cases (140 patients) the physician considered the patient fully competent.[22] In cases where treatment was withheld/withdrawn with the explicit intent to shorten life, the physician estimated that life was shortened by 1–7 days in 34% of cases, by 1–4 weeks in 18% and by more than a month in 9%.[23]

Neonates

The Survey stated that over 1,000 newborns die in the Netherlands before their first birthday and estimated that the lives of about 15 were actively and intentionally terminated by doctors.[24] The figure of 15 seems, however, a significant underestimate. The Survey showed that in 10 cases (1%) doctors administered a drug with the explicit intention of shortening life. But it also revealed a further 80 cases in which, also with the explicit intention of shortening life, doctors administered a drug and withdrew/withheld a life-prolonging treatment. In total, therefore, it appears to have been the explicit intention of doctors to shorten the lives of 90 neonates, not 15.[25]

Moreover, in no fewer than 41% of the 1,000 cases, treatment was withdrawn/withheld with the explicit intention of shortening life. In a significant proportion of these cases, life was terminated because the babies' lives were not thought bearable. Forty-five per cent of these babies were expected to live more than four weeks, and some of them more than half a year.[26]

In around a fifth of cases in which doctors intentionally withheld/withdrew treatment with the explicit purpose of shortening life because the baby's life was thought unbearable, there had been no discussion with the parents.[27] Doctors said that in most cases this was because the situation was so clear that discussion was unnecessary or because there was no

---

[22] Ibid., tables 8.1; 8.3.   [23] Ibid., table 8.2.   [24] Ibid., 189.

[25] The researchers' estimate of 15 cases may be traced to their observation that in 17% of cases in which drugs were administered with the explicit intent to shorten life (totalling 15 cases), one of the drugs administered paralysed muscles and therefore caused death almost immediately whereas in a majority of cases in which drugs were administered in combination with the withdrawal of treatment, the treatment withdrawn was artificial ventilation and the medication may have been administered to prevent suffocation.

[26] Ibid., table 17.3.   [27] Ibid., table 17.5.

time, though these reasons are not elaborated. Finally, doctors reported hardly any cases of neonatal NVAE to the authorities.

Forty-five per cent of neonatologists and intensive care specialists and 31% of general paediatricians said they had given drugs explicitly to end the life of a neonate or infant, and 29% and 49% respectively who had not done so said they could conceive of situations in which they would do so.[28]

Assisted suicide of psychiatric patients

Based on the replies of psychiatrists in respect of the year 1995, the Survey estimated that, although some 320 psychiatric patients explicitly requested PAS per year, only 2 to 5 were assisted to commit suicide by psychiatrists. Among psychiatrists who would never grant a request for assisted suicide on the basis of mental suffering (almost a third of the respondents) 'professional opinion' was cited by 88% as the most important reason. Only 2% of psychiatrists had ever assisted suicide.[29] This relatively restrictive approach of psychiatrists may owe not a little to the controversy generated by the case of the psychiatrist Dr Chabot who, it will be recalled from chapter 10, assisted a grieving 50-year-old woman to commit suicide. Dr Chabot's conduct was later criticised by a Medical Disciplinary Court.[30] Disclosing statistics testifying to the prudence of a restrictive approach, the Survey also indicated that of those patients not assisted in suicide, 16% committed suicide without assistance by a physician but that, of those patients still living, 35% no longer wished for death and that the death wish in a further 10% had diminished.

Consultation

It will be recalled that the guidelines for VAE and PAS require the doctor, before agreeing to either, to engage in a formal consultation with a colleague (*consultatie*) and not merely an informal discussion (*overleg*). In cases of VAE and PAS, 92% of doctors had, according to the Survey, discussed the case with a colleague.[31] In 13% of these cases, however, the discussion did not amount to a formal consultation. Consultation took

---

[28] Agnes van der Heide et al., 'Medical End-of-Life Decisions Made for Neonates and Infants in the Netherlands' (1997) 350 *Lancet* 251, 253.

[29] Ibid., table 18.1.   [30] See p. 87 n. 17; p. 109 n. 45; Hendin, chapter 3.

[31] Survey 2, table 10.1.

place, therefore, in 79% of cases. However, other figures in the Survey suggested that consultation occurred in a significantly smaller percentage of cases, for the Survey indicated that consultation occurred in 99% of reported cases but only 18% of unreported cases[32] and that almost 60% of all cases of VAE and PAS were not reported.[33] It therefore seems that consultation occurred in only around half of all cases.[34]

In cases of NVAE, a discussion occurred in 43% of cases but in 40% this did not amount to consultation. Consequently, there was no consultation in 97% of such cases. Moreover, even when consultation did take place, it was usually with a physician living locally and the most important reasons given for consulting such a physician were the doctor's geographical proximity and views on life-ending decisions: expertise in palliative care was hardly mentioned. Further, in the overwhelming majority of cases, the first doctor had come to a decision before consulting and the doctor consulted disagreed in only 7% of cases.[35] In short, the requirement of consultation, even when it was satisfied, hardly appeared to operate as a rigorous check.

Reporting

Of the 3,600 cases of VAE and PAS in 1995, only 1,466 (41%) were reported by doctors to the local medical examiner.[36] While 41% was an improvement on the figure of 18% reported in 1990, it meant that a clear majority of cases, almost 60%, still went unreported. The most important reasons given by doctors for failing to report in 1995 were (as in 1990), the wish to avoid the inconvenience (for the doctor and/or the relatives) of an investigation by the authorities, and to avoid the risk of prosecution (though, as the consistently tiny number of prosecutions indicated, this risk was negligible). Thirty per cent of doctors stated that they did not report because they had failed to observe the requirements and 12% because they considered VAE was a private matter between doctor and patient.[37]

---

[32] Ibid., table 10.2.   [33] See section on 'Reporting', p. 132 below.

[34] The reason for the discrepancy between the two totals might be a certain bias in the physicians' responses. The authors of the survey suggest that some of the physicians interviewed, when asked to discuss their *most* recent case of VAE, in fact discussed *a* recent case which had a stronger impact, probably because it was reported. See Survey 2, 113.

[35] Ibid., 102–7.

[36] Ibid., tables 11.1 and 11.2. Moreover, the Survey confirmed that the legal requirements were breached more frequently in unreported cases, in which there was less often a written request by the patient, a written record by the doctor, or consultation by the doctor (table 11.6).

[37] Ibid., table 11.8; 225.

Analysing the data

The second Survey showed that there had been some improvement in compliance with procedural requirements since 1990. However, it confirmed at least three disturbing findings of the first Survey: the significant incidence of intentional life-shortening, both with and without explicit request; the use of VAE as an alternative to palliative care; and the lack of reporting. We shall examine each in turn.

Incidence of VAE and NVAE

Like the first Survey, the second indicated that intentional life-shortening by Dutch doctors was far from rare. Even adopting the unusually narrow Dutch definition of 'euthanasia' as VAE, there were no fewer than 3,200 cases in 1995 (2.4% of all deaths), an increase of almost a thousand on the 1990 total of 2,300 (1.8% of all deaths). Adding the cases of PAS (400), NVAE (900) and the intensification of pain and symptom treatment with the explicit intent to shorten life (2,000), the total more than doubles from 3,200 to 6,500.[38] And although the number of cases of NVAE had fallen, the fall was only 10%.

VAE as an alternative to palliative care

The Survey's comment that 'the quality of medical treatment near the end of life has improved'[39] might not unreasonably be thought to display a certain complacency, particularly in a country which (like many if not all others) still has a considerable way to go in the provision of adequate palliative care. The high incidence of intentional life-shortening disclosed by the Survey and the reasons for VAE given in many cases by the doctors, reasons which fall short of what many would think of as 'unbearable suffering', tend to suggest that VAE has not been confined to cases of 'last resort' and has at least sometimes been used as an alternative to palliative care. And, as we noted in chapters 8 and 10, cases like those

---

[38] On a wider definition of 'euthanasia', embracing all intentional life-shortening by act or omission and with or without request, it would be appropriate to add those (90) cases in which the lives of neonates were intentionally terminated. Were it possible to ascertain which of the 18,000 cases of withholding/withdrawing treatment involved a primary intention to end life, rather than not to prolong life, it would be proper to include those too.
[39] Ibid., 240.

of Dr Chabot and Dr Sutorius illustrate the elasticity of the concept of 'unbearable suffering' and the readiness of some Dutch doctors to resort to VAE.

The Survey confirmed that, even when doctors believed that treatment alternatives were available, they not infrequently resorted to VAE. The opinion of the Supreme Court, the Ministers of Justice and Health, and the KNMG, that VAE is impermissible when treatment alternatives are available, even if the patient refuses them, has clearly not prevented its administration in such circumstances. In a move that would make the prospect of prosecution even more remote, the Minister of Justice appeared to reverse her earlier position and instructed the Attorneys-General that the refusal by the patient of available treatment alternatives did not render VAE unlawful.[40] The bill which was passed by the Dutch legislature on 10 April 2001 (discussed in chapter 8) enshrines this view.

Widespread failure to report

Although 41% of cases (1,466) were reported in 1995 as opposed to 18% (486) in 1990, it remained true that in both years, as in every year in between, *a clear majority of cases went unreported*. There was, in short, not even the *opportunity* for official scrutiny of the majority of cases of VAE, PAS or NVAE. Nor should the alleged increase in reporting be accepted uncritically. First, the Survey recorded an increase in cases of VAE between 1990 and 1995 (900 cases) almost as large as the increase in cases reported (980 cases). Secondly, if the total of 6,500 cases of active, intentional life-shortening is used, then the proportion of unreported cases rises from 59% to 77%.

It will be recalled that the purpose of the reporting procedure is to allow for scrutiny of the intentional termination of life by doctors and to promote observance of the legal and professional requirements for VAE. The undisputed fact that a clear majority of cases (59% according to the survey, at least 77% on the calculations in this chapter) still went unreported in 1995 serves only to reinforce doubts about the ability of the procedure to fulfil its purpose, and to undermine Dutch claims of effective regulation, scrutiny and control. Further, even those cases which *were* reported were

---

[40] Ibid., 144–5.

reported by the doctor who was, unless exceptionally honest or exceptionally stupid, most unlikely to disclose evidence of non-compliance with the guidelines.

Conclusion

The second Survey, like the first, produced a wealth of valuable data on the practice of intentional termination of life by Dutch doctors. The first Survey revealed significant non-compliance with the guidelines and a lack of effective control over VAE, PAS and NVAE. The second showed that, although there had been some improvement in compliance with some procedural requirements, control remained largely ineffective.[41]

---

[41] Two prominent advocates of VAE and NVAE, Dr Helga Kuhse and Professor Peter Singer, conducted a survey in 1996 into medical decision-making at the end of life in Australia from 1995 to 1996. Helga Kuhse et al., 'End-of-Life Decisions in Australian Medical Practice' (1997) 166 *Med J Aust* 191. They claimed that their survey was comparable to the Van der Maas Survey of the same year, and showed that in 30% of all deaths a medical end-of-life decision was made with the explicit intention of ending, by act or omission, the patient's life. They claimed that VAE and PAS accounted for 1.8% of all deaths; that doctors actively and intentionally ended patients' lives without explicit request in 3.5% of all deaths; and that 24.7% of all deaths involved a decision not to treat, with the intention of explicitly ending life (ibid., 195, box 4). The reliability of the survey has been seriously questioned. See e.g. Nicholas Tonti-Filippini et al., *Joint Supplementary Submission to the Senate Legal and Constitutional Legislation Committee Re: Euthanasia Laws Bill 1996*, who point out that the survey was not comparable in either size, scope or design to the Van der Maas Survey in the same year; that the Kuhse survey involved only a mailed questionnaire, not physician interviews, and that an important question conflated (far more seriously than did the corresponding Dutch question) an intention not to prolong life with an intention to hasten death. See also A. Fisher et al., 'End-of-Life Decisions in Australian Medical Practice' (1997) 166 *Med J Aust* 506 (letters); Robert Manne, 'How Data on Death Became a Numbers Game' *The Australian*, 17 February 1997. The Federal President of the Australian Medical Association commented that the Kuhse survey showed that only 1.8% of deaths involving a medical end-of-life decision involved VAE, and that 'euthanasia is not an important factor in end-of-life decision-making in Australia' (Dr Keith Woollard, AMA Media Release, 14 February 1997).

In November 2000, *The Lancet* published a survey into end-of-life decision-making in Belgium: Luc Deliens et al., 'End-of-Life Decisions in Medical Practice in Flanders, Belgium: A Nationwide Survey' (2000) 356 *Lancet* 1806. The survey sought to replicate the death certificate study of the Van der Maas Survey. The authors estimated that 1.3% of deaths (705) resulted from VAE or PAS and that 3.2% of deaths (1796) resulted from the intentional administration of lethal drugs without the explicit request of the patient. The response rate was, however, only 52% and the survey did not involve physician interviews. If accurate, the figures indicate that VAE and NVAE are practised to a certain extent in Belgium. Were Belgium to legalise VAE, however, there is every reason to believe that these figures would be substantially higher.

13

The Dutch in denial?

The increasing body of evidence which has emerged from the Netherlands over the past fifteen or so years, not least the wealth of data produced by the two surveys, shows that the guidelines have been extensively breached and that there has been a marked lack of control by the authorities. Yet the disturbing reality of inadequate control still seems lost on many. As we saw in the Introduction to this book, even one of the Justices of the US Supreme Court who was referred to the leading exposés of Dutch practice nevertheless thought that the picture from the Netherlands was still unclear and that further evidence was needed.[1] Why such hesitation given the mass of disturbing evidence already in the public domain?

One reason is that the Dutch (and non-Dutch) supporters of VAE have often, not surprisingly, placed a misleadingly benign interpretation on the evidence. They have persistently sought to portray the Dutch experience in the best possible light, denying or at least downplaying its negative aspects. This is predictable but not productive and has inevitably served to muddy the waters. In particular, anyone who had uncritically read the benign interpretation of the data either by Professor Van der Maas or by the Remmelink Commission could be forgiven for thinking that VAE was under effective control.

Van der Maas and Remmelink

As we have seen, Van der Maas concluded that his surveys showed that decision-making by Dutch doctors was of high quality and that they were prepared to account for their conduct. His lack of criticism of the widespread breaches of the guidelines was remarkable and contrasts with his readiness to criticise those who identified a higher incidence of

---

[1] See p. 4.

intentional life-shortening disclosed by his surveys.[2] It will also be re-called that the Remmelink Commission placed a no less benign gloss on the data, not least on the 1,000 cases of NVAE, despite the fact that these cases drove a coach and horses through a fundamental guideline and that their revelation had initially come as a 'terrible shock' to the Commission's members.[3]

Dutch diplomacy

In view of the fact that the Remmelink Commission was a government-appointed body, it is not surprising that its report should have reflected the complacent views of the Dutch political establishment. Another channel for those views and another source of information which may well have led many to adopt a misguidedly favourable view of Dutch euthanasia is the Dutch diplomatic corps, which seems primed to counter any criticism of their country's slide down the slippery slope. This was certainly the impression given by the reaction of the Dutch Ambassador in London to English criticism of a Dutch television programme sympathetic to the Dutch experience – *Death on Request*.

Death on Request

Death on Request was screened by the BBC on 15 March 1995.[4] This pro-gramme, produced by a Dutch company, told the moving story of a patient with motor neurone disease, Cees van Wendel de Joode, who asked for and was given VAE by his GP, Dr Van Oijen. The programme implied that this case, in which the guidelines were apparently followed, was typical of prac-tice generally. That the broadcast was intended to represent that practice in the best light is suggested by the fact that the protagonists were rec-ommended to the programme makers by the Dutch Society for Voluntary Euthanasia.[5] Psychiatrist Herbert Hendin, a leading expert on suicidology and on the Dutch experience, has produced a disturbing analysis of the broadcast. For example, Hendin questions whether the patient was given a real choice. The doctor says he had to offer VAE because 'what else can I offer the man? I can give him wonderful equipment so he can make himself

---

[2] See pp. 99–101.   [3] See p. 116, n. 8.   [4] *Modern Times*, BBC2, 15 March 1995.
[5] Hendin, 127.

understood. I can give him the finest wheelchair there is, but in the end it is only a stopgap. He's going to die and he knows it'.[6]

But, as Hendin points out, Professor Stephen Hawking is alive twenty-five years after he was diagnosed with the same illness and, while far more incapacitated than Cees, has managed to live a brilliantly productive life, with meaningful relationships. Hendin concludes: 'Hawking, however, has been surrounded by people who have wanted him to live, and who have not considered mechanical aids worthless because he was destined to die eventually'.[7]

Moreover, Cees seems to have been given a misleadingly bleak prognosis. A second doctor, as required by the guidelines, was consulted by the first, and the programme contains a scene in which the second doctor talks with Cees and his wife. The doctor tells Cees that to qualify for VAE he must be experiencing 'hopeless suffering with no chance of a cure' and that he satisfied this criterion. The doctor adds: 'You have an incurable disease which will soon end in death. And unless something is done you will suffer terribly. You will probably suffocate.'

Commenting on the case in an ensuing studio discussion, Dr Nigel Sykes, a consultant in palliative medicine at St Christopher's Hospice, London, said that one of the things that struck him most about this film was the lack of real choice that Cees had: he was essentially presented with the choice of terrible suffering or death. Dr Sykes said:

> What I would want to do for this man is to give him a further choice. To acknowledge the suffering that he is going through, his pain, his breathlessness, and tell him what could be done for that. At St Christopher's we've now looked after at least 300 patients with motor neurone disease over more than a quarter of a century, and 120 of those we studied especially carefully. We were able to improve their pain in absolutely every case.[8]

The BBC sustained heavy criticism for screening *Death on Request*. A powerful letter to *The Times* criticised the programme as misleading in that it failed to show 'the wider implications of a legally permissive attitude towards euthanasia'.[9] Its signatories included Lord Walton, who chaired the House of Lords Select Committee on Medical Ethics, Lord Habgood, one of its members, and Dame Cicely Saunders, foundress of

---

[6] Ibid., 132.   [7] Ibid., 133.   [8] *The Late Show*, BBC2, 15 March 1995.
[9] *The Times*, 16 March 1995, Letters.

the hospice movement. The letter stated: 'Having embraced the practice of euthanasia, the Dutch now find themselves on a slippery slope which not only involves euthanasia for those who are not dying but also euthanasia without request.' It concluded that 'facts from the Netherlands show clearly why euthanasia should not be legally sanctioned in this country'.

The programme also prompted an Early Day Motion in the House of Commons. Tabled by Mrs Marion Roe, Chairwoman of the House of Commons Select Committee on Health, and signed by 117 Members of the House, the Motion called on the BBC to report 'the real situation in the Netherlands where in a substantial number of cases euthanasia is carried out without a request from the patients, where the hospice and specialist palliative care movement is very much less developed than in the United Kingdom with the result that patients may request euthanasia in the absence of effective specialist palliative care'. It urged the BBC 'to give a complete and balanced picture of the situation'.[10]

Given the misleading impression which such programmes inevitably convey to viewers unfamiliar with the reality of the Dutch experience, the MPs' call for balance was welcome.

The Dutch Ambassador

The Motion provoked a response from the Dutch Ambassador. He wrote that he 'felt obliged to dispel some serious misconceptions of the Netherlands euthanasia policy'.[11] The Ambassador's response was, however, even more misleading than the programme he sought to defend.

---

[10] 'Euthanasia in the Netherlands', EDM 740 of Session 1994–5, tabled on 7 March 1995. As an interesting postscript to the programme, it was reported in March 2001 that the doctor who starred in it, Dr Van Oijen, had been convicted of murdering a comatose and dying 84-year-old patient by injecting her with 50 mg of the drug alloferine. Expert witnesses testified that this could not be considered palliative treatment. The patient had made no request for VAE and had in fact said she did not want to die. There had, moreover, been no second opinion and Dr Van Oijen had reported that death had been due to natural causes. For misreporting the death, he was given a suspended fine of 5,000 guilders, but he was not punished for the murder. The court said he had made an 'error of judgment' and had acted 'honourably and according to his conscience'. The KNMG defended his actions as having 'complete integrity' (Tony Sheldon, 'Dutch GP Found Guilty of Murder Faces no Penalty' (2001) 322 *BMJ* 509).

[11] Letter from the Dutch Ambassador, Mr J. H. R. D. van Roijen, dated 24 April 1995. I am grateful to one of the recipients of the letter, Professor Luke Gormally of the Linacre Centre for Healthcare Ethics, for sending me a copy.

The Ambassador asserted that VAE in his country was 'rare'.[12] But 3,600 cases in 1995 indicate the contrary. He added: 'In the Netherlands *all* cases of euthanasia . . . *must* be notified to the Public Prosecutor.'[13] He omitted to mention that a clear majority were *not* in fact so notified. He went on to say that a doctor would in general be prosecuted for performing either VAE or NVAE.[14] The reality was and is, however, precisely the reverse: it is prosecution, not VAE, which is a rarity. As Griffiths has pointed out, prosecutors 'practically always' decide not to prosecute reported cases. Fewer than five per year are prosecuted, of which half are 'test' cases brought to clarify the law. From 1981 to 1998 there were only twenty final judgments. In nine the doctor was convicted, but no punishment was imposed in six and only a suspended sentence was imposed in the other three. Such a control regime, Griffiths aptly comments, seems on its face to be 'all bark and no bite'.[15]

Turning to NVAE, the Ambassador wrote that it was common knowledge that doctors all over the world sometimes decide to stop further medical treatment, or to increase the doses of drugs which will have the effect of shortening the life of a terminally ill patient. According to the Remmelink Report, he claimed, there were 1,000 cases in which doctors had so acted. But the 1,000 cases were *not* cases of stopping treatment or increasing doses of sedatives to alleviate pain but cases of doctors taking active steps to terminate patients' lives (without their explicit request).

His Excellency continued that patients in Dutch hospitals were provided with 'excellent palliative or terminal care' and that 'In medical student training, much attention is focussed on sedatives and palliative care'.[16] The Ambassador cited no evidence to support either of these assertions. They sit uneasily with Dutch research indicating that the pain of a high proportion of cancer patients is inadequately treated,[17] with the recognition by the Remmelink Commission that Dutch doctors lacked expertise in palliative care,[18] and with the views of the leading Dutch hospice doctor, Dr Zylic.

Dr Zylic recently wrote that 'Palliative care is virtually unknown in Holland'.[19] He added: 'Almost seventy percent of physicians in the

---

[12] Ibid.   [13] Ibid. (original emphasis).   [14] Ibid.   [15] Griffiths, 268.   [16] Ibid.
[17] See p. 111.   [18] See p. 112 n. 61.
[19] Zbigniew Zylic, 'Palliative Care: Dutch Hospices and Euthanasia' in David C. Thomasma et al. (eds.), *Asking to Die* (1998) 187 at 196.

Netherlands have been involved in euthanasia of some sort. Yet there is virtually no training in treating dying patients and coping with the impending death. None of the medical schools offer any thorough training for their young students. It is unbelievable how we deny the importance of such training.'[20] He continued: 'we see poor symptom control among physicians',[21] and 'we see cases frequently enough of ignorance about palliative care that are causes of profound concern'.[22] 'Euthanasia', he argued, 'should never be seen as an alternative to good care. It was never meant to be this in Holland. It originated at the end of such care, when all else failed. But today it is growing to be seen as an alternative to the more difficult task of caring for the dying.'[23]

Finally, commenting on the *Chabot* case, the Ambassador asserted: 'Although the Supreme Court has opened the possibility of a discussion on euthanasia for [the] mentally ill, it has at the same time formulated such strict conditions that it will be extremely difficult at all times to perform euthanasia for [the] mentally ill.'[24]

This is a questionable interpretation of the *Chabot* case. The reality is that the Supreme Court held that the defence of necessity can apply in cases of mental illness, with the proviso that the second doctor must examine the patient and agree that the request is voluntary and that there is no other way to alleviate suffering. These conditions may not be so easy to satisfy if strictly applied. Nevertheless, the case did open the door to PAS for purely mental suffering, and although hitherto psychiatrists appear to have been hesitant to assist suicide on this ground there is no logical reason why the guidelines in relation to mental suffering should prove any more 'precise' or 'strict' than those in relation to physical suffering.

Whatever the explanation for the Ambassador's confusion, his misleading response to the House of Commons Motion seems not atypical of the reaction which the Dutch political establishment tends to exhibit in the face of any criticism, however cogent, of its inadequate control of VAE. Such reaction, which could not unreasonably be described as political propaganda, can only sow confusion, and helps to explain why so many in the Netherlands and abroad labour under an unduly favourable impression of the Dutch experience.

---

[20] Ibid., 198–9.   [21] Ibid., 195.   [22] Ibid., 200.

[23] Ibid., 199. See also Rien J. P. A. Janssens et al., 'Hospice and Euthanasia in the Netherlands: An Ethical Point of View' (1999) 25 *J Med Ethics* 408.

[24] Letter from the Dutch Ambassador, 24 April 1995.

Dutch reluctance to engage with criticism from abroad has been fairly acknowledged by Professor Griffiths, who has written:

> To a large extent, the Dutch tend simply to ignore foreign criticism. The more or less 'official' Dutch reaction, when there is one, amounts essentially to denial. Denial in the first place that there has been major legal change in the Netherlands: euthanasia, it is insisted, remains 'illegal'. This position is essentially disingenuous: it relies on the fact that the articles of the Criminal Code prohibiting euthanasia and assistance with suicide have not been amended and ignores the fact that another article of the Code has been interpreted to afford a defence of justification, so that if the relevant conditions are met, the behavior concerned is effectively *not* illegal.[25]

He continued:

> Denial, in the second place, that 'non-voluntary euthanasia' is taking place . . . Denial, most importantly, that there are problems of control. It is insisted that 'carefully and precisely drafted rules' make abuse impossible. But even a passing acquaintance with the applicable rules . . . shows that they can hardly be described as watertight, and in any case a precise rule is quite a different matter from an effectively enforced one. It is well known in the Netherlands, and since the early 1990s this has become a subject of increasing concern, that the existing control system, depending as it does on self-reporting, cannot be regarded as adequate.[26]

Dr Van Delden

To be sure, the Dutch approach has many *non*-Dutch defenders such as the American philosopher Professor Margaret Battin. Professor Battin, who has written widely on the subject of Dutch euthanasia, has gone so far as to claim that the Netherlands is 'virtually abuse-free'.[27] Conversely, though rarely, a Dutch defender of VAE may concede the lack of control. Professor Leenen, Emeritus Professor of Health Law at the University of

---

[25] Griffiths, 28–9 (footnotes omitted; original emphasis).   [26] Ibid., 29.

[27] Margaret Battin, 'Should We Copy the Dutch?' in Robert Misbin (ed.), *Euthanasia: The Good of the Patient, the Good of Society* (1992) 95, 102. See also Battin, 'Voluntary Euthanasia and the Risk of Abuse: Can We Learn Anything from the Netherlands?' (1992) 20 *L Med & Health Care* 133; Ludovic Kennedy, *Euthanasia: The Good Death* (1990) 32–54. Otlowski asserts that there is 'no evidence of large scale abuses or extensions of the practice' (*Voluntary Euthanasia and the Common Law* (1997) 451). Cf. the review of her book in (1998) 57(1) *Camb L J* 209.

Amsterdam and a very influential figure in Dutch health law and policy, bravely admitted in 1990 that there was an '*almost total lack of control* on the administration of euthanasia' in his country.[28] Similarly, as we have just noted, Professor Griffiths has acknowledged the ineffectiveness of the Dutch regulatory regime.[29] Commenting on the two Van der Maas surveys, he observed that it seems fair to describe the results of that research 'as far as the effectiveness of control is concerned, as pretty devastating'.[30] More recently, Dr Van Delden, a member of the Van der Maas research team, replied in the *Journal of Medical Ethics* to some of the criticisms which have been made in this chapter.[31] Interestingly, he nowhere sought to question the central criticism that the guidelines have been widely breached and have failed to ensure effective control.

Van Delden rightly identified three of the major concerns which support that contention: first, the practice of NVAE; secondly, the use of VAE when palliative care could have provided an alternative; and, thirdly, underreporting.

As for the first concern, he agreed that NVAE was 'a very serious problem'.[32] As for the second, he did not dispute the frequent performance of VAE in cases where palliative care could have alleviated the suffering. He stated that there had been a 'shift' (his word) towards using VAE even when palliative care would have provided an alternative.[33] Thirdly, he nowhere sought to controvert the argument, based on the fact that the majority of cases of VAE were not reported by doctors, that the

---

[28] 'Legal Aspects of Euthanasia, Assistance to Suicide and Terminating the Medical Treatment of Incompetent Patients' (paper delivered at a conference on euthanasia held at the Institute for Bioethics, Maastricht, 2–4 December 1990) 6 (emphasis added). The Ministry of Justice civil servant who wrote the Remmelink Report agreed that there was no control over cases which had not been reported and that even in relation to the reported cases the prosecutor did not know whether the doctor was telling the truth. He maintained that VAE occurred even if the law prohibited it, as was the case outside the Netherlands, and that it was preferable to try to control it (interview by author with Mr Kors, 29 November 1991).

[29] See p. 142 n. 26. See also Griffiths at 298: 'the current system of criminal enforcement of the legal requirements governing euthanasia and termination of life is ineffective'.

[30] Ibid., 268.

[31] J. J. M. van Delden, 'Slippery Slopes in Flat Countries – a Response' (1999) 25 *J Med Ethics* 22.

[32] Ibid., 24.

[33] Ibid., 23. His view was that this 'shift' was due to an increasing emphasis on patient autonomy. Even if his explanation were accurate, it would in no way detract from the force of the criticism that, whereas the guidelines require VAE to be applied only as a 'last resort' in cases of 'unbearable suffering', in a considerable number of cases in which palliative care could have made the situation bearable, VAE has nevertheless been carried out.

reporting procedure has failed to ensure effective control. The recent research by Cuperus-Bosma,[34] revealing inconsistent decision-making by
prosecutors in VAE cases even in cases where important guidelines have
been obviously breached, has served only to heighten doubts about the efficacy of the Dutch regulatory system. Van Delden noted the introduction
of the modified reporting procedure, whereby the report is sent to an interdisciplinary committee rather than to the prosecutor, and commented
that the effect of this change was not yet clear. There seems little reason
to believe, however, that this modification, which renders the procedure
even less strict, will ensure any greater control *even if* it turns out in time
to encourage more reporting. Indeed, the change may lead to *less* control:
under the revised procedure, although the medical examiner informs the
prosecutor about the case, the report of the doctor who administered VAE
is no longer sent to the prosecutor but to the committee.

In May 2000 the first annual report of the interdisciplinary appraisal
committees was published.[35] Echoing Dr Van Delden, the national chairwoman of the committees concluded that it was too early to say whether
the revised procedure will encourage doctors to report cases. In 1999,
2,216 cases were reported. This is a clear increase on the 1,466 reported
in 1995. If there were the same number of cases of VAE and PAS as in
1995 (3,600), then 60% were reported in 1999 compared to 41% in 1995.
It has been questioned, however, whether any increase was attributable to
the revision of the procedure in view of the fact that 2,241 cases were reported in the first ten months of 1998, *before* the procedure was revised.[36]
Moreover, slightly fewer cases were reported in 2000 (2,123) than in 1999
(2,216).[37]

The first annual report goes on to claim that the doctors' reports showed
that the guidelines had been followed in nearly all cases. This is, of course,
unsurprising: doctors are hardly likely to expose their own wrongdoing. Moreover, the report revealed that the information provided by the

---

[34] M. Cuperus-Bosma et al., 'Assessment of Physician-Assisted Death by Members of the Public
Prosecution in the Netherlands' (1999) 25 *J Med Ethics* 8.

[35] *Regionale Toetsingscommissies Euthanasie, Javerslaag 1998–1999* (2000).

[36] Tony Sheldon, 'New Reporting Procedure for Euthanasia Shows Doctors Follow the Rules'
(2000) 320 *BMJ* 1362.

[37] Agence France-Presse, 30 May 2001, reporting a statement made the previous day by a
spokesman for the Dutch Ministry of Health. The spokesman added that three cases had
been referred by the committees to the prosecutorial authorities, who had decided not to
prosecute.

physicians about the criterion of 'unbearable suffering' was often quite brief; that the second opinion was almost always from a colleague in the same field (for example, general practitioners usually consulted other general practitioners); and that information about the second doctor's opinion was often very brief.[38]

To return to Dr Van Delden, he continued that 'there is no rule that cannot (and will not) be broken' and that this is true of the prohibition on drunken driving.[39] But it is precisely because of the high value the law has traditionally attached to innocent human life that killing, even by drunk-driving, is a serious crime. The mere fact that the prohibition is broken is hardly an argument for *relaxing* that prohibition. Moreover, decriminalising VAE in certain circumstances *compounds* the difficulties of enforcing the prohibition on killing. It is vain to cite the fact of breach in support of a change which would make breaches not only more likely but also more difficult to detect and prosecute.

Finally, Van Delden asserted that the interpretation of the data 'remains largely dependent upon our moral views'.[40] Moral views (whether for or against) can indeed (though they need not) influence interpretation of the facts. There appears, however, to be a growing acceptance, even among those in favour of VAE in principle, that it is inadequately controlled in the Netherlands. Van Delden's response could be said to reflect this acceptance. It is also reflected by the views of the former editor of the *Journal of Medical Ethics*, Raanan Gillon. Professor Gillon used to favour the legalisation of VAE but changed his mind because of the difficulties of effective regulation. He agrees that the evidence shows that the Dutch guidelines are being 'extensively ignored' and that it is surely justifiable to conclude that Dutch euthanasia is 'in poor control'.[41] And that is the central contention of Part III of this book.

---

[38] *Regionale Toetsingscommissies Euthanasie* 10–14.
[39] 'Slippery Slopes in Flat Countries' 24.   [40] Ibid.
[41] R. Gillon, 'Euthanasia in the Netherlands – Down the Slippery Slope?' (1999) 25 *J Med Ethics* 3, 4. The pro-euthanasia editor of the *N Engl J Med*, commenting on the second Survey, opined that the similarity between the findings in respect of 1990 and 1995 showed that the Dutch were apparently *not* descending a slippery slope (M. Angell, 'Euthanasia in the Netherlands – Good News or Bad?' (1996) 335 *N Engl J Med* 1677). Such sympathetic interpretations are, however, unpersuasive. A more plausible interpretation of the evidence is that the descent had already occurred by 1990 and that the second Survey, far from showing that there had been no descent from 1984 to 1995, merely showed that there has been no significant ascent from 1990 to 1995. In any event, that the data from both surveys showed widespread breach of the guidelines is unarguable.

Professor Gillon echoed the point often made by defenders of the Dutch that in view of the absence of statistics before 1984 there is no way of proving statistically that there is a higher incidence of NVAE now than then.[42] This is true. However, there is good reason to think that NVAE has indeed increased since 1984. Breach of the guideline requiring a request is more likely to occur in a situation in which some VAE is allowed than when none is allowed, if only because of the greater problems in policing a practice allowed according to professional guidelines than a practice which is legally prohibited. Moreover, the *official endorsement* of NVAE by, for example, the Remmelink Commission can only have served to lessen doctors' inhibitions against it. Despite the absence of prior statistics it is, therefore, more plausible to conclude that NVAE has increased since 1984 rather than remained static.

That slippage has occurred in the guideline requiring 'unbearable suffering' is even harder to deny. This guideline has not only been breached in practice by the performance of VAE as an alternative to palliative care (and it is relevant to recall Van Delden's acknowledgment that there has been a 'shift' in practice towards relaxation of this guideline), but the guideline has arguably, as the *Chabot* and *Sutorius* cases illustrate, been interpreted beyond breaking-point. In short, the only hard evidence we have is that since VAE was permitted NVAE has been commonly practised, and that the requirement of 'unbearable suffering' has been, in practice and in theory, substantially relaxed. In any event, the absence of statistics before 1984 is no answer to the *logical* slippery slope argument, the argument which, as we noted in chapter 11, was endorsed by Van der Maas and Van Delden themselves.[43] As that chapter showed, there is no shortage of evidence from the Netherlands, independent of statistics, which indicates *official condonation* of NVAE.

Conclusion

Part III has subjected the Dutch experience to close scrutiny. Having questioned the Dutch claim that their guidelines are sufficiently 'precise' or 'strict' to ensure effective control, it has reviewed the empirical evidence. That evidence, which comprises mainly the two valuable Van der Maas surveys (but also the research of Gomez,[44] Hendin[45] and the author[46]), amply

---

[42] Gillon, 'Euthanasia in the Netherlands' 3.   [43] See p. 123 n. 38.   [44] Gomez.   [45] Hendin.
[46] See, e.g., Keown, chapter 16. See also the colloquy in (1992) 22(2) *Hastings Cent Rep.*

demonstrates that the guidelines have conspicuously failed. Despite Dutch representations to the contrary, whether in the form of sympathetic documentaries or diplomatic reassurances, the reality is that guidelines have been widely breached, and with effective impunity.

More particularly, the evidence points to the following three conclusions. First, VAE is far from a rarity[47] and is increasingly performed. Rather than being truly a 'last resort', it has quickly become an established part of mainstream Dutch medical practice to which doctors have resorted even when palliative care could have offered an alternative. As Professor Griffiths, a defender of Dutch euthanasia, has written: '[E]uthanasia and assistance with suicide have become essentially normal procedures in Dutch medicine. Dutch doctors receive some 34,500 requests "in general terms" per year, and 96% of them have at some time discussed euthanasia or assistance with suicide with a patient.'[48] He added: 'They receive about 9700 concrete requests per year, and 77% of them have at some time had such a request. About a third of all requests are refused (in about an equal number of cases the patient dies before the euthanasia request can be carried out).'[49]

Secondly, despite the insistent claims by proponents of VAE, inside and outside the Netherlands, that allowing it subject to 'safeguards' brings it from the shadows and 'into the open' where it can be controlled, the evidence indicates that such claims merit scepticism. The reality is that most cases of VAE, until recently a substantial majority, have gone unreported and unchecked. In view of the intractable fact that in a clear majority of cases there has not even been an *opportunity* for official scrutiny, Dutch reassurances of effective regulation ring hollow. The fact, which surely can only be disputed by those 'in denial', is that since its inception VAE in the Netherlands has been and remains, in Professor Gillon's words, 'in poor control'. More people would undoubtedly appreciate this fact were it not for the tendency of some defenders of the Dutch to paint a picture so persuasively misleading as to be worthy of a Dutch master. The reassuring picture of the euthanasia landscape portrayed by the Dutch is surreal. As Dan Callahan, a leading American bioethicist, has pointed out, the reality

---

[47] In 1977 as VAE was beginning to gain acceptance in the Netherlands, a leading physician there wrote: 'One can be sure that [VAE]...occurs extremely seldom. I presume that the majority of family physicians has never applied euthanasia' (J. C. van Es, 'Huisarts en de preventie van euthanasie' [The family physician and the prevention of euthanasia] in P. Muntendam (ed.), *Euthanasie* (1977) 159).
[48] Griffiths, 253.   [49] Ibid.

is quite different: 'The Dutch situation is a regulatory Potemkin village, a great facade hiding non-enforcement.'[50]

Thirdly, the guidelines have not only been ignored in practice, but they have been diluted in theory. The *Chabot* and *Sutorius* cases illustrated the expansive interpretation placed by the courts on 'unbearable suffering' and, as the court decisions condoning the killing of disabled babies show, the requirement of a request in all cases has now been jettisoned.

The undeniable want of effective control lends strong support to the empirical slippery slope argument. That the Dutch experience supports the empirical argument should come as little surprise given that the slide was predicted almost thirty years ago, it will be remembered, by Lord Habgood.[51] Habgood later became a member of the Select Committee of the House of Lords which was set up in 1993 to consider the euthanasia question. A fact-finding delegation from the Committee visited the Netherlands in October that year.[52] Having witnessed the Dutch experience at first hand, the Committee went on to recommend[53] that the UK should not follow suit. An important reason was that 'it would not be possible to frame adequate safeguards against non-voluntary euthanasia'.[54] To its credit, the Committee obviously saw through the Dutch rhetoric to the Dutch reality.

In the debate on the Report in the House of Lords, the Committee's Chairman, Lord Walton, observed that those members of the Committee who had visited the Netherlands had returned 'feeling uncomfortable, especially in the light of evidence indicating that non-voluntary euthanasia...was commonly performed'.[55] He added that they were 'particularly uncomfortable'[56] about the *Chabot* case.[57] Another member of the

---

[50] *The Troubled Dream of Life* (1993) 115.

[51] Rt. Revd J. S. Habgood, 'Euthanasia – A Christian View' (1974) 3 *J R Soc Health* 124, 126.

[52] A Dutch Ministry of Justice spokesman assured the delegation that 'the government held strongly to the position that euthanasia was not possible for incompetent patients' (Lords' Report, Appendix 3, 68). Remarkably, this statement was made eight months after the change in the law to provide a mechanism for the reporting of NVAE had been approved by the lower house of the Dutch Parliament and one month before its approval by the upper house. If euthanasia was 'not possible' for incompetent patients, why was the government making provision for its reporting? Or was the spokesman simply using the Dutch definition of 'euthanasia' which, perhaps unbeknown to the Lords' delegation, makes euthanasia *definitionally* impossible for incompetent patients?

[53] See chapter 16.   [54] Lords' Report, para. 238.

[55] (1993–4) 554 Parl. Deb., HL, col. 1345 at 1346.   [56] Ibid.

[57] See p. 109. His Lordship could, of course, have gone much further but expressed the view that it would not be proper for him to criticise the decisions of the 'medical and legal authorities in another sovereign state' ((1993–4) 554 Parl. Deb., HL, col. 1346).

Committee to comment unfavourably on the Dutch experience was Lord Meston. He said:

> it did not seem possible to find any other place beyond the existing law for a firm foothold on an otherwise slippery slope. The evidence of the Dutch experience was not encouraging: in the Netherlands, which apparently lacks much in the way of a hospice movement, there seems to be a gap between the theory and practice of voluntary euthanasia. One cannot escape the fear that the same could happen here, with pressures on the vulnerable sick and elderly, who may perceive themselves to have become a burden on others, and pressures on the doctors and nurses from relatives and from those who are concerned with resources.[58]

Of course, the reality of the slippery slope may not have been lost on at least some Dutch advocates of VAE, who may have thought it desirable to maintain a discreet silence about it for tactical reasons. Indeed, Professor Alexander Capron, a leading American health lawyer, has related how this was in fact conceded at a conference in the Netherlands by a leading Dutch figure who had been influential in gaining acceptance for VAE. This person revealed that the Dutch proponents of euthanasia began with a narrow definition of euthanasia 'as a strategy for winning acceptance of the general practice, which would then turn to ... relief of suffering as its justification in cases in which patients are unable to request euthanasia'.[59] Capron observes: 'It was an instance, or so it seemed to me, when the candour of our hosts was a little chilling.'[60]

In short, the failure of the Dutch effectively to control VAE lends weighty support to the empirical slippery slope argument, and their growing approval of NVAE illustrates the force of the logical slippery slope argument.

---

[58] Ibid., col. 1398. In *Rodriguez* v. *Attorney-General* (1994) 107 DLR (4th) 342, which rejected an alleged right to PAS, Mr Justice Sopinka, delivering the majority judgment of the Canadian Supreme Court, noted (at 403) the 'worrisome trend' in the Netherlands towards NVAE, which supported the view that 'a relaxation of the absolute prohibition takes us down the "slippery slope"'.

[59] Alexander Morgan Capron, 'Euthanasia and Assisted Suicide' (1992) 22(2) *Hastings Cent Rep* 30, 31.

[60] Ibid.

PART IV

Australia and the United States

Although VAE and PAS have been legally condoned in the Netherlands since 1984, this condonation was effected by caselaw rather than legislation. The world's first legislation permitting PAS was enacted by a referendum in Oregon, USA, in 1994. Its implementation was, however, delayed pending legal challenge until 1997 when it was confirmed by a second referendum. The first PAS legislation to come into force was enacted by the legislature of the Northern Territory of Australia in 1995. Seven people sought to make use of this Act before it was repealed by the Federal Parliament of Australia in 1997.

Part IV, comprising chapters 14 and 15, considers whether the legislation as framed and enforced in these two jurisdictions meets the criticisms about lack of effective control to which the Dutch approach has proved so vulnerable.

14

The Northern Territory: ROTTI

The Northern Territory (NT) is a vast but sparsely populated area in Australia, occupying a sixth of the continent but with a population of less than 200,000. In 1995, its legislature of twenty-five enacted (by a small majority) the Rights of the Terminally Ill Act ('ROTTI').[1] The Act permitted both PAS and VAE.

ROTTI

ROTTI was a long and complex Act. This chapter will first outline its main provisions and then consider whether they were any more capable of preventing abuse than the Dutch guidelines.

The Act stated that it sought 'to confirm the right of a terminally ill person to request assistance from a medically qualified person to voluntarily terminate his or her life in a humane manner; to allow for such assistance to be given in certain circumstances without legal impediment to the person rendering the assistance' and 'to provide procedural protection against the possibility of abuse of the rights recognised by this Act'.

The patient's request

Section 4 provided that a patient who 'in the course of a terminal illness' was experiencing 'pain, suffering and/or distress to an extent unacceptable to the patient' could 'request the patient's medical practitioner to assist the patient to terminate the patient's life'. The Act defined 'terminal illness' as an illness which 'in reasonable medical judgment will, in the normal

---

[1] Northern Territory of Australia, Act No. 12 of 1995. For an overview of developments in Australia see John Fleming, 'Death, Dying and Euthanasia: Australia versus the Northern Territory' (2000) 15 *Issues Law Med* 291.

course, without the application of extraordinary measures or of treatment unacceptable to the patient, result in the death of the patient'.[2] It defined 'assist' to include 'the prescribing of a substance, the preparation of a substance and the giving of a substance to the patient for self-administration, *and the administration of a substance to the patient*'.[3] It is clear from the italicised words that the Act allowed not only PAS but also VAE.

The first doctor's opinion

Section 5 stated that a medical practitioner who received such a request could, if satisfied that certain conditions had been met, assist the patient to terminate the patient's life in accordance with the Act.[4] The conditions were laid down by section 7. First, the patient must have attained the age of 18.[5] Secondly, the doctor must have been satisfied, on reasonable grounds, that:

- the patient was suffering from an illness that would, in the normal course and without the application of extraordinary measures, result in the death of the patient;[6]
- in reasonable medical judgment, there was no medical measure acceptable to the patient that could reasonably be undertaken in the hope of effecting a cure;[7] and
- any medical treatment reasonably available to the patient was confined to the relief of pain, suffering and/or distress with the object of allowing the patient to die a comfortable death.[8]

The second and third doctors' opinions

Thirdly, a second doctor (who was not a relative or employee of, or a member of the same medical practice as, the first) who held a 'diploma of psychological medicine or its equivalent' must have examined the patient and confirmed:

- the first doctor's opinion as to the existence and seriousness of the illness;
- that the patient was likely to die as a result of the illness;

---

[2] Section 3.   [3] Section 3 (emphasis added).
[4] Section 6(1) made it an offence to seek by specified means to persuade a doctor to assist or refuse to assist in the termination of a patient's life.
[5] Section 7(1)(a).   [6] Section 7(1)(b)(i).   [7] Section 7(1)(b)(ii).   [8] Section 7(1)(b)(iii).

- the first doctor's prognosis; and
- that the patient was not suffering from a treatable clinical depression in respect of the illness.

One problem with this part of the Act was that there was no such qualification as a 'diploma of psychological medicine' in the NT. Section 7(1)(c) was therefore amended in 1996. The Act as amended required the patient to be examined by *two* other doctors, one a 'qualified psychiatrist', to confirm the final criterion, and the other a medical practitioner who held the prescribed qualification or had the prescribed experience in the treatment of the terminal illness from which the patient was suffering, to confirm the first three.[9]

Other conditions

The Act also required that certain other conditions be satisfied:

- the illness was causing the patient severe pain or suffering;
- the first doctor had informed the patient of the nature of the illness and its likely course, and the medical treatment, including palliative care, counselling and psychiatric support and extraordinary measures for keeping the patient alive which might have been available to the patient.[10] Where the doctor had no special qualifications in the field of palliative care, the information to be provided to the patient about the availability of palliative care was to be given by a doctor (who could be the second doctor with expertise in the patient's terminal illness[11] or any other doctor) who had such special qualifications as prescribed;[12]
- after being so informed, the patient indicated to the doctor that the patient had decided to end his or her life;
- the doctor was satisfied that the patient had considered the possible implications of the decision to his or her family;
- the doctor was satisfied, on reasonable grounds, that the patient was of sound mind and that the patient's decision had been made freely, voluntarily and after due consideration;

---

[9] Rights of the Terminally Ill Amendment Act 1996, section 4(a).
[10] Rights of the Terminally Ill Act, section 7(1)(e).
[11] Rights of the Terminally Ill Amendment Act 1996, section 4(c).
[12] Rights of the Terminally Ill Act, section 7(3).

- the patient[13] had, not earlier than seven days after indicating his or her decision to the doctor, signed a 'certificate of request';
- the doctor had witnessed the patient's signature on the certificate and had completed and signed the relevant declaration on the certificate;
- the certificate of request had been signed in the presence of the patient and the first doctor by another doctor (who could be the 'second doctor' referred to above with expertise in the patient's terminal illness)[14] after that other doctor had discussed the case with the first doctor and the patient and was satisfied, on reasonable grounds, that the certificate was in order, that the patient was of sound mind and that the patient's decision to end his or her life had been made freely, voluntarily and after due consideration, and that the above conditions laid down by section 7 had been satisfied;
- the first doctor had no reason to believe that he or she; the countersigning doctor; or a close relative or associate of either of them, would gain a financial or other advantage (other than a reasonable payment for medical services) as a result of the patient's death;
- no less than 48 hours had elapsed since the signing of the completed certificate of request;
- at no time before the doctor assisted the patient to end his or her life had the patient indicated a change of mind to the doctor;
- the doctor himself or herself provided the assistance and/or was and remained present while the assistance was given and until the death of the patient.

Palliative care

Section 8(1) stipulated that a doctor should not provide assistance if, in his or her opinion and after considering the advice of the second doctor

---

[13] Or a person acting on the patient's behalf in accordance with section 9. Section 9(1) provided that if a patient who had requested assistance to end life was physically unable to sign the certificate of request, any person over 18 (other than the first or second doctors or a person likely to receive a financial benefit as a result of the patient's death) could, at the patient's request and in the presence of the patient and both the medical practitioner witnesses (see next point but one in text), sign the certificate of request on the patient's behalf. Section 9(2) provided that a person signing a certificate of request on behalf of a patient would forfeit any financial or other benefit the person would otherwise have obtained as a result of the patient's death.

[14] Rights of the Terminally Ill Amendment Act 1996, section 4(b).

with expertise in the patient's terminal illness,[15] there were palliative care options reasonably available to the patient to alleviate the patient's pain and suffering to levels acceptable to the patient. Section 8(2) stated that where a patient had requested assistance and had later been provided with palliative care alleviating pain and suffering, the doctor should not, in pursuance of the patient's original request, provide assistance to end the patient's life. If subsequently the palliative care ceased to provide alleviation acceptable to the patient, the doctor could continue the process of providing assistance to end the patient's life only if the patient indicated a wish to proceed in pursuance of the request.

Withdrawal of request

Section 10 provided that a patient could rescind a request for assistance at any time and in any manner and that where this occurred, the doctor must destroy the certificate of request and note that fact on the patient's medical records. Section 11 made it an offence to procure, by deception or improper influence, the signing or witnessing of a certificate of request.

Records and reporting

Part Three of the Act laid down procedures governing record-keeping and the reporting of death. Section 12 required a doctor who assisted a patient to terminate his or her life under the Act to file certain documentation in the patient's medical records:

- a note of any oral request by the patient for assistance;
- the certificate of request;
- a record of the doctor's opinion as to the patient's state of mind at the time of signing the certificate of request, and certification of the doctor's opinion that the patient's decision was made freely, voluntarily and after due consideration;
- the report of the second doctor and the psychiatrist;[16]
- a note by the first doctor
  - certifying the independence of the second doctor and the psychiatrist[17] and the residential and period of practice qualifications of the first doctor;

[15] Ibid., section 5.   [16] Ibid., section 7.   [17] Ibid.

– indicating that all requirements of the Act had been met;
– indicating the steps taken to carry out the request for assistance; and
– containing a notation of the substance prescribed.

Section 14(1) provided that, as soon as practicable after the death of the patient, the doctor who provided the assistance must report the death to the coroner by sending the coroner a copy of the death certificate and so much of the medical record as related to the terminal illness and death of the patient. Section 14(2) required the coroner annually to advise the Attorney-General how many patients had been assisted under the Act, and the Attorney-General to report the number, in such manner as he or she thought appropriate, to the Legislative Assembly. Section 15 provided that the coroner might, at any time and at his or her absolute discretion, report to the Attorney-General on the operation or on any matter affecting the operation of the Act and that the Attorney-General must table a copy of the report in the Legislative Assembly.

Miscellaneous

Part Four of the Act provided immunity from civil, criminal or disciplinary action to anyone for anything they had done, in good faith and without negligence, in compliance with the Act.

A vague and lax Act

The Act was much more detailed than the Dutch guidelines. But whether it was any more 'precise' and 'strict' is open to question. Scrutiny of its wording and procedures reveals that the Act was both vague and lax, and was no more able to confine PAS/VAE to 'hard cases' than the Dutch guidelines.

Precise?

'Terminal illness'

The Act defined 'terminal illness' in an unusually elastic way, not limited to the condition of those who were close to death. It was defined by section 3 as any illness which would result in death without the application of 'extraordinary measures' or of other treatment 'unacceptable to the patient':

- 'extraordinary measures'
  The term 'extraordinary measures' was left undefined by the Act, which produced serious vagueness.
- 'treatment unacceptable to the patient'
  The Act did not limit the sorts of treatment a patient might reject as 'unacceptable'. Consequently, patients refusing to accept even simple life-saving medication, such as a depressed diabetic rejecting insulin, apparently qualified as 'terminally ill' under the Act.

Treatment 'reasonably available'

Section 7(1)(b) required a doctor to be satisfied, before performing PAS/VAE, not only that the patient was suffering from a 'terminal illness' and that there was no medical treatment 'acceptable to the patient' that could reasonably be undertaken in the hope of effecting a cure, but also that 'any medical treatment reasonably available to the patient' was confined to the relief of pain, suffering and/or distress with the object of allowing the patient to die a comfortable death. It is unclear what this third requirement meant. Did it mean that a treatment was not 'reasonably available' if it was refused by the patient, in which case the diabetic who refused insulin might qualify for assisted death? Or did it refer only to a treatment which a patient would like but which was unavailable (due to expense, distance, etc.), in which case the diabetic would not qualify?

'In the course of a terminal illness'

Section 4 provided that patients 'in the course of a terminal illness' who were experiencing unacceptable pain, suffering and/or distress might request assistance in terminating their lives. But there was no requirement that their reason for requesting death need *be* their terminal illness. A patient in the course of a terminal illness whose pain, suffering and/or distress arose from a cause quite *unrelated* to the terminal illness (such as divorce, bereavement, or even unemployment) apparently qualified. Although section 7(1)(d) required the second doctor to confirm that the illness was causing the patient severe pain or suffering, there was nothing in the Act to require *that* source of pain or suffering to be the basis for the patient's request for assisted death. And even *that* source of suffering could arise solely from the patient's *anticipation* of pain. In short, a patient whose terminal illness was causing no pain, but who was experiencing mental suffering at the thought of *future* pain, and who was experiencing unacceptable suffering and/or distress from a cause *unrelated* to the illness (such as divorce), would evidently have qualified for VAE/PAS.

'Treatable clinical depression in respect of the illness'

Section 7(1)(c)(iv) required a qualified psychiatrist[18] to confirm that the patient was not suffering from a 'treatable clinical depression in respect of the illness'. A patient could, therefore, still qualify for VAE/PAS if the psychiatrist thought the depression were *untreatable*, or that it arose from a cause *unrelated* to the illness (such as divorce). Further, the Act nowhere required the psychiatrist to confirm that the patient was not suffering from a mental illness *other than* depression.

The Act did require that the first doctor (section 7(1)(h)) and the doctor who countersigned the certificate of request (section 7(1)(k)) be satisfied that the patient was of 'sound mind'. However, as the countersigning doctor need not be the qualified psychiatrist, the Act allowed the soundness of the patient's mind to be determined by two doctors without any qualification in psychiatry or psychology. Moreover, 'of sound mind' is an imprecise concept. And, in law, one may be competent to make a particular decision even though one is seriously mentally ill.[19] The term is not, therefore, anything like precise enough to exclude the mentally ill as candidates for VAE/PAS.

'Reasonably available' palliative care

Section 8(1) provided that the first doctor should not perform VAE/PAS if he thought, having consulted the second doctor, that there were 'palliative care options reasonably available to the patient to alleviate the patient's pain and suffering to levels acceptable to the patient'. What was meant by 'reasonably available' and 'levels acceptable to the patient' was unclear. At the time of the passage of the Act there appears to have been very little in the way of expert palliative care in the NT. Would such care in Sydney have qualified as 'reasonably available'? And what if such palliative care as might

---

[18] Ibid., section 4.
[19] In the case of *Re C* [1994] 1 All ER 819 a patient was held to be legally competent to refuse an amputation even though he suffered from paranoid schizophrenia.

have been available in the NT (or elsewhere) had simply been refused by a patient as a result of clinical depression (from a cause unrelated to the illness)? Would section 8 have been satisfied?

Strict?

The vagueness of the Act's wording is compounded by the remarkable laxity of the mechanism for supervising its operation. Section 14(1) required the doctor who performed PAS/VAE to send certain documentation to the coroner. The coroner normally has the power to investigate unnatural deaths. However, the Act *deprived* the coroner of the power to investigate deaths assisted under the Act. Section 13(2) provided that deaths assisted under the Act should not, for that reason only, be taken to be 'unexpected, unnatural or violent' for the purposes of being a 'reportable death' within the Coroner's Act 1993. Consequently, in the absence of evidence indicating a failure to comply with the Act coming to the attention of the coroner, the coroner's role was limited to filing a report with the Attorney-General stating the number of assisted deaths notified in that year (section 14(2)) and, at the coroner's discretion, reporting to the Attorney-General on the operation of the Act (section 15).

Summary

The above analysis of the wording of the Act indicates that the Act was not narrow and precise but broad and vague: even a diabetic who refused insulin because of serious depression would appear to have qualified for VAE/PAS. Such elasticity could only have promoted abuse and made the prospect of conviction for breach of the law remote.

Further, the Act's procedures for ensuring compliance with its provisions were remarkably lax, even more so than those in the Netherlands. The Dutch guidelines at least require the doctor to call in the medical examiner after the death to examine the body and file a report with an interdisciplinary committee. In the NT there was no possibility of *any* investigation by the coroner in the absence of evidence of non-compliance with the Act. Given that the relevant documentation was prepared by the doctors involved and that the patient need only have signed a standard form request, it is most unlikely that any such evidence would have emerged from that source.

In short, however benevolent the motives of those who drafted and voted for ROTTI, the Act's safeguards were seriously deficient. Although much more detailed than the Dutch guidelines, it was no more capable of ensuring that VAE/PAS was confined to cases where patients free of pressure or mental illness sought death to avoid unbearable suffering, not least because it did not even try to do so.

The Act in practice: seven deaths in Darwin

ROTTI came into force in July 1996. It was overturned by the Federal Parliament in March 1997. During the nine months it was in operation, seven patients sought to make use of the Act. Two died before it came into force; four died under it; and one after its repeal. The doctor involved in all these cases was Dr Philip Nitschke, a GP who was an ardent supporter of ROTTI.

After ROTTI was repealed, Dr Nitschke was approached by Professor David Kissane, a consultant psychiatrist and professor of palliative medicine at Melbourne University, and Dr Annette Street, a medical sociologist at the La Trobe University School of Nursing, who wanted to explore the decision-making process in the seven cases. They conducted in-depth interviews with Dr Nitschke and also drew on other sources including television interviews with the patients and letters written by them. The research resulted in a paper co-authored by Kissane, Street and Nitschke which was published in the *Lancet* in 1998.[20] The paper states that, given that Kissane and Street differed from Nitschke about the ethics of PAS, its aim was not to attempt a critique of the management of the patients but rather to place the case material on the public record. All of the seven patients described had cancer, mostly advanced. Cases three to six had their deaths hastened under ROTTI.

Case three,[21] the first patient to die under the legislation, involved a man with metastatic cancer of the prostate. During middle age he underwent counselling and took antidepressant medication for several years. His first marriage, which produced two sons, ended in divorce. He remarried and moved to the NT. During his last year anaemia aggravated breathlessness

---

[20] David W. Kissane, Annette Street and Philip Nitschke, 'Seven Deaths in Darwin: Case Studies under the Rights of the Terminally Ill Act, Northern Territory, Australia' (1998) 352 *Lancet* 1097.

[21] Ibid., 1099.

and was only temporarily eased by blood transfusion. There was a partial collapse of one lung and pathological fractures presented a further difficulty – on one occasion ribs broke during a hug. Neither radiotherapy nor strontium was available in the NT. The patient took morphine for generalised bone pain but was distressed by intermittent nausea, constipation, and diarrhoea, and he required catheterisation. He was cared for at home by a community palliative care team. He wept frequently, telling Dr Nitschke that he felt it pointless to continue suffering and that his oncologist and palliative care team minimised the severity of his predicament. He did not inform them he was being assessed for euthanasia. ('Euthanasia' is the word used in the paper, but by it the authors appear to mean PAS rather than VAE. In this summary of the paper, it will therefore appear in inverted commas.) A psychiatrist from another state certified the absence of treatable depression in respect of his illness. He was 'euthanized' on 22 September 1996. His second wife was present but only later did his two sons discover that he had been 'euthanized'.

Case four,[22] the second person to have death hastened under ROTTI, involved a woman who had developed an indolent rash, mycosis fungoides, twelve years before her request for death. She underwent chemotherapy but she still complained of fatigue and pruritis, which made her reluctant to continue with that therapy. Her oncologist advised her that the median survival of a patient with mycosis fungoides was nine months and that he had no further active management to offer. Her pain was well controlled but the dominant problem was pruritis which resulted in skin trauma, infection, eyelid oedema with closure and persistent aural discharge. Her dermatologist and an ear, nose and throat specialist suggested various symptomatic treatments.

A psychiatrist noted that she showed reduced reactivity to her surroundings, lowered mood, hopelessness, resignation about her future, and a desire to die. He judged that she was depressed but that her depression was consistent with her medical condition. Dr Nitschke also sought the required second opinion from a specialist in her condition. The physician who assessed her refused to certify that she was terminally ill. She made a public appeal for help on television. An orthopaedic surgeon then agreed to see her and certified that the terms of the Act had been satisfied. She was 'euthanized' on 2 January 1997.

---

[22] Ibid., 1099–1100.

Case five[23] concerned an elderly man living alone in the NT. He had never married and had no relatives in Australia. He had had a partial gastric resection for carcinoma of the stomach and sought death because he saw no point in continuing with pain and suffering when he learned he could not recover. His surgeon confirmed, and agreed to certify, the prognosis as hopeless. The patient was assessed by a psychiatrist on the day 'euthanasia' was to be carried out. The patient denied being depressed. He complained of mild background pain which was incompletely relieved by medication, and of nausea, intermittent vomiting, and of being able to keep down only liquids. The psychiatrist phoned Dr Nitschke within twenty minutes, saying the case was straightforward. The patient was taken back to his own home. Dr Nitschke recalled his sadness at the man's loneliness and isolation as he was 'euthanized'.

Case six involved a divorced woman with advanced metastatic cancer of the breast. She had recently seen her sister die from breast cancer and had been distressed by this, particularly by her sister's double incontinence. She feared she would die in a similar manner. She was also concerned about being a burden on her children even though her daughters were trained nurses. Despite chemotherapy, her cancer had progressed and regular analgesia was necessary for abdominal pain. She eventually became bedridden and although receiving palliative care said, 'I don't like being like this; I want to die.' Her children arranged her flight to Darwin. Once there, a general surgeon certified a prognosis of death in the near future. A psychiatrist certified that she was not clinically depressed and had full comprehension of her situation. A week after arriving in Darwin, she was moved to a hotel where she was 'euthanized'.

The authors conclude that the seven cases show that the assessment of depression is difficult in the terminally ill and that accurate prognosis is subject to disagreement.[24] With regard to prognosis, they note that case four showed the Act's inability to deal with differences of opinion: one oncologist gave the patient's prognosis as nine months whereas a dermatologist and another oncologist judged that the patient was not terminally ill.

Turning to the difficulty of diagnosing depression, the authors observe that, while several studies have shown that those with depression are more

---

[23] Ibid., 1100.   [24] Ibid., 1102.

likely than those without to request PAS,[25] the role of the psychiatrist in confirming the absence of treatable depression in respect of the illness was not easy since patients (understandably) perceived the assessment as a hurdle to be overcome. 'To what extent', the authors ask, 'was the psychiatrist trusted with important data and able to build an appropriate alliance that permitted a genuine understanding of a patient's plight?'[26] Four of the seven cases, they note, had symptoms of depression, including reduced reactivity, lowered mood, hopelessness, and suicidal thoughts. Although case four was receiving treatment for depression, 'no consideration was given to the efficacy of dose, change of medication, or psychotherapeutic management'. And, although Dr Nitschke thought that this patient was unlikely to respond to further treatment, 'continued psychiatric care appeared warranted – a psychiatrist can have an active therapeutic role in ameliorating suffering rather than being used only as a gatekeeper to euthanasia'.[27]

They note a survey of psychiatrists in Oregon which revealed that only 6% felt they could be a competent gatekeeper with a single assessment of a patient. This, then, is a central concern raised by the paper: 'a gatekeeping role may be flawed if seen as adversarial by patients and viewed as blocking successful treatment, rather than being one part of proper multidisciplinary care'.[28] Another concern raised by the paper is the authors' observation that 'palliative care services were underdeveloped in the Northern Territory, and the patients in our study needed palliative care'.[29] The force of these concerns is only heightened by the fact that one of the authors was, of course, none other than Dr Nitschke himself.

Conclusion

The experience of the NT lends little support to advocates of VAE/PAS who would claim that the deficiencies of Dutch regulation would be avoided if guidelines took the form of legislation rather than caselaw. The NT legislation was no more, and in some respects significantly less, precise and strict than the Dutch guidelines. In particular, ROTTI's lack of any mechanism for systematically supervising the application of the guidelines by medical practitioners meant that any prospect of effective regulation was even

[25] Ibid., 1101.   [26] Ibid.   [27] Ibid.   [28] Ibid.   [29] Ibid., 1102.

more distant than it has proved to be in the Netherlands. Moreover, the revealing study by Kissane, Street and Nitschke, albeit based on a handful of case histories, is far from reassuring.

In view of ROTTI's manifold deficiencies, it is not surprising that a bill to repeal it was introduced into the Federal Parliament. The Euthanasia Laws Bill, a private member's bill, was introduced by Kevin Andrews MP and sparked a nationwide debate. The bill was supported by those opposed to VAE in principle and to ROTTI's deficiencies in practice. It was opposed by supporters of VAE and opponents of federal intervention in state and territorial affairs. Having passed through the lower house, the bill was considered by the Senate, who referred it to the Senate's Legal and Constitutional Legislation Committee. By a majority, the Committee supported the bill.[30] By a narrow majority, so too did the Senate. ROTTI was repealed by the Euthanasia Laws Act in March 1997.

[30] Legal and Constitutional Legislation Committee of the Australian Senate, *Euthanasia Laws Bill 1996* (1997).

15

Oregon: the Death with Dignity Act

In November 1994 the Oregon Death with Dignity Act, a citizens' initiative, was passed in a referendum by the narrowest of margins: 51% to 49%. Implementation of the Act was delayed pending a court challenge to its constitutionality. On 27 October 1997 the injunction preventing its implementation was lifted by the Federal Court of Appeals for the Ninth Circuit. In November 1997 voters rejected a proposal to repeal the Act by 60% to 40%. Since then, several people have made use of the legislation to end their lives by PAS.

The requirements of the Act

The Act allows physicians to prescribe patients lethal drugs in certain circumstances. The Act provides:

> An adult who is capable, is a resident of Oregon, and has been determined by the attending physician and consulting physician to be suffering from a terminal disease, and who has voluntarily expressed his or her wish to die, may make a written request for medication for the purpose of ending his or her life in a humane and dignified manner.[1]

Some of the Act's requirements relate to patients, others to physicians.

Patients

Age

The patient must be an 'adult', which the Act defines as an individual aged 18 or over.[2]

---

[1] 127.805 s. 2.01. [2] 127.800 s. 1.01(1).

Residency

The patient must also be a 'resident of Oregon'.[3] The Act neither defines this nor lays down a minimum period of residence.

Terminally ill

The patient must be, in the opinion of the attending physician and a second doctor, 'suffering from a terminal disease'.[4] This is defined by the Act as 'an incurable and irreversible disease that has been medically confirmed and will, within reasonable medical judgment, produce death within six (6) months'.

Capable

The patient must be 'capable'. The Act originally defined this simply as 'not incapable', but this definition was amended in 1999 to denote the ability of a patient to make and communicate healthcare decisions.[5]

Request

The patient must have voluntarily expressed his or her wish to die and have requested medication for the purpose of committing suicide. The patient must have made both an oral request and a written request, and have reiterated the oral request to the attending physician no less than 15 days after making the initial oral request.[6] No less than 48 hours shall have elapsed between the written request and the writing of the prescription.[7] The Act states that a valid request for medication shall be in a specified form, signed and dated by the patient and witnessed by at least two people who attest, in the patient's presence, that to the best of their knowledge and belief the patient is capable, acting voluntarily and is not being coerced to sign the request.[8] Moreover, at least one of the witnesses must not be related to the patient, or entitled to benefit from the patient's estate, or an owner, operator or employee of a healthcare facility where the patient is receiving treatment or is resident.[9] Further, the attending physician may not be a witness.[10]

---

[3] 127.805 s. 2.01. 'Only requests made by Oregon residents . . . shall be granted' (127.860 s. 3.10).
[4] 127.800 s. 1.01(12).   [5] 127.800 s. 1.01(3), amending 127.800 s. 1.01(6).
[6] 127.840 s. 3.06.   [7] 127.850 s. 3.08.   [8] 127.810 s. 2.02(1).
[9] 127.810 s. 2.02(2).   [10] 127.810 s. 2.02(3).

Physicians

The Act requires the involvement of two physicians:[11] the 'attending physician' and the 'consulting physician'.

The attending physician

The attending physician is defined as 'the physician who has primary responsibility for the care of the patient and treatment of the patient's terminal disease'.[12] The Act requires this doctor to make the initial determination as to whether the patient has a terminal disease, is 'capable', and has made the request voluntarily.[13] The physician must also inform the patient of certain factors: the diagnosis and prognosis; the potential risks and probable result of taking the medication to be prescribed; and the feasible alternatives, including comfort care, hospice care and pain control.[14] Immediately before writing the prescription, the physician must verify that the patient is making an 'informed decision', that is, a decision 'based on an appreciation of the relevant facts and after being fully informed'[15] of these facts.[16] Prior to writing a lethal prescription, this doctor must also verify that all appropriate steps laid down in the Act have been carried out.[17] The doctor must also invite the patient to notify any next of kin;[18] inform the patient of the right to rescind the request at any time; offer the patient an opportunity to rescind at the end of the 15-day period,[19] and refer the patient to a 'consulting physician' for medical confirmation of the diagnosis and prognosis and that the patient is capable and acting voluntarily.[20]

The consulting physician

A 'consulting physician' is a doctor 'who is qualified by specialty or experience to make a professional diagnosis and prognosis regarding the

---

[11] 'Physician' is defined as a doctor of medicine or osteopathy licensed to practise medicine in Oregon (127.800 s. 1.01(10)).

[12] 127.800 s. 1.01(2).   [13] 127.815 s. 3.01(1).

[14] 127.815 s. 3.01(2).   [15] 127.800 s. 1.01(7).

[16] 127.830 s. 3.04 provides that no one shall receive a lethal prescription unless he or she has made an 'informed decision'.

[17] 127.815 s. 3.01(9).

[18] 127.815 s. 3.01(5). 'A patient who declines or is unable to notify next of kin shall not have his or her request denied for that reason' (127.835 s. 3.05).

[19] 127.815 s. 3.01(6). 'A patient may rescind his or her request at any time and in any manner without regard to his or her mental state' (127.845 s. 3.07).

[20] 127.815 s. 3.01(3).

patient's disease'.[21] This doctor's role is to 'examine the patient and his or her relevant medical records and confirm, in writing, the attending physician's diagnosis that the patient is suffering from a terminal disease, and verify that the patient is capable, is acting voluntarily and has made an informed decision'.[22]

Counselling

If either the attending or the consulting physician thinks that a patient may be suffering from 'a psychiatric or psychological disorder, or depression causing impaired judgment' he or she shall refer the patient for counselling. No lethal prescription may be written until the person performing the counselling determines that the patient is not so suffering.[23]

Documentation and reporting

The attending physician must satisfy certain requirements relating to documentation.[24] The Act requires the attending physician to document or file in the patient's medical records:

- all oral and written requests by the patient for lethal medication;
- the attending physician's and consulting physician's diagnoses, prognoses, and determinations that the patient is capable, acting voluntarily and has made an informed decision;
- a report of the outcome and determinations made during any counselling;
- the attending doctor's offer to the patient to rescind his or her request at the time of the patient's second request;
- and a note by the attending doctor indicating that all the steps required by the Act have been satisfied and the steps taken to carry out the request, including a description of the medication prescribed.[25] The prescribing doctor must also file a brief report with the Oregon Health Division (OHD).[26]

Immunity

The Act provides that no person acting 'in good faith' shall be subject to civil or criminal liability or professional disciplinary action for performing PAS.[27]

---

[21] 127.800 s. 1.01(3).   [22] 127.820. s. 3.02.   [23] 127.825 s. 3.03.
[24] 127.815 s. 3.01.   [25] 127.855 s. 3.09.
[26] Reporting Requirements of the Oregon Death with Dignity Act, 333-009-0010(1)(a).
[27] 127.885 s. 4.01.

Liability

The Act states that a person who without the authorisation of a patient wilfully alters or forges a request for medication or conceals or destroys a rescission of that request with the intent or effect of causing the patient's death,[28] or who coerces or exerts undue influence on a patient to request lethal medication for the purpose of ending the patient's life, or to destroy a rescission of such a request,[29] shall be guilty of a felony. The statute also declares that actions in accordance with its provisions shall not for any purposes constitute suicide or assisted suicide, and that it does not authorise active euthanasia.[30]

The *least* strict and precise?

The Oregon legislation seems even laxer and vaguer than the Dutch Guidelines or ROTTI.

Precise?

Important terms in the Act are foggy. For example, does the definition of 'terminal disease' mean a disease which will produce death within six months *with or without* treatment? If the latter then diabetes qualifies. Again, who is a 'resident of Oregon': someone who flew in the previous week from Alaska with a view to seeking a lethal prescription and who proposes, if successful, to take the lethal drug in a Portland motel? 'Consulting physician' is defined simply as a physician 'qualified by specialty or experience to make a professional diagnosis and prognosis regarding the patient's disease'. Which medical practitioner would *not* be so qualified? What are the criteria for diagnosing 'depression causing impaired judgment'? A person who exercises 'undue influence' on a patient to request a lethal prescription commits a felony. Would a doctor suggesting or even strongly recommending PAS to a patient thereby commit an offence?

Strict?

The Act appears as lax as it is vague. Unlike the Dutch guidelines or ROTTI, the Act does not require that the patient be experiencing *any suffering*

---

[28] 127.890 s. 4.02(1).   [29] 127.890 s. 4.02(2).   [30] 127.880 s. 3.14.

whatever. It requires simply that the patient have a terminal illness which will produce death within six months. Moreover, in one survey over 50% of Oregon doctors said they were not confident they could make such a prediction.[31]

The Act requires the two doctors to verify that the patient is 'capable' and has requested a lethal prescription 'voluntarily', and to refer the patient for counselling if the patient may be suffering from a psychiatric or psychological disorder, or depression causing impaired judgment. However, there is nothing in the Act to ensure that *at the time when the patient subsequently takes the lethal drugs,* which may be months later, the patient is then 'capable', acting 'voluntarily' or not suffering from mental disorder.

ROTTI required the patient to have been seen by others with some expertise in psychology and in palliative care. The Oregon Act does not require that either doctor specialise in the suspected terminal illness, or in psychiatry, or in palliative care. Even if either doctor suspects the patient may be suffering from mental disorder, and refers the patient for counselling, the Act allows a patient suffering from depression to be given a lethal prescription provided the depression is not then causing 'impaired judgment'.[32]

Further, the Dutch legislation requires that the second opinion be independent of the first: the Oregon Act does not. As for the requirement that two individuals (one of whom is neither a relative nor a beneficiary) witness the patient's signing of the written request and attest that to the best of their knowledge and belief the patient is capable, acting voluntarily and not being coerced, this is hardly an effective safeguard. An heir and the heir's best friend, or a couple of passers-by invited in off the street, could satisfy this requirement.

Finally, the documentation and reporting procedure is an administrative not an investigative process. Unlike in the Netherlands, the prescribing doctor is not interviewed and is merely required to submit to the OHD within seven days of making out the prescription a copy of the patient's written request together with a signed and dated report.[33] This report is, moreover, taciturn. It is largely a *pro forma* checklist of

---

[31] Melinda A. Lee et al., 'Legalizing Assisted Suicide – Views of Physicians in Oregon' (1996) 334 *N Engl J Med* 310 at 312.

[32] 127.825 s. 3.03.

[33] Reporting Requirements of the Oregon Death with Dignity Act, 333-009-0010(1)(a).

requirements to be ticked. It does not even seek the patient's reason for requesting PAS and, although it asks for the doctor's diagnosis and prognosis, it does not ask how the doctor arrived at them. The physician is even given the option of completing an alternative, shorter form which simply indicates agreement to make available the relevant parts of the patient's medical record to the OHD.

Additionally, the physician must submit a copy of the consulting physician's report and of any counselling report. After the patient's death, the OHD 'may' send the physician a confidential form to verify information concerning the patient's death.[34] No information is sought from any physician who has refused the patient's request or, if the prescribing doctor is not the patient's usual doctor, from that doctor.

As in the NT, the body to which any reports are sent – the OHD – has no investigative function. The Act simply requires that the OHD should 'annually review a sample of records maintained' under the Act[35] and publish an annual statistical report of information collected under the Act.[36] Although the statistical report is published, the information collected remains confidential,[37] which inevitably restricts the possibilities for conducting research into the operation of the Act and for detecting abuses. And given that, as in the Netherlands and the NT, any reports are filed by the doctors themselves, the reports are unlikely to contain evidence of non-compliance. Nor is the reporting system likely to detect non-compliance which is not reported.

In short, the Act is so lax that it would appear to allow a patient, X, who is 'terminally ill', to fly to Oregon solely to obtain PAS; to 'shop around' for two doctors willing to certify that the Act's requirements are met, even though neither doctor has any expertise in palliative care or psychiatry; to make a written request for a lethal prescription which is witnessed by the heir to X's estate and the heir's best friend, and to obtain a lethal prescription which is taken months later when X is seriously clinically depressed. One hopes that such a scenario would be most unlikely. But the fact that if PAS occurred in such circumstances it would appear to be protected by the Act shows just how permissive the Act is. And the unfolding evidence of the Act's operation is far from reassuring.

---

[34] Ibid., 333-009-0010(1)(b).   [35] 127.865 s. 3.11(1).   [36] 127.865 s. 3.11(3).
[37] 127.865 s. 3.11(2).

The Act in practice

The first reported case

The first case of PAS reported under the Act has been studied closely by Herbert Hendin (Medical Director of the American Foundation for Suicide Prevention), Kathleen Foley (Professor of Neurology and expert in palliative care) and Margot White (attorney and bioethicist).[38] They examined media interviews with the doctor who prescribed the medication, newspaper reports containing information supplied by Compassion in Dying (CID), a Portland-based advocacy group which supported the Act, and reports of a press conference called by that organisation.

The patient, referred to as Mrs A, was described as a woman in her mid-eighties with metastatic breast cancer who was in a hospice programme. Mrs A's own doctor refused to provide PAS and a second doctor refused on the ground that she was depressed. Mrs A's husband contacted CID. CID's medical director had two phone conversations with Mrs A. He said that Mrs A told him that she was not bedridden and was not in great pain but she could no longer do aerobics or tend her garden, one of her favourite pastimes. He doubted that she was depressed, concluded that her 'quality of life was just disappearing' and referred her to a doctor who was willing to assist suicide.[39] This doctor referred her to a specialist (of unstated speciality) and a psychiatrist who met her only once (though the meeting was said to be lengthy). Both these doctors confirmed that she satisfied the requirements of the Act. The physician who prescribed the medication said her physical condition was worse than described by CID's medical director, and the cancer had spread to her lungs, causing pain and making breathing difficult. He prescribed barbiturates, which she took in his presence. She was said to have died within thirty minutes.

Hendin et al. comment that although this case was presented by CID as a model of how well the Act works, it contains several disturbing features. The opinions of the doctor who knew her best, and of the doctor who diagnosed depression, were overridden. The CID medical director, on the basis of telephone conversations with Mrs A, questioned the diagnosis of depression and concluded her decision was appropriate. There is no

---

[38] Herbert Hendin et al., 'Physician-Assisted Suicide: Reflections on Oregon's First Case' (1998) 14(3) *Issues Law Med* 243.

[39] Ibid., 244–5.

evidence that the doctors recommended by CID either consulted the first two doctors or tried to find feasible alternatives to PAS. Hendin et al. observe that Mrs A appeared to have been presented, without discussion, with a 'perfunctory list' of alternatives. This is, they conclude, merely fulfilling a legal requirement, not presenting real medical choices.[40]

The paper adds that the apparent deficiencies in Mrs A's management illustrate some of the major inadequacies of the Act. As the Act does not require suffering, merely a terminal illness, it does not encourage doctors to enquire into the source of the desperation which generates a request for suicide.[41] As the Act does not require either of the doctors to be a specialist in palliative care, it does not encourage the expert, knowledgeable presentation of alternatives.[42] The Act requires psychological/psychiatric evaluation only in cases of mental disorder detected by physicians – physicians who need have no psychiatric expertise whatever. Given that two-thirds of patients requesting PAS are depressed,[43] and that physicians are not reliably able to diagnose depression, let alone whether it is causing impaired judgment,[44] the Act is likely to facilitate the suicide of many patients whose request is the result of a treatable mental illness.

Hendin et al. add, moreover, that there are in fact no agreed standards for identifying the impairment that may make a patient incapable of requesting suicide.[45] And even though Mrs A did consult a psychiatrist, there was only one consultation, however 'lengthy' it was. A survey of Oregon psychiatrists revealed that only 6% felt confident that, in the absence of a long-term relationship with a patient, they could satisfactorily determine in a single visit whether a patient was competent to commit suicide.[46] Moreover, in the absence of a discussion with experts in palliative care and in psychiatry, how 'informed' can a patient's request for PAS be? Hendin et al. conclude that under the Act 'substandard medical practice is

---

[40] Ibid., 249–50. [41] Ibid., 249. [42] Ibid.

[43] Ibid., 252, citing Harvey M. Chochinov et al., 'Desire for Death in the Terminally Ill' (1995) 152 *Am J Psychiatry* 1185; Ezekiel J. Emanuel et al., 'Euthanasia and Physician-Assisted Suicide: Attitudes and Experiences of Oncology Patients, Oncologists, and the Public' (1996) 347 *Lancet* 1805.

[44] Hendin et al., 'Physician-Assisted Suicide' 251, citing George E. Murphy, 'The Physician's Responsibility for Suicide: (1) An Error of Commission and (2) Errors of Omission' (1975) 82 *Ann Intern Med* 301.

[45] Ibid., 252.

[46] Ibid., 253, citing Linda Ganzini et al., 'Attitudes of Oregon Psychiatrists towards Physician-Assisted Suicide' (1996) 153 *Am J Psychiatry* 1496.

encouraged, physicians are protected from the consequences, and patients are left unprotected while believing they have acquired a new right'.[47]

The OHD reports

The OHD has produced three reports on the working of the Act. The first two were published in 1999 and 2000 respectively. Both reports appeared in the *New England Journal of Medicine*.[48]

The first report: practice in 1998

The report on the first year contained data on 23 notified prescriptions of lethal drugs. Of these 23 patients, 15 had died by taking the drug, 6 had died naturally, and 2 were alive as of 1 January 1999. Thirteen of the 15 patients had cancer and their median age was 69.[49] (In its second report, the OHD increased the number to 16 because one further death was reported in 1999.)[50]

The OHD compared those prescribed lethal drugs with a control group suffering from similar illnesses who did not seek PAS. The data for the study came from physicians' reports, death certificates and interviews with physicians. Comparison revealed that those who had made use of the Act were more concerned than the control group about loss of autonomy due to illness and loss of control of bodily functions, such as incontinence and vomiting. The study concluded that the decision to request PAS 'was associated with concern about *loss of autonomy or control of bodily functions, not with fear of intractable pain* or concern about financial loss'.[51] The authors also concluded that the study did not provide evidence to support fears that PAS would be disproportionately chosen by or forced on terminally ill patients who were poor, uneducated, uninsured, or fearful of the financial consequences of their illness.[52] Moreover, all the reports filed by the prescribing physicians stated that the Act had been complied with.[53]

---

[47] Ibid., 267.
[48] Arthur E. Chin et al., 'Legalized Physician-Assisted Suicide in Oregon – the First Year's Experience' (1999) 340 *N Engl J Med* 577; Amy D. Sullivan et al., 'Legalized Physician-Assisted Suicide in Oregon – the Second Year' (2000) 342 *N Engl J Med* 598.
[49] Chin et al., 'Legalized Physician-Assisted Suicide in Oregon – the First Year's Experience' 577.
[50] Sullivan et al., 'Legalized Physician-Assisted Suicide in Oregon – the Second Year' 598, 600.
[51] Chin et al., 'Legalized Physician-Assisted Suicide in Oregon – the First Year's Experience' 577 (emphasis added).
[52] Ibid., 582.   [53] Ibid., 578.

The authors cautioned that the results of the study were based on a small number of patients. The report does not, in any event, prove that all cases of PAS in Oregon that year satisfied the Act. First, it is hardly surprising that in the reported cases physicians stated that they had complied with the Act. Secondly, the study suggests that other doctors would have disagreed with the prescribing doctor about the appropriateness of PAS: not only were 40% of the patients who obtained a lethal prescription refused by one or two physicians before finding one who would provide assistance, but fewer than a quarter of physicians treating the control patients would have granted a request for a lethal prescription by their patients.[54] Thirdly, the OHD does not know how many cases were *not* reported. The study conceded that the OHD's duty to report any evidence of non-compliance to the Oregon Board of Medical Examiners 'makes it difficult, if not impossible, to detect accurately and comment on underreporting'.[55] It added: '*We cannot determine whether physician-assisted suicide is being practiced outside the framework of the Death with Dignity Act.*'[56]

The second report – practice in 1999

In 2000 the OHD published the results of a second survey into cases of PAS notified in 1999. The methodology of this survey was broader than that of the first in that it included interviews with family members of the deceased. The report contained data on 33 people who received lethal prescriptions in 1999 (compared to 24 in 1998), 26 of whom died after taking the prescribed drugs, 5 of whom died naturally, and 2 of whom were still alive as of 1 January 2000. One patient who had obtained a lethal prescription in 1998 took it in 1999, bringing the total number of such deaths that year to 27 (9 per 10,000 deaths in Oregon) as opposed to 16 (6 per 10,000) in 1998. Of those 27, 21 were receiving hospice care.[57]

The most common illness was cancer (in 17 cases), followed by amyotrophic lateral sclerosis (4 cases) and obstructive pulmonary disease (4 cases), and the median age of patients who died was 71. The median interval between the first request for PAS and death in 1999 was 83 days, compared to 22 days in 1998, though one patient took the drug more than six months after the prescription was written.[58] Eight of 26 patients received

---

[54] Ibid., 582.   [55] Ibid., 583.   [56] Ibid. (emphasis added).

[57] Sullivan et al., 'Legalized Physician-Assisted Suicide in Oregon – the Second Year' 598. See also www.ohd.hr.state.or.us/cdpe/chs/pas/ar-index.htm

[58] Sullivan et al., 'Legalized Physician-Assisted Suicide in Oregon – the Second Year' 599.

prescriptions from the first physician they asked. Of the 22 physicians who issued prescriptions, 14 were general practitioners, 5 oncologists, and 3 in other specialities. Of the other 18 patients, 10 asked one other physician, and 8 asked two or three other physicians.[59]

Eighteen patients (67%) discussed three or more reasons for their request with the physicians: 13 mentioned loss of autonomy, an inability to participate in activities that make life enjoyable, and loss of control of bodily functions. The most frequently cited reasons in both years were '*loss of autonomy* (cited by 81 percent of patients in 1999 and by 75 percent in 1998) and *an inability to participate in activities that make life enjoyable* (81 percent in 1999 and 69 percent in 1998).'[60] In 1999, 7 patients (26%) expressed concern about inadequate control of pain, compared to 2 patients (12%) in 1998, but this difference was not statistically significant.[61]

Between 15 September 1998 and 15 October 1999, 24 patients died after taking a lethal drug. The authors interviewed family members of 19 of these patients (the family member to be interviewed was generally chosen by the physician). Like the physicians, the relatives often cited multiple reasons. Twelve of the family members noted at least three reasons: 'Overall, the most frequently cited reasons were concern about *loss of control of bodily functions* (68 percent), *loss of autonomy* (63 percent), physical suffering (53 percent), an *inability to participate in activities that make life enjoyable* (47 percent), and *concern about being a burden on others* (47 percent).'[62] Fourteen of 19 family members added that the patient was determined to control the circumstances of death.

The authors concluded that although concern about possible abuse persists, their data indicated that poverty, lack of education or health insurance and poor care at the end of life were not important factors in patients' requests for PAS.[63] Moreover, they added: 'As best we could determine, all the physicians who provided assistance with suicide complied with the provisions of the Oregon Death with Dignity Act.'[64] However, the report frankly acknowledged: 'Underreporting cannot be assessed, and non-compliance is difficult to assess because of the possible repercussions for noncompliant physicians reporting data' to the OHD.[65] Indeed, it conceded that each doctor's report 'could have been a cock-and-bull story'.[66]

---

[59] Ibid.   [60] Ibid., 600 (emphasis added).   [61] Ibid.
[62] Ibid., 601 (emphasis added).   [63] Ibid., 602.   [64] Ibid., 603.   [65] Ibid.
[66] www.ohd.hr.state.or.us/chs/pas/year2/ar-index.htm. CD Summary 16 March 1999.

The third report – practice in 2000

The third report disclosed that, in 2000, a total of 39 prescriptions for lethal doses of medication were written, compared to 33 in 1999 and 24 in 1998. Twenty-seven patients committed suicide in 2000 (26 who received prescriptions in 2000, 1 who had received a prescription in 1999). The researchers interviewed by telephone the 22 physicians who prescribed the lethal medication for the 27 patients. Thirteen of the doctors (59%) were in family practice or internal medicine.[67]

The physicians were asked if, based on discussions with patients, any of six concerns might have contributed to the patients' requests for lethal drugs. In all cases, physicians reported multiple concerns among patients. Eleven (41%) patients expressed at least four concerns: becoming a burden on family, friends or caregivers; loss of autonomy; decreasing ability to participate in activities which make life enjoyable; and losing control of bodily functions. Another 15 (56%) mentioned at least two or three of these concerns. Most frequently mentioned across all three years of the Act's operation were loss of autonomy (93% in 2000; 78% in 1999; 75% in 1998), and inability to participate in enjoyable activities (78% in 2000; 81% in 1999; 69% in 1998).

The report detected three worrying developments. First, it revealed an increase in concern about being a burden to family, friends or caregivers. Only 12% had expressed this concern in 1998 and 26% in 1999, but 63% in 2000. Secondly, and despite the evidence that many of those requesting PAS are clinically depressed, only 19% of those requesting lethal medication in 2000 were referred for psychological evaluation (compared to 37% in 1999). Thirdly, the median time between a patient's initial request for PAS and his or her death by overdose declined from 83 days to 30 days.

Conclusion

The Oregon Act can claim to be the most permissive regime for PAS yet devised. Unlike the Netherlands and the NT there is no requirement that the patient be suffering, let alone be suffering severely or unbearably. Unlike the NT, there is no requirement that the patient be seen by doctors

---

[67] 'Oregon's Death with Dignity Act: Three Years of Legalized Physician-Assisted Suicide' www.ohd.hr.state.or.us/chs/pas/pas.htm. See also Sullivan et al., 'Legalized Physician-Assisted Suicide in Oregon, 1998–2000' (2001) 344 *N Engl J Med* 605.

with expertise in psychiatry and in palliative care. Unlike the Netherlands, the doctor is not interviewed and is required only to notify the OHD. As the OHD has itself acknowledged, non-compliance is difficult to assess, and the physician's report could be a 'cock-and-bull story'. In short, the Act cannot seriously hope to prevent abuse, either by doctors who notify the OHD or by those who fail to do so. Moreover, the news media have reported a number of cases which have raised serious doubts about compliance with the Act.[68]

The empirical evidence, both the in-depth analysis of the first case by Hendin et al. and the three reports by the OHD, is worrying and illustrates several weaknesses of the Act. It confirms that a significant proportion of patients 'shop around' to find a compliant doctor. It also shows that the stereotypical case standardly presented by campaigners for PAS, the cancer patient dying in agony, is in Oregon atypical. The most frequent reasons for obtaining PAS were loss of autonomy and an inability to participate in activities that make life enjoyable. And, while it appears that financial concerns were not a motivating factor, concern about being a burden on others has come to motivate a majority. Further, despite the fact that most patients seeking PAS are clinically depressed, a clear majority of Oregon patients were not referred for counselling. Did any of the physicians involved, most of whom were general practitioners, possess sufficient expertise to detect the symptoms of psychiatric illness?

It is difficult to disagree with Hendin et al. when they observe that the Act serves to give more power to doctors, not patients, and that it belies the claim that decriminalising PAS 'brings it out into the open'.[69] Or with Capron, who concludes that the Oregon safeguards are 'largely illusory'.[70] As in the Netherlands and in the NT, but even more so, PAS in Oregon could not unreasonably be said to be more a matter of the secret, unaccountable exercise of medical power than the open, regulated exercise of patients' rights. It is not surprising that a number of other states have rejected proposals to follow Oregon's example.[71]

---

[68] See (2000) 10(2) *Life at Risk* 1.   [69] Hendin et al., 'Physician-Assisted Suicide' 264–8.

[70] Alexander M. Capron, 'Legalizing Physician-Aided Death' (1996) 5(1) *Camb Q Healthc Ethics* 10.

[71] Ezekiel J. Emanuel, 'Euthanasia: Where the Netherlands Leads Will the World Follow?' (2001) 322 *BMJ* 1376.

PART V

Expert opinion

The question whether the law against VAE and PAS should be relaxed has been considered by expert committees, superior courts and medical associations around the globe. Their conclusions have typically been reached after exhaustive consideration of the arguments and evidence. Fortifying the conclusions reached hitherto in this book, these bodies have concluded almost without exception that the legal prohibition should be retained. A vital factor in their reasoning has been the dangers of abuse. This section will outline developments in three jurisdictions: England, Canada and the USA. Chapter 16 will consider the reports of expert committees; chapter 17 the views of the highest national courts, and chapter 18 the positions of the national medical associations.

16

Expert committees

The House of Lords Select Committee

In 1993 in the wake of the controversy generated by the *Bland* case, the House of Lords (the upper chamber of the legislature as distinct from its Appellate Committee comprising the Law Lords) appointed an expert Select Committee to address issues raised by the case. A central issue the Committee was charged to consider was 'whether and in what circumstances actions that have as their intention or a likely consequence the shortening of another person's life may be justified on the grounds that they accord with that person's wishes or with that person's best interests'.[1] The Committee's terms of reference also required it 'to pay regard to the likely effects of changes in law or medical practice on society as a whole'.[2]

The Select Committee on Medical Ethics comprised fourteen members and was chaired by Lord Walton, an eminent physician and former President of the General Medical Council. The composition of the Committee suggested it might well be sympathetic to reform. Lady Warnock was a well-known liberal philosopher who had chaired a government committee which had recommended destructive research on human embryos *in vitro*. Lord Mustill was one of the Law Lords who had permitted the withdrawal of Tony Bland's tube-feeding. Only one member was confidently thought to be opposed to euthanasia: Lord Rawlinson, a Roman Catholic and former Attorney-General. Although Lord Habgood had written against decriminalisation, that had been some twenty years before[3] and, like Lady Warnock, he had supported permitting non-therapeutic research on human *in vitro* embryos. In short, the Committee was far from 'pro-life'.

---

[1] Lords' Report, 7.   [2] Ibid.
[3] Rt. Revd J. S. Habgood, 'Euthanasia – A Christian View' (1974) 3 *J R Soc Health* 124, 126. See p. 71 n. 2.

For a year the Committee received voluminous evidence. It examined witnesses in favour of and against reform. A delegation of its members went to the Netherlands. Its report was published in 1994. To the surprise of many, the Committee unanimously recommended that the law should not be relaxed to permit either VAE or PAS. Given the importance of this report to the contemporary debate, its reasons merit extensive quotation.

One reason was the Committee's endorsement of the principle of the sanctity or inviolability of life. The arguments for VAE and PAS were, the Committee concluded, insufficient to justify weakening society's prohibition of intentional killing: 'That prohibition is the cornerstone of law and of social relationships. It protects each one of us impartially, embodying the belief that all are equal. We do not wish that protection to be diminished and we therefore recommend that there should be no change in the law to permit euthanasia.' It went on:

> We acknowledge that there are individual cases in which euthanasia may be seen by some to be appropriate. But individual cases cannot reasonably establish the foundation of a policy which would have such serious and widespread repercussions. Moreover dying is not only a personal or individual affair. The death of a person affects the lives of others, often in ways and to an extent which cannot be foreseen. We believe that the issue of euthanasia is one in which the interest of the individual cannot be separated from the interest of society as a whole.[4]

Another reason was the Committee's concern about the dangers of the slippery slope:

> [W]e do not think it possible to set secure limits on voluntary euthanasia. Some witnesses told us that to legalise voluntary euthanasia was a discrete step which need have no other consequences. But . . . issues of life and death do not lend themselves to clear definition, and without that *it would not be possible to frame adequate safeguards against non-voluntary euthanasia if voluntary euthanasia were to be legalised. It would be next to impossible to ensure that all acts of euthanasia were truly voluntary, and that any liberalisation of the law was not abused.*[5]

It continued:

> Moreover to create an exception to the general prohibition of intentional killing would inevitably open the way to its further erosion whether by

[4] Lords' Report, para. 237.   [5] Ibid., para. 238 (emphasis added).

design, by inadvertence, or by the human tendency to test the limits of any regulation. These dangers are such that we believe that *any decriminalisation of voluntary euthanasia would give rise to more, and more grave, problems than those it sought to address.* Fear of what some witnesses referred to as a 'slippery slope' could in itself be damaging.[6]

The Committee added: 'We are also concerned that vulnerable people – the elderly, lonely, sick or distressed – would feel pressure, whether real or imagined, to request early death.[7] ... [T]he message which society sends to vulnerable and disadvantaged people should not, however obliquely, encourage them to seek death, but should assure them of our care and support in life.'[8]

The Special Committee of the Canadian Senate

This Committee of nine senators, chaired by Senator Joan Neiman QC, was appointed by the Canadian Senate in February 1994. Its remit was 'to examine and report on the legal, social and ethical issues relating to euthanasia and assisted suicide'.[9] The Committee received written and oral evidence and held a video-conference with a number of Dutch legal and medical experts in October 1994. The Committee's report appeared in May 1995. By a majority, the Committee recommended that the law should not allow VAE or PAS.

The majority opposed PAS because they were 'primarily concerned with maintaining the fundamental social value of respect for life'. They were also concerned about the risks of decriminalisation. They commented that 'legalization could result in abuses, especially with respect to the most vulnerable members of society' and noted: 'The Netherlands experience illustrates that guidelines are not always followed.'[10] The majority opposed the decriminalisation of VAE for the same reasons. But they also mentioned an additional reason. Since a second person was directly involved in VAE, they did not think that adequate safeguards could ever be established

---

[6] Ibid. (emphasis added).   [7] Ibid., para. 239.

[8] Ibid. The Committee's conclusion that the law should not be relaxed to permit VAE or PAS was accepted by the government: *Government Response to the Report of the Select Committee on Medical Ethics* (Cm 2553, 1994).

[9] *Of Life and Death: Report of the Special Senate Committee on Euthanasia and Assisted Suicide* (1995) 2.

[10] Ibid., 71.

to ensure that the consent of the patient was given freely and voluntarily. Among the majority, some thought that while there was a small number of patients who could not be dealt with adequately by palliative care they were 'not sufficient to justify legalizing euthanasia because it could create serious risks for the most vulnerable and threaten the fundamental value of life in society'.[11]

The minority favoured allowing PAS because of the pain and suffering of those with debilitating and irreversible illnesses which could not always be adequately alleviated and the loss of autonomy many such patients experienced. The minority thought that PAS was already taking place anyway without adequate control and that this created more potential for abuse than would permitting it subject to 'clearly defined safeguards'.[12] They proposed a number of minimum conditions, strikingly similar to the Dutch guidelines.[13] The same criticisms which have been made about the vagueness and laxity of the Dutch guidelines, and their inability effectively to control VAE, apply with no less force to those proposed conditions. The minority also concluded that VAE should be permitted. If PAS should be allowed, they reasoned, then so should VAE so as to 'avoid the unequal treatment of those who are physically incapable of committing assisted suicide'.[14] Their argument that acceptance of PAS involves acceptance

---

[11] Ibid., 86.   [12] Ibid., 73.

[13]
- The individual must be competent and must be suffering from an irreversible illness that has reached an intolerable stage, as certified by a medical practitioner.
- The individual must make a free and informed request for assistance, without coercive pressures.
- The individual must have been informed of and fully understand his or her condition, prognosis and the alternative comfort care arrangements, such as palliative care, which are available.
- The individual must have been informed of and must fully understand that he or she has a continuing right to change his or her mind about committing assisted suicide.
- A health care professional must assess and certify that all of the above conditions have been met.
- No person should be obligated to provide assistance with suicide.

Ibid.

The minority added that regulations must be established to deal with the monitoring and enforcement of the safeguards by the 'appropriate level of government' and that records must be maintained of all applications for and instances of assisted suicide. In order to avoid abuse, moreover, the safeguards must provide for review both prior to and subsequent to the act of assisted suicide (ibid., 73–4). Neither the form nor substance of this review was specified.

[14] Ibid., 87.

of VAE confirms the close link between the two practices identified in chapter 3.

They also had other reasons:

> Those in favour of changes believe the principle of autonomy that justifies allowing the withholding and withdrawing of life-sustaining treatment also justifies permitting voluntary euthanasia. These members believe that the provision of treatment aimed at the alleviation of suffering that may hasten death is also similar to voluntary euthanasia. The death of the patient in all of these activities is a foreseeable consequence.[15]

This reasoning illustrates the conflation of intention and foresight criticised in chapter 2. As we noted there, the conflation places those who support VAE and the administration of life-shortening palliative drugs, but who oppose NVAE, in some logical difficulty. If the minority equate, on the one hand, the administration to a competent patient of palliative drugs which foreseeably hasten death and, on the other hand, VAE, do they not equally have to equate the administration to an incompetent patient of palliative drugs which foreseeably hasten death and NVAE? If so, must they not either oppose the administration of such drugs or approve NVAE?

The New York State Task Force

The New York State Task Force was appointed by Governor Mario Cuomo in 1985 to make recommendations on public policy aspects of issues raised by medical advances.[16] Its twenty-four members, whose expertise included medicine, nursing, law, philosophy and theology, turned their attention to VAE and PAS in order to inform the growing public debate.

Some members regarded VAE and PAS as inherently wrong, as violating the prohibition on ending life, and some felt that they violated the values fundamental to the practice of medicine and the doctor–patient relationship. Others disagreed, and felt that providing a quick death for some patients could respect their autonomy and demonstrate care and commitment by doctors. *All* agreed, however, that permitting VAE and PAS would be 'unwise and dangerous public policy'.[17] Given that the report of the Task Force is no less important a contribution to the debate

---

[15] Ibid.   [16] Task Force, vii.   [17] Ibid., xii–xiii.

than that of the House of Lords Select Committee, its conclusions merit equally extensive quotation:

> After lengthy deliberations, the Task Force unanimously concluded that *the dangers of such a dramatic change in public policy would far outweigh any possible benefits.* In light of the pervasive failure of our health care system to treat pain and diagnose and treat depression, legalizing assisted suicide and euthanasia would be profoundly dangerous for many individuals who are ill and vulnerable. The risks would be most severe for those who are elderly, poor, socially disadvantaged, or without access to good medical care.[18]

In reaching the unanimous conclusion that legalisation would 'pose profound risks to many patients', the Task Force members recognised that for the purposes of public debate it was possible to imagine cases of PAS in which all the safeguards would be satisfied. But, they added, 'positing an "ideal" or "good" case' was insufficient for public policy if it bore 'little relation to prevalent social and medical practices'. The 'social risks of legalisation' identified by the Task Force included the following:

- No matter how carefully any guidelines are framed, assisted suicide and euthanasia will be practiced through the prism of social inequality and bias that characterizes the delivery of services in all segments of our society, including health care. The practices will pose the greatest risks to those who are poor, elderly, members of a minority group, or without access to good medical care.
- The growing concern about health care costs increases the risks presented by legalizing assisted suicide and euthanasia. This cost consciousness will not be diminished, and may well be exacerbated, by health care reform.
- The clinical safeguards that have been proposed to prevent abuse and errors would not be realized in many cases. For example, most doctors do not have a long-standing relationship with their patients or information about the complex personal factors relevant to evaluating a request for suicide assistance or a lethal injection. In addition, neither treatment for pain nor the diagnosis of and treatment for depression is widely available in clinical practice.
- In debating public policies, our society often focuses on dramatic individual cases. With assisted suicide and euthanasia, this approach obscures

---

[18] Ibid., ix (emphasis added).

the impact of what it would mean for the state to sanction assisted suicide or direct killing under the auspices of the medical community.

- From the perspective of good health, many individuals may believe that they would opt for suicide or euthanasia rather than endure a vastly diminished quality of life. Yet, once patients are confronted with illness, continued life often becomes more precious; given access to appropriate relief from pain and other debilitating symptoms, many of those who consider suicide during the course of a terminal illness abandon their desire for a quicker death in favor of a longer life made more tolerable with effective treatment . . .

- Depression accompanied by feelings of hopelessness is the strongest predictor of suicide for both individuals who are terminally ill and those who are not. Most doctors, however, are not trained to diagnose depression, especially in complex cases such as patients who are terminally ill. Even if diagnosed, depression is often not treated. In elderly patients as well as the terminally and chronically ill, depression is grossly underdiagnosed and undertreated.

- The presence of unrelieved pain also increases susceptibility to suicide. The undertreatment of pain is a widespread failure of current medical practice, with far-reaching implications for proposals to legalize assisted suicide and euthanasia.

- If assisted suicide and euthanasia are legalized, it will blunt our perception of what it means for one individual to assist another to commit suicide or to take another person's life. Over time, as the practices are incorporated into the standard arsenal of medical treatments, the sense of gravity about the practices would dissipate.

- The criteria and safeguards that have been proposed for assisted suicide and euthanasia would prove elastic in clinical practice and in law. Policies limiting suicide to the terminally ill, for example, would be inconsistent with the notion that suicide is a compassionate choice for patients who are in pain or suffering. As long as the policies hinge on notions of pain and suffering, they are uncontainable; neither pain nor suffering can be gauged objectively, nor are they subject to the kind of judgments needed to fashion coherent public policy. Euthanasia to cover those who are incapable of consenting would also be a likely, if not inevitable, extension of any policy permitting the practice for those who can consent.

- These concerns are heightened by experience in the Netherlands, where the practices have been legally sanctioned. Although Dutch law requires an explicit request for euthanasia by the patient, a national study in the Netherlands [the first Van der Maas Survey] found that of approximately

3,300 deaths annually resulting from mercy killing, 1,000 deaths from euthanasia occurred without an explicit request. Moreover, in some cases, doctors have provided assisted suicide in response to suffering caused solely by psychiatric illness, including severe depression.[19]

The Task Force concluded that the risks of permitting VAE or PAS were likely to be 'extraordinary'.[20]

Conclusion

The reports of the House of Lords Select Committee, the Canadian Special Senate Committee and the New York State Task Force illustrate a widespread international concern among a battery of expert committees who have studied the question closely[21] that relaxing the law would prove counter-productive. Even members of these bodies who support VAE and PAS in principle have often been persuaded by the arguments and evidence, including evidence from the Netherlands, that relaxation of the law would be bad public policy.

---

[19] Ibid., xiii–xv.   [20] Ibid., viii.

[21] Other committees which have recommended against permitting VAE and PAS include the Law Reform Commission of Canada, *Euthanasia, Aiding Suicide and Cessation of Treatment* (Report 20, 1983); and a majority of the Legal and Constitutional Legislation Committee of the Australian Senate, *Euthanasia Laws Bill 1996* (1997).

17

Supreme Courts

The Law Lords

As we saw while reviewing the Dutch experience, the courts in at least one jurisdiction have changed the law to permit VAE and PAS. However, such judicial law-making is rare. In many countries judges would regard any relaxation of the prohibition as a matter properly to be left to elected legislatures, not only because the criminal prohibition is so long-established, but also because repeal is thought to involve profound issues of principle and complex issues of social policy better suited to legislative than judicial determination.

The English courts provide a good illustration of judicial reluctance to relax the law to permit doctors to administer or hand lethal injections to patients. The courts undoubtedly have the power to do so for, as an eminent judge once wrote, the law is what the judges say it is. It would, for example, be possible for the English courts to follow their Dutch counterparts and extend the defence of necessity. It is, however, unlikely that they would do so, not least because the defence of necessity in English law has traditionally been used to justify the conduct of those who save life, not take it. In the *Bland* case, Lord Goff, having noted that 'euthanasia' (by which he clearly meant *active* medical killing) was illegal at common law, observed:

> It is of course well known that there are many responsible members of our society who believe that euthanasia should be made lawful; but that result could, I believe, only be achieved by legislation which expresses the democratic will that so fundamental a change should be made in our law, and can, if enacted, ensure that such legalised killing can only be carried out subject to appropriate supervision and control.[1]

[1] *Airedale NHS Trust* v. *Bland* [1993] 1 AC 789 at 865. The Judicial Committee of the House of Lords is not, technically, the 'Supreme Court', but it is the final court of appeal and therefore occupies a position similar to what are called Supreme Courts in other jurisdictions.

In another leading case, one which raised the propriety of judges over-turning long-established legal rules, Lord Lowry (who also, incidentally, sat in *Bland*) laid down guidelines governing judicial law-making:

> (1) if the solution is doubtful, the judges should beware of imposing their own remedy; (2) caution should prevail if Parliament has rejected oppor-tunities of clearing up a known difficulty or has legislated while leaving the difficulty untouched; (3) disputed matters of social policy are less suitable areas for judicial intervention than purely legal problems; (4) fundamental legal doctrines should not be lightly set aside; (5) judges should not make a change unless they can achieve finality and certainty.[2]

Judicial endorsement of VAE would surely breach all of these guidelines.

However, the incorporation of the European Convention on Human Rights into English law in 2000 opened up new possibilities for challenging the law prohibiting VAE and PAS. Does that prohibition infringe the right to liberty and security of the person guaranteed by Article 5? Does it contravene the right to respect for private life guaranteed by Article 8? Or, on the other hand, does the provision in Article 2 that everyone's life shall be protected by law and that no one shall be deprived of his life intentionally justify if not require that prohibition? Is it not the Dutch law permitting VAE and PAS, and especially NVAE, which breaches the Convention? As this book went to press, Diane Pretty, a woman dying from motor neurone disease, invited the English courts to rule that she enjoyed a right to assisted suicide under the Convention.[3] Her case is discussed in the Afterword.

The Canadian Supreme Court

Judicial disinclination to permit VAE and PAS is not limited to countries like England, in which even the highest court does not have the power to strike down legislation. The Supreme Courts of Canada and the United States have such power and have been invited to exercise it to overturn legislation against PAS. Yet they have declined to do so. An important reason for their refusal has been the risk of abuse.

As we saw in chapter 3, in the *Rodriguez* case the Canadian Supreme Court held, albeit by a bare majority, that the law against assisted suicide

---

[2] *C* v. *DPP* [1995] 2 All ER 43 at 52.   [3] See pp. 282–91.

did not breach the Canadian Charter of Rights and Freedoms. The majority was clearly substantially influenced by the dangers of the slippery slope. Delivering the majority judgment, Mr Justice Sopinka cited the report of the Canadian Law Reform Commission and the views of the Law Lords in *Bland*. While both of these bodies had great sympathy for the plight of those who wished to end their lives because of significant suffering, he noted, neither had been prepared to countenance the provision of active assistance in suicide. The basis for this refusal, he added, appeared to be twofold: 'first, the active participation by one individual in the death of another is intrinsically morally and legally wrong, and secondly, there is no certainty that abuses can be prevented by anything less than a complete prohibition'.[4] He observed that critics of the Dutch experience had pointed to evidence suggesting that NVAE was being increasingly practised. 'This worrisome trend', added Mr Justice Sopinka, 'supports the view that a relaxation of the absolute prohibition takes us down the "slippery slope".'[5]

The US Supreme Court

We noted in the Introduction to the book that in June 1997 the US Supreme Court upheld legislation prohibiting assisted suicide in the states of Washington and New York. As with the Canadian Supreme Court, the principle of the sanctity of human life played an important part in the court's reasoning. So too did concern about the slippery slope. The Supreme Court was faced with two cases in which federal appellate courts had struck down laws prohibiting PAS: *Glucksberg* and *Quill*.

The Supreme Court opinion

Glucksberg

In *Glucksberg* the Court of Appeals for the Ninth Circuit found a liberty interest, protected by the due process clause of the Fourteenth Amendment, in controlling the time and manner of one's death. It held that the law against assisted suicide in Washington State was unconstitutional

---

[4] *Rodriguez v. British Columbia (Attorney-General)* (1993) 107 DLR (4th) 342 at 401.
[5] At 403. For a commentary on the case see John Keown, 'No Charter for Assisted Suicide' [1994] 53(1) *Camb LJ* 234.

as applied to terminally ill competent adults who wished to hasten their deaths with medication prescribed by their physicians.[6] Reversing the decision, the Supreme Court rejected a constitutional right to PAS. Delivering the judgment of the court,[7] Chief Justice Rehnquist began by examining the nation's history and traditions and found therein no basis for any such right. On the contrary, he observed: 'for over 700 years, the Anglo-American common-law tradition has punished or otherwise disapproved of both suicide and assisting suicide'.[8] He added: 'we are confronted with a consistent and almost universal tradition that has long rejected the asserted right, and continues explicitly to reject it today, even for terminally ill, mentally competent adults'. To uphold such a right, 'we would have to reverse centuries of legal doctrine and practice, and strike down the considered policy choice of almost every State'.[9] He rejected the assimilation of the right to refuse medical treatment with a right to PAS: the two were 'widely and reasonably regarded as quite distinct'.[10]

Quill

In this case the Court of Appeals for the Second Circuit struck down the New York State prohibition on assisted suicide on the ground that it violated the equal protection clause of the Fourteenth Amendment. The court held that the prohibition did not treat equally all competent people in the final stages of terminal illness who wanted to hasten their deaths. Those who were on life-support systems were allowed to hasten their deaths by ordering their removal, but those who were not on life-support were not allowed to hasten their deaths by self-administering prescribed drugs.[11] In the Appeal Court's view, such ending of life by the withdrawal of life-support amounted to assisted suicide.[12]

The Supreme Court disagreed. It concluded that the New York ban did not treat people differently. *Everyone* was entitled to refuse unwanted treatment; *no one* was permitted to assist suicide.[13] The distinction between assisting suicide and withdrawing life-sustaining treatment, which was widely recognised and endorsed in the medical profession and in legal

---

[6] *Washington* v. *Glucksberg* 138 L Ed 2d 772 (1997).

[7] In which Justices O'Connor, Scalia, Kennedy and Thomas joined.

[8] *Washington* v. *Glucksberg* 138 L Ed 2d 772 at 782 (footnote omitted).

[9] At 789. [10] At 791.

[11] *Vacco, Attorney-General of New York et al.* v. *Quill et al.* 138 L Ed 2d 834 at 834–5 (1997).

[12] At 834. [13] At 841.

tradition, was important, logical and rational.[14] Chief Justice Rehnquist noted that the distinction tracked fundamental legal principles of causation and intent. When a patient died after refusing life-sustaining treatment the patient died from the underlying disease, but when a patient died after taking lethal medication, the cause of death was the medication. Further, a doctor who withdrew, or respected a patient's refusal to begin, life-sustaining treatment purposefully intended, or may have intended, only to respect the patient's wishes and to cease futile treatment. The same was true when a doctor administered palliative drugs which hastened death when the doctor's intent was, or may have been, only to ease pain.[15] The law had long used the agent's intent or purpose to distinguish between two acts with the same result.[16] Moreover, the overwhelming majority of state legislatures had drawn a clear line between, on the one hand, assisting suicide and, on the other, withdrawing or permitting the refusal of unwanted life-sustaining treatment, by prohibiting the former and permitting the latter.[17]

State interests

Although he rejected the claim that a right to assistance in suicide was constitutionally protected, Chief Justice Rehnquist continued that in order to pass constitutional muster the legislation against assisted suicide had nevertheless to be 'rationally related to legitimate government interests'.[18] He listed several such interests, of which one was the interest in 'protecting vulnerable groups – including the poor, the elderly, and disabled persons – from abuse, neglect, and mistakes'.[19] He cited the New York State Task Force report which warned that legalising PAS 'would pose profound risks to many individuals who are ill and vulnerable' and he added that the state's interest went beyond protecting the vulnerable from coercion and extended to protecting disabled and terminally ill people from prejudice, negative and inaccurate stereotypes, and societal indifference.[20]

He added that the state 'may fear that permitting assisted suicide will start it down the path to voluntary and perhaps even involuntary euthanasia'. Although the Court of Appeals had struck down the Washington statute only in so far as it applied to 'competent, terminally ill adults who

---

[14] At 842.   [15] At 842–3.   [16] At 843.   [17] At 844.
[18] *Washington* v. *Glucksberg* 138 L Ed 2d 772 at 792.   [19] At 795.   [20] Ibid.

wish to hasten their deaths by obtaining medication prescribed by their doctors', the state had argued that the impact of its decision would not and could not be so limited: if there were a constitutional right to suicide, it must be enjoyed by everyone. The Appeal Court's expansive reasoning, Rehnquist said, amply supported the state's concerns. That reasoning noted that the decision of a surrogate was as valid as that of the patient; that some patients might be unable to self-administer lethal drugs and that administration by a physician was the only alternative; and that not only doctors but also family members would inevitably participate in the decision-making process. 'Thus', concluded the Chief Justice, 'it turns out that what is couched as a limited right to "physician-assisted suicide" is likely, in effect, a much broader license, which could prove extremely difficult to police and contain.'[21]

This concern was, moreover, 'further supported by evidence about the practice of euthanasia in the Netherlands'. Rehnquist observed that: 'despite the existence of various reporting procedures, euthanasia in the Netherlands has not been limited to competent, terminally ill adults who are enduring physical suffering'. He added that 'regulation of the practice may not have prevented abuses in cases involving vulnerable persons, including severely disabled neonates and elderly persons suffering from dementia'.[22] He concluded that the state of Washington, like most other states, reasonably ensured against this risk by banning, rather than regulating, physician-assisted suicide.[23]

Another judge, Justice Souter, found the state interest in protecting the terminally ill from 'involuntary suicide and euthanasia, both voluntary and non-voluntary', was, by itself, 'dispositive'.[24] He considered the slippery slope arguments at some length.

Justice Souter

Justice Souter noted the state-asserted interests in protecting patients from 'mistakenly and involuntarily' deciding to end their lives, and in guarding against euthanasia both with and without request:

> Leaving aside any difficulties in coming to a clear concept of imminent death, mistaken decisions may result from inadequate palliative care or a terminal prognosis that turns out to be error; coercion and abuse may stem from

[21] At 795–6 (footnote omitted).   [22] At 796.   [23] Ibid.   [24] At 827.

the large medical bills that family members cannot bear or unreimbursed hospitals decline to shoulder. Voluntary and involuntary euthanasia may result once doctors are authorized to prescribe lethal medication in the first instance, for they might find it pointless to distinguish between patients who administer their own fatal drugs and those who wish not to, and their compassion for those who suffer may obscure the distinction between those who ask for death and those who may be unable to request it.[25]

The state argued that dependence on the vigilance of physicians to assess the patient's competence and any outside influence would be an insufficient safeguard. The limits proposed to the right to assisted suicide (particularly that of a knowing and voluntary request by the patient) would be harder to determine than the limits to other due process rights, such as the trimester measurements limiting the right to abortion. The 'knowing and responsible mind' was harder to assess than the stage of pregnancy.[26] Further, this difficulty could be compounded by the possibility that doctors would not be assiduous in preserving the line:

> They have compassion, and those who would be willing to assist in suicide at all might be the most susceptible to the wishes of a patient, whether the patient were technically quite responsible or not. Physicians, and their hospitals, have their own financial incentives, too, in this new age of managed care. Whether acting from compassion or under some other influence, a physician who would provide a drug for a patient to administer might well go the further step of administering the drug himself; so the barrier between assisted suicide and euthanasia could become porous, and the line between voluntary and involuntary euthanasia as well.[27]

He concluded:

> The case for the slippery slope is fairly made out here, not because recognizing one due process right would leave a court with no principled basis to avoid recognizing another, but because there is a plausible case that the right claimed would not be readily containable by reference to facts about the mind that are matters of difficult judgment, or by gatekeepers who are subject to temptation, noble or not.[28]

The respondents claimed that the answer to these problems was 'state regulation with teeth'. But the judge countered that 'at least at this moment'

[25] Ibid.   [26] At 828.   [27] Ibid. (footnote omitted).   [28] At 828–9.

there were reasons for caution in predicting the effectiveness of the teeth which the respondents proposed. He noted that their proposals seemed similar to the Dutch guidelines, and that some commentators on Dutch euthanasia (Gomez, Hendin and the author) had marshalled evidence that those guidelines had been violated with impunity and that NVAE was widely practised and increasingly condoned.[29] The judge added that this evidence had been contested by Richard Epstein (an American law professor); Judge Richard Posner (Chief Judge of the Court of Appeals for the Seventh Circuit), and by Dr Van der Wal (the Dutch health inspector who, as we saw in chapter 12, has carried out surveys into end-of-life decision-making in the Netherlands). Although, said Justice Souter, the day might come when it could be said 'with some assurance' which side was right, 'for now it is the substantiality of the factual disagreement, and the alternatives for resolving it, that matter. They are, for me, dispositive of the due process claim at this time.'[30]

He went on to say that, given the serious factual controversy, and given that the facts necessary to resolve it were more readily ascertainable through legislative fact-finding and experimentation than by the judicial process, the court should not hold that the state had acted arbitrarily and declare the legislation unconstitutional.[31] He observed:

> The principal enquiry at the moment is into the Dutch experience, and I question whether an independent front-line investigation into the facts of a foreign country's legal administration can be soundly undertaken through American courtroom litigation. While an extensive literature on any subject can raise the hopes for judicial understanding, the literature on this subject is only nascent.[32]

Souter's sources

Justice Souter's concern about the Dutch experience is well founded. However, whereas those justices who joined the opinion of the Chief Justice appear to have been persuaded that the Dutch guidelines have been widely breached, Justice Souter preferred to rest his judgment on the disagreement about whether they have been. His hesitation is surprising. First, as Part III of this book has shown, there was already at the time the case was decided in 1997 substantial evidence about the Dutch

[29] At 829.   [30] Ibid.   [31] At 830.   [32] Ibid.

experience – certainly sufficient to conclude that control was poor. The evidence available even some years before that had been sufficient to enable bodies such as the Canadian Supreme Court and the House of Lords Select Committee to conclude that the Dutch had failed to prevent NVAE. Secondly, that evidence indicates, and the Dutch themselves do not deny, that thousands of patients have been actively and intentionally killed without request, and there has been widespread under-reporting. *In short, that there has been frequent breach of the guidelines is not really a matter of dispute at all.* One wonders, therefore, what further evidence Justice Souter was awaiting before arriving at the conclusion which other courts and committees had already reached. Thirdly, it is revealing to examine the three sources which were thought by Souter to 'contest' the evidence that the Dutch guidelines have been widely breached.

Professor Epstein

Justice Souter quoted Professor Epstein as claiming: 'Dutch physicians are not euthanasia enthusiasts and they are slow to practice it in individual cases.'[33] Epstein's assertion is taken from his book which deals with several healthcare issues. Only one chapter addresses the Dutch experience – unlike the books by Gomez and Hendin which are devoted entirely to the subject. Before we analyse Epstein's assertion, it is worth sketching the background to his consideration of VAE.

Epstein favours the legalisation of VAE and does so because he thinks that 'the principle of patient autonomy that undergirds the right to refuse treatment also supports the right to active euthanasia'.[34] This assimilation of refusing treatment and VAE was, as we saw above, explicitly rejected by the Supreme Court. And rightly so. For Epstein rejects the crucial moral distinction between intending to put an end to treatment and intending to put an end to life. Were there no moral distinction, there would hardly be a debate about VAE at all.

His unwarranted assimilation of the nature of the two decisions also leads him to conclude that the safeguards relating to both decisions should be the same. Although some 'modest procedural safeguards' should surround these decisions, he writes, 'It does not matter whether the patient asks to receive an injection of morphine or pentobarbital, or to withdraw

---

[33] At 829, citing *Mortal Peril* (1997) 322. [34] *Mortal Peril* 284.

feeding and breathing tubes. In both cases, the best set of safeguards is likely to be informal and consultative, as is now the norm in cases to refuse treatment.'[35] Given the sweeping nature of the patient's right to refuse treatment in Anglo-American law, it is difficult to see what limits Epstein would place on the patient's right to request and obtain VAE.[36] Further, Epstein makes it clear that he himself condones NVAE in certain cases.[37]

To return to his assertion that Dutch doctors are 'not euthanasia enthusiasts' and that they are 'slow' to practise it, what does he mean by 'slow'? If he means that they do not euthanise everyone who asks for it, he is right: the Van der Maas surveys indicated that Dutch doctors denied around one out of three requests.[38] But if he means that Dutch doctors do not administer lethal injections until they have satisfied the guidelines, he is demonstrably wrong. The reality, which he nowhere denies, is that in many cases Dutch doctors have administered lethal injections without a request from the patient and without exhausting alternatives. In such cases, therefore, they *do* practise it too quickly when judged by their own guidelines. Indeed, not only should they be 'slow' to perform it in those circumstances; they should not be performing it at all.

Epstein dismisses the allegation of inadequate regulation made by Professor Gomez in his book *Regulating Death: Euthanasia and the Case of the Netherlands*.[39] Gomez's pioneering critique of the Dutch experience is perceptive and impressive. Drawing on twenty-six case-histories he gleaned through interviews with Dutch doctors who performed VAE, Gomez argued persuasively that the Dutch guidelines were inadequate to ensure effective control. He pointed out, for example, that twenty-one of

---

[35] Ibid., 289.

[36] 'Once we have recognized that it may be rational for some individuals to seek death in extreme circumstances, why shouldn't they be allowed to do so at the lowest cost to themselves, by whatever means they see fit, and at whatever time they regard as appropriate?' (ibid., 305–6). If patients have a right to refuse treatment in any circumstances, 'extreme' or not, why should they not have an equal right to request and obtain VAE?

[37] Discussing disabled babies he writes: 'If additional surgery is not worth the candle, then why balk at active euthanasia if it is honestly invoked to avoid the pain and suffering that would otherwise follow? The fate of the incompetent should lie exclusively in the hands of her guardian' (ibid., 358). He adds: 'State intervention must be used to preserve lives known to be worth living, but it should be rejected as a tool to preserve lives haunted by pain or doomed to eerie silence. Imperfect utilitarian judgments as to the prospects and quality of life are inescapable whenever life and death decisions are made, for ourselves as well as for others' (ibid.).

[38] Griffiths, 213.

[39] (1991). See John Keown, 'On Regulating Death' in (1992) 22(2) *Hastings Cent Rep* 39.

the twenty-six cases were not reported.[40] Epstein writes that only two of those cases merit separate comment as they were cases of NVAE. Remarkably, he concludes that precisely *because* they were not cases of VAE they should have been excluded from the sample![41] Perhaps this explains why Epstein, although mentioning the Remmelink Report and citing some of the statistics it discusses,[42] remains strangely silent about the 1,000 cases of NVAE. Epstein goes on to concede that Gomez's twenty-four remaining cases did show 'systematic departures from the formal guidelines requiring public and independent review' but adds that review is not an end in itself because 'the ultimate question is whether patient self-determination was violated'.[43] This will hardly do.

First, the question is not whether patient self-determination was violated, but whether doctors respected the guideline requiring a request by the patient. Secondly, as the 1,000 cases disclosed, Dutch doctors frequently end life actively and intentionally without request, mostly in the case of incompetent patients but sometimes even in the case of competent patients. Thirdly, without systematic review, how is Epstein or anyone else to *know* whether doctors have complied with the guideline requiring an explicit request? He asserts that legalising VAE and PAS 'takes the process out of the closet and brings it forward into the light of day'[44] but this assertion is contradicted by the systematic non-reporting which he himself concedes. Epstein further claims that Dutch VAE is practised as its proponents predicted: 'when pain is unbearable'; 'when palliation cannot be achieved'; and 'after all other alternatives are considered and rejected'.[45] These claims are refuted by the evidence in Part III, not least that from the two surveys by Van der Maas, neither of which is even mentioned by Epstein.

It is perhaps not surprising, in view of Professor Epstein's support for VAE and NVAE, his assimilation of the active, intentional shortening of life with the refusal of treatment and his consequent support for 'modest procedural safeguards', that he should view the Dutch experience so benignly. But his omission of much important evidence renders his analysis flawed.

Judge Posner

Justice Souter cites Judge Posner's assertion that the fear of doctors 'rushing patients to their death' in the Netherlands 'has not been substantiated and

---

[40] Gomez, 89.   [41] *Mortal Peril*, 322–3.   [42] Ibid., 321.   [43] Ibid., 323.   [44] Ibid., 311.
[45] Ibid., 323.

does not appear realistic'.[46] This assertion is taken from Posner's book, on the subject of old age, in which the issue of the Dutch experience receives only passing consideration.[47] Of the thirteen chapters of his book, only one discusses euthanasia and only part of that chapter touches on Dutch euthanasia. Put another way, of the 360 pages of his book the subject of Dutch euthanasia occupies about three.[48]

Posner attributes the fear of patients being 'rushed to their death' (the emotive language is Posner's) to Gomez's book.[49] Posner claims that only one of Gomez's case-histories, concerning a young woman who may not have been informed about alternatives to chemotherapy, 'provides even a modicum of support' for the thesis that the guidelines are insufficient to ensure that euthanasia is always voluntary.[50] Inexplicably, Posner quite overlooks the two cases (noted by Epstein) in which there was no explicit request. One was the case of a 56-year-old man who was admitted to hospital after a car crash and whose life was terminated by an injection of potassium chloride to minimise the relatives' distress.[51] The second concerned a baby born with Down's syndrome and an intestinal blockage who was given large doses of benzodiazepines 'just to help the child along'.[52] Three other cases involved no contemporaneous request.[53]

Posner largely evades Gomez's well-grounded concerns about Dutch regulation including the lack of reporting. Posner's four reasons for dismissing those concerns as 'not realistic' are weak indeed. First, claims Posner, such behaviour 'would go against the grain of the medical profession, which strongly favors treatment, however unlikely of success'.[54] However, whether or not many American doctors tend to overtreat, many Dutch doctors do not. As the thousands of cases per year of VAE indicate, VAE has quickly become part of mainstream Dutch medical practice. And once termination, both with and to a significant extent without consent, has become part of the grain the generalisation that doctors prefer to treat than to terminate, however true it may be in other contexts, does not hold.

Posner's second argument is no stronger. He says that breaching the guidelines 'might also be contrary to the profession's financial self-interest',

---

[46] *Washington* v. *Glucksberg* 138 L Ed 2d 772 at 829.   [47] *Aging and Old Age* (1995).
[48] Ibid., 241–3.   [49] Gomez.   [50] Posner, *Aging and Old Age* 242.
[51] Gomez, 85–6.   [52] Ibid., 83–4.
[53] Case 19 (ibid., 83); Case 21 (ibid., 84–5); Case 23 (ibid., 86).
[54] *Aging and Old Age* 242.

though he immediately qualifies this with the observation that 'this depends on the method of financing medical services'.[55] Given that Dutch doctors are not paid on a fee-for-service basis this speculation is no more relevant than the first. Indeed, it is double-edged, for Posner goes on to concede that, in the case of many patients who are not treated on a fee-for-service basis in the USA, 'the financial incentive is to avoid expensive end-of-life treatments, for which euthanasia might be a cheap alternative'.[56] Incidentally, even leading Dutch practitioners of VAE have cautioned against its export to countries, like the USA, without state-funded healthcare systems.[57]

Thirdly, Posner argues that hospices provide an alternative to VAE. He seems to overlook the fact that hospices are rare in the Netherlands. Moreover, it does not follow that the alternative of palliative care, whether provided in a hospice setting or otherwise, will prevent abuse. Indeed, VAE has been not infrequently performed in the Netherlands when it was not a 'last resort' and when palliative care could have offered an alternative. Further, Posner does not address the argument, often advanced by palliative care experts, that VAE is antagonistic to palliative care. Why should patients undergo palliative care, and why should doctors strive to advance its frontiers, when there is the 'quick fix' of VAE? Why should society fund expensive hospices instead of cheap injections?

Fourthly, Posner argues:

> The danger of the abuses that Gomez fears can be minimized by relatively simple regulations, such as a requirement that the patient's consent to euthanasia be witnessed or in writing, that the physician performing euthanasia report any case in which he performs it to a hospital committee, and that before performing it he consult with a duly certified specialist in the ethics of dealing with dying patients.[58]

But the inadequacy of his proposal is easy to demonstrate, for his suggested regulations are similar to the Dutch guidelines which have patently failed to prevent abuse. Indeed, the Dutch guidelines, although they do not require the patient's request to be witnessed, are somewhat stricter in that they require the doctor to consult with another doctor, not just an ethicist,

---

[55] Ibid.   [56] Ibid.   [57] For a summary of this and other arguments, see Griffiths, 304–5.
[58] Posner, *Aging and Old Age* 243.

and the notification of a prosecutor or, more recently, an interdisciplinary committee, not just a hospital committee.

In short, Posner does not adequately address the concerns legitimately raised by Gomez (and others) about breach of the guidelines requiring a voluntary request and that VAE be a last resort. Posner does not even attempt to meet the concern about lack of reporting. These concerns have, of course, been confirmed by the wealth of further evidence which has emerged subsequent to the publication of Gomez's book in 1991, including the Van der Maas surveys. Unlike Epstein, Posner cites the first Survey in a footnote but, like Epstein, curiously omits to mention any of its disturbing findings.[59] He also fails to mention the reports of either the House of Lords Select Committee or the New York State Task Force.

In sum, Posner's assertion, like Epstein's, is not only vague and unsubstantiated; it is falsified by the stark fact that in many cases Dutch doctors have actively and intentionally killed patients without a request and/or without exhausting alternatives. These patients' lives have been prematurely terminated (or, in Posner's emotive phrase, they have been 'rushed to their death') without the guidelines being satisfied.

It is remarkable that Justice Souter should apparently put the views of Epstein and Posner, neither of whom claims to have conducted any original research into the Dutch situation, on a par with those who have spent years doing precisely that. What, then, of the third source cited by Justice Souter?

Van der Wal

The third source is Dr Van der Wal who, as we saw in chapter 12, conducted, with Professor Van der Maas, the second major survey into end-of-life decision-making in the Netherlands. Posner cites a different survey carried out by Van der Wal and other prominent Dutch defenders of VAE.[60] This research, which is cited by Posner in his attempt to counter Gomez's study, is said by Posner to have 'found no serious abuses'.[61] Posner's reassuring observation requires heavy qualification.

First, Van der Wal himself acknowledged the limitations of his survey, which took the form of an anonymous postal questionnaire to family

---

[59] Ibid., 241 n. 16.

[60] G. van der Wal et al., 'Euthanasia and Assisted Suicide, 2, Do Dutch Family Doctors Act Prudently?' (1992) 9 *Fam Pract* 135, cited in *Washington v. Glucksberg* 138 L Ed 2d 772 at 829.

[61] *Aging and Old Age* 242 n. 23.

doctors. He conceded that it 'could reveal only indirectly to what extent the family doctors observed the material requirements for prudent practice. For instance, there were no specific questions about the voluntary nature of the request.'[62] Moreover, 'No direct questions were asked about whether the request was well considered and whether the desire for death was persistently present'.[63] Van der Wal conceded that it was difficult to tell from his survey to what extent family doctors ensured that patients had a clear understanding of their diagnosis and prognosis.[64] Advising caution in drawing conclusions from the study he added: 'it should be remembered that the results are based on the replies given by the family doctors themselves'.[65]

Secondly, the survey in fact contains several findings which cast serious doubt on whether, when doctors actively and intentionally killed patients, those patients were suffering unbearably, had made a free and informed request and were killed as a last resort. The survey revealed that in two-thirds of cases the request was purely oral;[66] that in 22% of cases there was only one request;[67] that in 13% of cases less than a day elapsed between the first request and its implementation and in a further 35% of cases less than a week;[68] and that more patients cited 'pointless' suffering and 'fear of/avoidance of humiliation' than 'unbearable suffering' as their most important reason for requesting euthanasia. 'Pain' was cited as the most important reason by only 5%.[69]

Turning to the requirement of consultation, Van der Wal pointed out: 'One quarter of the family doctors say that they did not ask for a second opinion before applying euthanasia or assisting with suicide. More serious is the finding that 12% of the family doctors who applied euthanasia or assisted suicide had no kind of consultation with any professional health worker.'[70] He continued:

> A striking aspect in our study is that in most cases the doctor consulted for a second opinion was a partner in the practice, a locum or was the specialist assisting in the patient's treatment. The question, however, is whether the conditions for an independent opinion have been adequately met here, particularly since the point at issue is not only the independence of the consultant *vis-à-vis* the patient's doctor but also his independence with regard

---

[62] Van der Wal et al., 'Euthanasia and Assisted Suicide' 136.   [63] Ibid.   [64] Ibid., 139.
[65] Ibid., 138.   [66] Ibid., 136.   [67] Ibid., 137.   [68] Ibid.   [69] Ibid., 138, table 4.
[70] Ibid., 140.

to the patient. More than 60% of the 'consultants' already knew the patient before the (first) consultation.[71]

It could be assumed, he continued, that the independence of the second opinion was greater if it was given in writing but this was so in only about a quarter of cases.[72] Although the treating doctor should have kept a written record of events, almost half the doctors surveyed had not done so.[73] Finally, 74% had certified that death had been due to natural causes and had not, therefore, reported the case to the authorities.[74]

Van der Wal concluded that those who observed the procedural requirements usually observed others as well and that the majority of family doctors did satisfy the material requirements for prudent practice.[75] This conclusion is difficult to square with the evidence of his survey, not least the widespread breach of procedural requirements he exposed. Those requirements were laid down precisely to promote prudent practice. If those requirements were ignored, which they were, what evidence is there (apart from the doctors' self-serving replies) that the material requirements were satisfied?

Thirdly, the evidence of widespread breach of the procedural requirements disclosed by the Van der Wal survey was, as we have seen, subsequently confirmed by the more comprehensive research by Van der Maas examining practice in 1990. It is odd indeed that Posner did not address the findings of this survey, findings which were largely confirmed by the second Van der Maas Survey (in which Van der Wal participated) examining practice in 1995.

Finally, Posner seems unaware that Van der Wal himself has never denied the evidence that many patients have been terminated without request, or that VAE has not always been a last resort, or that the majority of cases have not been reported. For example, in 1993, commenting on the finding of the first Van der Maas Survey that some competent patients had been killed without request, Van der Wal wrote that their right to self-determination was 'seriously undermined'[76] (or, to use Epstein's word, 'violated').

In sum, Justice Souter's hesitation in joining his colleagues' criticism of the Dutch is unwarranted. He need not have waited for the evidence showing widespread breach of the guidelines: it was already in. It shows

---

[71] Ibid.   [72] Ibid.   [73] Ibid.   [74] Ibid., 135.   [75] Ibid., 140.

[76] Gerrit van der Wal, 'Unrequested Termination of Life: Is It Permissible?' (1993) 7 *Bioethics* 330, 337.

beyond dispute that VAE has been used as an alternative to palliative care, that most cases have gone unreported, and that NVAE is not uncommon. On closer inspection, not one of the three sources he thinks contest that evidence convincingly does so.

Conclusion

The highest courts in England, Canada and the USA have declined to relax the law against doctors administering or handing lethal medication to their patients. A major reason has been concern about the dangers of abuse, and a major reason for that concern, at least in North America, has been the evidence from the Netherlands.

18

Medical associations

To please no one will I prescribe a deadly drug, nor give advice which
may cause his death.

The Hippocratic Oath[1]

Maintaining a tradition dating from the Hippocratic Oath in the fifth
century BC forbidding doctors to give any deadly poison to patients, even
if asked, the vast majority of medical associations oppose both VAE and
PAS. This is reflected by the policy of the World Medical Association. In
May 2001, in the wake of the passage of the Dutch euthanasia legislation,
the WMA reaffirmed its strong belief that euthanasia conflicts with basic
ethical principles of medical practice and called on doctors to refrain from
participating in it, even when it is permitted by national law.[2] The previous
chapter outlined decisions of Supreme Courts in the UK, Canada and the
USA. This chapter will outline the policies of their respective medical
associations.

The British Medical Association

The BMA has consistently opposed VAE and PAS. In 1987, in response to a
motion passed at its Annual Representative Meeting (ARM) the previous
year urging the Association to reconsider its opposition, the Association
set up a working party under the chairmanship of Sir Henry Yellowlees, a
former Chief Medical Officer at the Department of Health. The Working
Party identified four major arguments for VAE.[3] The first – respect for
autonomy – was rejected on the ground that autonomy has limits. The
second – the desire for a kind death – was countered by the fact that

---

[1] Reproduced in J. K. Mason and R. A. McCall Smith, *Law and Medical Ethics* (5th edn, 1999) 551.

[2] Veronica English, Jessica Gardner, Gillian Romano-Critchley and Ann Sommerville, 'Legislation
on Euthanasia' (2001) 27 *J Med Ethics* 284.

[3] *Euthanasia: Report of the Working Party to Review the British Medical Association's Guidance on
Euthanasia* (1988) 39.

those caring for the dying were usually able to provide a gentle death without resorting to intentional killing. The third – respect for persons – was an argument which was felt to tell against rather than for VAE: 'It is precisely because human life has depths, and a value that may take fresh and unexpected form, even up until the moment of death, that it must not be cut short.'[4] The fourth argument was that the sanctity of life was an outmoded religious concept. The Working Party commented that, while the religious conviction which underlay the concept was no longer a universally accepted basis for medical practice, the humility induced by the principle was nevertheless fundamental to the ethos of medical practice.[5] As for the invocation of public opinion polls which purported to show widespread support for reform, the report questioned their reliability and, citing the example of slavery, rejected the notion that what was right should be determined by majority opinion.[6] The Working Party was, moreover, concerned to protect the doctor–patient relationship and to affirm that the life of each individual had unique and irreplaceable value even when that individual had lost sight of it.[7] The report concluded:

> The law should not be changed and the deliberate taking of a human life should remain a crime. This rejection of a change in the law to permit doctors to intervene to end a person's life is not just a subordination of individual wellbeing to social policy. It is, instead, an affirmation of the supreme value of the individual, no matter how worthless and hopeless that individual may feel.[8]

1993 saw the publication of the BMA's guide to doctors on medical ethics – *Medical Ethics Today*.[9] The book reaffirmed that authorising doctors to kill or help kill, however carefully circumscribed the circumstances, invited them to adopt a role alien to that of healer and act in a way radically inconsistent with the dignity which belongs to each human being.[10] Autonomy had limits and the rights of one group could not be allowed to undermine the rights of others.[11] Moreover, permitting VAE could result in NVAE, either because the safeguards would not prevent the slide or because the case for the former could easily be made into a case for the latter.[12] Noting the trends in the Netherlands, where the KNMG had canvassed NVAE for neonates, minors, the mentally retarded and those

---

[4] Ibid., 40.   [5] Ibid., 41.   [6] Ibid., 42.   [7] Ibid., 59.   [8] Ibid., 69.
[9] Ann Sommerville, *Medical Ethics Today: Its Practice and Philosophy* (1993) chapter 6.
[10] Ibid., 150.   [11] Ibid., 151.   [12] Ibid., 151–2.

with dementia, it observed: 'The BMA opposes such views, not least on the grounds that such comments appear to classify whole groups of people as particularly eligible for premature death.'[13]

Other concerns were expressed. If VAE were permitted it might prove an obstacle to improved palliative care: eliminating the patient might seem an easier option than striving to eliminate the pain.[14] Some might seek VAE because they felt a burden on others[15] and many requests were based on the patient's increasing sense of worthlessness and dependence. 'Willingness by society to supply or condone euthanasia', the book observed, 'will merely confirm the patient's sense of worthlessness, resulting in a society where individuals are not deemed valuable unless demonstrably useful.'[16]

In 1993 the BMA's ARM passed a motion categorically rejecting the legalisation of VAE and in 1995 a motion reaffirming its opposition to legalisation. The terms of the motion passed in 1997, however, suggested a softening: 'That this Meeting recognises that there is a wide spectrum of views about the issues of physician assisted suicide and euthanasia and strongly opposes a change in the law for the time being.'[17] That the Association might be willing to reconsider its opposition was further suggested by the fact that its 1998 ARM voted for a conference 'to promote the development of consensus' on PAS. In preparation for this conference, a website, open to the public, was set up.[18] Dr Wilks, the Chairman of the Medical Ethics Committee, explained that his remit was not to change BMA policy but to find a common language and identify common values.[19] The conference took place on 3–4 March 2000. Fifty BMA members, nominated by their local divisions, participated. They were selected to reflect a range of age, speciality and professional seniority and came with a wide variety of views.

A discussion paper written by the BMA Medical Ethics Department in 1998 and made available on the website and to conference delegates set out the bases of the Association's opposition:

> The BMA's position is based on two main strands of argument. The moral arguments that killing is intrinsically wrong, alien to the ethos of medicine and potentially diminishes societies that permit it as a solution for social problems are reinforced, in the BMA's published view, by practical concerns. Prominent among these is the view that toleration of euthanasia would

---

[13] Ibid., 152.   [14] Ibid., 155.   [15] Ibid., 154.   [16] Ibid., 156.
[17] www.bma.org.uk/public/bmapas.nsf   [18] Ibid.   [19] Ibid., Chairman's introduction.

irrevocably change the context of health care for everyone but especially for vulnerable patients.[20]

It added that the opportunities for manipulation and abuse would be unacceptable. Moreover, it would be difficult to limit VAE to those who asked for it. Referring to the 1,000 cases of NVAE exposed by the first Van der Maas Survey, the discussion paper commented that the acknowledged contravention of the permissive Dutch rules could be seen as a cause for concern. Establishing a right to VAE would, moreover, inevitably raise questions about why such a right should be denied to others such as the senile.[21] Endorsing the conclusion of the House of Lords Select Committee that the arguments for VAE were not sufficient to weaken the social prohibition against intentional killing, the BMA concluded that the societal price for legalisation would, by reducing the protection of the majority of vulnerable people, be injustice.[22] Turning specifically to PAS, the document considered some of the arguments for distinguishing it from VAE, including the argument that, because PAS requires the patient's co-operation, it is less open to potential abuse.[23] The paper concluded, however, that in many cases there was little practical difference between the two, and that similar arguments about the potential for abuse could be levelled against PAS, though they 'may be thought to carry less weight in practical terms'.[24]

After two days of intense and thorough debate, the conference produced several consensus statements. The final document is a collection of those statements.[25] The document began: 'Drawing together a wide range of moral viewpoints and practical considerations, the conference cannot agree to recommend a change in law to allow physician assisted suicide.'[26] Commenting on the outcome, Dr Wilks said:

> This weekend's conference has firmly rejected any move to change the law on physician assisted suicide. That may appear to be a simple reaffirmation of existing law and policy, but behind the decision lies two days of

---

[20] 'Euthanasia and Physician Assisted Suicide: Do the Moral Arguments Differ?' In *Physician Assisted Suicide Debating Pack PAS4* (2000) 1.
[21] Ibid., 2.   [22] Ibid., 2–3.
[23] Ibid., 4. It could, however, be countered that a patient could just as easily be pressured into taking a lethal substance as into being injected with it, and that abuse lies not in the method of delivery but in the manipulation of the mind.
[24] Ibid., 6.   [25] www.bma.org.uk/public/pubother.nsf/webdocsvw/PASConf
[26] Ibid.

intense and thorough debate. The consensus statement is remarkable for the fact that delegates with fundamentally and diametrically opposing views on end of life issues were able to agree a position with which they all feel comfortable.[27]

The Canadian Medical Association

The Canadian Medical Association (CMA) is also opposed to VAE and PAS, though its formally stated opposition seems more recent and less deeply rooted than that of the BMA. In 1991 the General Council of the CMA directed the Association's Committee on Ethics to prepare a discussion paper on VAE and PAS. A working group of the Committee, which sought to adopt a morally neutral stance, wrote five articles intended to provide information which would assist individual doctors and the CMA to formulate a position. The articles were published in the form of a report in 1993.[28] In 1995 the CMA issued a policy statement expressing its opposition to VAE and PAS, a statement updated in 1998. The statement pointed out that, while neither was specifically mentioned in its Code of Ethics, the Code had traditionally been interpreted as opposing these practices.[29] The statement expressly advised its members to avoid them: 'The CMA does not support euthanasia and assisted suicide. It urges its members to support the principles of palliative care.'[30] Canadian physicians should not, it advised, participate in either VAE or PAS.[31]

However, just as the CMA's explicit policy was more recent than that of the BMA it also appeared less deeply rooted, for it appeared to acknowledge the possibility of change. It urged that, in deciding whether the law should be relaxed, society should consider a number of concerns physicians had, such as the provision of adequate palliative care to all Canadians, and the question whether any proposed legislation could restrict VAE and PAS to the indications intended.[32] It added that any legislation which was limited to competent, suffering, terminally ill patients might be challenged and extended under the Canadian Charter of Rights and Freedoms.[33]

---

[27] www.bma.org/pressrel.nsf/webpubvwlink/SGOY-4H6DYK

[28] Frederick H. Lowy, Douglas M. Sawyer and John R. Williams, *Canadian Physicians and Euthanasia* (1993).

[29] CMA, 'Euthanasia and Assisted Suicide (Update 1998)'. www.cma.ca/inside/policybase/1998/06-19f.htm page 2.

[30] Ibid., 1.   [31] Ibid., 3.   [32] Ibid., 3–4.   [33] Ibid., 4–5.

The American Medical Association

The American Medical Association (AMA) is also opposed to both VAE and PAS. Its current policy affirms that permitting doctors to engage in VAE or PAS would be harmful. It explains that both are fundamentally incompatible with the physician's role as healer, would be difficult or impossible to control, and would pose serious social risks. Moreover, active, intentional killing could also easily be extended to incompetent patients and other vulnerable populations. Instead of resorting to VAE and PAS, the AMA urges, doctors should aggressively respond to the needs of patients at the end of life, who must not be abandoned and who must continue to receive emotional support, comfort care, adequate pain control, respect for their autonomy, and good communication.[34] To this end, the AMA has embarked on an educational campaign to improve the provision of palliative care by, for example, establishing a faculty of doctors with expertise in end-of-life care who can provide consultations for other doctors in caring for patients at the end of life.[35] The AMA's Institute for Ethics has collaborated with the Robert Wood Johnson Foundation to create the EPEC Project: Education for Physicians on End-of-Life Care. The project aims to provide all US doctors with the knowledge and skills required to provide quality care to patients at the end of life.[36]

Conclusion

Despite the fact that many individual doctors support VAE and PAS, the professional medical associations in Britain, Canada and the USA echo their respective Supreme Courts in maintaining an unbroken tradition of opposition to the legalisation of either. As the last three chapters reveal, there is an impressive phalanx of expert interdisciplinary opinion ranged against legalisation.

[34] E-2.21 Euthanasia; E-2.211 Physician-Assisted Suicide. See also H-270.965; www.ama-assn.org
[35] Ibid., H-140.949.
[36] Ibid., News release: AMA testifies on pain management, end-of-life care, 13 October 1999.

PART VI

Passive euthanasia: withholding/withdrawing treatment and tube-feeding with intent to kill

It was tempting to stop writing at the end of the last chapter and to limit the book to an elucidation and exploration of the slippery slope arguments against legalising VAE and PAS. To have stopped writing would, however, have been to ignore an aspect of the debate which, despite its importance, commands relatively little attention. This is the question whether the law and professional medical ethics do, and should, permit doctors intentionally to end patients' lives, and intentionally assist them to commit suicide, *by withholding/withdrawing treatment and tube-feeding*. Without at least some consideration of this question, this book would have overlooked an important dimension of the euthanasia debate. Part VI therefore considers whether English law and professional medical ethics permit *passive* euthanasia (PE), that is, *the withholding/withdrawing of medical treatment (or tube-delivered food and fluids) by a doctor with intent to kill*. It concludes that they do and that this is inconsistent with their continued opposition to the active, intentional killing of patients. What is said in this part in relation to English law has important implications for other jurisdictions – not least the USA – in which (as will be suggested in the conclusions to this Part) some courts have also moved from 'inviolability' towards 'Quality'.

Chapter 19 illustrates the English courts' condonation of PE by examining the landmark decision of the Law Lords in the *Tony Bland* case in 1993. Chapter 20, by analysing the BMA's recent Guidance on Withholding and Withdrawing Medical Treatment, illustrates the medical profession's acceptance of the proposition, central to the case for both VAE and NVAE, that the lives of certain patients are not worth living and that it is permissible for that reason to withhold/withdraw life-preserving treatment, or tube-feeding, from them. Chapter 21 discusses a private member's bill which sought to restore 'moral and intellectual shape' to law and medical ethics after the *Bland* case and the BMA guidance, and suggests that the opposition to that bill by the government and the BMA was confused and inconsistent.

19

The *Tony Bland* case

We mentioned this case in chapter 1 to illustrate the second definition of 'euthanasia' as including intentional termination of life *by omission*. We revisit it now to focus on its legal and ethical significance as a landmark decision condoning PE. It merits repetition that PE means (at any rate as used in this book) the withholding/withdrawal of medical treatment (or tube-feeding) *with the intention (aim) of hastening death*. It does *not* mean withholding/withdrawing treatment *because the treatment is either futile or too burdensome, or in order to respect the patient's refusal of treatment*, which everyone (except a vitalist) agrees is perfectly proper both ethically and legally.

The facts

Before his death on 3 March 1993, Tony Bland had lain in Airedale Hospital for over three years in a 'persistent vegetative state' (pvs), a state in which, it was believed, he could neither see, hear nor feel. The medical consensus was that he would never regain consciousness. Neither dead nor dying, his brain stem still functioned and he breathed and digested naturally. He was fed by nasogastric tube, his excretory functions regulated by catheter and enemas. Infections were treated with antibiotics. His doctor and parents wanted to stop the feeding and antibiotics and the Hospital Trust applied for a declaration that it would be lawful to do so. The application, supported by an *amicus curiae* (a 'friend of the court') instructed by the Attorney-General, was opposed by the Official Solicitor, who represented Tony. The declaration was granted by Sir Stephen Brown, whose decision was unanimously affirmed by the Court of Appeal and the House of Lords.

The courts' reasoning

Tony's counsel, James Munby QC, argued that stopping treatment and feeding would be murder or at least manslaughter. Three of the five Law Lords accepted his argument that the doctor's intention would be to kill Tony, a submission which the remaining two neither rejected nor accepted. One of the three, Lord Browne-Wilkinson, said:[1]

> Murder consists of causing the death of another with intent to do so. What is proposed in the present case is to adopt a course with the intention of bringing about Anthony Bland's death. As to the element of intention . . . in my judgment there can be no real doubt that it is present in this case: the whole purpose of stopping artificial feeding is to bring about the death of Anthony Bland.[2]

Why, then, would this not be murder? Because stopping treatment and feeding was not a positive act but an omission. Lord Goff said[3] that withdrawing life-support was no different from withholding it in the first place; the doctor was simply allowing the patient to die as a result of his pre-existing condition. Further, tube-feeding was medical treatment: there was, he said, 'overwhelming evidence' that in the medical profession tube-feeding was so regarded and, even if it were not strictly treatment, it formed part of the patient's medical care. The provision of food by tube was, he added, analogous to the provision of air by a ventilator. The House of Lords held that the doctor was under no duty to continue tube-feeding. The earlier case of Re F[4] had decided that a doctor could treat an incompetent patient only if it was in the patient's best interests; Bland held that the same criterion should govern the withdrawal of treatment. As continued feeding was no longer in the patient's interests, the doctor was under no duty to continue it.

Why was the tube-feeding not in Tony's best interests? Because it was 'futile'. Why was it futile? Because, in the words of Lord Goff,[5] 'the patient is unconscious and there is no prospect of any improvement in his condition'. In deciding whether treatment was futile, the doctor had to act in accordance with a responsible body of medical opinion. More precisely, the

---

[1] [1993] AC 789 at 876 per Lord Browne-Wilkinson; at 887 per Lord Mustill.
[2] Why the majority assumed it was the doctor's purpose to kill is unclear. A doctor who withdraws tube-feeding in such circumstances may do so with the sole purpose of removing what he or she regards as a futile treatment. Whether the doctor would be right in so regarding it is another matter and is discussed later in this chapter.
[3] [1993] AC 789 at 866.   [4] [1990] 2 AC 1.   [5] [1993] AC 789 at 869.

doctor had to satisfy the so-called *Bolam* test – the test which determines whether, in an action for medical negligence, a doctor has fallen below the standard of care required by the law.[6]

From inviolability to Quality

Their Lordships' reasoning appears, with respect, vulnerable to several criticisms. The main criticism is that, wittingly or unwittingly, they shifted the law from its axis of inviolability of life towards an axis of Quality of life. We distinguished these competing approaches to the valuation of human life in chapter 4.

Tube-feeding: futile treatment or basic care?

First, why did the judges regard tube-feeding as medical treatment, which could be withdrawn because it could not improve Tony's condition, rather than as basic care which the hospital and its medical and nursing staff were duty-bound to provide regardless of whether his condition would improve? The Law Lords held that tube-feeding was part of a regime of 'medical treatment and care'.[7]

The insertion of a gastrostomy tube into the stomach requires a minor operation which is clearly a medical procedure. But it is not at all clear that the insertion of a nasogastric tube is a medical intervention. It is, after all, something that even relatives can be shown how to do. And, even if it were a medical procedure, the intervention had already been carried out in Tony's case. The question in such a case is surely why *the pouring of food and water down the tube* constitutes medical treatment. What is the pouring of food and water supposed to be *treating*? Nor does the difficulty evaporate by classifying it, as did the Law Lords, as medical treatment *or* medical care. As Professor Finnis has observed:

> The judgments all seem to embrace a fallacious inference, that if tube-feeding *is* part of medical 'treatment or care', tube-feeding is therefore *not* part of the non-medical (home or nursing) care which decent families and communities provide or arrange for their utterly dependent members. The non-sequitur is compounded by failure to note that although naso-gastric tube-feeding will not normally be established without a doctor's decision,

---

[6] *Bolam* v. *Friern HMC* [1957] 1 WLR 582. Lord Mustill reserved judgment about the appropriateness of this test in this context: see text p. 225.
[7] See e.g. [1993] AC 789 at 858 *per* Lord Keith.

no distinctively medical skills are needed to insert a naso-gastric tube or to maintain the supply of nutrients through it.[8]

Their Lordships seemed to place great weight on the fact that tube-feeding is regarded by the medical profession as medical treatment.[9] But whether an intervention is medical is not a matter to be determined by medical opinion nor by the mere fact that it is an intervention typically performed by doctors. A doctor may do many things in the course of his practice, such as reassuring patients, which are not distinctively 'medical' in nature. And, if it is opinion which is crucial, the answer one gets may well depend on whom one asks. Tube-feeding may be regarded as medical treatment by many doctors, but many nurses regard it as ordinary care.[10]

Further, Lord Goff's analogy between tube-feeding and mechanical ventilation is (although accepted by Mr Munby QC)[11] unpersuasive. Ventilation is standardly part of a therapeutic attempt to stabilise, treat and cure: tube-feeding is not. Moreover, ventilation replaces the patient's capacity to breathe whereas a tube does not replace the capacity to digest and merely delivers food to the stomach. Nor have all patients who are tube-fed (including, it appears, those in pvs) lost the capacity to swallow. Tube-feeding may be instituted solely to minimise the risk of the patient inhaling food and/or because spoon-feeding is thought to be too time-consuming. Even if the particular patient has lost the capacity to swallow, the tube will still not be treating anything. A feeding-tube by which liquid is delivered to the patient's stomach is, it could reasonably be argued, no more medical treatment than a catheter by which it is drained from the patient's bladder.

Even if tube-feeding *were* 'medical treatment', why was it futile? Was it because it would do nothing to restore Tony Bland to the condition towards which *medical* practice and procedures are directed, namely some level of health – an explanation consistent with the inviolability ethic?[12] Or was it rather because Tony's *life* was thought futile – an explanation inconsistent with that ethic? Dr Keith Andrews, director of medical services at the Royal Hospital for Neurodisability, and a leading authority on pvs, has commented:

---

[8] '*Bland*: Crossing the Rubicon?' (1993) 109 *LQR* 329 at 335 (original emphasis).
[9] See e.g. [1993] AC 789 at 870 *per* Lord Goff.
[10] See e.g. *Nursing Times*, 10 February 1993 at 7.   [11] [1993] AC 789 at 822.
[12] See Luke Gormally, 'Reflections on Horan and Boyle' in Luke Gormally (ed.), *The Dependent Elderly* (1992) at 47. It will be recalled that in the case of *Adams*, Mr Justice Devlin said that the 'first purpose' of medicine was the 'restoration of health'. See p. 24.

It is ironic that the only reason that tube feeding has been identified as 'treatment' has been so that it can be withdrawn ... I would argue that tube-feeding is extremely effective since it achieves all the things we intend it to do. What is really being argued is whether the patient's life is futile – hence the need to find some way of ending that life.[13]

Are there, then, grounds for concluding that the judges in *Bland* condoned the withdrawal of tube-feeding because they felt the patient's life, rather than the 'treatment', was futile?

Misunderstanding the inviolability of life

Lord Mustill rejected the notion that the state's interest in preserving life was diminished 'where the "quality" of the life is diminished by disease or incapacity'. If correct, he added, that argument would justify active as well as passive euthanasia and thus require a change in the law of murder.[14] The proposition that because of incapacity or infirmity one life was intrinsically worth less than another was, he said, the first step on a 'very dangerous road indeed' and one he was unwilling to take.[15] Yet even he held that Tony had no interest in being kept alive[16] and no best interests of any kind.[17] How do these propositions differ from a judgment that Tony's life was no longer worth while?

The view that the lives of certain patients are no longer worth living is even more pronounced in other judgments, particularly in those passages which espouse what one may call 'dualism', the notion that human beings comprise two separate entities: a 'body' and a 'person', the former being of merely instrumental value as a vehicle for the latter. In the High Court, Sir Stephen Brown described Tony thus: 'His spirit has left him and all that remains is the shell of his body ... [which is] kept functioning as a biological unit.'[18] In the Court of Appeal Lord Justice Hoffmann said: 'His body is alive, but he has no life in the sense that even the most pitifully handicapped but conscious human being has a life.'[19] Bland's existence was, he added, a 'humiliation'; he was 'grotesquely alive'.[20]

---

[13] (1995) 311 *BMJ* 1437 (letters).   [14] [1993] AC 789 at 894.   [15] Ibid.
[16] At 898.   [17] At 897.   [18] At 804.
[19] At 825. He admitted he had been influenced by reading the manuscript of Professor Dworkin's book *Life's Dominion*, a book which espouses dualism and misunderstands the sanctity of life (see (1994) 110 *LQR* 671).
[20] See also [1993] AC 789 at 863 *per* Lord Goff; at 879 *per* Lord Browne-Wilkinson; at 897 *per* Lord Mustill.

Such judicial endorsement of dualism is both novel and surprising, not only because (as Finnis points out)[21] dualism enjoys relatively little support among philosophers but also because the law has historically rejected the notion of 'biological units' which are 'inhabited' by a non-bodily person and has, on the contrary, taken the traditional, common-sense view that human bodily life *is* personal life, that living human beings are persons and that persons are, applying standard biological criteria, either alive or dead. As the judges recognised, it would be murder actively to kill Tony, regardless of his permanent unconsciousness. The law does not deny personhood and the rights it attracts because the person has lost the ability to think. We are *all* 'biological units', and our mental acts, far from being a separate form of life, something 'added to' our body (from where?), intrinsically involve, just like our physical acts, biological processes and are an expression of our one life as a human being, a human person.

For example, the judge who listens to and evaluates an argument from counsel is not a biological machine with a little mental person inside but an integrated, dynamic unity, a living human body exercising the capacities (intellectual and physical) which are inherent in his or her nature as a human being. It is because we are human beings, human 'biological units', that we have the radical capacity for acts both physical and mental. The fact that a human being has lost the ability to think does not mean he or she has lost his or her life. As Finnis puts it:

> One's living body is intrinsic, not merely instrumental, to one's personal life. Each of us has a human life (not a vegetable life plus an animal life plus a personal life); when it is flourishing that life includes all one's vital functions including speech, deliberation and choice; when gravely impaired it lacks some of those functions without ceasing to be the life of the person so impaired.[22]

Further, he adds, the fact that one is in pvs, although a gravely impairing condition which may prevent participation in basic human goods such as friendship or aesthetic experience, does not mean that one is not participating in the good, the benefit, of life.

But could it have been beneficial to feed and care for Tony even though he could not appreciate it? It is, in fact, perfectly possible to benefit

---

[21] '*Bland*: Crossing the Rubicon?' 334.   [22] Ibid.

someone, even if they are unaware of it. An example would be where Mr A, unbeknown to Ms B, deposits a large amount in Ms B's bank account, or speaks well of her to Mrs C.[23] And to say, as did Lord Mustill,[24] that Tony had 'no best interests of any kind' is open to the objection that it would surely have been contrary to his interests to use him as a sideboard, or as a sex object, or to make a spectacle of him by selling tickets to ghoulish spectators.

Given the dualistic reasoning uncritically engaged in by some of the judges, their conclusion that Tony's life was of no benefit – indeed may even have been a harm, a humiliation – comes as little surprise. That it was his *life*, and not his *tube-feeding*, that was adjudged worthless is clearly illustrated by the following passage from the speech of Lord Keith:

> [I]t is, of course, true that in general it would not be lawful for a medical practitioner who assumed responsibility for the care of an unconscious patient simply to give up treatment in circumstances where continuance of it would confer some benefit on the patient. On the other hand a medical practitioner is under no duty to continue to treat such a patient where a large body of informed and responsible medical opinion is to the effect that no benefit at all would be conferred by continuance. *Existence in a vegetative state with no prospect of recovery is by that opinion regarded as not being a benefit*, and that, if not unarguably correct, at least forms a proper basis for the decision to discontinue treatment and care: *Bolam* v. *Friern Hospital Management Committee.*[25]

But why was discontinuance not a breach of the principle of the sanctity of life, a principle which Lord Keith accepted[26] it was the concern of the state, and the judiciary as an arm of the state, to uphold? What is remarkable is that, while their Lordships agreed with the fundamental importance of the principle, none of them accurately articulated it. Lord Goff, for example, in setting out the fundamental principles of law relevant to the case, stated[27] that the 'fundamental principle is the principle of the sanctity of life'. But he then went on to claim[28] that, although this principle was fundamental, it was 'not absolute'. In support of this surprising claim,

---

[23] See Joseph Boyle, 'A Case for Sometimes Tube-Feeding Patients in Persistent Vegetative State' in Keown, chapter 13.

[24] [1993] AC 789 at 897.

[25] At 858–9 (emphasis added). See also 857, where he implies that Tony's life was meaningless; and 878–9 and 884–5 *per* Lord Browne-Wilkinson.

[26] At 859.   [27] At 863.   [28] At 864.

he made a number of observations which suggest that even this eminent Law Lord misunderstood the principle.

He observed, first, that it is lawful to kill in self-defence and, secondly, that, in the medical context, there is no absolute rule that a patient's life must be prolonged by treatment or care regardless of the circumstances. Both statements are accurate, as the discussion in Part II of the book made clear. But they do not show that the principle of the sanctity of life is 'not absolute' unless one thinks, as his Lordship appeared to, that the principle prohibits *all* killings or requires the preservation of life *at all costs*. Neither proposition is, of course, consistent with the principle as traditionally formulated and understood. His Lordship observed, thirdly, that the fact that a doctor must respect a patient's refusal of life-prolonging treatment showed that the sanctity of life yielded to the right to self-determination. Again, his Lordship seemed to think that the sanctity of life requires the preservation of life by medical treatment even when a competent patient declines treatment designed to secure that end. Again, this is not so. Fourthly, he distinguished between a doctor, on the one hand, omitting to provide life-prolonging treatment or care and, on the other, administering a lethal drug. 'So to act', he said, 'is to cross the Rubicon which runs between on the one hand the care of the living patient and on the other hand euthanasia – actively causing his death to avoid or to end his suffering.'[29] But, as we saw in chapter 4, the intentional killing by one person of another person in his care, even if carried out by omission, breaches the principle of the sanctity or inviolability of life.

Responsible medical opinion: the 'Bolam test'

The Law Lords decided that Tony's doctor was under no duty to continue treatment and tube-feeding if he felt that continuation was no longer in the patient's best interests and if his opinion was supported (as it was) by a 'responsible body' of medical opinion. Indeed, as Lord Browne-Wilkinson pointed out,[30] if the doctor decided that treatment was no longer in the patient's best interests, he was under a *duty* to withdraw it. Since the doctor could only lawfully treat the patient if he believed it was in the patient's best interests, continuing treatment when he did not believe it to be so would constitute the crime and tort of battery.

[29] At 865.   [30] At 883.

But why should a judgment about which patients have lives 'worth living' be delegated to a 'responsible body' of medical opinion? Even if this comprehensive judgment about the worth of another could indeed be made (which the inviolability principle denies), what qualifies *a doctor* to make it? Lord Mustill aptly observed[31] that the decision could be said to be ethical and that there was no logical reason why the opinions of doctors should be decisive. His was, however, a lone voice. Lord Browne-Wilkinson expressly stated[32] that one doctor could decide, because of his ethical views about the sanctity of life, that his patient was 'entitled to stay alive' whereas another doctor who saw 'no merit in perpetuating a life of which the patient is unaware' could lawfully stop his patient's treatment.

Their Lordships did observe that, for the present, all cases like Tony's should be brought before the High Court for a declaration. But what is the court's role? Is it, as it appears to be, essentially to confirm that the doctor's opinion is supported by a responsible body of medical opinion? Or is it to lay down judicial criteria for deciding which lives are worth while? If the latter, what are those criteria?[33]

A slippery slope?

In the Court of Appeal, Lord Justice Hoffmann said[34] that it was 'absurd to conjure up the spectre of eugenics' as a reason against the decision in *Bland*. However, once Quality supplants inviolability there is no reason in principle why the Quality threshold should stop at pvs. Finnis has observed that it is one thing to say that one should not treat people in ways which affront their inalienable dignity but quite another to say that, because of their physical or mental disabilty, they *have* no dignity or, worse, that they *are* an indignity. How can the latter judgment logically be limited to those in pvs? As he pointed out: 'Epithets of indignity and humiliation could easily be applied (as in recent history) to various classes of severely handicapped people, many of whom, moreover, cannot exercise the distinctively human or "personal" forms of understanding and response.'[35] Lord Mustill raised,[36] without resolving, the case of the patient who has 'glimmerings of awareness' and Lord Browne-Wilkinson[37] the case of the

---

[31] At 898–9.   [32] At 884.   [33] See *Frenchay NHS Healthcare Trust* v. *S* [1994] 1 WLR 601.
[34] [1993] AC 789 at 831.   [35] '*Bland*: Crossing the Rubicon?' 336.
[36] [1993] AC 789 at 899.   [37] At 885.

patient with slight chances of improvement or with 'very slight sensate awareness'.

In May 1995, the Irish Supreme Court, following *Bland*, permitted (by a 4-1 majority) the withdrawal of tube-feeding from a patient who was not in pvs and retained some cognitive function.[38] It affirmed the decision of the first-instance judge who stated that if the patient were aware of her condition 'that would be a terrible torment to her and her situation would be *worse* than if she were fully P.V.S.'.[39] Leaving aside the reasoning of the judges who favoured withdrawal (which is more, rather than less, vulnerable to criticism than the reasoning in *Bland*), the Irish case illustrates the inherently arbitrary nature of Quality of life judgments. The criticism bites even more deeply when the judgment is, *via* the *Bolam* test, delegated to 'responsible' medical opinion. The question then simply becomes whether there is a body of 'responsible' medical opinion which supports the doctor's view that the patient's life is worthless, whether or not a larger body of medical opinion disagrees. The arbitrariness is underlined by the fact that medical opinion is often divided and in a state of flux. A patient may be treated by a doctor who thinks his life worth while but that doctor's ethical views may change or the patient may come under the care of a doctor with different ethical views. The upshot would appear to be that if a doctor responsible, say, for a patient with advanced Alzheimer's disease thinks the patient's life is of no benefit, and the doctor's opinion coincides with that of a 'responsible body' of medical opinion, the doctor may – if not *must* – cease treating the patient.

The risk of a slippery slope is aggravated by the practical difficulties involved in accurately diagnosing the condition which is thought to justify non-treatment. Even pvs is not a clear-cut syndrome and misdiagnoses are not uncommon. A study carried out by Dr Keith Andrews, published in July 1996, disclosed that of 40 patients referred to the Royal Hospital for Neurodisability as in pvs between 1992 and 1995, no fewer than 17 (43%) had been misdiagnosed. All but one of the 17 had been referred by a hospital consultant, mostly by a neurologist, neurosurgeon or rehabilitation specialist. The study concluded that accurate diagnosis is possible but requires the skills of a multidisciplinary team experienced

---

[38] *In the Matter of a Ward of Court* [1995] 2 ILRM 410; John Keown, 'Life and Death in Dublin' [1996] 55 (1) *Camb LJ* 6.

[39] Lynch J., quoted by O'Flaherty J. in [1995] 2 ILRM 401 at 432 (emphasis added).

in the management of people with complex disabilities.[40] The procedural rules governing applications for declarations in cases of pvs state that there should be two neurological reports on the patient, one commissioned by the Official Solicitor. However, the rules do not require the involvement of such a team.[41] Furthermore, the risks of misdiagnosis must increase if time is short. In one case in which the Court of Appeal declared that it would be lawful not to reinsert a feeding-tube which had become disconnected, the court did so even though there had been insufficient time for the Official Solicitor to obtain an independent neurological opinion.[42] There is room for doubt as to whether the patient in that case was in fact in pvs.

In a later case the patient did not wholly fulfil the Royal College of Physicians guidelines for pvs as she was apparently able to track movement with her eyes and to demonstrate a 'menace' response. Two experts did not, therefore, diagnose her as being in a 'permanent vegetative state' though a third did. Counsel for the Official Solicitor therefore opposed the granting of a declaration. The judge, Sir Stephen Brown, noted that all the witnesses agreed that the patient was totally unaware and he concluded that 'for all practical purposes' she was in a 'permanent vegetative state'. He added: 'there is no evidence of any meaningful life whatsoever'.[43] His Lordship omitted to lay down the criteria for determining when a patient's life was 'meaningful'. Such cases do little to assuage concerns about the prospect of a slippery slope.

Misunderstanding autonomy

The courts in *Bland* undervalued human life. But they also appeared to *over*value individual autonomy, even to the extent of suggesting that the latter trumped the former. We noted above Lord Goff's statement that the patient's right to self-determination overrides the sanctity of life and we observed that this statement is misleading if it suggests that the sanctity of life is breached whenever a doctor allows a patient to refuse a life-saving treatment. What *would* breach the principle, however, is a *suicidal* refusal

---

[40] Keith Andrews et al., 'Misdiagnosis of the Vegetative State: Retrospective Study in a Rehabilitation Unit' (1996) 313 *BMJ* 13.
[41] [1994] 2 All ER 413.
[42] *Frenchay Healthcare NHS Trust* v. *S* [1994] 2 All ER 403; John Keown, 'Applying *Bland*' [1994] 53 (3) *Camb LJ* 456.
[43] *Re D* (1997) 38 BMLR 1 at 10. See also *Re H* (1997) 38 BMLR 11; *Re R* [1996] 2 Fam LR 99.

of treatment by the patient and the intentional assistance or encourage-
ment of that refusal by the doctor, whether by act or omission. Whether
his Lordship was intending to condone such refusals and assistance in
them is unclear. He said that where a patient refused life-prolonging treatment: 'there is no question of the patient having committed suicide, nor
therefore of the doctor having aided or abetted him in doing so'.[44]

If his Lordship was referring to the refusal of a treatment because it
is futile or too burdensome, this is uncontroversial. But if he included a
refusal *by which the patient intends to commit suicide*, the statement suggests
that patients may now lawfully commit suicide by refusals of treatment
(or care?) and that doctors may lawfully intentionally assist or encourage
such refusals, albeit by omission. This interpretation could look for support to the statement of Lord Justice Hoffmann in the Court of Appeal
that the decriminalisation of suicide by the Suicide Act 1961 'was a recognition that the principle of self-determination should in that case prevail
over the sanctity of life'.[45] However, as we saw in chapter 6, the reason for
decriminalisation was *not* respect for self-determination but a belief that
the suicidal needed help rather than punishment. In other words, suicide
was decriminalised not to help people to commit suicide but to help them
not to.[46]

In *Secretary of State for the Home Department* v. *Robb*,[47] Mr Justice Thorpe
cited *Bland* as authority for the proposition that a patient who refuses life-
prolonging treatment which results in death does not commit suicide
and that the doctor who complies with the patient's wishes does not aid or
abet suicide. Granting a declaration that the Home Office and medical and
nursing staff might lawfully abide by a prisoner's refusal to take food and
water, he observed that '[t]he principle of the sanctity of human life in this
jurisdiction is seen to yield to the principle of self-determination',[48] adding
that, although the state interest in preventing suicide was recognisable, it
had no application to a case such as that before him where the refusal of
food and treatment 'in the exercise of the right of self-determination does
not constitute an act of suicide'.

If Mr Justice Thorpe was of the opinion, as he seems to have been, that
suicide may only be committed by an *act* and not by a refusal of food

---

[44] [1993] AC 789 at 864.
[45] At 827. See also 814 *per* Sir Thomas Bingham MR, who assumed that a refusal of tube-feeding
is not suicidal.
[46] See pp. 64–6.   [47] [1995] 1 All ER 677.   [48] At 682.

and treatment, then he advances no argument or authority in support, beyond the comments in *Bland*. But this is bootstrap authority: those comments are themselves either ambiguous or bereft of authority and the point was simply not argued in that case. Moreover, the apparently unqualified proposition that the right to self-determination takes precedence over the sanctity of life is difficult to square with the prohibition on assisted suicide and murder on request.[49] It also sits uneasily with the later decision of the House of Lords in *Reeves* v. *Commissioner of Police of the Metropolis* in which the House held that police and prison authorities owe prisoners, even if they are competent, a duty to take care to prevent them from committing suicide.[50]

A more recent case still throws further doubt on the existence of any right of a prisoner intentionally to starve himself to death: *R* v. *Collins and Ashworth Hospital Authority ex parte Brady*.[51] It concerned Ian Brady who was serving a life sentence for his part in the gruesome 'Moors Murders'. Diagnosed as mentally ill, Brady had been transferred to the Ashworth secure mental hospital. The proceedings arose out of his decision to go on hunger strike in protest at the way he had been dealt with in the hospital. The hospital initiated force-feeding and Brady sought judicial review of that decision. Mr Justice Maurice Kay held that the force-feeding was justified on two grounds. The first was the Mental Health Act 1983, which permits treatment for mental disorder to be given without the patient's consent. The second was that Brady was mentally incompetent to refuse force-feeding and his doctors were therefore justified in treating him in accordance with what they, in their reasonable clinical judgment, considered to be in his best interests. Interestingly, the judge went on to consider the argument of counsel for the hospital authority that there was a third ground on which the force-feeding could be justified: that the patient's right to self-determination was not absolute and had to be balanced

---

[49] For an ethical and legal analysis of pre-incompetence refusals of treatment see Stuart Hornett, 'Advance Directives: A Legal and Ethical Analysis' in Keown, chapter 17; John Finnis, 'Living Will Legislation' in Gormally, 167–76.

[50] [1999] 3 All ER 897. Lord Hoffmann said (at 902–3) that a duty to protect a person of full understanding from causing harm to himself was very rare but that it arose in this case from the complete control which the police or prison authorities had over the prisoner, combined with the special danger of people in prison taking their own lives. See also Lord Hope at 913 (the duty is owed to the prisoner if it is known he may engage in self-mutilation or suicide while he is in their custody, 'irrespective of whether he is mentally disordered or of sound mind').

[51] [2000] 8 Lloyd's Rep Med 355.

against public interests such as the preservation of life, the prevention of suicide, the maintenance of the integrity of the medical profession, and the preservation of institutional discipline. Counsel argued that *Robb* did no more than establish that, on its facts, there was no *duty* to force-feed: it did not consider whether there was a *power* to do so.

The judge, noting the Law Lords' decision in *Reeves*, observed:

> It would be somewhat odd if there is a duty to prevent suicide by an act (for example, the use of a knife left in the cell) but not even a power to intervene to prevent self-destruction by starvation. I can see no moral justification for the law indulging its fascination with the difference between acts and omissions in a context such as this and no logical need for it to do so.[52]

Without deciding the point, his Lordship added that it seemed to him that in the case of a mentally ill but legally competent patient who was detained in hospital for treatment for mental disorder, there should be circumstances in which state or public interests such as those mentioned by counsel 'would properly prevail over a self-determined hunger strike so as to enable, even if not to require, intervention'.[53]

His Lordship's observations are, with respect, a welcome corrective to the earlier judicial *dicta* which seem to suggest that the right to refuse treatment or sustenance, even with a suicidal intent, is absolute. There is indeed much to be said for the view that there is at least a power, if not a duty, to intervene to prevent even competent patients in hospital from committing suicide by refusing treatment or basic care.[54] And whether or not there is a duty to prevent them from doing this, there is at least a duty not intentionally to assist them.

From Quality to inviolability

Explaining the shift from inviolability

What accounts for the judges' misunderstanding in the *Bland* case of the inviolability principle, a principle which has long been at the heart of the common law? One plausible explanation is that the principle does not appear to have been accurately set out before them by any of the counsel who appeared in the case. Even learned and experienced counsel for the

---

[52] At 367.   [53] Ibid.

[54] See P. D. G. Skegg, *Law, Ethics and Medicine* (revised edn, 1988) 111. Cf. Ian Kennedy and Andrew Grubb (eds.), *Medical Law: Text with Materials* (3rd edn, 2000) 910–24.

Official Solicitor appears to have confused inviolability with vitalism. In the Court of Appeal, for example, he argued that if Tony showed signs of life-threatening failure of, in succession, heart, lungs, liver, kidneys, spleen, bladder and pancreas, the doctor would be under a duty to perform surgery to rectify the failure. The presiding judge, Sir Thomas Bingham MR, observed: 'Such a suggestion is in my view so repugnant to one's sense of how one individual should behave towards another that I would reject it as possibly representing the law.'[55] This observation was correct since counsel's argument was surely vitalistic.

Bland was not the first time Mr Munby QC had, as counsel for the Official Solicitor, advanced a vitalistic understanding of the sanctity of life. In *Re J (A Minor)*,[56] the previous leading case on withholding/withdrawing medical treatment, the question was whether a disabled baby, who had been made a ward of court, should be artificially ventilated. Mr Munby made two alternative submissions. The first, his 'absolute' (or vitalist) submission, was 'that a court is never justified in withholding consent to treatment which could enable a child to survive a life-threatening condition, whatever the pain or other side-effects inherent in the treatment, and whatever the quality of the life which it would experience thereafter'.[57]

The alternative, 'qualified' (or Quality of life) submission[58] (based on the reasoning of the Court of Appeal in the earlier case of *Re B*)[59] was that a court could withhold consent to treatment only if it was certain that the Quality of the child's life would be 'intolerable' to the child. In *Re J*, then, the court was presented with only two alternatives: vitalism or Quality of life. It preferred the latter, with the rider that the Quality of life was to be judged from the perspective of the child. As Lord Justice Taylor put it:

> the correct approach is for the court to judge the quality of life the child would have to endure if given the treatment, and decide whether in all the circumstances such a life would be so afflicted as to be intolerable to that child. I say 'to that child' because the test should not be whether the life would be tolerable to the decider. The test must be whether the child in question, if capable of exercising sound judgment, would consider the life tolerable.[60]

---

[55] [1993] AC 789 at 815. See also Butler-Sloss LJ at 822–3.
[56] *Re J (A Minor)(Wardship: Medical Treatment)* [1991] 1 Fam LR 366.
[57] At 370–1.   [58] At 373.   [59] [1981] 1 WLR 1421.
[60] [1991] 1 Fam LR 366 at 383–4. Given that the child had never been capable of making any judgment, asking what the child would decide is something of a fiction. It is remarkable that the courts should import 'substituted judgment' in the case of a child who has never been competent and reject it in the case of an adult like Tony Bland who once was. If the court

It appears, then, that in *Bland*, as in *Re J* before it, the inviolability of life was not heard; that the choice as presented and perceived was between vitalism and Quality of life, and that the judges (unsurprisingly) opted for Quality of life. Despite the fundamental importance attached to the inviolability of life by the judges who sat in *Bland*, it is by no means clear that any had the benefit of an accurate appreciation of it.

This is not to single out Mr Munby for criticism. He was a leading, respected practitioner with probably unrivalled experience of acting for the Official Solicitor in medico-legal matters.[61] The fact that even he misunderstood the inviolability principle suggests how widespread such misunderstanding is within the legal profession, even among specialists in medical law. Indeed, *none* of the specialist counsel involved in *Bland* accurately articulated the principle.[62] It may be that the shift from inviolability in this case has other explanations, such as judicial deference to medical opinion or changing social values. But the fact that the judges misunderstood the principle meant that the Quality of life approach won the day without its opponent even having taken to the field.

Applying inviolability

What answer would the traditional ethic, accurately understood and applied, have yielded in the *Bland* case? Many advocates of inviolability agree that since medical treatment such as ventilation and/or antibiotics can do nothing to restore those in pvs to a state of health or some approximation to it, they are medically futile and need not be provided. On the question whether tube-feeding is simply medical treatment or basic care, there is less agreement: some classify tube-feeding as medical treatment which may,

had applied substituted judgment in *Bland*, and declared that the feeding should be stopped because Tony would have chosen to be starved to death rather than live in pvs, and if the court endorsed this choice as reasonable, it would still have been endorsing a Quality of life approach.

[61] His distinction was later recognised by his elevation to the High Court bench.

[62] A major source of the misunderstanding may well have been Kennedy and Grubb's *Medical Law: Text and Materials* (1st edn, 1989). This was then, and remains, the leading reference work on medical law in England among academics and practitioners alike. Unfortunately, citing extracts from some of the sanctity of life's leading critics, it seriously misstated the principle, confusing it with vitalism (see 941–6). The editors also misunderstood the principle of 'double effect'. They wrote: 'if an act may have two effects and the actor *desires* only one of them, which is considered a *good* effect, then he should be regarded as blameless even though his act also produces a bad effect' (at 938, original emphasis). Cf. the discussion of double effect in chapter 2 of this book.

therefore, be withdrawn; others (probably advancing the more representative viewpoint) claim that it is basic care which ought, therefore, to be provided.[63] Although the traditional ethic does not, as yet, unequivocally rule out the withdrawal of tube-feeding on the ground that it is futile medical treatment, it certainly rules out its withdrawal on the ground that the *patient* is futile. While the ethic may currently allow for a legitimate range of answers on tube-feeding those in pvs, it does insist on asking the right question: 'Is tube-feeding "treatment" and, if so, is it worth while?' and not 'Is the patient's life worth while?'

How, then, could their Lordships have developed the law in accordance with the sanctity of life principle? As Finnis has pointed out, cases such as *Gibbins and Proctor*[64] establish that one who undertakes the care of a dependent person and omits to provide necessary food or clothing with the intention of causing death (or serious harm) commits murder if death results. He adds that those cases do not confront the argument successfully raised in *Bland* – that one who has undertaken a duty of care may yet have no duty to exercise it so as to sustain life – but that 'the proper application or extension of their rule to meet that argument was surely this: those who have a duty to care for someone may never exercise it in a manner intended to bring about that person's death'.[65]

Bland decides the opposite. And it does so at the expense of radical inconsistency, prohibiting as murder intentional killing by an act but permitting intentional killing by omission. Imagine the following scenario. X is a patient in pvs who is free of any suffering and who has made no request to be killed. X's doctor decides that X's life is no longer worth living and stops his tube-feeding with intent to kill him. In the next bed is Y, a patient dying in agony who, after serious reflection, begs the doctor to kill him by lethal injection. The doctor, fearful of prosecution, refuses. A third patient, Z, moved by Y's predicament, produces a gun, holds it to the doctor's head and threatens, 'If you don't kill Y, I will shoot you dead.' The doctor, to save his own life, administers a lethal drug to Y. The doctor's killing of X is lawful; his killing of Y is murder.

Small wonder that Lord Mustill expressed his 'acute unease' about resting his decision on a distinction between acts and omissions, given that

---

[63] See e.g. Luke Gormally, 'Definitions of Personhood: Implications for the Care of PVS Patients' (1993) 9.3 *Ethics and Medicine* 44 at 47; Boyle, 'A Case for Sometimes Tube-Feeding Patients in Persistent Vegetative State'.
[64] See p. 59, n. 6.   [65] Finnis, '*Bland*: Crossing the Rubicon?' 333.

'however much the terminologies may differ the ethical status of the two courses of action is for all relevant purposes indistinguishable'.[66] But is it not the judges' reasoning in *Bland* which has distorted the legal structure, rather than vice versa? *Bland* is the culmination of a series of cases in which the courts have veered away from the traditional ethic, which coherently combines sanctity and quality in a consistent and principled legal opposition to intentional killing, towards a new ethic which incoherently combines sanctity and Quality and produces a misshapen opposition to active killing but not intentional killing by omission.

The Law Lords in *Bland* urged Parliament to consider the issues it raised. As we noted earlier, a Select Committee of the House of Lords, which included Lord Mustill, was established in the wake of the case by the House of Lords and the Committee recommended that the law should not be relaxed to permit active intentional killing. Reaffirming the prohibition on intentional killing, the Committee observed: 'That prohibition is the cornerstone of law and of social relationships. It protects each one of us impartially, embodying the belief that all are equal.'[67] On the question of tube-feeding patients in pvs, the Committee was divided between those who regarded it as basic care which should be provided and those who regarded it as medical treatment which could properly be withdrawn. Nevertheless, the Committee was unanimous that the question need not, indeed should not, usually arise since it was proper to withdraw medical treatment, including antibiotics, from such patients.[68] However, by confining itself to considering *active* killing and ignoring intentional killing by omission the Committee did little to resolve the inconsistency in the law created by *Bland*.[69] Consequently, the law remains in the same misshapen state in which the Law Lords left it.

Lord Lowry referred[70] in *Bland* to a gap between 'old law' and 'new medicine' and observed that it was the role of the legislature to remedy any disparity between society's notions of what the law is and what is right. But if their Lordships were looking to the legislature to render the law consistent by decriminalising active intentional killing, the legislature

---

[66] [1993] AC 789 at 887. See also 865 *per* Lord Goff; 877 *per* Lord Lowry; 885 *per* Lord Browne-Wilkinson.

[67] Lords' Report, para. 237.   [68] Ibid., para. 257.

[69] The Committee gave no reason for limiting its definition of euthanasia to active killing (ibid., para. 20) nor did it rule out Quality of life judgments (see e.g. ibid., para. 255). It did not, therefore, advance a consistent inviolability ethic.

[70] [1993] AC 789 at 877.

has declined the invitation and bounced the misshapen ball back into the judicial forum. The question which the Committee said should not arise has continued to do so as courts continue to permit hospitals to terminate the lives of those considered to be in pvs.[71] Not even the incorporation of the European Convention of Human Rights into English law – with its clear requirement in Article 2 that everyone's right to life shall be protected by law, and that 'No one shall be deprived of his life intentionally' – has induced the courts to reverse the ruling in *Bland* that patients in pvs may lawfully be intentionally killed.

In *NHS Trust A* v. *M; NHS Trust B* v. *H*,[72] the new President of the Family Division of the High Court, Dame Elizabeth Butler-Sloss, held that withdrawing tube-feeding from a pvs patient does not breach Article 2 because, although it is 'intentional' (purposeful) killing, it does not amount to a 'deprivation' of the patient's life: 'Although the intention in withdrawing artificial nutrition and hydration in PVS cases is to hasten death, in my judgment the phrase "deprivation of life" must import a deliberate act, as opposed to an omission.'[73]

Her Ladyship's reasoning tracks the same 'morally and intellectually misshapen' distinction between acts and omissions exhibited by the Law Lords in *Bland*. An ideal opportunity to restore the law's moral and intellectual shape was therefore missed. It is to be hoped that the European Court of Human Rights soon has and takes the opportunity to effect that restoration.

Conclusions

First, the ethical principle of the inviolability of life, which has long informed the common law, offers a middle way between the poles of vitalism on the one hand and Quality of life on the other. *Bland* represented a swerve towards Quality of life, accepting that certain lives are of no benefit and may lawfully be intentionally terminated by starvation and dehydration.

Secondly, accentuating the swerve was a shift from a traditional understanding of the value of autonomy – autonomy as enabling individuals to participate in the moral enterprise of making choiceworthy decisions, decisions which respect objective moral norms and promote the flourishing

---

[71] See p. 227.   [72] [2001] 1 Lloyd's Rep Med 27.
[73] At 33. See John Keown, 'Dehydration and Human Rights' [2001] 60(1) *Camb LJ* 53.

of the decision-maker and others – to an essentially self-justificatory understanding of autonomy in which choices merit respect simply by virtue of being choices.

Thirdly, *Bland* has indeed left the law in a 'morally and intellectually misshapen' state. The law prohibits doctors caring for patients in pvs from actively killing them but permits (if not requires) them to kill by omission. The case also suggests that, while doctors may not actively assist competent patients to commit suicide, they may assist them to do so by omission – by intentionally assisting suicidal refusals of treatment. The significance of *Bland* is profound: although the House of Lords Select Committee reaffirmed that intentional killing by an act, even on request, should not be made lawful, the Law Lords have decided that intentional killing by omission, even without request, already is. The making of such a fundamental change in the law seems, moreover, difficult to reconcile with the guidelines for judicial development of the law laid down by Lord Lowry in the case of *C* v. *DPP* which we noted in chapter 17.[74]

Fourthly, given that the Law Lords have embraced the Quality of life principle and effectively delegated the judgment as to which lives are of no benefit to medical opinion, there is little reason to expect that judgment to be confined to patients in pvs. Moreover, the ramifications of the courts' adoption of an individualist and amoral understanding of autonomy may also prove profound, not least in its potentially corrosive effect on the legal prohibition of assisted suicide and consensual murder.

Fifthly, the Law Lords' rejection of the sanctity principle and their apparent endorsement of an amoral concept of autonomy appear to have been based on a misunderstanding of the traditional ethic. Lord Mustill, surely rightly, observed[75] that it was a great pity that the Attorney-General had not appeared to represent the interests of the state in maintaining citizens' lives. It is to be hoped that the Attorney-General will appear in an appropriate future case to ensure that the inviolability of life at least gets a fair hearing. The hearing may be receptive: it is encouraging that in the conjoined twins case the presiding judge in the Court of Appeal, Lord Justice Ward, criticised the view of the judge in the lower court that the life of the weaker twin was a harm rather than a benefit and also expressly approved the inviolability principle as it has been set out in this book.[76]

---

[74] [1995] 2 All ER 43 at 52. See p. 192, n. 2. See also *Airedale NHS Trust* v. *Bland* [1993] AC 789 at 865 *per* Lord Goff; at 880 *per* Lord Browne-Wilkinson; at 890 *per* Lord Mustill.
[75] [1993] AC 789 at 889.   [76] *Re A (Children)* [2000] 4 All ER 961 at 997–1004.

Sixthly, the decision whether to withdraw treatment and tube-feeding from a patient in pvs should be based on an evaluation of the worthwhileness of the treatment, not the supposed worthwhileness of the patient. While there appears to be something approaching a consensus that it is proper to withdraw treatment in such a case, there is a good argument that tube-feeding constitutes basic care and that it should, at least presumptively, be provided. Even if it were the better view that tube-feeding may properly be withdrawn, this should be because it, and not the patient, is judged futile.

Bland rendered the law morally and intellectually misshapen, hypocritical rather than Hippocratic. But the Law Lords are not alone in promoting this legal revolution. For, as the decision of the Irish Supreme Court illustrates, *Bland* is but one of several leading cases in common law jurisdictions that could have been used to illustrate the tendency of judges across the Western world to undermine the traditional ethic.[77] Judges, often regarded

---

[77] For example, Professor Larry Gostin wrote in 1985 that the term 'quality of life' had entered Anglo-American jurisprudence to justify the withholding of medically indicated treatment from severely handicapped infants 'whose life would be so bereft of enjoyment as not to be worth living'. He added that it was difficult to argue with the premise underlying the 'quality of life' position as there must come a point when life is 'so devoid of meaning and contentment that it is not worth living' ('A Moment in Human Development: Legal Protection, Ethical Standards and Social Policy on the Selective Non-Treatment of Handicapped Neonates' (1985) 11 *Am J Law Med* 32, 39–40).

Examples of US cases which accommodate (or at the very least are reasonably open to the interpretation of accommodating) the notions that the supposed 'worth' of a patient's life can be a justifiable reason for withdrawing life-saving treatment or tube-feeding, and that patients have an absolute right to refuse treatment or tube-feeding even with intent to commit suicide, include: *In the Matter of Claire Conroy* (1985) 486 A 2d 1209 and *Bouvia* v. *Superior Court* (1986) 225 Cal Rptr 297 (Cal CA).

In *Conroy*, the New Jersey Supreme Court held (at 1229) that treatment or tube-feeding could lawfully be withdrawn from an incompetent patient when it was clear that the patient would have refused it in the circumstances. It said (at 1224) that refusing treatment 'may not properly be viewed as an attempt to commit suicide. Refusing medical intervention merely allows the disease to take its natural course' and added that patients who refuse life-sustaining treatment 'may not harbor a specific intent to die'. But equally, of course, they *may*, and the court evaded the question of why refusals *with* such intent would not be suicidal. It is obviously no answer to say that they are merely 'letting nature take its course' since death is hastened by, and is intended to be hastened by, the decision to refuse treatment. If a diabetic refuses insulin in order to kill himself so his wife can claim his life insurance, why is this not suicide? If a father intentionally starves his baby to death, would the court acquit him on the ground that he was 'merely letting nature take its course'?

The court went on that, in the absence of any evidence that the patient would have refused it, treatment or tube-feeding could still lawfully be withheld or withdrawn if the 'net burdens *of the patient's life* with the treatment should clearly and markedly outweigh the benefits that

as one of the most conservative arms of the state, are, it could reasonably be argued, playing a role no less significant than legislatures in subverting that ethic by converting a right *not* to be killed into a duty *to* kill and a right to self-determination into a right to self-termination.

the patient derives from life' (at 1232, emphasis added). Despite the court's denial that it was thereby authorising non-treatment based on assessments of personal worth or social utility, its reasoning, focussing on the worth of the patient's *life* rather than the worth of the *treatment*, clearly endorses a Quality approach.

In *Bouvia*, the California Court of Appeal allowed a 28-year-old quadriplegic patient with severe cerebral palsy to demand the withdrawal of tube-feeding. The court rejected the hospital's argument that she intended thereby to commit suicide. Despite a finding to the contrary by the trial judge, the court, echoing the court in *Conroy*, concluded (at 306) that she merely wanted 'to allow nature to take its course'. Similarly evading the importance of intention, the court in *Bouvia*, in a question-begging criticism of the trial judge's finding, stated: 'If a right exists, it matters not what "motivates" its exercise.' By contrast, the concurring opinion of Justice Compton squarely addressed the issue, and in so doing, illustrates the extent to which some judges have rejected the inviolability principle. The judge said (at 307):

> I have no doubt that Elizabeth Bouvia wants to die; and if she had the full use of even one hand, could probably find a way to end her life – in a word – commit suicide. In order to seek the assistance which she needs in ending her life by the only means she sees available – starvation she has had to stultify her position before this court by disavowing her desire to end her life in such a fashion and proclaiming that she will eat all that she can physically tolerate. Even the majority opinion here must necessarily 'dance' around the issue.

Justice Compton added: 'Elizabeth apparently has made a conscious and informed choice that she prefers death to continued existence in her helpless and, to her, intolerable condition. I believe she has an absolute right to effectuate that decision.' The judge continued: 'The right to die is an integral part of our right to control our own destinies so long as the rights of others are not affected. That right should, in my opinion, include the ability to enlist assistance from others, including the medical profession, in making death as painless and quick as possible.'

Further, the decisions of the Federal Courts of Appeal for the Second and Ninth Circuits in *Quill* and *Glucksberg* respectively, considered in chapter 17, show just how far, and how fast, some courts in the USA have moved from inviolability to Quality.

20

Beyond *Bland*: the BMA guidance on withholding/withdrawing medical treatment

In June 1999 the BMA published important guidance on the withholding/withdrawal of 'medical treatment', so defined as to include food and water delivered by tube.[1] The guidance endorses the withholding/withdrawal of tube-delivered food and water not only from patients in pvs but also from other non-terminally ill patients such as those with severe dementia or serious stroke.[2] The underlying justification for non-treatment appears (as in *Bland*) to be that such lives are not worth living and that it is right to end them by purposeful omission.

Published by the Medical Ethics Committee of the BMA, the guidance was prepared by a working group comprising nine of the Committee's twenty-five members and was written by three members of the BMA administrative staff.[3] The Foreword states that a consultation exercise which the BMA had carried out in 1998,[4] and which had generated over 2,000 responses, has revealed a need for guidance and that one of the most difficult issues was withholding/withdrawing tube-delivered food and water. Confusion had arisen from the fact that judicial guidance on this question related only to patients in pvs, and the BMA therefore wanted to provide guidance outlining the criteria to be applied in other conditions, such as advanced dementia or severe stroke.[5] The guidance sought to 'document

---

[1] *Withholding and Withdrawing Life-Prolonging Medical Treatment. Guidance for Decision Making* (1999) (hereafter 'Guidance').

[2] Indeed, the main focus of the guidance is not on the terminally ill, but on those who could live for months or even years (Guidance, 4 para. 2.1).

[3] The Working Group comprised: Dr Michael Wilks (Chairman of the Medical Ethics Committee), Dr Andrew Carney, Professor Len Doyal, Professor Raanan Gillon, Professor Sheila McLean, Mr Derek Morgan, Dr Jane Richards, Dr Jeremy Wight and Ms Rosie Wilkinson. It was written by Veronica English, Gillian Romano-Critchley and Ann Sommerville (Guidance, xi–xiii).

[4] Guidance, xv (refering to *Withholding and Withdrawing Treatment: A Consultation Paper from the BMA's Medical Ethics Committee* (1998)).

[5] Guidance, ix.

the type of factors which should be taken into account, the process which should be followed and the safeguards which should be in place to ensure that these decisions, and decisions to withhold or withdraw other life-prolonging treatments, are made appropriately'.[6]

The BMA is to be commended for seeking to provide guidance on what can prove complex ethical, legal, medical and personal decisions. The guidance has not, however, proved uncontroversial. More than 6,000 doctors reportedly supported the launch of an organisation, the 'Medical Ethics Alliance', to oppose it.[7] Religious leaders such the Chief Rabbi, Dr Jonathan Sacks, have also been critical.[8]

Some of the guidance is uncontroversially good, such as its emphasis on the importance of communication between doctors, patients and relatives.[9] The main focus of this chapter, however, is on its most controversial aspect, namely, its endorsement of the withholding/withdrawal of tube-delivered food and water not only from patients with no awareness, such as those in pvs, but also from those with severely impaired mental capacity, such as those with severe dementia. The chapter, which is divided into five sections, advances three criticisms. First it questions the guidance's reasons for holding that the delivery of food and water by tube constitutes 'medical treatment'. Secondly it criticises, as incompatible with the BMA's opposition to the active, intentional termination of any patient's life, the guidance's endorsement of withdrawing treatment and tube-feeding from some incompetent patients on the ground that their lives lack worth. Similarly, it criticises, as inconsistent with the BMA's opposition to active assisted suicide, the guidance's apparent endorsement of assisting refusals of treatment and tube-feeding which are suicidal. Thirdly it observes that the vulnerability of the guidance to such criticisms is a reflection of the guidance's heavy reliance on legal precedent rather than ethical reasoning, and ethically controversial legal precedent at that.

Centrally, the chapter challenges the guidance's apparent endorsement of withholding/withdrawing tube-delivered food and water from non-terminally ill patients with no awareness or with severely limited mental capacity, who will as an inevitable result die from dehydration and

---

[6] Ibid., x.
[7] 'BMA's Policy Condemned as "Euthanasia"' *The Times*, 12 July 1999.
[8] Press Release, Office of the Chief Rabbi, 5 July 1999.
[9] See, e.g., Guidance, 48 para. 18.4.

starvation, *because their lives are thought to lack worth.* Like the report of the BMA Working Party on euthanasia in 1988,[10] the guidance is vulnerable to the charge of ethical incoherence by opposing the intentional termination of any patient's life *by an act* but allowing the intentional termination of some patients' lives *by omission.*

Tube-feeding as medical treatment not basic care

The guidance applies to the withholding/withdrawal of 'medical treatment' and it regards tube-feeding as 'medical treatment'. It contrasts 'medical treatment' with 'basic care', which it defines as 'those procedures essential to keep an individual comfortable', including the 'administration of medication or the performance of any procedure which is solely or primarily designed to provide comfort to the patient or alleviate that person's pain, symptoms or distress'. Basic care includes 'warmth, shelter, pain relief, management of distressing symptoms ... hygiene measures (such as the management of incontinence) and the offer of oral nutrition and hydration'.[11] This definition is, however, at once too broad and too narrow: too broad in that it is wide enough to include palliative *medicine*;[12] too narrow in that it excludes pouring food and water down a tube. The classification of tube-feeding as 'medical treatment' or 'basic care' is no mere semantic exercise: it will influence if not determine whether thousands of incompetent patients are given food and water or are left to die from dehydration. Given that profound consequence, the guidance must surely advance correspondingly weighty argumentation to support its classification. What, then, is the guidance's argument?

Remarkably, it is brief and heavily reliant on caselaw. The guidance quotes[13] the statement by Lord Goff in *Bland* that[14] 'There is overwhelming evidence that, in the medical profession, artificial feeding is regarded as a form of medical treatment; and even if it is not strictly medical treatment,

---

[10] *Euthanasia. Report of the Working Party to Review the British Medical Association's Guidance on Euthanasia* (1988). For a thorough critique of the Report see Luke Gormally, 'The BMA Report and the Case against Legalization' in Gormally, 177.

[11] Guidance, 6 para. 3.3.

[12] While it is true that if patients do not receive basic care, such as warmth and sustenance, they will experience discomfort, keeping them comfortable is not a goal only of basic care: ensuring comfort may require the application of medical treatments, such as the administration of morphine.

[13] Guidance, 7 para. 3.4.   [14] [1993] AC 789 at 870.

it must form part of the medical care of the patient'. Whether the evidence about medical opinion was 'overwhelming' is, with respect, doubtful. As we noted in the last chapter, Dr Keith Andrews, a leading expert in the care of patients in pvs, wrote after *Bland*: 'It is ironic that the only reason that tube feeding has been identified as "treatment" has been so that it can be withdrawn.'[15] The establishment of the Medical Ethics Alliance suggests that many doctors still regard tube-feeding as basic care. And a recent report on tube-feeding, which the guidance itself cites but not on this point, acknowledges that while tube-feeding is regarded in law as a medical treatment 'some professionals consider tube-feeding, especially of infants, to be part of basic medical care'.[16]

What, then, of the guidance's own reasoning? It argues: 'The provision of nutrition and hydration by artificial means requires the use of medical or nursing skills to overcome a pathology in the swallowing mechanism, in the same way that the artificial provision of insulin is given to diabetic patients to overcome the body's own inability to produce that substance.'[17]

Even if all pvs patients have lost the ability to swallow, which seems not to be the case,[18] not everyone will find the analogy persuasive. Insulin is a drug which is required because of the failure of an organ to function properly. A tube is not a drug. A more obvious and apt analogy would surely be between a feeding-tube and a catheter: the former allows liquid to pass into the stomach, the latter allows it to pass out of the bladder. Catheters (especially those already in place) are surely basic care rather than medical treatment. The guidance's own definition of 'basic care', it will be recalled, includes 'hygiene measures (such as the management of incontinence)'.[19]

Moreover, given that tube-feeding may, at least in some cases, prevent an uncomfortable death from dehydration (possibly even in cases of pvs),[20] why does it not qualify as 'basic care' on the guidance's own

---

[15] See p. 221 n. 13. See also 'RCN Favours Stopping Active Care for Bland' (1993) 89(6) *Nursing Times* 7; Graham Scott, 'In the Patient's Best Interests' (1993) 7(22) *Nursing Standard* 19.

[16] J. E. Lennard-Jones, 'Giving or Withholding Fluid and Nutrients: Ethical and Legal Aspects' (1999) 33(1) *J R Coll Physicians Lond* 39 at 43, cited in the Guidance, 78 n. 58.

[17] Guidance, 8 para. 3.4.

[18] Describing the syndrome of pvs, the then Principal Medical Officer at the Royal Hospital for Neurodisability wrote: 'Food and/or liquids placed in the mouth may be swallowed' (Maureen Tudor, 'Persistent Vegetative State' (1991) 42(1) *Cath Med Q* 10). And, apart from those patients in pvs, how many of those patients with advanced dementia or serious stroke have lost the ability to swallow?

[19] See p. 241.

[20] 'Death from dehydration is a lingering death that can be unpleasant for both patient and observers' (G. Craig, 'No Man Is an *Island*: Some Thoughts on Advance Directives'

definition? The guidance's argument that tube-feeding is 'medical treatment' is cursory and unpersuasive. However, even if the argument were thought convincing, it would still be contrary to traditional medical ethics to deny tube-feeding on the ground that the *patient*, rather than the *treatment*, is not worth while. Yet this is precisely what the guidance appears to do.

From inviolability to Quality

The ethical alternatives

Any guidance on withholding/withdrawing life-prolonging medical treatment needs to be clear-headed about which of the three ethical approaches to the valuation of human life outlined in chapter 4 it is adopting, not least because these approaches are mutually inconsistent and have significantly different implications for treatment decisions. Which approach does the BMA guidance adopt?

Worthless treatments or worthless lives?

A superficial reading of the guidance might suggest that it rejects both 'vitalism' and 'Quality' in favour of the middle way of 'inviolability'. There is little doubt that the guidance rejects 'vitalism'. It states: 'It is not an appropriate goal of medicine to prolong life at all costs, with no regard to its quality or the burdens of treatment.'[21] And in an apparent rejection of 'Quality' the guidance advises: 'It must always be clear that the doctor's role is not to assess the value or worth of the *patient* but that of the *treatment*.'[22] In an apparent endorsement of 'inviolability' it reiterates its opposition to 'active, intentional measures taken with the purpose of ending a patient's life'.[23]

But a closer reading (which is necessary if only to attempt to decipher the guidance's sometimes cryptic expression) indicates a preference for 'Quality' at the expense of 'inviolability'. The guidance condones the withholding/withdrawal of treatment on the ground that the patient's life is no

---

(1999) 49(3) *Cath Med Q* 7 at 11); Craig, 'On Withholding Artificial Hydration and Nutrition from Terminally Ill Sedated Patients: The Debate Continues' (1996) 22 *J Med Ethics* 147; P. McCullagh, 'Thirst in Relation to the Withdrawal of Hydration' (1996) 46(3) *Cath Med Q* 5.

[21] Guidance, 2 para. 1.2.

[22] Ibid., 3 para. 1.2 (original emphasis). See also 28 para. 14.2.

[23] Ibid., 1 para. 1.1. See also 50 para. 19.2.

longer thought worth while. Further, it appears to condone non-treatment when at least one of the doctor's purposes in withholding/withdrawing treatment is to kill the patient. The notion that the lives of certain groups of patients lack worth and that non-treatment of such patients is justified for that reason could not unfairly be described as a central theme of the guidance.

The guidance recognises the doctor's duty to act in the 'best interests' of an incompetent patient.[24] And it states that the primary goal of medical treatment is to benefit the patient by restoring or maintaining the patient's health as far as possible, maximising benefit and minimising harm.[25] However, it seems clear that it does not regard preserving the lives of patients with severely impaired mental capacity as a benefit, even when all that is required to preserve their lives is to pour food and water down a tube. The guidance states that it is not an appropriate goal to prolong life 'with no regard to its quality'.[26] Does this reference to 'quality' refer to the patient's condition as part of an assessment of the worthwhileness of a proposed or pending treatment or to a judgment about the worthwhileness of the patient's life? The guidance notes that terms such as 'quality of life' are 'problematic and ambivalent' and can imply that some people are less valued. But rather than explaining its use of the term, the guidance simply observes that its usage is 'unavoidable'.[27] It soon becomes clear, however, that 'quality' bears the latter meaning.

The guidance's endorsement of judgments about the worth of patients' lives is illustrated by its incorporation of judicial decisions which have 'specifically stated that the "quality of life" which could reasonably be expected following treatment is an appropriate factor to take into account when making treatment decisions'.[28] In these court cases the term is used to assess the worth of the patient's life rather than the worth of the treatment. In *Re J*, for example, the test laid down by the Court of Appeal was, it will be recalled, whether life would be 'so afflicted as to be intolerable'.[29] In

---

[24] Ibid., 22–3 para. 13.3.   [25] Ibid., 1 para. 1.1.   [26] Ibid., 2 para. 1.2.

[27] Ibid. It is doubtful whether the term is unavoidable. Other formerly frequently used terms such as 'ordinary' and 'extraordinary' treatments have been widely replaced by the more helpful adjectives 'proportionate' and 'disproportionate'. Indeed, the guidance itself avoids the long-established word 'futile' in favour of asking whether treatment would provide a net 'benefit'.

[28] Ibid., 3 para. 1.2.

[29] [1991] 1 Fam LR 366 at 383–4, discussed on pp. 231–2. See also *Re R* [1996] 2 Fam LR 99, referred to in the Guidance at 51–2 para. 19.3.

its discussion of non-treatment of babies the guidance again endorses *Re J* and states that the criteria for deciding whether treatment is in the best interests of a child are the same as for incompetent adults, 'including whether the child has the potential to develop awareness, the ability to interact and the capacity for self-directed action and whether the child will suffer severe unavoidable pain and distress'.[30] Again focussing on the burdens of the *disability* rather than on the burdens of the *treatment*, it adds that in some cases 'the severity and burdens of the condition' may not be sufficient to justify non-treatment.[31]

The guidance observes that where patients are so disabled that they have 'no or minimal levels of awareness of their own existence and no hope of recovering awareness, or where they suffer severe untreatable pain or other distress',[32] the question arises whether life-prolonging treatment would benefit them. It adds that an important factor in making this decision is whether the patient is thought to be aware of his or her environment or existence, as demonstrated by, for example:

- being able to interact with others;
- being aware of his or her own existence and having an ability to take pleasure in the fact of that existence; and
- having the ability to achieve some purposeful or self-directed action or to achieve some goal of importance to him or herself.[33]

Later on the guidance lists the 'type of factors which should be taken into account' in assessing whether treatment would benefit the patient, including 'the patient's own wishes and values (where these can be ascertained)'; 'the level of awareness the individual has of his or her existence and surroundings as demonstrated by, for example: an ability to interact with others, however expressed; capacity for self-directed action or ability to take control of any aspect of his or her life'; ' the views of the parents, if the patient is a child'; and 'the views of people close to the patient, especially close relatives, partners and carers, about what the patient is likely to see as beneficial'.[34] While such factors may well be relevant in determining the patient's 'quality of life' in order to decide whether treatment would

---

[30] Guidance, 26 para. 14.2.

[31] Ibid., 29 para. 15.1. The guidance seems implicitly to approve of the reasoning in *Re T* [1997] 1 All ER 906: 31 para. 15.3. This case has, however, been subjected to cogent criticism: see Andrew Bainham, 'Do Babies have Rights?' [1997] 56(1) *Camb LJ* 48.

[32] Guidance, 3 para. 1.2.   [33] Ibid., 4 para. 1.2.   [34] Ibid., 44–5 para. 18.1.

be worth while, the guidance appears to endorse their use to determine the patient's 'Quality of life' in order to decide whether the patient's life is thought to be worth living.

Equal dignity and rights?

The Foreword rightly states that the guiding principle underlying decisions to withhold or withdraw life-preserving treatment must be 'to protect the dignity, comfort and rights of the patient; to take into account the wishes – if known – of the patient and, where the patient is not competent, the views of those close to the patient'.[35] However, it seems clear from the foregoing discussion that the guidance rejects the traditional ethical view that all patients, however disabled, share, simply by virtue of their common humanity, the same fundamental dignity and rights. The guidance appears to adopt instead the radically different philosophy that dignity and rights attach only to those patients who have a certain 'Quality of life'. Those who do not, because of severe mental incapacity, are simply not worth tube-feeding.

The guidance even appears to condone withholding or withdrawing treatment and tube-feeding *when one of the doctor's intentions in so doing is to put an end to a life which he thinks is not worth while.* In a discussion of legal considerations, the guidance rejects the argument that a doctor who foresees that withdrawing life-preserving treatment will result in death *must* be doing so with the purpose of ending the patient's life. It goes on: 'In law, a doctor may foresee – be able to predict – that the patient will die if treatment is not provided but this *cannot* be the sole reason for withholding it; the *overriding* purpose or objective is to ensure that treatment which is not in the best interests of the patient is avoided.' The guidance continues that it is only when this condition is satisfied that withholding/withdrawing treatment without the patient's consent will be lawful.[36] Although the guidance is right to stress that foresight is not intention,[37] it nevertheless appears to allow doctors to have an intention to

---

[35] Ibid., ix.

[36] Ibid., 50 para. 19.1 (original emphasis; footnote omitted).

[37] Even though, as we saw in chapter 2, the Law Lords in *Woollin* [1998] 4 All ER 103 appear to have largely elided this crucial distinction in the criminal law.

kill as at least one of their purposes in withholding/withdrawing treatment and tube-feeding.

First, the guidance here appears to be legal rather than ethical: the guidance does not explicitly state that it is *unethical* to withhold/withdraw treatment even if the sole or predominant purpose is to kill. Secondly, it is far from clear that non-treatment with intent to kill is always illegal. As we saw in the previous chapter, a majority of the Law Lords in *Bland* explicitly stated that the doctor's intention (purpose) in withdrawing the patient's tube-feeding was to kill (the other two judges expressing neither agreement nor dissent), and the House unanimously declared withdrawal lawful. Thirdly, the guidance advises that the patient's death cannot be the 'sole' or 'overriding' reason for withdrawal; but this is not to say it cannot be *a* reason. In reality, it is surely likely to be (as the majority took it to be in *Bland* itself) the sole or overriding reason. Why else, in practice, is a doctor likely to withhold/withdraw tube-feeding from a patient whose life he thinks is no longer a benefit except in order to put an end to that life?

This was acknowledged some years ago by Derek Morgan, Reader in Healthcare Law at Cardiff University, who would later become a member of the BMA Working Group. Commenting on *Bland*, he wrote with characteristic candour: 'Withdrawing nutrition and hydration can have only one effect, indeed it is intended to have one effect – to kill the patient.'[38] Rejecting as dishonest any suggestion that withdrawal is in the pvs patient's interests, he and his co-author observed: 'Insofar as plants can be said to have interests, perishing from drought is not among them.'[39] They went on to argue that ending the lives of pvs patients was justified by two reasons which were not otherwise sufficient in law or morals to justify killing: saving resources and ending strain on the patient's family and friends. They added that saving money was the reason which the courts should openly adopt, rather than 'hiding behind the dubious niceties of acts and omissions'.[40] As *Bland* illustrates, the courts preferred the 'dubious niceties'. So does the BMA.

---

[38] Derek Morgan, 'The Greatest Danger' (1992) 142 *New LJ* 1652. Though this is true of many cases, it is not true of cases where the doctor withdraws tube-feeding because it is disproportionate.

[39] Peter Alldridge and Derek Morgan, 'Ending Life' (1992) 142 *New LJ* 1536.

[40] Ibid., 1537.

Going beyond *Bland* ?

From 'no awareness' to 'limited mental capacity'

The guidance appears to go significantly beyond *Bland* in two respects. First, it condones the withdrawal of tube-feeding from certain patients who are not in pvs. In *Bland*, Lord Mustill said that he had no doubt that Tony Bland's best interests no longer required continued treatment and care, but added: 'This is not at all to say that I would reach the same conclusion in less extreme cases, where the glimmerings of awareness may give the patient an interest which cannot be regarded as null. The issues, both legal and ethical, will then be altogether more difficult.'[41] Similarly, Lord Browne-Wilkinson emphasised that *Bland* was an extreme case where it could be overwhelmingly proved that the patient was and would remain insensate. His Lordship said that he expressed no view on cases where the chances of improvement were slight or the patient had 'very slight sensate awareness'.[42] Yet the guidance baldly states, without reference to these judicial reservations, that 'the BMA can see no reason to differentiate between decisions for patients in PVS and those for patients with other serious conditions'[43] such as serious stroke or severe dementia.[44]

Secondly, the guidance advises that 'a body of medical opinion' has developed that withdrawal of tube-feeding is appropriate in such cases and that the BMA does not think that (in the absence of any serious conflict of opinion or uncertainty about the patient's diagnosis) 'all' (or any?) such decisions require legal review,[45] unlike cases of pvs or conditions 'closely resembling' pvs.[46] The guidance states that where guidelines exist for the diagnosis and management of a condition, they should be consulted. Where none are available, and there is reasonable doubt about diagnosis or prognosis, or the healthcare team has limited experience of the condition, advice should be sought from a senior clinician with experience of the condition. Where assessments are required about the extent of brain damage and the likelihood of any recovery, advice will 'usually' be required from a clinician with expertise in the long-term consequences of and management of brain injury.[47] Before a decision is made to withhold or withdraw

---

[41] [1993] AC 789 at 899.   [42] At 885.   [43] Guidance, 54 para. 21.1.
[44] Ibid., 56 para. 21.4.   [45] Ibid., 56–7 para. 21.4.   [46] Ibid., 58 para. 22.1(b).
[47] Ibid., 38–9 para. 17.2.

life-prolonging treatment, adequate time, resources and facilities should be made available to permit a thorough assessment of the patient's condition. The assessment should 'ideally' be undertaken over a period by a multidisciplinary team with expertise in such assessment.[48] In relation to withholding or withdrawing artificial nutrition, the guidance proposes as an additional 'safeguard' that all such decisions, whether in hospital or not, should be subject to 'formal clinical review by a senior clinician who has experience of the condition from which the patient is suffering and who is not part of the treating team'.[49] For rarer conditions, it adds, this 'may' involve seeking advice from an expert from a particular speciality; for more common conditions, the 'senior clinician' could be a GP.[50] All such cases should, moreover, be reviewed at a local level to ensure that the appropriate procedures and guidelines are followed.[51]

A major criticism of *Bland* was its condonation of withdrawing tube-feeding from a patient, with intent to kill him, because his life was judged to be no longer worth living. To the extent that the BMA guidance endorses *Bland*, it is no less vulnerable to the same objection. To the extent that it goes beyond *Bland*, it is vulnerable to correspondingly greater objection. Moreover, the Law Lords in *Bland* were concerned to lay down strict procedures to ensure that patients from whom it was proposed to withdraw tube-feeding were indeed in pvs, urging doctors to apply for a High Court declaration. The 'safeguard' proposed by the BMA guidance is obviously far less demanding. Further, it implicitly calls into question the need for court declarations in relation to pvs: if there is thought to be no need for a declaration in cases of limited mental capacity, why legally review cases where the patient is thought totally unaware?

The guidance is remarkably unclear about what conditions other than pvs, and what degree of those conditions, are thought to merit withdrawal of tube-feeding. The list of factors which the guidance advises doctors to take into account is hardly precise, and leaves many questions unanswered. For example, how are the respective factors to be 'taken into account'? How are they to be weighed where they conflict? Are the criteria of 'awareness' and 'intolerability' alternative grounds for non-treatment? What 'level of awareness' is sufficient to merit treatment? What if a patient is aware but severely mentally impaired? What is meant by 'ability to interact with

---

[48] Ibid., 41–2 para. 17.8.   [49] Ibid., 57–8 para. 22.1 (a).   [50] Ibid., 58 para. 22.1 (a).
[51] Ibid., 58–9 para. 21.1(c).

others, however expressed' and 'ability to take control of any aspect of his or her life'? How are these to be assessed? What degree of either is ethically relevant? Need the interaction be 'intentional', as the guidance suggests at one point (but not at others)?[52] In the case of a child, what weight should the views of the parents have? If a doctor thinks a child's life is not 'intolerable' but the parents disagree, to what extent should the doctor be influenced by the parents' assessment? These questions disclose the inherent vagueness of the guidance, which is likely to promote decision-making that is not only unprincipled but also inconsistent. The guidance states that 'Without clear guidance, the public may feel that different standards are being applied in similar cases'.[53] Quite so.

Moreover, not all will agree that the requirement of a second GP's opinion is a sufficient 'safeguard' against misdiagnosis and misprognosis. Even consultant neurologists have mistakenly diagnosed pvs.[54] Several patients so diagnosed have recovered consciousness.[55] If consultant neurologists can err in diagnosis and prognosis in relation to pvs, are GPs not at least as liable to err in their diagnoses and prognoses of other conditions, and of patients' 'awareness' and 'ability to interact'?

Experience with pvs also raises questions about whether legal procedures and clinical guidelines have been strictly and consistently applied. The reader will recall that in one case the Court of Appeal granted a declaration without a full exploration of the facts even though counsel for the Official Solicitor questioned whether the patient was in pvs[56] and that in a later case the patient did not wholly fulfil the Royal College of Physicians guidelines for diagnosing pvs as she was apparently able to track movement with her eyes and to demonstrate a 'menace' response. The judge, having noted that all the medical witnesses agreed she was totally unaware, concluded that 'for all practical purposes' she was in a 'permanent vegetative state' and that there was 'no evidence of any meaningful life whatsoever'.[57] The guidance's criteria of 'minimal awareness' and 'intolerability'

---

[52] Ibid., 1 para. 1.1. Cf. 4 para. 1.2; 45 para. 18.1.
[53] Ibid., xvii.
[54] Keith Andrews et al., 'Misdiagnosis of the Vegetative State: Retrospective Study in a Rehabilitation Unit' (1996) 313 *BMJ* 13.
[55] See, e.g., Nancy L. Childs and Walt N. Mercer, 'Brief Report: Late Improvement in Consciousness after Post-Traumatic Vegetative State' (1996) 334 *N Engl J Med* 24; Keith Andrews, 'Managing the Persistent Vegetative State' (1992) 305 *BMJ* 486; '"Dead" Woman Casts Vote for Right to Stay Alive' *The Sunday Times*, 7 January 1996, 3; p. 13 n. 8.
[56] See p. 227 n. 42.   [57] Ibid., n. 43.

(not to mention the judge's concept of 'meaningful life') are even more imprecise than 'pvs'.

Further, if life with 'minimal awareness' is of no benefit, what about life with *a little more than minimal* awareness? Or life with profound mental handicap? Or life with *quite* profound handicap? In short, the inherent arbitrariness of 'Quality of life' judgments means that it seems impossible to draw any principled line to safeguard the vulnerable. After *Bland* it was predicted that the case carried the seeds of its own extension:

> The upshot would appear to be that if a doctor responsible, say, for a patient with advanced Alzheimer's disease thinks the patient's life is of no bene-fit, and the doctor's opinion coincides with that of a 'responsible body' of medical opinion, the doctor may, indeed must, cease treating the patient.[58]

In the light of this interpretation of *Bland*; of cases like *Re J*[59] which have allowed non-treatment of patients who were not in pvs; and of the consid-erable weight attached by the courts, *via* the *Bolam* test,[60] to a 'responsible body' of medical opinion,[61] it is surely likely that, were a case involving the withdrawal of tube-feeding from a patient with serious stroke or severe dementia to come before a court, the court would declare the withdrawal lawful if the doctor had complied with the BMA guidance.

As the guidance notes, lack of guidance had led to anxiety among health professionals about the scope of their discretion.[62] By granting consider-able discretion to doctors, through guidance which is so vague as to make compliance relatively easy, particularly if the decision is not to treat or tube-feed, and by requiring comparatively little in the way of consulta-tion and review, the guidance affords greater protection to doctors than patients.

Imposition of the new ethic?

This chapter has criticised the guidance for encouraging doctors to base decisions to withdraw life-preserving treatment (including tube-feeding)

---

[58] John Keown, 'Restoring Moral and Intellectual Shape to the Law after *Bland*' (1997) 113 *LQR* 481 at 497.

[59] See also *Re R* [1996] 2 Fam LR 99.   [60] *Bolam* v. *Friern HMC* [1957] 1 WLR 582.

[61] See John Keown, 'Doctor Knows Best: The Rise and Rise of the *Bolam* Test' (1995) *Singapore J Legal Stud* 342.

[62] Guidance, xviii.

on the basis of essentially arbitrary, unjust judgments about the worth of their patients' lives. The launching of the Medical Ethics Alliance suggests that a significant number of doctors favour the traditional approach which considers the worth of the treatment not the worth of the patient. But to what extent will the guidance allow them to maintain that ethic in practice? Is there not a risk that the guidance may be imposed on *all* doctors regardless of their ethical views, particularly by cost-conscious health service managers?

The guidance recognises the possibility of divergent medical opinion.[63] Moreover, it explicitly rejects the argument that tube-feeding can never be in the best interests of patients in pvs and should always be withdrawn: 'As stressed throughout this document . . . the BMA believes that such important decisions must only be made after very careful consideration of the individual circumstances in each case, rather than applying blanket decisions to certain categories of patients.'[64] On the other hand, the guidance does propose 'standard policies' and 'guidelines' in order 'to ensure that proper and transparent procedures are followed'.[65] Moreover, it recommends:

> Health Authorities should be encouraged to provide local guidelines addressing the decision-making process with a *system of audit to ensure that the guidelines are being followed. Doctors must be able to demonstrate that their treatment recommendations comply with a responsible body of medical opinion.* Advice *must* be sought from professional bodies and the General Medical Council if *anomalous patterns of decision-making* are identified in comparison with those of other clinicians or other similar facilities. *Managers have an obligation to investigate promptly* such trends in their facilities.[66]

Implicitly if not explicitly, the guidance advances the view that tube-feeding is not in the best interests of patients with severe mental disability. Will doctors who disagree be required by cost-conscious health service managers to justify their 'anomalous' practice? The guidance itself

---

[63] Ibid.   [64] Ibid., 44 para. 18.1.   [65] Ibid., ix–x.

[66] Ibid., 63 para. 25.3 (emphasis added). In *Bland*, Lord Browne-Wilkinson said ([1993] AC 789 at 879) that there were an estimated 1,000 to 1,500 patients in pvs in the country. However, the guidance points out that by the end of 1998 only eighteen applications had been made to the courts for declarations in such cases (Guidance, 44 para. 18.1). Whether this indicates that doctors who think tube-feeding appropriate have indeed interpreted *Bland* as giving them a discretion, rather than imposing a duty, to withhold tube-feeding, or whether doctors have been omitting tube-feeding without applying for a declaration, is unclear.

expresses the BMA's concern that 'cost factors probably have a disproportionate influence on decision-making for this very vulnerable patient
group'.[67] Some managers may not be slow to act on the guidance's encour-
agement to investigate promptly 'anomalous patterns of decision-making'.
Will the exceptional withdrawal of tube-feeding, as in cases like *Bland*, now
become the rule?

The guidance does propose that any member of a healthcare team who
has a conscientious objection to withdrawing life-prolonging treatment,
particularly tube-feeding, should 'wherever possible' be permitted 'to
hand over his or her role in the care of the patient to a colleague'.[68] This may
not, of course, always be 'possible'. And, as the guidance implies,[69] will doctors who oppose withdrawing tube-feeding in principle be marginalised
as a minority body of moral opinion rather than as a 'responsible body'
of medical opinion?

Assisting suicidal refusals of treatment

Just as the guidance's endorsement of withholding/withdrawing medical
treatment and tube-feeding from incompetent patients compromises the
BMA's opposition to VAE, so too its apparent endorsement of assisting
even suicidal refusals of treatment by competent patients compromises its
opposition to active PAS. The guidance asserts that the right of competent
adults to refuse medical treatment, even if the refusal results in death, is
well established in law and ethics.[70] Unqualified, this statement goes too
far, for there are *limits* to that right, in both ethics and law. Some of these
have been discussed earlier.[71] Suffice it here to point out one important
limit: a doctor is not ethically bound (indeed, is ethically bound *not*) to
assist a refusal of treatment which is suicidal, that is, made not because the
treatment is futile or excessively burdensome *but in order to hasten death*.
Moreover, it is submitted that a doctor who intentionally assists such a
refusal, even by withholding or withdrawing life-preserving treatment,
may incur criminal liability for assisting suicide. Were it otherwise and

---

[67] Guidance, 49 para. 18.5. Indeed, there is credible evidence that elderly patients in some hospitals
are undernourished because there are insufficient staff to help them feed themselves orally.
[68] Ibid., 62 para. 24.1.   [69] Ibid.   [70] Ibid., 13 para. 9.1.
[71] See pp. 53–5, 60–1 and 227–30; and John Keown and Luke Gormally, 'Human Dignity,
Autonomy and Mentally-Incapacitated Patients: A Critique of *Who Decides?*' (1999) 4 *Web
Journal of Current Legal Issues* (www.webjcli.ncl.ac.uk).

were doctors allowed, let alone required, intentionally to assist suicidal refusals by omission of treatment, the prohibition on assistance in suicide by the Suicide Act 1961 would be seriously compromised.

The BMA's Working Party on euthanasia in 1988 was alive to this issue. It cautioned doctors who were requested by patients paralysed by high spinal injury, who were respirator-dependent, and who requested disconnection, to refuse the request until authorised by a court to comply. A court order should be sought, it advised, so as to avoid complicity in suicide.[72] By contrast, the present guidance is silent on the question of liability for complicity in suicide. Indeed, in its unqualified endorsement of the right to refuse treatment, the guidance may be thought implicitly to condone suicidal refusals. The guidance advises that even when a patient is capable of eating and drinking normally, their refusal of food and water should be respected and they should not be force-fed.[73] But, unless the patient is close to death, such a refusal is likely to be suicidal: why else would the patient refuse? Is the guidance advising that healthcare professionals may or should *intentionally* assist such suicides by, say, keeping the patient comfortable while they starve themselves to death? The guidance is certainly open to that interpretation. The guidance also seems to condone intentional assistance by omission in suicidal refusals of treatment made by patients in advance of incompetence, where treatment would not provide 'a level of recovery, or length and quality of life, they would find acceptable'.[74]

This chapter is not arguing that doctors should automatically force-treat or force-feed but merely that recognition of an absolute right to refuse treatment, even in order to commit suicide, could dragoon health professionals into assisting in suicide by omission. The right to refuse treatment should be recognised as a shield, not as a sword. It is one thing to say that doctors need not force treatment/feeding in the case of even an obviously suicidal refusal; quite another to say that they may intentionally assist such a refusal. The distinction is crucial; the guidance overlooks it. If the guidance is indeed condoning intentional assistance in suicide by deliberate omission, how can this square with the BMA's opposition to active PAS? The guidance does not think that advance refusals of basic care should be binding:[75] neither should suicidal refusals, whether or not made in advance of incompetence.

---

[72] *Euthanasia*, 22 paras. 83–4; 63 para. 258.   [73] *Guidance*, 9 para. 3.5.
[74] Ibid., 15 para. 10.1. See also 24 para. 13.5.   [75] Ibid., 16 para. 10.1.

Law-led ethics?

One of the most striking aspects of the Ethics Committee's guidance is its dearth of ethical reasoning and its tendency to rely instead on legal precedent. Much if not most of the guidance is in fact legal. This is unsatisfactory for two reasons: first, without an ethical foundation, the guidance is little more than ungrounded assertion; secondly, legal precedent is no substitute for ethical argument. One cannot derive an ethical 'ought' from a legal 'is'. This is particularly so when the legal precedent is itself ethically controversial.[76] A reliance on legal precedent at the expense of ethical argument permeates the guidance's discussion of the three major issues addressed in this chapter: the classification of tube-feeding; the value of patients' lives; and assistance in suicidal refusals of treatment.

In relation to the value of patients' lives, for example, the guidance nowhere seeks to *justify* its criteria for what makes life no longer a benefit, whether 'intolerability' or lack of sufficient 'awareness' or whatever. These criteria are largely assumed. No less importantly, the traditional view that *all* patients share the same worth in virtue of their common humanity, whatever their level of awareness or ability to interact, is nowhere rebutted. *Bland* was criticised in the last chapter for being inconsistent with the traditional ethic which has historically informed the criminal law: the guidance is also at odds with that very same ethic which has also historically shaped medical practice.

While there is little ethics in the guidance, there is much law. Much of the guidance is devoted to court decisions which have held that considerations of the 'Quality' and 'intolerability' of the patient's life may be taken into account.[77] Tellingly, that part of the guidance devoted to withholding/withdrawing tube-feeding contains a section addressing 'Legal considerations' in which *Bland* features prominently but there is no corresponding section dealing with 'Ethical considerations'.[78] Moreover, *Bland* is hardly an uncontroversial basis for moral guidance. As we noted in the previous chapter, Lord Mustill pointed out in that case that its reasoning relied on 'the *morally* and intellectually dubious' distinction between acts

---

[76] Occasionally, the guidance criticises a court decision (see e.g. ibid., 35 para. 16.2). This reinforces the impression that, when it does not do so, it agrees with the ethical position adopted by the court and is content to let the legal decision do the work of ethical argument.

[77] Ibid., 3 para. 1.2. See also 26–7 para. 14.2.   [78] Ibid., 53–9 paras. 20–2.

and omissions[79] and left the law in a '*morally* and intellectually misshapen' state.[80] He expressed his 'acute unease' at adopting this approach, given that 'the *ethical* status of the two courses' – active killing on the one hand and starvation on the other – was 'for all relevant purposes indistinguishable'.[81]

Similarly, Sheila McLean, International Bar Association Professor of the Law and Ethics of Medicine at Glasgow University (another important legal member of the BMA Working Group and a prominent advocate of PAS), has accurately commented that the case of Tony Bland and the Scots equivalent, Janet Johnstone, have created a 'massive paradox' in the law, and have developed tests which are '*philosophically* and *ethically* flawed'.[82]

Conclusion

The guidance appears to endorse the non-treatment not only of those with no awareness but also those with severely impaired mental capacity on the ground that their lives lack any or sufficient worth and even if, it seems, one of the doctor's purposes is to kill. How can this square with the BMA's unqualified opposition to the *active* intentional termination of patients' lives whatever their level of awareness? The guidance also appears to invite if not require doctors intentionally to assist even suicidal refusals of medical treatment. How is this consistent with the BMA's opposition to *active* PAS?

And when patients of limited mental capacity are denied food and fluids and experience slow deaths from starvation and dehydration, how will the BMA respond to the argument that it would be kinder to give them a quick death by lethal injection? As Professor McLean has put it: 'Mrs Johnstone's death was not dignified – dehydration is certainly not that. But if we do feel that her existence should not be extended, what might have been

---

[79] [1993] AC 789 at 898 (emphasis added).

[80] [1993] AC 789 at 887 (emphasis added). Though he did say (at 899) that he thought the result was ethically justified 'since the continued treatment of Anthony Bland can no longer serve to maintain that combination of manifold characteristics which we call a personality'.

[81] [1993] AC 789 at 887 (emphasis added). See also Lord Lowry's reference (at 877) to a 'distinction without a difference'; and Lord Browne-Wilkinson's admission (at 885) that he found it 'difficult to find a moral answer' to criticism that the decision was 'almost irrational'.

[82] Sheila McLean, 'End-of-Life Decisions and the Law' (1996) 22 *J Med Ethics* 261–2 (emphasis added). For Professor McLean's views on PAS see Sheila McLean and Alison Britton, *The Case for Physician Assisted Suicide* (1997). The Scots case is *Law Hospital NHS Trust* v. *Lord Advocate* (1996) 39 BMLR 166.

dignified would have been a single act which ended it.'[83] In short, the guidance appears to condone passive non-voluntary euthanasia and compromises the profession's opposition to VAE and NVAE.[84] Moreover, the criteria identifying lives thought to lack benefit are inherently arbitrary and vague. They are liable to extension, in principle and in practice, to patients with lesser disabilities. Nor is it fanciful to suggest that doctors who disagree with the criteria may nevertheless come under pressure to apply them.

The guidance stresses the importance of doctors not appearing to abandon patients.[85] Yet doctors who follow the guidance may not unreasonably be thought by many relatives to be doing precisely that: abandoning their loved ones to a slow death from dehydration because their lives are thought worthless. The perception of abandonment may be all the greater given that what is being withheld/withdrawn is not modern medical technology but food and water. Providing food and water to those who hunger and thirst is a powerful expression and symbol of care and solidarity; its denial can no less powerfully express and symbolise abandonment. The guidance therefore risks undermining the trust which is so essential to the relationship between doctors, patients and relatives. The guidance also risks undermining the disposition, which has long been thought essential to the ethical practice of medicine, to respect and care equally for all patients, regardless of disability. It has been argued here that the guidance invites doctors to discriminate against certain patients because of their severe mental disability. But *even if* that were a misreading of the guidance, the guidance is at the very least *open* to that interpretation and there can be little doubt that that is how it will be interpreted by many if not most doctors, patients and relatives. Nor are all doctors and relatives immune to selfish motives: some doctors may be tempted to give up on patients either at the behest of impatient, grasping relatives, or to avoid the undeniable effort involved in caring for the severely disabled, particularly in our crumbling health service.

Given the Association's unqualified and long-standing opposition to VAE it is not easy to account for this guidance. Is it simply a result of

---

[83] McLean, 'End-of-Life Decisions and the Law' 262.

[84] As did the report of the BMA Working Party on euthanasia (see p. 241 n. 10). For similar inconsistency see the report by the Royal College of Paediatrics and Child Health, *Withholding or Withdrawing Life Saving Treatment in Children. A Framework for Practice* (1997).

[85] Guidance, xviii; 4 para. 1.3; 28 para. 14.2.

inconsistent ethical reasoning? Or is it a reflection of the BMA's role as a trade union seeking to further its members' interests by maximising their discretion so as to minimise their potential civil and criminal liability? The effect of the guidance is certainly to accommodate doctors who withhold/withdraw treatment and tube-feeding from certain patients because they think their lives are no longer worth while. Indeed, in paediatrics, the sedation and starvation of disabled babies, by denial of ordinary *oral* feeding, is by no means unknown. In its report on euthanasia in 1988, the BMA Working Party noted, without disapproval, that children with severe spina bifida were '*encouraged to die* as a result of sedation and "demand feeding"'.[86] The testimony of eminent medical witnesses in the *Arthur* case (a case in which a paediatrician was tried for attempting to murder a Down's syndrome baby by sedation and starvation) disclosed that sedation and starvation of newborn babies with Down's syndrome was accepted as ethical by a 'responsible' body of medical opinion. Citing this testimony, the judge directed that it was lawful for a doctor intentionally to starve such a baby to death if the doctor and parents decided to do so.[87]

The guidance notes that 'a practice has developed'[88] whereby some doctors already withhold/withdraw tube-feeding from patients with low awareness. The guidance lends powerful professional support to such practice. It is unlikely that the practice, which now has the blessing of the BMA, will be questioned by the courts, particularly in the light of the courts' ingrained and largely uncritical deference to medical opinion.[89]

Whatever the explanation for the inconsistent position adopted by the BMA, the flaws in the guidance indicate that the gravity and complexity of the issues warrant further consultation and deliberation. The guidance has fallen short of its aim of providing a 'coherent and comprehensive set of principles',[90] and there is a strong case for it to be reconsidered.

A second edition of the guidance, revised to take account of the incorporation into English law of the European Convention on Human Rights,

---

[86] *Euthanasia*, 46 para. 174 (emphasis added).

[87] See M. J. Gunn and J. C. Smith, '*Arthur's* Case and the Right to Life of a Down's Syndrome Child' [1985] *Crim LR* 705 who conclude (at 715) that, according to *Arthur*, such a baby has no right to be fed if the doctor and parents decide to let it die. Cf. David Poole QC, '*Arthur's* Case (1) A Comment' [1986] *Crim LR* 383. For a withering analysis of the summing-up see the LIFE publication: Anon., *REGINA* v. *ARTHUR: A Verdict on the Judge's Summing-up in the Trial of Dr. Leonard Arthur, November 1981* (n.d.).

[88] Guidance, ix. See also 56 para. 21.4.   [89] Keown, 'Doctor Knows Best'.

[90] Guidance, xvii.

was published in 2001.[91] The revised guidance notes the prohibition in Article 2 on the intentional taking of life[92] and in Article 3 on 'inhuman or degrading treatment'.[93] It also states that the Convention binds public authorities in relation not only to their acts but also their omissions.[94] And it observes that Article 14 provides that the enjoyment of the rights and freedoms set out in the Convention shall be secured 'without discrimination on any ground', and that therefore special care should be taken when treatment decisions are being made 'to avoid making such decisions on a discriminatory basis which cannot subsequently be objectively justified'.[95]

These provisions provided a timely opportunity for the BMA to reconsider its guidance in the light of the sort of criticisms made in this chapter. If the guidance encourages doctors to withdraw tube-feeding from certain patients on the ground that their lives are of no or insufficient worth because of their mental disability, and even with intent to kill them, why does it not breach Articles 2, 3 and 14? Unfortunately, the revised guidance does not say. Indeed, nothing in the revision even addresses, let alone answers, the criticisms made in this chapter against the original version. This is so, moreover, even though these criticisms were first published a year before the revised version.[96] The guidance takes a significant step beyond *Bland*. It is now too late for it to be withheld, but it should certainly be withdrawn.

---

[91] *Withholding and Withdrawing Life-Prolonging Medical Treatment* (2nd edn, 2001). Also at: bmjpg.com/withwith/ww.htm

[92] Ibid., 2 para. 1.2.   [93] Ibid., 3 para. 1(2).

[94] Ibid., 13 para. 6.1, citing Human Rights Act 1998 s. 6(6).

[95] Ibid., 23–4 para. 11.1(d).

[96] 'Beyond *Bland*: A Critique of the BMA Guidance on Withholding and Withdrawing Medical Treatment' (2000) 20(1) *Legal Stud* 66.

21

The Winterton Bill

Chapter 19 showed how the *Bland* case left the law in a 'morally and intellectually inconsistent' shape, prohibiting the purposeful termination of patients' lives by an act but permitting it, at least in the case of patients in pvs, by omission. In chapter 20 we saw how the recent guidance issued by the BMA appears to have embraced that inconsistency and extended it to patients with less serious degrees of mental disability. In December 1999, in an attempt to restore the law's consistency, Ann Winterton MP introduced the Medical Treatment (Prevention of Euthanasia) Bill. This chapter outlines the bill's provisions, identifies criticisms of it which were made by the BMA and the government, and evaluates those criticisms.

The bill

The bill was short, comprising three brief clauses. Clause 1 provided:

> It shall be unlawful for any person responsible for the care of a patient to withdraw or withhold from the patient medical treatment or sustenance if his purpose or one of his purposes in doing so is to hasten or otherwise cause the death of the patient.

Clause 2 stated:

> In this Act –
>
> 'medical treatment' means any medical or surgical treatment, including the administration of drugs or the use of any mechanical or other apparatus for the provision or support of ventilation or of any other bodily function;
> 'patient' means a person suffering from mental or physical illness or debility;
> 'sustenance' means the provision of nutrition or hydration, howsoever delivered.

Clause 3 provided that the Act should be cited as the Medical Treatment (Prevention of Euthanasia) Act 2000; that it should come into force at the end of one month beginning with the day on which the Act was passed; and that it extended to England, Wales and Northern Ireland only.

The bill was concise, clear and focussed. It would, quite simply, have made it clearly unlawful for those responsible for the care of patients to withhold/withdraw medical treatment, including tube-feeding, *with the (or a) purpose of hastening death.*

Criticisms by the BMA and the government

Both the BMA and the government have long reiterated their opposition to 'euthanasia', by which they mean the intentional termination of patients' lives by an act. It was, therefore, odd that both should have opposed a bill which would have restored the law prohibiting the intentional termination of patients' lives by omission. Their criticisms were, moreover, ill-founded.

The BMA's criticisms

On 21 January 2000, shortly before the bill's Second Reading in the House of Commons, the Chairman of the BMA Council, Dr Ian Bogle, wrote to all MPs.[1] The letter expressed the BMA's opposition to the bill and made a number of criticisms of it.

The competent patient's right to refuse treatment

Dr Bogle wrote:

> The current legal position is that questions of treatment withdrawal are resolved either by agreeing to the wishes of a competent patient or, for a patient who is unable at the time to indicate his/her wishes, by considering their best interests. For any person, 'best interests' encompass a range of factors such as the individual's own moral values, religious or cultural beliefs, views of their own aim and purpose in life, as well as the degree and type of medical treatment they want. The Bill would diminish consideration of these values and make worthless any valid refusal by restricting the law to have regard only for the 'purpose or one of his purposes' of the doctor (Clause 1). Our interpretation of the Bill is that it has no regard for the autonomy of patients.

Dr Bogle was mistaken. The bill would not have made 'worthless any valid refusal' of treatment (or tube-feeding) by a competent patient (whether

---

[1] Letter from Dr Ian Bogle, 21 January 2000 (ref. IB/GR/wb).

made while competent or prior to incompetence by way of advance directive or 'living will'). For one thing, most patients no doubt refuse treatment because they think it would either be futile or too burdensome for them rather than with the purpose of hastening their deaths. For another, even if in a particular case the doctor had good reason to think that the *patient's* purpose were to hasten death, the bill was concerned only with the *doctor's* purpose, not the patient's purpose. The bill would in no way have prevented doctors from withholding/withdrawing treatment *with the purpose of respecting a patient's refusal.* It would only have prevented doctors from withholding/withdrawing treatment (or tube-feeding)*with the (or a) purpose of hastening death.* And, as we saw in chapter 2, the mere fact that the doctor foresees that if treatment is withheld/withdrawn the patient will die sooner than would otherwise have been the case does not mean that hastening death is the doctor's purpose.[2]

The incompetent patient's best interests

Dr Bogle was also wrong in claiming that, in the case of incompetent patients, the bill would 'diminish consideration' of the patient's values, beliefs and wishes. The law has always forbidden doctors to *give* treatment with a purpose of hastening death. That prohibition in no way diminishes the doctor's duty and right to take into account the patient's best interests, values and views in deciding whether and what treatment *to give.* Equally, the bill's prohibition on withholding/withdrawing treatment with a purpose to kill would in no way have diminished the doctor's duty and right to take those same factors into account in deciding whether and what treatment *to withhold or withdraw.* Moreover, the bill would simply have restored the prohibition which was long part of the law before the *Bland* case in 1993. Dr Bogle produced no evidence that this prohibition in any way prevented doctors before 1993 from taking into account those factors in deciding whether to withhold/withdraw treatment.

Complexity

Dr Bogle also claimed: 'This is a complex area where simplistic statements are unhelpful and increase confusion. By seeking to remove the emphasis in law from the wishes of the patient to the "purpose or one of his purposes"

---

[2] *Pace* the Law Lords' equation in *Woollin* [1998] 4 All ER 103, noted in chapter 2, of effects which are intended and those which are foreseen as virtually certain.

of the doctor, the Bill further complicates an already complex decision making process.'

Yet the prohibition on *active* killing, which focusses on the doctor's purpose irrespective of the patient's wishes, is simple and creates clarity, not confusion. So too would the bill's simple prohibition on purposeful killing by omission.

Dr Bogle noted that the BMA issued guidance on withholding/withdrawing treatment in 1999. But, as we saw in chapter 20, the guidance is vague and inconsistent. It invites doctors to deprive patients of life-saving treatment (and tube-feeding) on the basis of an opinion that they would be 'better off dead' and even appears to condone the purposeful ending of life, albeit by omission. The guidance is part of the problem, not part of the solution. It strengthened rather than weakened the case for the bill.

Two scenarios

To illustrate his arguments, Dr Bogle presented two scenarios. The first was as follows:

> Doctors caring for a patient with chronic kidney disease, controlled with dialysis, who develops a rapidly progressive and terminal cancer would not be permitted to agree to the withdrawal of dialysis at the request of the patient. The doctor in so doing would be acquiescing to [*sic*] the patient's purpose of hastening death although the patient is already dying; agreeing to the patient's wishes in this instance would open the doctor to the accusation that his purpose was to hasten the death of the patient.

The second scenario was:

> A patient with a long standing but progressive cancer of the breast may wish to indicate in advance what treatment should be given, withheld or withdrawn should the cancer spread to other organs and the patient be unable to express a view. To follow the patient's informed and expressed view would clearly be open to the interpretation as [*sic*] having the purpose of bringing about the patient's death.

Dr Bogle was, yet again, mistaken. For one thing, why did he assume that in either case the patient's purpose in refusing treatment would be to hasten death rather than simply to refuse a treatment which – given the patient's terminal condition – no longer offered a reasonable hope of benefit? For another, even if the *patient's* purpose were to hasten death, it by no means follows that this would be the *doctor's* purpose. So long as the doctor's purpose were to respect the patient's refusal and not to hasten the patient's death, the doctor would commit no offence. In the (most unlikely) event that he or she were to be accused of having the purpose of hastening death, the prosecution would have difficulty even getting off the ground. How could the Crown prove that the doctor's purpose was to hasten death when it was not? Any insinuation that, because doctors may falsely be accused of seeking to hasten death by omission, the prohibition should not exist is no stronger than the argument that because doctors administering palliative drugs to alleviate pain may falsely be accused of seeking to hasten death by an act, the prohibition on active killing should be abrogated.

The government's criticisms

The government also opposed the bill, and for reasons similar to, and no better than, those advanced by the BMA. During the Second Reading debate on the bill, the Parliamentary Under-Secretary of State for Health, Yvette Cooper MP, started by reiterating the government's opposition to euthanasia: 'At the outset, I emphasise that the Government remain completely opposed to euthanasia, by which we mean the *intentional taking of life*, albeit at the patient's request or for a merciful motive.'[3] Addressing the doctor's duty, she pointed out: 'When a patient is in hospital there is no doubt that the doctor owes the patient a duty of care. *That certainly includes a requirement not to kill the patient intentionally by any means, action or omission.*'[4] She recognised that a doctor was under no duty to provide treatment which would not benefit the patient, but that a doctor's omission to provide beneficial treatment to a patient so that the patient would die could be 'just as culpable – just as unlawful – as a positive attempt to kill that patient using a toxic drug.'[5] So far, so good. However, having expressed the government's opposition to intentional killing by act or by omission, Ms Cooper went on, inconsistently, to express the government's opposition to the bill and its reasons for that opposition. Those reasons were a tangled skein of error and misunderstanding.

[3] (2000) 343 Parl. Deb., HC, 743 (emphasis added).   [4] Ibid. (emphasis added).
[5] At 742–4.

The competent patient's right to refuse treatment

A central reason for the government's opposition was:

> It would switch the focus from the rights and best interests of the patient to the purpose or one of the purposes of the doctors. If it were passed, the law would judge a situation in which treatment was withdrawn or withheld not according to the decisions, rights and interests of the patient, but according to what was in the mind of the doctor.[6]

The present law was, the Minister added, based firmly on the rights of patients to consent to or refuse treatment. Competent patients had the right to refuse treatment, including tube-feeding. That right could be exercised even if a refusal would lead to death, and even if it were exercised 'to bring about' death.[7] The bill she said, introduced 'a new test of "purpose", as distinct from the existing tests based on the rights and interests of the patient or, alternatively, the criminal-law concept of intention' applied by the law of homicide.

The Minister's argument was seriously confused. First, her claim that the bill would 'switch the focus' from the rights and best interests of the patient to the purpose or one of the purposes of the doctors betrayed a strange understanding of the criminal law. The criminal law typically protects rights and interests *by* framing prohibitions against conduct performed with specified states of mind, not least intention. The most important rights are protected by prohibitions against *purposeful* interference. For example, the right to life is protected by the crime of murder which prohibits *intentionally* causing death. Indeed, the bill sought merely to restore the criminal law to its long-standing condition before *Bland*; to restore the fullness and consistency of its protection of patients' rights and interests; *to switch the focus back* to the rights of patients not to be intentionally killed by omission. The law as amended by the bill would indeed have judged 'a situation in which treatment was withdrawn or withheld' according to 'what was in the mind of the doctor' but there would be nothing novel in this. The criminal law would equally judge the lawfulness or otherwise of a doctor *giving* a treatment which hastened death according to 'what was in the mind of the doctor'. The Minister claimed that the patient's right to

---

[6] At 744.

[7] Ibid. This unsubstantiated proposition is contrary to principle and authority. As we noted in chapter 19, there is in law no right to commit suicide (much less to be assisted in so doing) either by act or by omission.

refuse treatment would be undermined if a purpose of the doctor was to hasten death. She argued:

> The doctor's main purpose may be to respect the competent patient's right to refuse treatment. The Bill means that any other purposes that the doctor may have in respecting that request should be relevant, too. That would make the lawfulness of respecting the patient's rights dependent on the mindset of the doctor, not the patient's right in the first place. The Hon. Lady [Mrs Winterton] has made it clear that she does not intend the Bill to have any such impact, but making acts and omissions identical and focusing on the doctor's purpose would do exactly that.[8]

She illustrated this argument as follows:

> A patient with advanced motor neurone disease, for example, may develop disabilities that make it necessary for her to receive increasing help with the tasks of daily living, such as bathing and feeding. If the person subsequently develops pneumonia, which without treatment could be fatal, she may decide that she does not want to receive that treatment, in full knowledge of the likely consequences. If the doctor understands the patient's position and desire to hasten her own death, could it be held that the doctor's purpose, or one of the doctor's purposes, was also to hasten death? For fear of that, would the doctor feel compelled to provide treatment?[9]

The objection is similar to that advanced by the BMA; it is no more persuasive.

First, the fact that the patient has 'full knowledge' of the likely consequence of refusing treatment does not mean she has the 'desire to hasten her own death'.

Secondly, even if the patient's purpose in refusing treatment *were* to hasten her own death, a doctor who withheld/withdrew treatment *with the purpose of respecting the patient's refusal and not with the purpose of hastening the patient's death* would commit no offence. The Minister's speculation that the doctor might fear that a lawful purpose might be misconstrued as unlawful and decide to impose treatment is unsubstantiated and, surely, fanciful. Indeed, forcing treatment on the patient would be much more likely to attract accusations of illegality, accusations which would be all

---

[8] At 746. It was misleading for Ms Cooper to state that 'The bill means that any other purposes that the doctor may have in respecting that request should be relevant, too'. The bill was concerned only with one purpose which would be unlawful, not others which were lawful.

[9] At 747.

the more to be feared as being well grounded rather than groundless. Further, is there any evidence that doctors omit to prescribe palliative drugs for fear that their lawful purpose of alleviating pain might be misconstrued as an intent to kill?[10]

Thirdly, even if the doctor's purpose, or one of the doctor's purposes, were to hasten the patient's death, this would affect the *doctor's criminal liability* not the *patient's right to refuse treatment*. The bill would in no way have permitted, much less required, a doctor with such an unlawful purpose to force treatment on a patient who has refused it.[11] It simply proscribed *one* purpose for non-treatment: the doctor could lawfully be motivated by others, not least respect for the patient's refusal. Patients currently have a right to refuse treatment which doctors must respect. Nothing in the bill would have deprived them of that right.

Fourthly, the fallacy of Ms Cooper's argument that the lawfulness of respecting the patient's right to refuse treatment would have been compromised by a doctor's purpose of hastening death can be illustrated by an analogy with the administration of palliative drugs to ease suffering where the drugs will also have the effect of shortening the patient's life. The present law allows doctors to administer such drugs with the purpose of alleviating suffering *but not with the purpose of hastening death*. This in no way compromises the lawfulness of giving patients life-shortening palliative care *without that unlawful purpose*. Indeed, the analogy shows that the patient's legal right to refuse treatment is more powerful than his right to be given life-shortening palliative care. While a doctor *may not give* life-shortening palliative drugs with a purpose of shortening life, a doctor *must withhold/withdraw* treatment in the face of the patient's valid refusal.

The incompetent patient's best interests

The Minister applied her central criticism, that the bill would 'switch the focus' from the patient's rights and interests to the doctor's purposes,

---

[10] Even if there were evidence of such hesitation, it would point to the need to elucidate confusions in practice, not create them in principle.

[11] Whether and in what circumstances a doctor *may* lawfully override a suicidal refusal in order to keep the patient alive is an interesting question, touched on in chapter 19, but it is not in issue here. The issue here is whether under the bill a doctor would *have to* override a suicidal refusal to keep the patient alive for fear of falling foul of the bill's prohibition on non-treatment with the purpose of hastening death. The criticism fails: nothing in the bill would have prohibited the doctor from withholding/withdrawing treatment with the purpose of respecting the patient's refusal, nor have allowed let alone required the doctor to override that refusal.

to both competent and incompetent patients. She criticised the bill for not containing any reference to the 'patient's interests' or the 'welfare' of children, and for not stating that treatment could be withdrawn if it was 'burdensome'.[12]

As we saw above, the bill would in no way have diminished the doctor's duty and right to take into account all relevant factors in deciding whether treatment would be, or would not be, in the best interests of an incompetent patient. Doctors would have remained completely free to take those considerations into account and it was not a goal of the bill to limit them. Just as it was not the goal of the bill to *limit* those considerations nor was it its function to *list* them. The bill sought to amend and clarify the criminal law. It is not the role of the blunt instrument of the criminal law to spell out to people what they may do but, rather, to specify what they may not do. For example, the Road Traffic Acts tell us how we may not drive by setting out several offences such as dangerous driving. They do not try to go beyond that and explain how to be a good driver. That is better left to driving instructors and the Highway Code. The criminal law's limited role is no less apposite in relation to more complex, delicate and subtle areas of conduct such as medical ethics. The criminal law properly lays down a basic framework of prohibitions. Educating doctors how to act ethically is largely the responsibility of medical schools and professional codes of conduct. In the tradition of the criminal law's limited but nevertheless vital function, the bill did not seek to provide a treatise on medical ethics but simply to repair a flaw in the basic framework of criminal law within which ethical medicine could be defined, refined and practised. To that end, the bill confined itself to prohibiting one form of conduct as not being in the patient's best interests: *trying to kill the patient* by withholding/withdrawing treatment or tube-feeding.

The Minister went on to claim that: 'The lack of reference in the Bill to consideration of the patient's interests means that there is a risk that doctors, to ensure that there could be no doubt about any of their purposes, may feel pressurised to provide treatment beyond the point at which it is in the patient's best interests.'[13] This fanciful speculation echoes the one she raised that doctors might force treatment on a competent patient who refuses treatment for fear of their lawful purposes being misconstrued. It

[12] (2000) 343 Parl. Deb., HC, 748.   [13] Ibid.

is equally vulnerable to the type of criticisms levelled against that earlier speculation.

Ms Cooper continued that the bill would have changed the present law under which artificial nutrition and hydration may not be continued if they are agreed not to be in the patient's best interests.[14] She was mistaken. All the bill provided was that sustenance could not be withheld/withdrawn with the or a purpose of hastening death. If a doctor judged that tube-feeding was not in the patient's best interests because, for example, the patient could not tolerate the tube or because the doctor regarded it, given the patient's condition, as a futile medical treatment, it would have re-mained lawful for the doctor to withhold/withdraw the tube. The doctor's purpose would be to withhold/withdraw what the doctor judged to be a futile or excessively burdensome treatment, not to hasten the patient's death. This would be so even if the doctor foresaw, for certain, that as a consequence death would come sooner than it otherwise would. Purpose is not foresight. Which brings us to yet another criticism advanced by the Minister.

Purpose and intention

Avoiding the ambiguity of 'intention'   In ordinary usage, the word 'in-tention' connotes 'purpose'.[15] However, as we noted in chapter 2, in legal usage the word may also include foresight of a virtually certain con-sequence.[16] Had the bill used the word 'intention' rather than 'purpose', it could well have attracted the criticism of being over-broad, of prohibit-ing doctors from withholding/withdrawing treatment and sustenance not only when hastening death was their purpose *but also when they foresaw the hastening of death as certain.* There are, of course, many cases in which it is agreed (except by vitalists) that doctors behave properly in with-holding/withdrawing treatment even though they foresee the consequent hastening of death as certain. Any bill which sought to criminalise such be-haviour would indeed be objectionable. Avoiding the ambiguity created by the differences between the ordinary and the legal meanings of 'intention', and avoiding any criticism that the bill sought to prohibit the foreseen hastening of death, the bill wisely used the word 'purpose' which has the

---

[14] At 749.
[15] The *OED* defines 'intent' as 'the act or fact of intending; intention, purpose' (*The New Shorter Oxford English Dictionary* (1993) I, 1389). See also 'intention'.
[16] *Woollin* [1998] 4 All ER 103.

clear meaning, in ordinary (and legal) usage of 'aim' not foresight.[17] Had the bill used the word 'intention', it would have been open to the criticism of being ambiguous and over-broad. But it did not, and it was not.

Remarkably, however, this did not prevent the Minister from advancing these very criticisms. Ms Cooper claimed: 'It introduces a new test of "purpose", as distinct from the existing tests based on the rights and interests of the patient or, alternatively, the criminal-law concept of intention, which is applicable to, for example, homicide laws.'[18]

The test of 'purpose' is hardly new: it has for centuries been at the heart of the criminal-law concept of 'intention'. What *is* new is the use of the word 'purpose' in a bill explicitly to avoid the confusion which the courts have created by their stretching of 'intention' to cover foresight of virtual certainty.

Ms Cooper added that 'given that the criminal laws relating to murder and manslaughter use the concept of primary intention and gross negligence rather than the concept of purpose, it is not clear how the Bill would, in practice, fit in with those existing laws'.[19] It was, on the contrary, crystal clear. The bill would have prohibited doctors from aiming to hasten death by withholding/withdrawing treatment or feeding. Apart from that single amendment the law would have remained unchanged. The lawfulness of doctors hastening death by an act, purposefully or not, would have been determined by the existing law. So too would the lawfulness of doctors hastening death by omission when this was not one of their purposes.

The Minister claimed that it was not clear what 'purpose' meant, and that it appeared to mean 'motive'.[20] She was wrong on both counts. In statutory interpretation there is a presumption that words bear their ordinary meaning. The ordinary meaning of 'purpose' is 'aim'. Further, a judge interpreting the word would be aware that the criminal law distinguishes between aims and motives and is generally concerned with the former not the latter. The Minister went on that attempts could well be made to interpret 'purpose' in line with the legal meaning of 'intention'.[21] So, having criticised the bill for being *too narrow* in using 'purpose' rather than 'intention' in its broader legal meaning, in the next breath she seemed to criticise the bill because it *might not be narrow enough* to avoid misconstrual as 'intention' in its broader legal meaning!

---

[17] 'A thing to be done; an object to be attained, an intention, an aim' (*OED* II, 2421).
[18] (2000) 343 Parl. Deb., HC, 744.   [19] Ibid.   [20] At 745.   [21] Ibid.

In addition to criticising the word 'purpose' for being ambiguous, she argued that its use made the bill over-broad. She went on to consider 'some of the consequences of the change, whether it is to "purpose" or to "intent"'.[22]

'If a doctor knew, virtually for certain, that withholding or withdrawing treatment – even at the patient's request – would result in the patient's death, and if the current legal concept of intention were applied, the doctor could be held to have intended the patient's death. The Bill would make it unlawful for a doctor to respect a patient's rights.'[23]

However, the bill used the word 'purpose' *not* 'intent'. Secondly, if the legal meaning of 'intent' does include foresight of virtual certainty and if, as Ms Cooper stated, a doctor is under a duty not to kill a patient 'intentionally' by omission,[24] *then the doctor is liable under the existing law*. Thirdly, under the bill the doctor would *not* be liable for foreseeing rather than aiming at the hastening of death. In other words, the bill *could only have improved* the position of doctors in such circumstances.

Ms Cooper continued that even if 'purpose' were given 'a more everyday meaning' the bill 'requires every one of the doctor's purposes to be considered before it is decided whether withholding treatment at the patient's request is lawful'.[25] But this is as misleading as saying that the present law against active killing 'requires every one of the doctor's purposes to be considered before it is decided whether' the doctor's administering of life-shortening doses of morphine to the dying is lawful. In either case, only if there were grounds to suspect a homicidal purpose would the doctor's respective states of mind merit investigation.

Finally, the Minister's objections to the bill seemed inconsistent with her statement of the government's opposition to 'euthanasia'. She began, it will be recalled, by reiterating the government's opposition to 'the intentional taking of life' and accepted that the doctor's duty of care to the patient 'certainly includes a requirement not to kill the patient intentionally by any means, action or omission'.[26] This raises three questions about the Minister's criticism of the bill.

First, by the government's opposition to the 'intentional' taking of life, she presumably meant the 'purposeful' taking of life. The government is surely not opposed to doctors giving or withholding/withdrawing

[22] Ibid.   [23] Ibid.   [24] See p. 264   [25] (2000) 343 Parl. Deb., HC, 745.
[26] At 743.

treatment which they merely *foresee* will hasten death. Why, then, did the Minister object to the bill's use of the word 'purpose' which accurately conveys the scope of the government's opposition? Secondly, if it is indeed the case (as it may well be) that the current legal meaning of intention extends beyond purpose to include foresight of virtual certainty, and that doctors may currently be criminally liable merely for foreseeing that their omission, or indeed act, will hasten death, why did the minister oppose a bill which could only have *narrowed* the law so as to prohibit only purposeful killing? Thirdly, if the existing law does prohibit doctors from intentionally ending life by deliberate omission, why did she oppose a bill which would, at the very least, have clarified that prohibition?

Ascertaining purposes   Another criticism levelled by the Minister was that the bill would have been unworkable. A doctor could state one purpose. 'But how can we know whether the doctor has another purpose as well?' She added: 'the law has no mechanism for finding out every purpose of the doctor'.[27] This is another distracting and irrelevant criticism. For one thing, the criminal law does not need to ascertain 'every purpose' of the doctor, only any *criminal* purpose. For another, the practical difficulty of ascertaining a defendant's state of mind is no argument against the criminal law requiring proof of that state of mind. The principle of *mens rea* (the need to prove a blameworthy state of mind) is foundational to the criminal law. Many criminal offences require proof of a state of mind, whether intention or recklessness. We noted in chapter 2 that the House of Lords Select Committee on Medical Ethics considered, and rejected, the same criticism when it was levelled against the ethical principle of double effect.[28]

Conclusions

The criticisms of the bill raised by the BMA and the government were misconceived.[29] Regrettably, however, the bill was 'talked out' at Report stage on 14 April 2000. The law therefore remains in the morally and intellectually misshapen state fashioned by the Law Lords in *Bland*.

---

[27] At 745.   [28] Lords' Report, para. 243.

[29] For more recent but no less misconceived criticism, see Anne Morris, 'Easing the Passing: End of Life Decisions and the Medical Treatment (Prevention of Euthanasia) Bill' (2000) 8(3) *Med L Rev* 300.

Conclusions

Given that each chapter in the book has its own conclusions, this concluding chapter will be brief, and confine itself to drawing together some of the main threads of the argument the book has advanced against legalising VAE or PAS.

Part VI highlighted a corner of the euthanasia debate which is too often overlooked – passive euthanasia – and argued that it deserves greater consideration, not least in view of cases such as *Bland* and the guidance produced by the BMA. If it is wrong intentionally to kill patients by an act, why should doctors be allowed intentionally to kill patients by withholding or withdrawing treatment or tube-feeding? Is it not gravely inconsistent for the law to prohibit doctors from administering a lethal injection to a patient at the patient's request, but to allow doctors intentionally to starve a patient to death without request? Although the bulk of this book has been concerned with VAE rather than PE, intellectually consistent opposition to the former requires opposition to the latter.

The Introduction noted that many people support the legalisation of VAE and/or PAS. Those people, many of whom have seen their loved ones die in distress, campaign for the law to be relaxed to allow doctors actively and intentionally to hasten the deaths of competent patients who freely request death as a last resort to avoid unbearable suffering. The book began in Part I by stressing the importance of clarity in definition, and of distinguishing (as do the Dutch) intentional (purposeful) from merely foreseen life-shortening. Part II outlined the central moral arguments advanced to support VAE in principle, and concluded that those arguments are unpersuasive. It went on to argue that, even if VAE or PAS were morally acceptable in certain, rare 'hard cases', it would be bad public policy to relax the law in order to accommodate those cases. The lawyer's adage 'hard cases make bad law' is particularly apt in response to the campaign for VAE.

Supporting this conclusion, Part III of the book considered the Dutch experience in some detail and Part IV outlined the experiences in the Northern Territory and Oregon. As the experience of the Netherlands in particular vividly illustrates, VAE resists effective regulation. This is not only because it is, as a practical matter, difficult to control, but also because, logically, the case for VAE is also a case for NVAE. The Dutch guidelines have been widely breached, and with impunity. NVAE is not only frequently performed in the Netherlands: it is now officially condoned, and VAE has been performed in many cases where palliative care would have offered an alternative. As Professor Leenen conceded in 1990, there has been an 'almost total lack of control' over euthanasia in the Netherlands.[1] Similarly, Professor Griffiths, another supporter of Dutch euthanasia, rightly acknowledged, referring to Dutch claims of effective control, that the results of the two Van der Maas surveys were 'pretty devastating'.[2]

As Part V showed, the central argument in this book also draws impressive support from those expert committees, Supreme Courts, and professional medical associations which have thoroughly evaluated the arguments for legalisation. As the New York State Task Force noted, legalisation would be 'unwise and dangerous public policy'.[3] The conclusion of this distinguished body, many of whose members, it will be recalled, support VAE in principle, bear repetition:

> After lengthy deliberations, the Task Force unanimously concluded that *the dangers of such a dramatic change in public policy would far outweigh any possible benefits.* In light of the pervasive failure of our health care system to treat pain and diagnose and treat depression, legalizing assisted suicide and euthanasia would be profoundly dangerous for many individuals who are ill and vulnerable. The risks would be most severe for those who are elderly, poor, socially disadvantaged, or without access to good medical care.[4]

The decision of the US Supreme Court rejecting the asserted constitutional right to PAS also offers weighty support to the central argument

---

[1] See p. 143 n. 28.

[2] See ibid., n. 30. The experiences of the Northern Territory and Oregon serve further to illustrate the intractable problem of effective regulation.

[3] Task Force, xii–xiii.

[4] Ibid., ix (emphasis added). And as John Arras has pointed out, the victims of a policy of legalised VAE would largely be hidden from view, unlike those who claim to be victims of the current policy (John Arras, 'Physician-Assisted Suicide: A Tragic View' in Margaret P. Battin et al., *Physician-Assisted Suicide: Expanding the Debate* (1998) 279, 293).

advanced in this book. The opinion of the court not only strongly reaffirmed the traditional distinction between intentional and merely foreseen life-shortening, but was clearly influenced by the reality of abuse
in the Netherlands and the difficulties of effective regulation. The findings of these distinguished bodies can only drive the unbiased observer to
the conclusion that respect for individual autonomy and concern for the
alleviation of suffering tell *against* not *for* the legalisation of VAE.

Moreover, an important point to stress when we are considering the
likely effects of legalising VAE in certain 'hard cases' is that, if VAE were
legalised, it is not as if everything else would remain the same. Legalisation
would change the entire context in which decisions at the end of life were
made. It would transform the legal, medical and social culture of death
and dying. We may recall Lord Habgood's perceptive prediction:

> Legislation to permit euthanasia would in the long run bring about profound
> changes in social attitudes towards death, illness, old age and the role of the
> medical profession. The Abortion Act has shown what happens. Abortion
> has now become a live option for *anybody* who is pregnant. This does not
> imply that everyone who is facing an unwanted pregnancy automatically
> attempts to procure an abortion. But because abortion is now on the agenda,
> the climate of opinion in which such a pregnancy must be faced has radically
> altered.

One could, he added, expect 'similarly far-reaching and potentially more
dangerous consequences from legalized euthanasia'.[5]

Supporting this prediction, Professor Patricia Mann has reflected upon
how cultural expectations about death are likely to be transformed by the
legalisation of PAS.[6] She begins by noting that 'Autonomy, understood
as freedom from interference of others, ceases to be a meaningful value,
insofar as it ignores the fabric of relationships, good and bad, within which
our actions necessarily occur'.[7]

If PAS were to be legalised, she continues,

> many doctors will adjust their practices, and gradually their values, as
> well ... Insofar as assisted suicide is a cost-efficient means of death, doc-
> tors are also likely to be rewarded by healthcare companies for participating

---

[5] Rt. Revd J. S. Habgood, 'Euthanasia – A Christian View' (1974) 3 *J R Soc Health* 124, 126 (original
emphasis).
[6] Patricia S. Mann, 'Meanings of Death' in Battin et al., *Physician-Assisted Suicide* 11.
[7] Ibid., 19.

in it. As institutional expectations and rewards increasingly favor assisted suicide, expectations and rewards within the medical profession itself will gradually shift to reflect this. Medical students will learn about assisted suicide as an important patient option from the beginning of their training. We may expect that a growing proportion of doctors will find themselves sympathetic to this practice, and will find themselves comfortable with recommending it to their patients.[8]

Families, she adds, will also be affected by legalisation: 'Once assisted suicide ceases to be illegal, its many advantages to busy relatives will become readily apparent. More than merely an acceptable form of ending, relatives and friends may come to see it as a preferred or praiseworthy form of death.'[9]

Managed care organisations will, she says, also be involved: their profit-based concerns, and their responsibility to shareholders, will make them prefer patients to choose PAS.[10] Mann adds that, in this changed climate of opinion, 'A lingering death may come to seem an extravagance, a frivolous indulgence'.[11] She observes that, if one doubts that views on death could change so rapidly, one only needs to remember how strong the expectations were for even highly educated women to become homemakers in the 1950s and 1960s, and 'how rapidly we have come to consider it somewhat indulgent and eccentric' for such a woman to decide to give up work and remain at home caring for her children full-time. 'We can', she argues, 'be relatively certain that our views of dying will change quite radically if and when assisted suicide is legalized.'[12] If it is legalised, she concludes, 'strong social expectations are likely to develop for individuals to choose assisted suicide as soon as their physical capacities decline to a point where they become extremely dependent upon others in an expensive, inconvenient way'.[13]

Many will find Professor Mann's predictions even more persuasive given that her essay takes no moral position for or against legalisation.[14]

Professor Margaret Battin is, it will be recalled, a prominent supporter of VAE and the Dutch experience. Yet even she has wondered whether we are not witnessing 'the first breaking waves of a sea-change from one perspective on death and dying to another, a far more autonomist and

---

[8] Ibid., 21.   [9] Ibid., 21–2.

[10] Ibid., 22. The financial savings to be made from VAE would not, one may add, be lost on public health service providers.

[11] Ibid., 23.   [12] Ibid.   [13] Ibid., 25.   [14] Ibid., 11; 25.

directive one much as we have seen changes in reproduction'.[15] She adds that if this trend (a trend which she says she would welcome) is real, then the widespread assumption that PAS would or should be rare collapses.[16] Such a trend could, surely, only be reinforced by legalisation.

In short, it would be misguided to assume that, if VAE were legalised, current attitudes among patients, doctors and health providers would remain the same and that VAE would be limited to rare 'hard cases'. Like abortion, VAE would probably become a commonly performed elective procedure. The evidence from the Netherlands, not least the 'shift' noted by Dr Van Delden towards the increasing performance of VAE as an alternative to palliative care,[17] strengthens this prediction.

Nor is society faced with a stark choice of leaving some patients to suffer or legalising VAE. There is a middle path. Bodies like the New York State Task Force and the House of Lords Select Committee have shown the way forward. The Lords Select Committee concluded: 'the rejection of euthanasia as an option for the individual, in the interest of our wider social good, entails a compelling social responsibility to care adequately for those who are elderly, dying or disabled. Such a responsibility is costly to discharge, but is not one which we can afford to neglect.'[18]

To this end, the Committee recommended that high-quality palliative care services should be made more widely available by improving public support for hospices, ensuring that all general practitioners and hospital doctors had access to specialist advice, and providing more support for relevant training at all levels. It also called for more research into new and improved methods of pain relief and symptom control.[19] The enormous contribution made by the hospice movement shows what can be done, given sufficient commitment, skill, training and resources, to provide quality care for patients at the end of life. There is no need for any dying person to experience unbearable suffering. The inadequate care that too many patients experience, even in wealthy, developed countries like the UK and the USA, is a shameful indictment of the shortcomings of society's attitude towards the sick and the dying. It is, however, an indictment of society's failure to provide adequate care, not society's prohibition of intentional killing. It is, moreover, significant that those doctors and nurses at the forefront of caring for those who are often cited as typical

---

[15] Margaret Battin, 'Physician-Assisted Suicide: Safe, Legal, Rare?' in Battin et al., *Physician-Assisted Suicide* 63, 71.
[16] Ibid.   [17] See p. 143 n. 33.   [18] Lords' Report, para. 276.   [19] Ibid.

candidates for VAE, such as the terminally ill cancer patient, are in the vanguard of opposition to VAE and perceive, surely rightly, that killing is incompatible with their vocation of healing and caring.

Linda Emanuel, Vice-President of Ethics Standards at the AMA, has rightly pointed out that policy-makers should discern and address the underlying causes of calls for VAE, whether made by individuals or society. She stresses that most requests for VAE are motivated not by pain but by fear: fear of future suffering, of indignity, of burdensomeness, of abandonment and of loss of control. She observes: 'psychosocial suffering should be treated by ameliorating its sources, not by eliminating the victim. Unfortunately, the widely acknowledged difficulty of assessing and lessening psychosocial suffering is a factor that could make physicians more prone to misuse of physician-assisted suicide and euthanasia if it were legalized.'[20] She adds that, to develop an understanding of the root causes of the fears which generate requests for VAE, doctors and others should learn how to discuss, plan for and manage dying, not only with patients but with their relatives, thereby building a care unit for patients who lack one. And society should promote care networks for the dying, whether provided by family, professionals, volunteers or others.[21]

In an editorial in the *BMJ* in June 2001 in the wake of the passage of the Dutch bill, Ezekiel Emanuel, Director of the Warren G. Magnuson Clinical Center at the National Institutes of Health, USA, commented that 'if the objective is to improve the quality of care at the end of life then the battle over legalising euthanasia is an emotionally charged irrelevance'. He added that legalisation might well be counter-productive, diverting effort away from the reforms needed to improve the care of those 90% or more of dying patients who will never even vaguely desire VAE. He concluded: 'It is time to eschew the spotlight of euthanasia and focus on the unglamorous process of systematic change to help the majority of dying patients.'[22] Similarly, an editorial in the *Lancet* concluded that the passage of the Dutch bill pushed the debate about end-of-life care, not euthanasia, higher up national health agendas.[23]

---

[20] Linda L. Emanuel, 'A Question of Balance' in Emanuel, *Regulating How We Die* 234, 258–9.
[21] Ibid., 260.
[22] Ezekiel J. Emanuel, 'Euthanasia: Where the Netherlands Leads Will the World Follow?' (2001) 322 *BMJ* 1376, 1377.
[23] 'Euthanasia and Assisted Suicide: What Does the Dutch Vote Mean?' (2001) 357 *Lancet* 1221, 1222.

It is to be hoped that the debate does indeed shift from euthanasia and towards end-of-life care. The campaign for VAE is, however, far from spent. Only the month before the *BMJ* editorial, Sir Ludovic Kennedy, President of the Voluntary Euthanasia Society, had written an article in *The Times* announcing his resignation from the Liberal Democrat Party, evidently because the leader of the party, Charles Kennedy, would not make legalisation of VAE party policy.[24] Sir Ludovic has long been a prominent campaigner for VAE. His arguments illustrate nicely several of the weaknesses of the case for legalisation which have been identified in this book.

He began by stating that Charles Kennedy is a Roman Catholic 'who believes that life must be preserved at all costs'. The accusation that opposition to legalisation is vitalist is, of course, a mere caricature, whether the reasons for the opposition are religious or, as in this book, secular.

He referred to the refusal of an English jury 'to convict a doctor who admitted that he had helped several patients end their sufferings'. If this was, as it appeared to be, a reference to the trial of Dr Moor, then the jury refused to convict precisely because they were not persuaded it was a case of VAE at all. Sir Ludovic seemed yet again[25] to be conflating VAE and palliative care.

He dismissed the prospect of abuse if VAE were to be permitted. 'Like the Dutch,' he wrote, 'we advocate strict safeguards.' As we have seen, however, the Dutch safeguards are lax. Revealingly, in a lecture to the Royal Society of Medicine, Sir Ludovic had already expressed the view that VAE should remain an 'essentially private' matter. Rejecting a requirement that the doctor should obtain the prior approval of a tribunal, he said: 'In my view the undesirable publicity that this would incur, would transfer into public consideration what should remain essentially private. For is this not strictly a medical matter, one to be discussed and resolved between the patient and his medical advisers . . . [?]'[26] No less revealingly, although he proposed that the first safeguard should be the sustained and written request of the patient, later in the very same lecture he implicitly condoned NVAE. Discussing the *Tony Bland* case, he said he could not see the need for court approval 'to terminate the life of the patient' in future pvs cases. What, he asked, was the point in keeping alive such a 'brain dead [*sic*]

[24] *The Times*, 19 May 2001.   [25] *The Times*, 18 May 1999.
[26] Ludovic Kennedy, *Euthanasia* (1993) 16.

person'? Why did Tony have to die from slow starvation and dehydration? How painful it was for his parents to have to endure his slow death 'when a lethal injection would have granted him and them a quick release'.[27]

He concluded his article by observing that his greatest concern was that neglect and abuse of the elderly was likely to increase and that if VAE was not legalised, 'economic pressure will lead to the acceptance of the idea that old people are expendable, with the inevitable corollary, *involuntary* euthanasia'.[28] But if his concern about increasing neglect and abuse is well grounded, this is hardly a reason for *weakening* the legal protection currently afforded to the elderly. And what kind of message would society send to the elderly by allowing them to be killed? Those who see the elderly as an undesirable, economic burden would surely welcome legalisation. As one witness to the Canadian Senate Committee testified, warning of the discriminatory message legalisation would send out to those with disabilities: 'Canada has identified a suicide problem among its youth, and we have responded "How can we prevent it?" Canada has identified a suicide problem among Aboriginal peoples and we have responded "How can we prevent it?" Canada has identified a suicide problem among people with disabilities and we have responded "How can we assist them to kill themselves?"'[29]

Apart from campaigning for VAE, Sir Ludovic has long been an opponent of the death penalty and has tirelessly fought to clear the names of those he believes were wrongly convicted and executed. Many opponents of the death penalty are rightly exercised by the risk that the innocent may be executed. Even if, they argue, the criminal justice system guarantees the most stringent safeguards against wrongful conviction, not least a fair trial in which guilt has to be proved beyond all reasonable doubt to the satisfaction of a jury, there is always a risk that a mistake will be made. The risk of patients being euthanised who do not fit the criteria for VAE is far greater than the risk of the innocent being executed.

The book started by noting the apparently widespread popular support for legalisation and the fact that, despite that support, it had actually enjoyed surprisingly little success in changing the law. In view of the evidence we have considered in this book, perhaps this failure is not so surprising

---

[27] Ibid., 21.

[28] *The Times*, 19 May 2001 (original emphasis).

[29] Special Senate Committee on Euthanasia and Assisted Suicide, *Of Life and Death: Report of the Special Senate Committee on Euthanasia and Assisted Suicide* (1995) 63.

after all. The formidable body of expert opinion which has concluded that, whatever the ethics of VAE, legalisation would be bad public policy has shown that, despite its superficial attractions, the case for legalisation is, on closer inspection, seriously flawed. This opinion, which could not unfairly be described as approaching an international consensus, may now be informing wider public opinion. As Emanuel observed, no other US state seems poised to follow Oregon. He added: 'Indeed, in the past five years 10 states have passed bills making euthanasia or physician assisted suicide illegal, and bills are pending in five more. In a referendum in 1998, Michigan voters overwhelmingly (70% to 30%) rejected the legalisation of physician assisted suicide, and in 2000, voters in Maine also rejected legalisation.'[30]

In 1992, Professor Battin wrote that the risk of potential abuse required much more careful and sensitive examination than it had received. She cautioned that it was morally responsible to advocate legalisation of VAE only if one could conscientiously argue either that abuse would not occur or that it could be prevented.[31] This book has attempted the careful examination she called for. It concludes that abuse is the child of legalisation and cannot be prevented.

---

[30] Emanuel, 'Euthanasia' 1376.

[31] Margaret Battin, 'Voluntary Euthanasia and the Risk of Abuse: Can We Learn Anything from the Netherlands?' (1992) 20 *L Med & Health Care* 133, 134. Professor Battin thinks that the Netherlands is 'virtually abuse free': see p. 142 n. 27. As Part III showed, however, such an interpretation is unsustainable.

AFTERWORD: THE DIANE PRETTY CASE

In late 2001, the English courts were confronted with the claim that a right to assisted suicide is guaranteed by the European Convention on Human Rights for the Protection of Human Rights and Fundamental Freedoms. The claim was made by Mrs Diane Pretty, aged 42. She was diagnosed in November 1999 with motor neurone disease, the same terminal neurodegenerative illness that afflicted Sue Rodriguez. Mrs Pretty's condition deteriorated rapidly and, though her intellect remained unimpaired, she became paralysed from the neck down. She had only months to live. Frightened at the prospect of a distressing death, she wanted her *husband* to help her commit suicide at a time of her choosing. He was willing to do so, but only if he could be sure he would not be prosecuted for assisting suicide contrary to section 2(1) of the Suicide Act 1961.

Under section 2(4) of the Act, prosecutions may be brought only with the consent of the Director of Public Prosecutions (DPP). Mrs Pretty asked the DPP to give an undertaking that he would not prosecute her husband. The DPP refused and Mrs Pretty challenged his refusal by way of judicial review. She sought an order quashing his refusal and requiring him to give the undertaking or, alternatively, a declaration that the Suicide Act was incompatible with the European Convention on Human Rights.

The Divisional Court unanimously dismissed her claim.[1] It held that the DPP had no power to give the undertaking sought. It also rejected the argument that the Suicide Act was incompatible with the Convention. Mrs Pretty appealed to the House of Lords. Unanimously, the Law Lords dismissed her appeal.[2] Lord Bingham, the Senior Law Lord, delivered the leading judgment with which Lords Steyn, Hope, Hobhouse and Scott agreed. Their Lordships affirmed the Divisional Court's ruling that the DPP had no power to grant the undertaking. Lord Bingham observed that

---

[1] http://porch.ccta.gov.uk/courtser/judgements.nsf/5cbcc578c01a . . . /Pretty_v_DPP_SSHD.ht
(hereafter 'DC', followed by relevant paragraph number from the judgment).

[2] The Queen on the Application of Mrs Diane Pretty (Appellant) v Director of Public Prosecutions (Respondent) and Secretary of State for the Home Department (Interested Party). http://www.parliament.the-stationery-office.co.uk/pa/ld200102/ldjudgmt/jd01 . . . /pretty-1.ht
(hereafter 'HL', followed by relevant paragraph number from judgment).

the DPP was not being asked for a statement of prosecuting policy but for an anticipatory grant of immunity from prosecution. The power to dispense with and suspend laws and the execution of laws without the consent of Parliament was denied to the crown and its servants by the Bill of Rights 1688.[3] The Law Lords also rejected Mrs Pretty's claim that the European Convention contained a right to assisted suicide.

In claiming this right for Mrs Pretty, her counsel relied principally on Articles 2 and 3 of the Convention but also on Articles 8, 9 and 14. Article 2 provides that 'Everyone's right to life shall be protected by law. No one shall be deprived of his life intentionally' save for certain purposes connected with criminal justice. Counsel argued that this article protected not life itself, but the right not to be deprived of life by third parties. The corollary of life, he argued, is death and thus the corollary of the right to life is the right to die at a time and in a manner of one's own choosing. The Divisional Court, noting that there was no case-law from the European Court of Human Rights to support his argument, had rejected it, observing that death is not the corollary of life but its antithesis.[4] The Law Lords also rejected counsel's argument.

Lord Bingham said that, as the language of article 2 made clear, it was 'framed to protect the sanctity of life'[5] and could not be interpreted as conferring a right to die or enlist the aid of another in bringing about one's death. Moreover, to the extent that there was any Convention case-law on the matter, it went against counsel's argument. In one case,[6] the European Court of Human Rights observed that article 2 not only prohibited the state from taking life intentionally but also enjoined it to take appropriate steps to safeguard the lives of those within its jurisidiction.[7] In another case,[8] the applicant had complained that, having gone on hunger strike in prison, he had been force-fed. His complaint was rejected on the ground that in certain circumstances article 2 required positive action, in particular to save the lives of those in custody. Lord Bingham commented that, although the state's positive obligation to protect the life of Mrs Pretty was weaker than its duty to protect the life of someone in custody, it would be

---

[3] HL, para. 39.   [4] DC, para. 42.

[5] HL, para. 6. Similarly, Lord Steyn said that article 2 'enunciates the principle of the sanctity of life' (HL, para. 59). Lord Hope observed that article 2 'does not create a right to life. The right to life is assumed to be inherent in the human condition which we all share' (HL, para. 87).

[6] *Osman* v. *United Kingdom* (1998) 29 EHRR 245.   [7] HL, para. 7.

[8] *X* v. *Germany* (1984) 7 EHRR 152.

'a very large, and in my view quite impermissible, step to proceed from acceptance of that proposition to acceptance of the assertion that the state has a duty to recognise a right for Mrs Pretty to be assisted to take her own life'.[9] He added that it was noteworthy that her argument was also inconsistent with two principles deeply embedded in English law. The first was a distinction between taking one's own life by one's own act, and the taking of life through the intervention or with the help of a third party. The former was permitted, the latter was prohibited.[10] The second was between the cessation of life-prolonging treatment and the taking of action lacking therapeutic or palliative justification and intended solely to terminate life. He cited Lord Donaldson MR, who had said in a previous case that the distinction between medical decisions which hastened death as a *side effect*, and those where death was the *primary purpose*, was 'fundamental'.[11] Concluding his analysis of article 2, Lord Bingham noted that it was not enough for Mrs Pretty to show that the UK would not breach the Convention by permitting assisted suicide; she had to go further and argue that it breached the Convention by *not* permitting it. Such an argument was, he concluded, 'untenable'.

His Lordship then turned to her counsel's reliance on article 3, which provides: 'No one shall be subjected to torture or to inhuman or degrading treatment or punishment.' Counsel argued that the state has an absolute obligation, first, not to inflict such treatment and, secondly, to take positive steps to prevent the subjection of individuals to such treatment; that suffering attributable to the progression of a disease may amount to such treatment if the state can prevent or improve such suffering and fails to do so; and that by denying Mrs Pretty the opportunity to bring her suffering to an end, the state would be subjecting her to inhuman or degrading treatment.

Lord Bingham observed that article 3 complemented article 2: as article 2 requires the state to respect and safeguard the lives of individuals within its jurisidiction, so article 3 requires the state to respect their physical integrity. There was, in his opinion, nothing in article 3 which bears on an individual's right to live or to choose not to live. Indeed, as was clear from the force-feeding case he referred to earlier, a state could on occasion justifiably inflict treatment which would otherwise be in breach of article 3 in order to serve the ends of article 2. Moreover, given that article 3 was

[9] HL, para. 8.   [10] Ibid., para. 9.   [11] Ibid.

(like article 2) absolute, the word 'treatment' should not be given an extravagant meaning: 'It cannot, in my opinion, be plausibly suggested that the Director or any other agent of the United Kingdom is inflicting the proscribed treatment on Mrs Pretty, whose suffering derives from her cruel disease.'[12] The judge went on to consider whether, if article 3 could be assumed to be applicable to the facts of the case, there was a breach of the state's *positive* obligation to prevent individuals being subjected to inhumane or degrading treatment. He noted that this positive obligation was not absolute and the steps required to fulfil it were prone to variation from state to state. He concluded that that obligation did not require the UK to permit assisted suicide for the terminally ill.[13]

Lord Bingham then addressed Mrs Pretty's argument that she enjoyed, under article 8, a right to choose when and how to die so as to avoid suffering and indignity. Article 8(1) provides that 'Everyone has the right to respect for his private and family life, his home and his correspondence' and 8(2) that there shall be no interference with this right except as is in accordance with the law and is necessary in a democratic society in the furtherance of certain interests, including the protection of health or morals, and the protection of the rights and freedoms of others. His Lordship concluded that the article was expressed in terms directed to the protection of personal autonomy while individuals are living their lives and there was nothing to suggest that the article protected the choice to live no longer.[14] Nor was there any Convention case-law to support counsel's argument.

Even if, the judge continued, Mrs Pretty's rights under article 8(1) were engaged, the law's prohibition of assisted suicide was justified under article 8(2). The case for relaxing that prohibition had, he observed, been rejected by the Criminal Law Revision Committee in 1980; by the House of Lords Select Committee on Medical Ethics in 1994; by the government in its response to the Select Committee's Report in the same year; and by the Council of Europe (the body which sponsored the European Convention) in 1999. The Council's Recommendation 1418, on the protection of the human rights and dignity of the terminally ill and the dying, declared that the Assembly of the Council of Europe recommended that member states 'respect and protect the dignity of terminally ill or dying persons' in all respects 'by upholding the prohibition against intentionally taking

---

[12] HL, para. 13.   [13] Ibid., para. 15.   [14] Ibid., para. 23.

the life of terminally ill or dying persons'.[15] His Lordship added that it would be by no means fatal to the UK's prohibition on assisted suicide if it were unique, but it was, on the contrary, 'in accordance with a very broad international consensus'.[16]

Counsel for Mrs Pretty had disclaimed any general attack on the prohibition and had sought to restrict his claim to the particular facts of her case: that of a mentally competent adult, free from any pressure, who has made a fully informed and voluntary decision. Whatever the need to protect the vulnerable, counsel had argued, Mrs Pretty was not vulnerable. Dismissing this argument, Lord Bingham cited Dr Samuel Johnson, who wrote that 'Laws are not made for particular cases but for men in general', and that 'To permit a law to be modified at discretion is to leave the community without law. It is to withdraw the direction of that public wisdom by which the deficiencies of private understanding are to be supplied.'[17] It was, said his Lordship, for the state to assess the risk of abuse, and the risk was, as the Lords Select Committee had shown, one which could not lightly be discounted. If the prohibition infringed any right of Mrs Pretty, the state had shown 'ample grounds to justify the existing law and the current application of it'.[18] Similarly, even if Mrs Pretty were able to show an infringement of article 9, protecting freedom of thought, conscience and religion, the justification shown by the state in relation to article 8 would again defeat her.[19]

As for article 14, prohibiting discrimination in the enjoyment of the rights and freedoms set out in the Convention, Lord Bingham rejected Mrs Pretty's argument that the prohibition on assisted suicide discriminated against those who, like her, were incapable of committing suicide without assistance. He pointed out that this article had no application unless she could show a breach of another article, which she could not.[20] Even if she could have shown such a breach, she would still have to show that the prohibition was discriminatory in that it prevented the disabled, but not the able-bodied, from exercising a right to commit suicide. Such an argument would, his Lordship observed, be based on a misconception, for the law conferred no right to commit suicide. Suicide was decriminalised because the offence was not thought to act as a deterrent, because it cast

---

[15] Ibid., para. 28.   [16] Ibid.   [17] Ibid., para. 29.   [18] Ibid., para. 30.
[19] Ibid., para. 31.   [20] Ibid., paras. 33–4.

an unwarranted stigma on innocent members of the suicide's family, and because it led to the distasteful result of prosecuting attempted suicides. While the Suicide Act abrogated the offence of suicide, it conferred no right to commit suicide, as was illustrated by the serious punishment it provided for assisting suicide.[21] The criminal law could not be criticised as discriminatory because it applied to everyone. The broad policy of the criminal law was to apply its offence-creating provisions to all. Provisions criminalising misuse of drugs did not exempt the addict. Moreover, 'mercy killing' was, in law, killing. He continued: 'If the criminal law sought to proscribe the conduct of those who assisted the suicide of the vulnerable, but exonerated those who assisted the suicide of the non-vulnerable, it could not be administered fairly and in a way which would command respect.'[22]

Lord Steyn noted that serious concerns had been expressed about the operation of euthanasia in the Netherlands, not least in a recent report of the UN Human Rights Committee.[23] This report expressed concern over whether the Dutch procedures could detect and prevent breach of the guidelines resulting from 'undue pressure' being applied to patients. It also voiced concern about the possible growth of 'routinization and insensitivity' in the application of the guidelines, and over the ability of the review committees adequately to scrutinise all the cases reported to them. It recommended that the control mechanism *before* euthanasia was carried out should be strengthened, and expressed grave concern over reports of disabled newborns being killed.[24] Lord Steyn concluded that English law's total prohibition on assisted suicide was 'a legitimate, rational and proportionate response to the wider problem of vulnerable people who would otherwise feel compelled to commit suicide'.[25]

Lord Hope accepted Mrs Pretty's assurance that she had reached her decision to end her life of her own free will,[26] but concluded that the blanket prohibition struck the right balance between the interests of the individual and the public interest in protecting the weak and vulnerable. He also held that, although the DPP's refusal was likely to expose Mrs Pretty to acute

[21] Ibid., para. 35.   [22] Ibid., para. 36.   [23] Ibid., para. 55.

[24] http://www.unhchr.ch/tbs/doc.nsf/(Symbol)/CCPR.CO.72.NET.En?Opendocument, paras. 5–6.

[25] HL, para. 63.

[26] Ibid., para. 71. It does not appear, however, that any psychiatric evidence was adduced to establish that she was not suffering from depression or other mental illness.

distress as she succumbed to her illness, his refusal could not be said to have infringed her right under article 3 more than reasonably necessary.[27]

The decision in *Pretty* is welcome for several reasons. Although their Lordships could have laid greater emphasis on the fundamental equality-in-dignity of all human beings which underlies the inviolability principle,[28] the case represents a further weighty judicial endorsement of that principle. Although their Lordships did not overturn the ruling in *Bland*, allowing intentional killing by omission, nor did they endorse it. Although they did not overrule *Woollin*'s conflation of foresight of virtual certainty with intention, they correctly understood the inviolability principle as distinguishing between intended and merely foreseen life-shortening.[29]

Further, their Lordships rightly did not endorse certain controversial aspects of the judgment of the Divisional Court, such as its formulation of the human rights issue as a conflict between the right to life and 'the right to decide what will and will not be done with one's own body'.[30] As the Archbishop of Wales pointed out in an impressive submission to the Law Lords, this does not accurately describe any true right, and is contrary to well-grounded precepts of public policy such as those excluding voluntary self-mutilation whether for pleasure or profit.[31] Nor did the Law Lords exhibit the Divisional Court's readiness to assume a breach of article 8.[32] Such an assumption is difficult to justify. As the Archbishop again pertinently observed:

> The State's very first duties include upholding respect for the life of everyone in its territory by ensuring that they are not privately killed by anyone else. It is therefore inconceivable that the act of killing another in purported exercise of a right to assist in suicide could be regarded as a private act, or an incident in merely private life.

---

[27] Ibid., para. 97.

[28] Not least as article 1 of the Universal Declaration on Human Rights, a Declaration which the European Convention (as its preamble makes clear) seeks to enforce, states that all human beings are born free and equal in dignity and rights. See the submission to the Law Lords by the Archbishop of Wales, p. 288, n. 31, para. 3.

[29] See p. 284 n. 11; HL, para. 55 *per* Lord Steyn. He seemed, however, to regard the principle of double effect as an 'inroad' on the sanctity of life, suggesting he may have confused sanctity with vitalism.

[30] DC, para. 37. [31] http://www.catholic-ew.org.uk/CN/01/011116-2.htm, para. 12.

[32] DC, para. 53.

He continued:

> As for one's right to bodily integrity, it can scarcely afford a rational basis
> for a right to assistance in bringing about one's death, for one's death is
> essentially the irreversible and complete disintegration of the body. A right
> of self-determination premised on the respect for private life or to bodily
> security would therefore contradict its own premises if it extended to a right
> to such assistance.[33]

Further, their Lordships acknowledged the very real risks of permitting
assisted suicide. They recognised, in the words of Lord Bingham, that prohibition was consistent with 'a very broad international consensus' and
that if the law were to allow assisted suicide for the 'non-vulnerable' it
'could not be administered fairly and in a way which would command
respect'. The risks to the vulnerable clearly played a major role in per-
suading the Law Lords that the blanket prohibition on assisted suicide was
consistent with the Convention.

The outcome of the case was perhaps as predictable as it was important.
For one thing, the courts are as reluctant to interfere with prosecutorial
discretion as they are to trespass on what they consider to be the province
of a democratically elected legislature. Lord Steyn observed that so fundamental a change as relaxing the law to permit assisted suicide could not
properly be effected by the judiciary.[34] For another, this was not a case
in which the applicant sought to establish that assisted suicide would be
openly and carefully performed by a doctor as a last resort to put an end
to otherwise unbearable suffering. As the Divisional Court put it: 'We are
being asked to allow a family member to help a loved one die, in circumstances of which we know nothing, in a way of which we know nothing,
and with no continuing scrutiny by any outside person.'[35] Lord Bingham
pointed out that even in the Netherlands Mrs Pretty's husband would not
be allowed to assist her suicide.[36]

---

[33] See p. 288, n. 31, para. 13.

[34] HL, para. 57. See also Lord Hope (ibid., para. 96); Lord Hobhouse, (ibid., para. 120).

[35] DC, para. 60.

[36] HL, para. 28. Lord Hobhouse, commenting on the 'highly unsatisfactory' approach adopted
by Mrs Pretty and her advisers, said that if assisted suicide were to be permitted it was essential
that the permission include 'suitable safeguards of an appropriate rigour and specificity'. He
referred to the Dutch scheme as including 'an elaborate medically supervised and executed
procedure' (ibid., para. 120), a description which is, with respect, overly generous.

Moreover, the court was provided with scant information about the palliative care which was or might be made available to Mrs Pretty to relieve her suffering.[37] It was unclear whether she had sought to avail herself of the expert palliative care which exists for those with her condition, and it was no part of her counsel's argument that such care would be unavailable to her.[38]

Finally, the risk of the slippery slope was evident in the arguments deployed by her own counsel. He argued that she had a 'right to self-determination in relation to issues of life and death'.[39] He sought to limit this right to assisted suicide, not voluntary euthanasia. But, as Lord Bingham countered, if article 2 contained a right to self-determination which extended to deciding when to die, there was no logic in drawing a line between the two.[40] If a person were so gravely disabled as to be unable to commit suicide, it logically followed that that person had the right to be killed. Indeed, his Lordship could have gone further. It would also logically follow that a person had a right to assisted suicide or euthanasia *whether or not* they were disabled, dying, or suffering. In short, *Pretty* again illustrates the cogency of the slippery slope arguments which continue to impede the decriminalisation of VAE and PAS around the world.

The continuing vigour of the debate is further illustrated by four other recent legal developments. The first is the decision of the US Attorney-General to prohibit the use of federally controlled drugs by doctors to assist suicide. Even doctors in Oregon who do so may lose their licences. The Oregon Attorney-General is challenging this decision in court.[41] The second is the decision of a Dutch Court of Appeal convicting Dr Sutorius, albeit without punishment, for assisting his elderly patient Mr Brongersma to commit suicide. The Appeal Court drew a line between suffering resulting from a medical condition and 'existential' suffering resulting from loneliness and fear of further decline. A committee of the KNMG is

[37] Lord Steyn noted the lack of agreement as to what palliative care was available to her. He said that she apparently visited a hospice where she received some medical and nursing care and in the final stages of her illness would reside in the hospice (ibid., para. 50). Lord Hope commented that it had not been possible to examine the relevant facts in detail but that the available information about what palliative care could offer cast serious doubt on her contention that refusing her claim to assisted suicide would result in 'inhuman or degrading treatment' within article 3 (ibid., para. 91).

[38] Ibid., para. 118, *per* Lord Hobhouse.

[39] Ibid., para. 4, *per* Lord Bingham.   [40] Ibid., para. 5.

[41] Fred Charatan, 'US Government Moves against Doctor Assisted Suicide' (2001) 323 *BMJ* 1149.

currently considering euthanasia for existential suffering.[42] The third development is the passage of a bill by the Belgian senate which, if it receives the approval of the lower house, will reportedly decriminalise VAE at the voluntary and repeated request of conscious patients over 18 who have an incurable illness.[43] The fourth development is the coming into force, on 1 January 2002, of the Dutch euthanasia legislation.[44]

As the debate continues, it is important that it be properly informed, and that, whenever the arguments for decriminalisation are put, the slippery slope arguments are also given a fair hearing. That has been a central purpose of this book.

[42] Tony Sheldon, '"Existential" Suffering not a Justification for Euthanasia' (2001) 323 *BMJ* 1384.
[43] Rory Watson, 'Belgium Gives Terminally Ill People the Right to Die' (2001) 323 *BMJ* 1024.
[44] *The Times*, 2 January 2002.

BIBLIOGRAPHY

Admiraal, Pieter, 'Justifiable Euthanasia' (1988) 3 *Issues Law Med* 361

Alldridge, Peter and Derek Morgan, 'Ending Life' (1992) 142 *New LJ* 1536

Andrews, Keith, 'Managing the Persistent Vegetative State' (1992) 305 *BMJ* 486
Letter (1995) 311 *BMJ* 1437

Andrews, Keith et al., 'Misdiagnosis of the Vegetative State: Retrospective Study
in a Rehabilitation Unit' (1996) 313 *BMJ* 13

Angell, M., 'Euthanasia in the Netherlands – Good News or Bad?' (1996) 335
N Engl J Med 1677

Annas, George J., 'The Bell Tolls for a Right to Assisted Suicide' in Linda L. Emanuel
(ed.), *Regulating How We Die* (Cambridge, Mass.: Harvard University Press,
1998) 203

Anonymous, *REGINA V. ARTHUR: A Verdict on the Judge's Summing-up in the Trial
of Dr. Leonard Arthur, November 1981* (Leamington Spa: LIFE, n.d.)

Arras, John, 'Physician-Assisted Suicide: A Tragic View' in Margaret Battin et al.
(eds.), *Physician-Assisted Suicide: Expanding the Debate* (New York: Routledge, 1998) 279

Ashworth, Andrew, 'Criminal Liability in a Medical Context: The Treatment of
Good Intentions' in A. P. Simester and A. T. H. Smith (eds.), *Harm and
Culpability* (Oxford: Clarendon Press, 1996) 173

Bainham, Andrew, 'Do Babies Have Rights?' [1997] 56 *Camb LJ* 48

Battin, Margaret, 'Should We Copy the Dutch?' in Robert Misbin (ed.), *Euthanasia:
The Good of the Patient, the Good of Society* (Frederick: UPG, 1992) 95
'Voluntary Euthanasia and the Risk of Abuse: Can We Learn Anything from
the Netherlands?' (1992) 20 *L Med & Health Care* 133
'Physician-Assisted Suicide: Safe, Legal, Rare?' in Margaret Battin et al. (eds.),
Physician-Assisted Suicide: Expanding the Debate (New York: Routledge,
1998) 63

Boyle, Joseph, 'A Case for Sometimes Tube-Feeding Patients in Persistent
Vegetative State' in John Keown (ed.), *Euthanasia Examined* (Cambridge:
Cambridge University Press, 1995) 189

Breibart, William and Barry D. Rosenfeld, 'Physician-Assisted Suicide: The Influence of Psychosocial Issues' (1999) 6 *Cancer Control* 146

British Medical Association, *Euthanasia: Report of the Working Party to Review
the British Medical Association's Guidance on Euthanasia* (London: BMA,
1988)

Withholding and Withdrawing Treatment: A Consultation Paper from the BMA's Medical Ethics Committee (London: BMA, 1998)

Withholding and Withdrawing Life-Prolonging Medical Treatment. Guidance for Decision Making (London: BMJ Books, 1999; revised edn, 2001)

'Euthanasia and Physician Assisted Suicide: Do the Moral Arguments Differ?' in *Physician Assisted Suicide Debating Pack PAS4* (London: BMA, 2000) 1

Burleigh, Michael, *Death and Deliverance: 'Euthanasia' in Germany c. 1900–1945* (New York: Cambridge University Press, 1994)

Ethics and Extermination: Reflections on Nazi Genocide (New York: Cambridge University Press, 1997)

Callahan, Daniel, 'When Self-Determination Runs Amok' (1992) 22(2) *Hastings Cent Rep* 52

The Troubled Dream of Life (New York: Simon and Schuster, 1993)

Callahan, Daniel and Margot White, 'The Legalization of Physician-Assisted Suicide: Creating a Regulatory Potemkin Village' (1996) 30 *U Rich L Rev* 1

Capron, Alexander Morgan, 'Euthanasia and Assisted Suicide' (1992) 22(2) *Hastings Cent Rep* 30

'Legalizing Physician-Aided Death' (1996) 5(1) *Camb Q Healthc Ethics* 10

Childs, Nancy L. and Walt N. Mercer, 'Brief Report: Late Improvement in Consciousness after Post-Traumatic Vegetative State' (1996) 334 *N Engl J Med* 24

Chin, Arthur E. et al., 'Legalized Physician-Assisted Suicide in Oregon – the First Year's Experience' (1999) 340 *N Engl J Med* 577

Chochinov, H. M. et al., 'Desire for Death in the Terminally Ill' (1995) 152 *Am J Psychiatry* 1185

'Will to Live in the Terminally Ill' (1999) 354 *Lancet* 816

Clough, A. H., 'The Latest Decalogue' in Carl Woodring and James Shapiro (eds.), *The Columbia Anthology of British Poetry* (New York: Columbia University Press, 1995) 615

Craig, G., 'On Withholding Artificial Hydration and Nutrition from Terminally Ill Sedated Patients: The Debate Continues' (1996) 22 *J Med Ethics* 147

'No Man Is an *Island*: Some Thoughts on Advance Directives' (1999) 49(3) *Cath Med Q* 7

Cuperus-Bosma, J. M. et al., 'Assessment of Physician-Assisted Death by Members of the Public Prosecution in the Netherlands' (1999) 25 *J Med Ethics* 8

Davies, Jean, 'Raping and Making Love Are Different Concepts: So are Killing and Voluntary Euthanasia' (1988) 14 *J Med Ethics* 148

Deliens, Luc et al., 'End-of-Life Decisions in Medical Practice in Flanders, Belgium: A Nationwide Survey' (2000) 356 *Lancet* 1806

Devlin, Patrick, *Easing the Passing: The Trial of Dr. John Bodkin Adams* (London: Bodley Head, 1985)

Dickenson, Donna and Mike Parker (eds.), *The Cambridge Medical Ethics Workbook: Case Studies, Commentaries and Activities* (Cambridge: Cambridge University Press, 2001)

Dorrepaal, Karin L. et al., 'Pain Experience and Pain Management among Hospitalized Cancer Patients' (1989) 63 *Cancer* 593

Dworkin, Ronald, *Life's Dominion: An Argument about Abortion and Euthanasia* (London: HarperCollins, 1993)

Emanuel, Ezekiel J., 'Euthanasia: Where the Netherlands Leads Will the World Follow?' (2001) 322 *BMJ* 1376

Emanuel, Ezekiel J. et al., 'Euthanasia and Physician-Assisted Suicide: Attitudes and Experiences of Oncology Patients, Oncologists, and the Public' (1996) 347 *Lancet* 1805

English, Veronica, Jessica Gardner, Gillian Romano-Critchley and Ann Sommerville, 'Legislation on Euthanasia' (2001) 27 *J Med Ethics* 284

Epstein, Richard, *Mortal Peril: Our Inalienable Right to Healthcare?* (Reading: Addison-Wesley, 1997)

Fenigsen, Richard, 'A Case against Dutch Euthanasia' (1989) 19(1) *Hastings Cent Rep* 22

  'The Report of the Dutch Governmental Committee on Euthanasia' (1991) 7 *Issues Law Med* 339

Finnis, J. M., 'Intention and Side-Effects' in R. G. Frey and Christopher W. Morris (eds.), *Liability and Responsibility* (Cambridge: Cambridge University Press, 1991) 32

  '*Bland*: Crossing the Rubicon?' (1993) 109 *LQR* 329

  'Living Will Legislation' in Luke Gormally (ed.), *Euthanasia, Clinical Practice and the Law* (London: The Linacre Centre, 1994) 167

Fisher, Anthony, John I. Fleming, Anna Krohn and Nicholas Tonti-Filippini, 'End-of-Life Decisions in Australian Medical Practice' (1997) 166 *Med J Aust* 506 (Letters)

Fitzpatrick, F. J., *Ethics in Nursing Practice: Basic Principles and Their Application* (London: The Linacre Centre, 1988)

Fleming, John, 'Death, Dying and Euthanasia: Australia versus the Northern Territory' (2000) 15 *Issues Law Med* 291

Freidson, Eliot, *Profession of Medicine: A Study of the Sociology of Applied Knowledge* (New York: Dodd, Mead and Co., 1970)

Ganzini, Linda et al., 'Attitudes of Oregon Psychiatrists towards Physician-Assisted Suicide' (1996) 153 *Am J Psychiatry* 1496

Garcia, J. L. A., 'Intentions in Medical Ethics' in D. S. Oderberg and J. H. Laing (eds.), *Human Lives: Critical Essays in Consequentialist Bioethics* (Basingstoke: Macmillan, 1997)

General Medical Council, 'Decision of the Professional Conduct Committee in the Case of Dr Nigel Cox' *General Medical Council News Review (Supplement)*, December 1992

George, Robert P., *Making Men Moral* (Oxford: Clarendon Press, 1993)

Gevers, J. K. M., 'Legal Developments Concerning Active Euthanasia on Request in the Netherlands' (1987) 1 *Bioethics* 156

'Legislation on Euthanasia: Recent Developments in the Netherlands' (1992) 18 *J Med Ethics* 138

Gillon, Raanon, 'Euthanasia in the Netherlands – Down the Slippery Slope?' (1999) 25 *J Med Ethics* 3

'When Doctors Might Kill their Patients: Foreseeing is not Necessarily the Same as Intending' (1999) 318 *BMJ* 1431

Glover, Jonathan, *Causing Death and Saving Lives* (Harmondsworth: Penguin Books, 1977)

Lord Goff, 'The Mental Element in the Crime of Murder' (1988) 104 *LQR* 30

'A Matter of Life and Death' (1995) 3 *Med L Rev* 1

Gomez, Carlos F., *Regulating Death: Euthanasia and the Case of the Netherlands* (New York: Free Press, 1991)

Gormally, Luke, 'Reflections on Horan and Boyle' in Luke Gormally (ed.), *The Dependent Elderly: Autonomy, Justice and Quality of Care* (Cambridge: Cambridge University Press, 1992) 47

'Definitions of Personhood: Implications for the Care of PVS Patients' (1993) 9(3) *Ethics & Medicine* 44

'The BMA Report on Euthanasia and the Case against Legalization' in Luke Gormally (ed.), *Euthanasia, Clinical Practice and the Law* (London: The Linacre Centre, 1994) 177

'Walton, Davies, Boyd and the Legalization of Euthanasia' in John Keown (ed.), *Euthanasia Examined* (Cambridge: Cambridge University Press, 1995) 113

(ed.), *Euthanasia, Clinical Practice and the Law* (London: The Linacre Centre, 1994)

Griffiths, John et al., *Euthanasia and Law in the Netherlands* (Amsterdam: Amsterdam University Press, 1998)

Groenewoud, Johanna H. et al., 'Clinical Problems with the Performance of Euthanasia and Physician-Assisted Suicide in the Netherlands' (2000) 342 *N Engl J Med* 551

Gunn, M. J. and J. C. Smith, '*Arthur*'s Case and the Right to Life of a Down's Syndrome Child' [1985] *Crim LR* 705

Habgood, Rt. Revd J. S., 'Euthanasia – A Christian View' (1974) 3 *J R Soc Health* 124

Harris, John, *The Value of Life* (London: Routledge and Kegan Paul; revised 1992)
'Euthanasia and the Value of Life' in John Keown (ed.), *Euthanasia Examined* (Cambridge: Cambridge University Press, 1995) 6
'The Philosophical Case [for] Euthanasia' in John Keown (ed.), *Euthanasia Examined* (Cambridge: Cambridge University Press, 1995) 36
'Final Thoughts on Final Acts' in John Keown (ed.), *Euthanasia Examined* (Cambridge: Cambridge University Press, 1995) 56
Hendin, Herbert, *Seduced by Death: Doctors, Patients and Assisted Suicide* (New York: W. W. Norton & Co., 1998)
Hendin, Herbert et al., 'Physician-Assisted Suicide: Reflections on Oregon's First Case' (1998) 14 *Issues Law Med* 243
Hornett, Stuart, 'Advance Directives: A Legal and Ethical Analysis' in John Keown (ed.), *Euthanasia Examined* (Cambridge: Cambridge University Press, 1995) 297
Horton, Richard, 'Euthanasia and Assisted Suicide: What Does the Dutch Vote Mean?' (2001) 357 *Lancet* 1221
House of Lords Select Committee, *Report of the Select Committee – Murder and Life Imprisonment* (London: HMSO, HL Paper 78 of 1988–9)
House of Lords Select Committee on Medical Ethics, *Report of the Select Committee on Medical Ethics* (London: HMSO, HL Paper 21-1 of 1993–4)
Janssens, Rien J. P. A. et al., 'Hospice and Euthanasia in the Netherlands: An Ethical Point of View' (1999) 25 *J Med Ethics* 408
Jochemsen, Henk, 'Life-Prolonging and Life-Terminating Treatment of Severely Handicapped Newborn Babies . . .' (1992) 8 *Issues Law Med* 167
'Euthanasia in Holland: An Ethical Critique of the New Law' (1994) 20 *J Med Ethics* 212
'The Netherlands Experiment' in J. F. Kilner et al. (eds.), *Dignity and Dying: A Christian Appraisal* (Carlisle: Paternoster Press, 1996) chapter 12
'Dutch Court Decisions on Nonvoluntary Euthanasia Critically Reviewed' (1998) 13 *Issues Law Med* 447
'Legalizing Euthanasia in the Netherlands' (1999) 5 *Dignity: the Newsletter of the Center for Bioethics and Human Dignity* 1
'Update: The Legalization of Euthanasia in the Netherlands' (2000) 17(1) *Ethics & Medicine* 7
Jochemsen, Henk and John Keown, 'Voluntary Euthanasia under Control? Further Empirical Evidence from the Netherlands' (1999) 25 *J Med Ethics* 16
Kamisar, Yale, 'Some Non-Religious Views against Proposed "Mercy-Killing" Legislation' (1958) 42 *Minn L Rev* 969; and in Dennis J. Horan and David Mall (eds.), *Death, Dying and Euthanasia* (Frederick, Md.: Aletheia Books, University Publications of America, 1980) 406.

'Physician-Assisted Suicide: The Last Bridge to Active Voluntary Euthanasia' in John Keown (ed.), *Euthanasia Examined* (Cambridge: Cambridge University Press, 1995) 225

Kastelijn, W. R., *Standpunt hoofdbestuur KNMG inzake euthanasie* [Position of the Central Committee of the KNMG with respect to euthanasia] (Utrecht: KNMG, 1995)

Kennedy, Ian, 'The Quality of Mercy: Patients, Doctors and Dying' (The Upjohn Lecture, 1994)

Kennedy, Ian and Andrew Grubb (eds.), *Medical Law: Text with Materials* (3rd edn) (London: Butterworths, 2000; 1st edn 1989)

Kennedy, Ludovic, *Euthanasia: The Good Death* (London: Chatto and Windus, 1990)

Euthanasia (London: Royal Society of Medicine, 1993)

Keown, Damien, *Buddhism and Bioethics* (Basingstoke: Macmillan, 1995)

Keown, John, *Abortion, Doctors and the Law: Some Aspects of the Legal Regulation of Abortion in England from 1803 to 1982* (Cambridge: Cambridge University Press, 1988)

'The Law and Practice of Euthanasia in the Netherlands' (1992) 108 *LQR* 51

'On Regulating Death' (1992) 22(2) *Hastings Cent Rep* 39

'Hard Case, Bad Law, "New" Ethics' [1993] 52 *Camb LJ* 209

'Applying *Bland*' [1994] 53 *Camb LJ* 456

'No Charter for Assisted Suicide' [1994] 53 *Camb LJ* 234

'Review of *Life's Dominion*' (1994) 110 *LQR* 671

'Some Reflections on Euthanasia in the Netherlands' in Luke Gormally (ed.), *Euthanasia, Clinical Practice and the Law* (London: The Linacre Centre, 1994) 193

'Doctor Knows Best: The Rise and Rise of the *Bolam* Test' (1995) *Singapore J Legal Stud* 342

'Physician-Assisted Suicide and the Dutch Supreme Court' (1995) 111 *LQR* 394

'Life and Death in Dublin' [1996] 55 *Camb LJ* 6

'The Tragic Truth about Dutch Death' in John Morgan (ed.), *An Easeful Death? Perspectives on Death, Dying and Euthanasia* (Sydney: The Federation Press, 1996) 172

'Restoring Moral and Intellectual Shape to the Law after *Bland*' (1997) 113 *LQR* 481

'The Legal Revolution: From "Sanctity of Life" to "Quality of Life" and "Autonomy"' (1998) 14 *J Contemp Health Law Policy* 253

'Beyond *Bland*: A Critique of the BMA Guidance on Withholding and Withdrawing Medical Treatment' (2000) 20 *Legal Stud* 66

'Dehydration and Human Rights' [2001] 60 *Camb LJ* 53

(ed.), *Euthanasia Examined: Ethical, Clinical and Legal Perspectives* (Cambridge: Cambridge University Press, 1995)

Keown, John and Luke Gormally, 'Human Dignity, Autonomy and Mentally-Incapacitated Patients: A Critique of *Who Decides?*' (1999) 4 *Web Journal of Current Legal Issues* (www.webjcli.ncl.ac.uk)

Kilner, J. F. et al. (eds.), *Dignity and Dying: A Christian Appraisal* (Carlisle: Paternoster Press, 1996)

Kimsma, Gerrit K., 'Euthanasia Drugs in the Netherlands' in David C. Thomasma et al. (eds.), *Asking to Die: Inside the Dutch Debate about Euthanasia* (Dordrecht: Kluwer Academic Publishers, 1998) 135

Kimsma, Gerrit K. and Evert van Leeuwen, 'Euthanasia and Assisted Suicide in the Netherlands and the USA: Comparing Practices, Justifications and Key Concepts in Bioethics and Law' in David C. Thomasma et al. (eds.), *Asking to Die: Inside the Dutch Debate about Euthanasia* (Dordrecht: Kluwer Academic Publishers, 1998) 35

Kissane, David W., Annette Street and Philip Nitschke, 'Seven Deaths in Darwin: Case Studies under the Rights of the Terminally Ill Act, Northern Territory, Australia' (1998) 352 *Lancet* 1097

Kissane, David W., D. M. Clarke and A. F. Street, 'Demoralisation Syndrome – a Relevant Psychiatric Diagnosis for Palliative Care' (2001) 17 *J Pall Care* 12

KNMG, 'Guidelines for Euthanasia' (translated by W. Lagerwey) (1988) 2 *Issues Law Med* 429

Vision on Euthanasia (KNMG: Utrecht, 1986)

Kuhse, Helga et al., 'End-of-Life Decisions in Australian Medical Practice' (1997) 166 *Med J Aust* 191

Lamb, David, *Down the Slippery Slope: Arguing in Applied Ethics* (New York: Croom Helm, 1988)

Law Reform Commission of Canada, *Report No. 20, Euthanasia, Aiding Suicide and the Cessation of Treatment* (Ottawa: Minister of Supply and Services, 1983)

Lee, Melinda A. et al., 'Legalizing Assisted Suicide – Views of Physicians in Oregon' (1996) 334 *N Engl J Med* 310

Leenen, H. J. J., 'The Definition of Euthanasia' (1984) 3 *Med Law* 333

'Euthanasia, Assistance to Suicide and the Law: Developments in the Netherlands' (1987) 8 *Health Policy* 197

'Dying with Dignity: Developments in the Field of Euthanasia in the Netherlands' (1989) 8 *Med Law* 517

'Legal Aspects of Euthanasia, Assistance to Suicide and Terminating the Medical Treatment of Incompetent Patients' (Unpublished paper delivered at a conference on euthanasia held at the Institute for Bioethics, Maastricht, 2–4 December 1990)

Leenen, H. J. J. and Chris Ciesielski-Carlucci, 'Force Majeure (Legal Necessity): Justification for Active Termination of Life in the Case of Severely Handicapped Newborns after Forgoing Treatment' (1993) 2(3) Camb Q Healthc Ethics 271

Legal and Constitutional Legislation Committee of the Australian Senate, Euthanasia Laws Bill 1996 (Australia, 1997)

Leng, Roger, 'Mercy Killing and the CLRC' (1982) 132 New LJ 76

Lennard-Jones, J. E., 'Giving or Withholding Fluid and Nutrients: Ethical and Legal Aspects' (1999) 33(1) J R Coll Physicians Lond 39

Lifton, Robert J., The Nazi Doctors: Medical Killing and the Psychology of Genocide (New York: Basic Books, 1986)

Lowy, Frederick H., Douglas M. Sawyer and John R. Williams, Canadian Physicians and Euthanasia (Ottawa: Canadian Medical Association, 1993)

McCullagh, P., 'Thirst in Relation to the Withdrawal of Hydration' (1996) 46(3) Cath Med Q 5

McLean, Sheila A. M., 'End-of-Life Decisions and the Law' (1996) 22 J Med Ethics 261

McLean, Sheila A. M. and Alison Britton, Sometimes a Small Victory (Glasgow: Institute of Law and Ethics in Medicine, 1996)

The Case for Physician Assisted Suicide (London: HarperCollins Publishers, 1997)

Making Decisions. The Government's Proposals for Making Decisions on Behalf of Mentally Incapacitated Adults (Cm 4465, 1999)

Mann, Patricia S., 'Meanings of Death' in Margaret Battin et al. (eds.), Physician-Assisted Suicide: Expanding the Debate (New York: Routledge, 1998) 11

Mason, J. K. and R. A. McCall Smith, Law and Medical Ethics (5th edn) (London: Butterworths, 1999)

Meier, Diane E. et al., 'A National Survey of Physician-Assisted Suicide and Euthanasia in the United States' (1998) 338 New Engl J Med 1193

Misbin, Robert (ed.), Euthanasia: The Good of the Patient, the Good of Society (Frederick: UPG, 1992)

Morgan, Derek, 'The Greatest Danger' (1992) 142 New LJ 1652

Morris, Anne, 'Easing the Passing: End of Life Decisions and the Medical Treatment (Prevention of Euthanasia) Bill' (2000) 8(3) Med L Rev 300

Muntendam, P. (ed.), Euthanasie [Euthanasia] (Leiden: Stafleu's Wetenschappelijke Uitgeversmaatschappij, 1977)

Murphy, George E., 'The Physician's Responsibility for Suicide: (1) An Error of Commission and (2) Errors of Omission' (1975) 82 Ann Intern Med 301

Nederlandse Vereniging voor Kindergeneeskunde, Doen of laten? (Utrecht: Nederlandse Vereniging voor Kindergeneeskunde, 1992)

The New Shorter Oxford English Dictionary (Oxford: Oxford University Press, 1993)

New York State Task Force on Life and the Law, *When Death is Sought: Assisted Suicide and Euthanasia in the Medical Context* (New York: NYSTF, 1994)
  When Death is Sought: Assisted Suicide and Euthanasia in the Medical Context (Supplement to Report) (New York: NYSTF, 1997)

Oregon Health Division, 'Oregon's Death with Dignity Act: Three Years of Legalized Physician-Assisted Suicide' (www.ohd.hr.state.or.us/chs/pas/pas.htm)

Otlowski, Margaret, *Voluntary Euthanasia and the Common Law* (Oxford: Clarendon Press, 1997)

Pijnenborg, Loes et al., 'Life-Terminating Acts without Explicit Request of Patient' (1993) 341 *Lancet* 1196

Poole, David, '*Arthur's* Case (1) A Comment' [1986] *Crim LR* 383

Posner, Richard, *Aging and Old Age* (Chicago: University of Chicago Press, 1995)

Regionale Toetsingscommissies Euthanasie, Javerslaag 1998–1999 (The Hague: Regionale Toetsingscommissies Euthanasie, 2000)

Rigter, Henk, 'Euthanasia in the Netherlands: Distinguishing Facts from Fiction' (1989) 19(1) *Hastings Cent Rep* 31

Royal College of Paediatrics and Child Health, *Withholding or Withdrawing Life Saving Treatment in Children. A Framework for Practice* (London: Royal College of Paediatrics and Child Health, 1997)

Savulescu, Julian, 'Rational Desires and the Limitation of Life-Sustaining Treatment' (1994) 8 *Bioethics* 191

Scott, Graham, 'In the Patient's Best Interests' (1993) 7(22) *Nursing Standard* 19

Sheldon, Tony, 'Dutch GP Cleared after Helping to End Man's "Hopeless Existence"' (2000) 321 *BMJ* 1174
  'New Reporting Procedure for Euthanasia Shows Doctors Follow the Rules' (2000) 320 *BMJ* 1362

Simester, A. P., 'Why Distinguish Intention from Foresight?' in A. P. Simester and A. T. H. Smith (eds.), *Harm and Culpability* (Oxford: Clarendon Press, 1996) 71

Singer, Peter and Helga Kuhse, *Should the Baby Live?: The Problem of the Handicapped Newborn* (Oxford: Oxford University Press, 1985)

Skegg, P. D. G., *Law, Ethics and Medicine: Studies in Medical Law* (rev. edn) (Oxford: Clarendon Press, 1988)

Smith, J. C. and B. Hogan, *Criminal Law* (9th edn) (London: Butterworths, 1999)

Sommerville, Ann, *Medical Ethics Today: Its Practice and Philosophy* (London: BMJ Publishing, 1993)

Sorgdrager, W. and E. Borst-Eilers, 'Euthanasie – de stand van zaken' (1995) 12 *Medisch Contact* 381

Special Senate Committee on Euthanasia and Assisted Suicide, *Of Life and Death* (Ottawa: Minister of Supply and Services, 1995)

Street, Annette and David Kissane, 'Dispensing Death, Desiring Death: An Exploration of Medical Roles and Patient Motivation during the Period of Legalised Euthanasia in Australia' (1999–2000) 40 *Omega* 231

Sullivan, Amy D., Katrina Hedberg and David W. Fleming, 'Legalized Physician-Assisted Suicide in Oregon – the Second Year' (2000) 342 *N Engl J Med* 598 'Legalized Physician-Assisted Suicide in Oregon, 1998–2000' (2001) 344 *N Engl J Med* 605 (Correspondence)

ten Have, Henk A. M. J. and Jos V. M. Welie, 'Euthanasia: Normal Medical Practice?' (1992) 22(2) *Hastings Cent Rep* 34

Thomasma, David C. et al. (eds.), *Asking to Die: Inside the Dutch Debate about Euthanasia* (Dordrecht: Kluwer Academic Publishers, 1998)

Tonti-Filippini, Nicholas, John I. Fleming, Anthony Fisher and Anna Krohn, *Joint Supplementary Submission to the Senate Legal and Constitutional Legislation Committee Re: Euthanasia Laws Bill 1996*

Tudor, Maureen, 'Persistent Vegetative State' (1991) 42(1) *Cath Med Q* 10

Twycross, Robert G., 'Where There is Hope There is Life: A View from the Hospice' in John Keown (ed.), *Euthanasia Examined* (Cambridge: Cambridge University Press, 1995) 141

van Delden, J. J. M., 'Slippery Slopes in Flat Countries – a Response' (1999) 25 *J Med Ethics* 22

van Delden, J. J. M., L. Pijnenborg and P. J. van der Maas, 'The Remmelink Study: Two Years Later' (1993) 23(6) *Hastings Cent Rep* 24 'Dances with Data' (1993) 7 *Bioethics* 323

van der Heide, Agnes et al., 'Medical End-of-Life Decisions Made for Neonates and Infants in the Netherlands' (1997) 350 *Lancet* 251

van der Maas, P. J., J. M. M. van Delden and L. Pijnenborg, *Medische beslissingen rond het levenseinde. Rapport van de Commissie onderzoek medische praktijk inzake euthanasie* ('s-Gravenhage: SDU Uitgeverij Plantijnstraat, 1991) *Medische beslissingen rond het levenseinde. Het onderzoek voor de Commissie onderzoek medische praktijk inzake euthanasie* ('s-Gravenhage: SDU Uitgeverij Plantijnstraat, 1991) *Euthanasia and Other Medical Decisions Concerning the End of Life* (Amsterdam: Elsevier, 1992)

van der Maas, P. J. et al., 'Euthanasia, Physician-Assisted Suicide, and Other Medical Practices Involving the End of Life in the Netherlands, 1990–1995' (1996) 335 *N Engl J Med* 1699

van der Wal, G., 'Unrequested Termination of Life: Is It Permissible?' (1993) 7 *Bioethics* 330

van der Wal, G. and P. J. van der Maas, *Euthanasie en andere medische beslissingen rond het levenseinde. De praktijk en de meldingsprocedure* [Euthanasia and other medical decisions concerning the end of life. Practice and reporting procedure] (Den Haag: SDU Uitgevers, 1996)

van der Wal, G. J. Th. M. van Eijk, H. J. J. Leenen and C. Spreeuwenberg, 'Euthanasia and Assisted Suicide, 2, Do Dutch Family Doctors Act Prudently?' (1992) 9 *Fam Pract* 135

van der Wal, G. et al., 'Evaluation of the Notification Procedure for Physician-Assisted Death in the Netherlands' (1996) 335 *N Engl J Med* 1706

van Es, J. C., 'Huisarts en de preventie van euthanasie' [The family physician and the prevention of euthanasia] in P. Muntendam (ed.), *Euthanasie* [Euthanasia] (Leiden: Stafleu's Wetenschappelijke Uitgeversmaatschappij, 1977)

Walton, Douglas N., *Slippery Slope Arguments* (Oxford: Clarendon Press, 1992)

Ward, B. J. and P. A. Tate, 'Attitudes among NHS Doctors to Requests for Euthanasia' (1994) 308 *BMJ* 1332

Watt, Helen, *Life and Death in Healthcare Ethics* (London: Routledge, 2000)

Welie, Jos V. M., 'The Medical Exception: Physicians, Euthanasia and the Dutch Criminal Law' (1992) *J Med Philos* 419

World Health Organisation, *Cancer Pain Relief and Palliative Care* (Geneva: WHO, 1990)

Zylic, Zbigniew, 'The Story behind the Blank Spot' (July/August 1993) 10 *Am J Hosp Pall Care* 30

'Palliative Care: Dutch Hospices and Euthanasia' in David C. Thomasma et al. (eds.), *Asking to Die: Inside the Dutch Debate about Euthanasia* (Dordrecht: Kluwer Academic Publishers, 1998) 187

'Survey: Doctor-Assisted Suicide is Rare' (1998) 8(3) *Life at Risk* 1

'Oregon: "Botched" Suicides, Flawed Reports' (2000) 10(2) *Life at Risk* 1

INDEX